A New History of Management

Concepts of 'good management' are generally derived from what is assumed to be a fundamental need to increase efficiency. But this approach is based on a specific and limited view of management's past. *A New History of Management* disputes these foundations. By reassessing conventional perspectives on the development of management theories and providing a critical outline of present-day management, it highlights alternative conceptions of good management focussed on ethical aims, sustainability and new views of good practice. This new history provides a platform from which scholars and reflective practitioners can develop alternative approaches for managing and organizing in the twenty-first century.

STEPHEN CUMMINGS is Professor of Management at Victoria University of Wellington. His previous books include *Recreating Strategy* (2002), *Images of Strategy* (2003), *Creative Strategy* (2010), *Handbook of Management and Creativity* (2014) and *Strategy Builder* (2015). Stephen is an Academic Fellow of the International Council of Management Consulting Institutes and Chair Elect of the Academy of Management's Critical Management Studies division.

TODD BRIDGMAN is Senior Lecturer in Management at Victoria University of Wellington, having previously held research fellowships at Judge Business School and Wolfson College, University of Cambridge. He co-edited *The Oxford Handbook of Critical Management Studies* (2009) and is currently co-editor-in-chief of *Management Learning*.

JOHN HASSARD (MBS) is Professor of Organizational Analysis at the University of Manchester. He has written several books, including *Sociology and Organization Theory* (2003) and *Managing in the*

Modern Corporation (2009) (both Cambridge University Press), as well as journal articles for leading business research journals such as *Academy of Management Review* and *Industrial Relations*.

MICHAEL ROWLINSON is Professor of Management and Organizational History at the University of Exeter. He co-founded the journal *Management & Organizational History* in 2006 and was an editor until 2013. He is currently an associate editor of *Organization Studies* and a member of the editorial board of *Academy of Management Review*. With John Hassard and Stephanie Decker, he authored the landmark article 'Research Strategies for Organizational History: A Dialogue between Historical Theory and Organization Theory' in *Academy of Management Review*.

A New History of Management

STEPHEN CUMMINGS
Victoria University of Wellington

TODD BRIDGMAN
Victoria University of Wellington

JOHN HASSARD
University of Manchester

MICHAEL ROWLINSON
University of Exeter

CAMBRIDGE
UNIVERSITY PRESS

CAMBRIDGE
UNIVERSITY PRESS

University Printing House, Cambridge CB2 8BS, United Kingdom

One Liberty Plaza, 20th Floor, New York, NY 10006, USA

477 Williamstown Road, Port Melbourne, VIC 3207, Australia

4843/24, 2nd Floor, Ansari Road, Daryaganj, Delhi – 110002, India

79 Anson Road, #06–04/06, Singapore 079906

Cambridge University Press is part of the University of Cambridge.

It furthers the University's mission by disseminating knowledge in the pursuit of
education, learning, and research at the highest international levels of excellence.

www.cambridge.org
Information on this title: www.cambridge.org/9781107138148
DOI: 10.1017/9781316481202

First published 2017

Printed in the United Kingdom by Clays, St Ives plc

A catalogue record for this publication is available from the British Library.

Library of Congress Cataloging-in-Publication Data
Names: Cummings, Stephen, author. | Bridgman, Todd, author.
Title: A new history of management / Stephen Cummings, Victoria University of
Wellington, Todd Bridgman, Victoria University of Wellington, John
Hassard, University of Manchester, Michael Rowlinson, University of Exeter.
Description: New York : Cambridge University Press, 2017. | Includes
bibliographical references and index.
Identifiers: LCCN 2017012133| ISBN 9781107138148 (hardback) | ISBN
9781316502907 (paperback)
Subjects: LCSH: Management – History. | Organizational behavior. | BISAC:
BUSINESS & ECONOMICS / Organizational Behavior.
Classification: LCC HD30.5 .C86 2017 | DDC 658.009–dc23
LC record available at https://lccn.loc.gov/2017012133

ISBN 978-1-107-13814-8 Hardback
ISBN 978-1-316-50290-7 Paperback

....

Every effort has been made to trace the owners of copyright material included in this
book. The publishers would be grateful for any omissions brought to their notice for
acknowledgement in future editions of the book.

Contents

Figures

Tables

Preface and Acknowledgements

And isn't the past inevitable,
now that we call the little
we remember of it 'the past'?

William Matthews, from the poem *Cows Grazing at Sunrise*

The object is to learn to what extent the effort to think one's
own history can free thought from what it silently thinks, and
so enable it to think differently.

Michel Foucault, from *The History of Sexuality*, Vol. 2

Charles (Chuck) Wrege passed away on 19 August 2014 as we were writing this book. Just before he died, he gave a presentation at an Academy of Management that we attended. In answer to a question from the floor about what advice he would offer to young management historians, Chuck said, 'You just have to work hard! Read and read the stuff again. It takes a long time. It's hard work.' We would like to dedicate *A New History of Management* to him.

   Chuck was critical. Some would say an iconoclast. But he wasn't against management history, he was for it. He just thought management history should be done with more curiosity and more rigour than was often the case, and is especially the case with the way history is presented in management textbooks. And it is these textbook histories, the only place that most managers and management scholars encounter a history of our field, which we take as our target in this book.

   A New History of Management is inspired by Chuck's spirit, but also by other pioneering management historians. We are critical of the little pieces of the past (to paraphrase William Flood) that have been distilled into a set of unquestioned and inevitable certainties that now bound the way management is presented to young scholars, and by association, limit their horizons for the future. But we are not necessarily critical of management historians like, for example, Lyndall Urwick and Daniel Wren. They were pioneers who wrote good management histories that were essential to moving the field forward in their times. Their insights have been reduced by later interpreters, but we have learned a lot from the coverage of the field in their original works.

What we present in this book is a new history of management written for our times. Throughout the chapters that follow, we develop an alternative history that counters those limited historical assumptions conveyed in management textbooks as foundations to management scholars and practitioners. We aim to show that these foundations are not as hard and fast as we might assume, and show that recognizing this can, in the words of Michel Foucault, 'free thought from what it silently thinks and enable thinking differently'.

We have chosen the title of the book and the cover image to illustrate this counter-intuitive idea: that rather than seeking innovation or thinking differently by running away from the past, we can, instead, seek innovation by looking more deeply at our interpretations of the past and how these limit our horizons.

The title *A New History of Management* indicates that what we are presenting is not intended to be a new orthodoxy or 'one best way'. It is 'a' history rather than 'the' history. In advocating that history is subjective and that any view of the past must be less than all that happened and based, at least partly, on the context of the present, we encourage the creation of other alternative management histories in addition to ours. Our history is not as comprehensive as Wren's histories, not even close: but our aim was not to be comprehensive. Rather, our aim was to investigate how looking again and more deeply at those elements that are conventionally seen as management's key foundations might highlight new insights and change the boundaries that our historical assumptions have, often unconsciously, placed

around the development of our field. It is, in this sense, a 'counter-history'.

The book's cover is a re-imagining of a classic image of the Bethlehem Steel works in Pennsylvania, where Frederick W. Taylor honed his management ideas. This image has often been used by management historians, perhaps drawn by the association with this new Bethlehem and the birth of a new subject for which Taylor was considered by many to be a messiah. Of course, the image that is traditionally used is an industrial working grey. The image on our cover, drawn by Brendon Palmer, is a colourful but decaying cartoon.

As Chuck put it in the words we quoted from him above, this approach to re-digging through the archive and rethinking management history is hard work. But while researching and writing this book has been difficult, we didn't do it all at once. It was a long time in the making.

Steve can recall going with a group from the University of Warwick to see John talk at a seminar at Keele University in 1992, when both of their research was beginning to engage with critical thinking and management history. Steve had just begun a PhD at Warwick focussed on how management's historical understanding of itself may limit present understandings and future endeavours in the subject. This led to a book called *Recreating Strategy*.

John's doctoral research at Aston was based on a multiple paradigm study of work behaviour in the UK Fire Service. One of the paradigm case accounts involved constructing a historical account of the labour process in fire-fighting based on archival materials held in Birmingham and London. John was completing his PhD research at Aston at the time Mick was starting his in the same department. After they completed their doctoral studies, they worked together on a study of the UK computer corporation, ICL, and then on a number of projects up to their recent papers on history in the *Academy of Management Review*.

Todd started his PhD at Cambridge in 2001. Exploring the possibility of academic freedom in an increasingly commodified higher education sector lead him to examine the history of business schools in the US and UK. Upon joining Steve at Victoria University of Wellington in 2006, they became aware of the common interest they shared in applying critical theory to question the institutions of management education and in the provenance of a number of the ideas and frameworks that they were teaching, such as Lewin's 'change as three steps', Maslow's 'hierarchy of needs', and Max Weber's theory of bureaucracy.

A number of meetings at various conferences eventually enabled the four of us to figure out that we were working in different ways with a similar purpose, and that we should join forces to create this book. So what we present here is the sum of many parts. But not only do we believe that the whole is greater than the sum of these parts, we are sure that it would not stand without all of the parts combined. In this respect, and because we all believe that it is a book that really did need to be written, it is a collaboration that we are all truly grateful for.

Given the length of time taken and the multiplicity of projects involved in the lead up, there is a large number of people to thank for helping us to get to this point: Gibson Burrell, Haridimos Tsoukas, Roger Dunbar, Gabrielle Durepos, Richard Dunford, Torkild Thanem, Scott Taylor, Donncha Kavanagh, Ellen O'Connor, Robert Cooper, Robert Chia, Elena Antonocopolou, Urs Daellenbach, David Wilson, Robin Wensley, Tom Cooper, Kenneth Brown, Duncan Angwin, Alex Faria, Rosemary Nixon, Kiren Shoman, Hugh Willmott, Chris Grey, Ann Cunliffe, Colm McLaughlin, Janet Tyson, John Ballard, John Alford, Albert Mills and Johnathan Brock.

We have drawn on the resources of many good archives and would also like to thank the librarians that have assisted us in our endeavours in various parts of the world: Leah Loscutoff at The Stevens Institute in New Jersey, Juliet Scott from the Tavistock Institute in London, Anne Woodrum from Brandeis University,

C. Vaughan-Stanley at Washington and Lee University, Katherine Fox from the Baker Library Historical Collection at Harvard Business School, and the archival team and Harvard University library. And thanks as well to our administrative and research support in our various institutions: Sophia Lum, Misa Ito, Luisa Acheson, Janet Keiler, Sheila Frost, Eve Stacey, Katherine Given, Phoebe Smith, Ben Walker, Clare Taylor and Victoria Bone.

We would also like to thank our team at Cambridge University Press: Paula Parish, Valerie Appleby, Bethany Johnson, Ellena Moriarty, Adam Hooper, Srilakshmi Gobidass, Sarah Driffill and James Gregory, and additionally the four reviewers of our original proposal. They provided very useful critical feedback, particularly with regard to how the book would benefit from a deeper investigation of Adam Smith's work and the development of theories with regard to corporate culture in the 1980s.

All of these people have contributed to the hard work of putting together a book with a simple message: if we want to think differently about management for the future, a good place to start would be to rethink what we assume to be its history.

1 Rethinking the Map of Management History

To think differently about management, we need to shake up the map of management history.

This book takes aim at an unnoticed barrier to innovation: the conventional history of management. We take as our particular target the form in which this history is most often experienced by management initiates: management textbooks. The purpose of these textbook histories, in the words of those who develop them, is to 'put the present in perspective' and 'to help us understand today's management theory and practice'. But this approach, we argue, justifies present practices as part of an evolutionary advance and makes it less likely that substantive change will occur. A New History of Management *seeks to counter the assumptions that this conventional view promotes in order to question the present, blur the boundaries defined by simplistic versions of the past and to encourage thinking differently for the future. This first chapter surveys the current narrow and homogeneous map of management history and outlines a methodology for a deeper historical understanding that can encourage people to think differently about management.*

As a starting point in our new exploration of the history of management, we sought a snapshot of what historians have previously seen as worthy of investigation.[1] We surveyed the most highly regarded journals of management and business history to ascertain the geographical locations that they focussed on. We coded the 859 articles from the journal *Business History* published over the past six decades; 894 from the journal *Business History Review* for the same period; and the 234 and 78 respectively published in the more recently established *Journal of Management History* and *Management and Organization History*. About 80 per cent of the articles could be coded for their geographic focus, or which part of the world the article was about. We sent the results to *Worldmapper.org* to create a map that depicted the world in terms of the relativities in the data. The picture on the page opposite is the world according to management and business history journals (Figure 1).[2] In this world, the two Anglo giants, the UK and the US, dominate. Japan, Australia, New Zealand and South Africa just about hold their own, while the rest of Africa, Asia and South America shrink to slivers.

This is obviously problematic from the perspective of wanting to encourage diversity. But where this is less obviously problematic is that this picture may be reflective of a potential decline in innovation in management and it is this that is the focus of this book. Our thesis may be summed up in a sentence: *if we are to think differently, truly innovatively, about management, we may have to look again at and rethink our historical assumptions about our field.*

This idea differs from those reasons put forward by scholars recently as to why we may have seen a decline of substantially new

---

[1] This chapter draws on material from Clark, P. & Rowlinson, M. (2004). The Treatment of History in Organisation Studies: Towards an 'Historic Turn'? *Business History*, 46(3), 331–52; Cummings, S. & Bridgman, T. (2016). The Limits and Possibilities of History: How a Wider, Deeper, and More Engaged Understanding of Business History Can Foster Innovative Thinking. *Academy of Management Learning & Education*, 15(2): 1–18.

[2] The authors wish to thank Benjamin D. Hennig and Danny Dorling at the University of Sheffield and www.worldmapper.org for kindly developing this map based on our data.

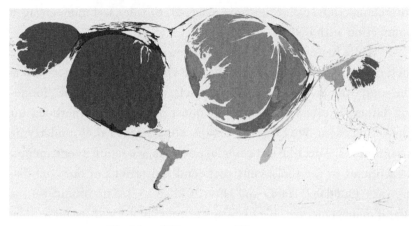

FIGURE I The Map of Management History
Source: Worldmapper.org (reproduced with permission from Worldmapp
er.org)

ideas in management studies. They have suggested a range of other
limits. For example, a low-risk inductive-deductive approach to copy-
ing 'best practice' rather than aiming abductively for next practice
(Martin, 2009; Nattermann, 2000; Prahalad and Ramaswamy, 2004);
theorizing in ways that are disconnected from the realities of management practice (Clark and Wright, 2009; Cornelissen and Floyd, 2009;
Sandberg and Tsoukas, 2011; Smith and Lewis, 2011); a desire to
borrow theories from other fields rather than develop unique theories
(Oswick, Fleming and Hanlon, 2011; Whetten, Felin and King, 2009);
professional norms that privilege research appealing to traditional
conventions and highly ranked forums (Alvesson and Sandberg,
2011; 2012; Bartunek, Rynes and Ireland, 2006; Grey, 2010; Shepherd
and Sutcliffe, 2011); and the limiting institutional conditions of theory development in business schools (Alvesson and Sandberg, 2012;
Clark and Wright, 2009; Grey, 2010). Our book provides another
reason: that the current lack of innovation has roots in the past, or
more specifically, in management research's narrow view of what in
its past is relevant. The limited way in which we have recorded our
past limits what we focus on and how we theorize in the present and
consequently   bounds   progression.   New   possibilities   and

interconnections can result from a deeper, broader and more engaged connection with history.

While history has occasionally been noted in debates about the lack of innovation in management, the view that looking forward is the source of new ideas is still promoted: 'we still look to the "founding fathers" for our fundamental questions and our methods for answering them. We carry the historical baggage of their underlying assumptions. And, like lost colonial outposts, we retain a sentimental attachment to the tools, constructs and limitations of our core disciplines' (Suddaby, Hardy and Huy, 2011, p.237). The implication is that if management is able to escape from its history, thinking will be freed to be more in keeping with new times and to be more innovative. We argue the opposite: rather than running away from history and paying it less attention, we should dive back in, take a broader look and uncover more than the narrow view recorded in conventional histories of management. More history rather than less could promote greater innovation.

A New History of Management subsequently advocates an approach that may seem contrary to logic: that looking back in this way can foster a greater plurality of ideas that can be debated, challenge one another and be combined to promote innovative thinking. We argue that the limited, one-dimensional, uni-cultural way in which we have recorded our field's past can limit what we focus on in the present and how we face the future.

The elements of this argument are not new. There is increasing awareness about the links between greater diversity leading to more innovation, idea generation and more creative problem solving. One of the first scholarly books on creativity, Arthur Koestler's (1970) *The Act of Creation*, links creativity to the Latin verb 'cogito' (to think), which, he explains, 'means to "shake together" ... the creative act, by connecting previously unrelated dimensions of experience is an act of liberation [and] defeat[er] of habit' (Koestler, 1970, p.96). As Koestler's work has been revisited in recent times, interest in this idea has grown. Scholarly research has promoted diversity of perspective as a means of countering the effects of 'dominant logic' and spurring creativity and innovation (e.g., Bettis and Prahalad, 1995; Jackson et al., 2003; Kearney and Gebert, 2009; Polanyi, 1981; Prahalad and Bettis, 1986; Shin and Zhou, 2007; Williams and O'Reilly, 1998). Others have linked a reducing range of citations, and a focus on recent articles and a faster forgetting of works from earlier ages (what is sometimes referred to now as 'attention decay'), to a narrowing of scholarship and a reduction in significant new knowledge development (Evans, 2008; Parolo et al., 2015). And a range of popular books have appeared trumpeting everything from the 'Medici Effect', or the Medici's ability to bring together leaders in a range of disciplines (Johansson, 2006); how a diversity of 'visions' contributed to the creation of the American Constitution (Ellis, 2012); Einstein's breadth of life experiences (White and Gribbin, 2005); and the range of personalities that Edison assembled (in addition to his own peculiarities) at Menlo Park (Baldwin, 1996).

Indeed, a good example of how innovation emerges from diverse characteristics combining or 'bisociating' (to use the Koestler's term for this idea) can be seen in Edison's notebooks. Edison's ideas books were divided in two. Edison would scrawl out his barely legible flashes of inspiration. And then, on the facing page, an associate, such as precise and highly organized Charles Batchelor, would work out these ideas more fully and start to plan out if and how they might be realized (Figure 2). Neither Batchelor nor Edison's approach, on its own, was innovative: innovation emerged when the two were 'shaken together'.

Furthermore, our argument that looking back can help us to better look forward is not completely new with respect to management history either. Some recent works have linked a neglect of historical awareness to a number of key skills business students are less likely to acquire. They argue that a better understanding of management's history helps students learn the lessons of past mistakes (Smith 2007; Thomson 2001; Wren 1987a); or establish a link with 'great minds' (Bedeian, 2004); or develop a 'collective memory', an

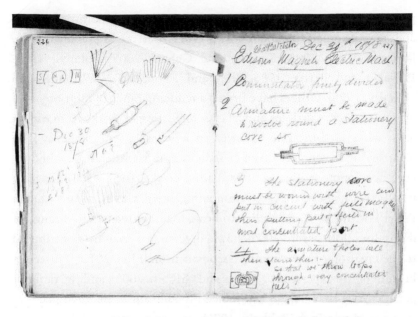

FIGURE 2 Edison's Ideas Book: Edison (left); Batchelor (right)
Source: This image is from Edison's Menlo Park notebooks and
reproduced from the freely available collection that has been compiled
and digitized by Rutgers University (http://edison.rutgers.edu/digital
.htm)

identity for the profession or an integrating framework (Khurana,
2007; Smith, 2007; Wren, 1987a); or that it provides a baseline for
evaluating the extent of change in management over time (Jones and
Khanna, 2006; Smith, 2007; Thomson, 2001; Wren, 2005; Wren,
1987a); or that a better understanding of history assists students to
think about how supposedly 'new' management practices really are
(Bedeian, 2004; Smith, 2007; Thomson, 2001; Wren, 2005).

We agree with these assessments. However, it is not just the
lack of history teaching that goes on in business schools and who is
teaching it that diminishes our field (Wren, 2005). It is also the quality
of teaching materials and, in particular, the lack of a critical and
creative attitude that prevents history having the positive effect on
management's future that it could. Addressing this by promoting

a search for greater diversity would, we argue, offer a further advantage of a historical engagement, which would result not only in better students in the present, but fundamental improvements for the future of our field. *A New History of Management* argues that encouraging people to think critically about the construction of management history will enable them to think more creatively about what management could be.

And the first and best place that we might start thinking critically about the presentation of management history is introductory management textbooks.

THE TARGET: THE TEXTBOOK VIEW OF MANAGEMENT HISTORY

> Students want to know what works and what doesn't ... they are not interested in the details of research, the historical evolution of our knowledge, or long discourses on competing ideas.

Stephen Robbins (1997, p.xvii)

Given most management students and scholars only encounter the history of the general field (as opposed to their specialization) in introductory courses and texts, and that textbooks in general play an essential role in codifying and disseminating the foundations and limits of what is important in a field (Kuhn, 1970; Stambaugh and Trank, 2010), management textbooks may provide the best insight into the conventional view of management's origins (Jones and Khanna, 2006; Payne, Youngcourt and Watrous, 2006; Smith, 2007; Wren, 2005). Subsequently, our new history of management starts with exploring how history is presented in these texts.

Typically, studies of textbooks have focussed on the accuracy of the representation of pioneers such as Taylor (Payne, Youngcourt and Watrous, 2006) and critical events such as the Hawthorne Studies (Adair, 1984; McQuarrie, 2005; Olsen, Verley, Salas and Santos, 2004). We, however, are not so much concerned to report on inaccuracies, but to highlight what is promoted, both in terms of the content and the process by which this content is seen to develop, and by association left out, so that we might think further about alternative origins.

The views expressed by Stephen Robbins at the head of this section reflect a general undertone in many management textbooks (Robbins goes on to claim that 'students' interest in history is minimal' and that 'the classical material in management textbooks has little value to today's students ...' 1997, p.xvii). This view resonates with broader assumptions about the ideal managers for the 'new economy': free floating identities, trained to constantly embrace change, unattached and unencumbered by history (assumptions recently critiqued by Sennett (2006) and Petriglieri and Petriglieri (2009; 2010)). Moreover, this view may be connected to debates in management education, suggesting that our curricula would be more relevant (i.e., better) if it was cut free from teaching subjects for tradition's sake and reflected what was actually happening in the world of business practice (Bennis and O'Toole, 2005; Mintzberg, 2004; Rubin and Dierdorff, 2009; Worrell, 2009).

But despite this antipathy, a simple 'potted history' is found in most introductory texts: almost always in 'chapter two' after an introductory chapter (Chapter One will define the field; Chapter Two reinforces this by outlining the history of these definitions). These histories typically identify the key kernel as the assertion of a mechanistic-industrial worldview (if cultures prior to the industrial revolution are incorporated, it is because modern management's staples, planning, directing, organizing and controlling, are discerned in their achievements, not because they looked at things differently – Tsoukas and Cummings, 1997); and a subsequent belief that since that point, progress has come from the development of a more humanistic and organic understanding. This continuity currently culminates in views about the discovery of contingency, systems approaches and culture, and importance of sustainability and an organization's responsibility to the wider environment, views claimed to oppose management's classical approaches. Figure 3 is

Era	Background to contemporary management	Classical	Human	Calculating	Values & beliefs	Future
Years	1530+	1910–30	1930–50	1950–70	1970–90	1990–
Key ideas associated with each era	Emphasis on materialism & individualism Industrial revolution Increasing prevalence & size of corporations	One best way Scientific mgmt -Taylor Time/Motion Gilbreth Bureaucracy Weber Principles of mgmt - Fayol	Interpersonal aspects	Mgmt science	Social construction, institutionalization, culture *etc.*	CSR; stakeholder theory Mainstream emphasis on maximizing materialist-individualist goals gets in the way of other forms of well-being (e.g., social, ecological)

FIGURE 3 Management History 'Road Map'
Source: Adapted from images and text in *Management: Current Practices and New Directions* (Dyck and Neubert 2008, pp.30–1)

a representation of a map from a recent textbook that illustrates the standard narrative.

While most texts do not outline a historical map as explicitly, one may be discerned in the origin stories told and the subsequent sequencing of chapters in other texts, from the simplest/oldest mechanistic theories to more recent international, diversity-encouraging, ecologically minded chapters towards the end. The content of their descriptions of their field's history and the process by which it is outlined is strikingly similar, as shown in Table 1.

Where are the key points of origin in the historical narrative outlined in management textbooks taken from? As Table 1 illustrates, sometimes no references are needed: this is common knowledge. But when references are cited, they are similar. They tend to be the few management history books that were written at the time most of these textbook's first editions were developed (the late 1960s and 1970s). The books written by C.S. George (1968/1972), Daniel Wren (1972), Sidney Pollard (1965) and Alfred Chandler (1962) are utilized to a great extent. Sometimes academic articles are also cited, either from business history journals or in other journals, but with a historical theme. Wren's books, in particular, cited academic journal research as a basis of his book which formed the basis of many of the histories in

Table 1 *Key Elements of Management's Origin Narrative in Textbooks*

Textbook	Precedents leading to management	Primary individuals	References to management histories
Bateman & Snell (2009) *Management*	Poor production efficiency, management decisions unsystematic	Adam Smith → Taylor → Fayol → Mayo → Weber → McGregor	Chandler (1990); George (1972)
Kinicki & Williams (2009) *Management*	Industrial expansion, labour in short supply, need to improve labour productivity	Taylor → Gilbreths → Weber → Mayo → McGregor →	None
Rue & Byars (2009) *Management*	Rapid industrialization but production methods crude, needed to be improved	Taylor → Barth → Cooke → Gantt → Gilbreths →Fayol → McGregor → Mayo → Peters & Waterman	Wren (1972, 1979); Chandler (1959); Mee (1963); Wrege & Hodgetts, (2000)
Robbins et al. (2012) *Management*	Popularity of division of labour, industrial revolution, need to maximize efficiency	Adam Smith → Taylor → Gilbreths → Weber → Fayol → Follet → Mayo → Maslow → McGregor	George (1972); Banta (1993); Kanigel (1997); Wagner-Tsukamoto (2007)

Table 1 (cont.)

Textbook	Precedents leading to management	Primary individuals	References to management histories
Samson & Daft (2012) *Management*	Factory systems that emerged in the 1800s posed new management challenges	Taylor → Gantt → Weber → Fayol → Follet → Barnard → Mayo → Maslow → McGregor	Wren (1979); George (1968); Metcalf & Urwick (1940); Van Fleet (1982)
Schermerhorn et al. (2014) *Management*	Workers produced less than they were capable of because of inefficient work methods	Adam Smith → Taylor → Gilbreths →Fayol → Follet →Weber →Mayo → Maslow→McGregor	Wren (2005); Kanigel (1997); Locke (1982); Wrege & Perroni (1974)

the textbooks. There was a convergence of interests here. The period post–World War II witnessed the spread of business schools at universities, and the first serious histories of management were written which outlined the fields' noble origins and helped legitimate them being seen as 'university worthy'. The Ford and Carnegie sponsored reports had prescribed the ideal form of a business school and its curricula (Gordon and Howell, 1959; Pierson, 1959). And with a further growth spurt in student numbers and advances in pedagogy and publishing, the first textbooks (as we know them) started to emerge *en masse*. Business Schools, management textbooks and a history of management grew quickly in this period and legitimated one another's existence.

It may be that these limited historical reference points lead to the homogeneity displayed in the world map at the head of this chapter (and we shall pay close attention to the influence of George and Wren in later chapters). However, before jumping to this conclusion, we did wonder after looking at the Worldmapper image if we were unreasonably harsh on the reporting of management history. Would it not be the case that historians writing in English and contributing to leading scholarly journals (given that highly rated journals tend to be based in places like the US and the UK) would be similarly predisposed to focus on 'their own'? Might it not be self-evident that management and business histories should focus on the regions where the industrial revolution or management consulting began? The Worldmapper result made us curious to investigate the presentation of business and management's history, relative to the presentation of history in comparable fields.

Consequently, as a next step, we set out to probe whether management history writing was any more limited than other types of history and whether there had been any changes of scope over a substantial period of time. We already knew that business had two highly regarded history journals that been published for over six decades: one based in the US, one in the UK (*Business History* and *Business History Review*). Having decided it would be useful to use these journals as representative of the field and leave aside the other two management history journals which were established far more recently, we required, as comparable sets, disciplines with more than one highly rated history journal devoted solely to the study of just its history (i.e., journals with a broader focus on the history of a group of subjects like science or art were not useful for our purposes) and for one of these journals to be based in the US and another in the UK or another country.

Economics, law, philosophy and many others fell short of our comparable academic history journal criterion for selecting comparators. However, the history of medicine and the history of architecture did meet our needs. Like management and business, these are stochastic fields where, while we may be guided by theories or principles, we must adjust our thinking and recalibrate our actions as our subjects or cases or stakeholders respond in individual ways to previous interventions in changing environments. Our initial investigations also revealed that there seemed to be no recent laments in these fields about the lack of new ideas. Consequently, we sought to analyse and contrast what their histories recorded with management and business history.

We constructed three sets of abstracts dating from 1951 to 2010. The business history set contained all 859 abstracts from articles published across this period in the UK-based *Business History*, and the 894 abstracts published in *Business History Review*. (The *Journal of Management History* and the *Journal of Management and Organizational History*, data from which we shall refer to on occasion later in this chapter, are based in the US and the UK, respectively). The medical history set was made up of 602 from the UK-based *Journal of the History of Medicine and Allied Sciences* and 1554 from the US-based *Bulletin of the History of Medicine*. The third set, of architectural history abstracts, comprised 1059 abstracts from the US-based *Journal of the Society of Architectural Historians* and 292 from the UK-based *Construction History*. While neither the medical nor architectural set contained the abstracts of all the articles published in this period (as we were reliant on downloading electronic versions of the abstracts, there were a couple of years that were not

Table 2 *Data for Six Business Management, Medical and Architectural Journals*

	Coded for time – Raw	Coded for time – %	Coded for place – Raw	Coded for place – %	Coded for both – Raw	Coded for both – %
BH	724/859	84.28	772	90	694	80.79
BHR	710/894	79.42	757	84.34	710	79.42
Total Coded Business	1434	81.80	1529	87.22	1404	80.09
JHMAS	580/602	96.34	480	79.73	463	76.91
BHM	728/1554	46.85	763	49.09	500	32.17
Total Coded Medicine	1308	60.67	1243	57.65	963	44.66
JSAH	443/1059	41.83	894	84.42	402	37.96
CH	288/292	98.63	259	88.70	257	88.01
Total Coded Architecture	731	54.10	1153	85.34	659	48.77

obtainable in both the medical and architectural history journals, often in the years surrounding a change of publisher), in both instances, we were able to gather the majority of all abstracts with representative samples across all six decades of our survey.

After discussing and ruling out potential criteria (such as whether the perspective being applied was conventional or unconventional) for being too difficult to determine reliably in our large data sets, we settled on two simple aspects: the geographical location focussed upon in the article, or 'place', and the temporal setting or age focussed upon, or 'time'.[3] Experienced researchers could quickly code for these aspects with extremely high inter-rater reliability, and given that our purpose was not to capture the truth of what happened in the past, but to seek comparison that would help to raise questions about how what we focus on in the past illuminates pathways in the present, time and place were effective dimensions with which to begin.

As we explain in the paragraphs to follow, our results for geographic place, time, and time and place together show that management and business history has a far more limited geographical and temporal perspective than either of its two comparator fields of inquiry. More encouragingly though, we found signs that greater diversity in management history is certainly possible and that it may now be emerging. Table 2 shows the numbers and percentages of the articles surveyed from the six business management, medical, and architectural history journals published between 1950 and 2010 that could be coded for time of focus, for place focus, and for both time and place.

Table 3 shows the numbers and percentages of the articles surveyed from the two additional management history journals that are referred to in this chapter that could be coded for time of focus, for place focus, and for both time and place.

---

[3] When an article focussed on two or more discrete geographical locations, we gave each of these locations a fraction of one (e.g., a focus on the US and Japan scored .5 for each location). When an article focussed on a very broad swathe of time, we recorded the median point.

Table 3 *Data for Two Additional Management History Journals*

	Coded for time – Raw	Coded for time – %	Coded for place – Raw	Coded for place – %	Coded for both – Raw	Coded for both – %
JMH	134/234	57.02	149/234	63.40	113/234	48.29
JM&OH	56/78	71.79	50/78	64.10	45/78	57.69

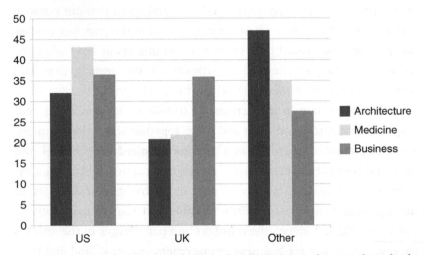

FIGURE 4 Percentages of Geographical Focus in Architectural, Medical and Business History Articles

CONVENTIONAL MANAGEMENT HISTORY'S RELATIVE LIMITS

Place

Our initial analysis on the places focussed upon indicated a far greater deal of geographical variety in journals of architecture and medical history (Figure 4). While the US and UK, respective home bases for the two journals chosen to represent each of these

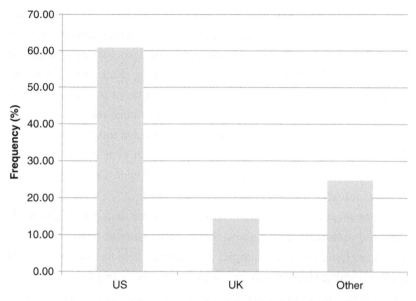

FIGURE 5 Total Percentages of Articles Coded for Place in the *History of Management Journal* and the *Journal of Management and Organizational History*

professions, were also the two most written about national settings, nearly half of the articles on architectural history were written about other locations, as were over a third of the medical history papers. Just over a quarter of all business history papers focussed on territories beyond the US and UK.

Moreover, there is a significant difference in the total number of countries focussed upon in that 'other' category. A total of eighty-four countries have been afforded at least some consideration by architectural historians: eighty in medicine, and only fifty in business. No other countries (apart from the US and the UK) have over 5 per cent representation in business history journals. In medicine and architecture, two other countries achieve this level of significance (Germany and France, and Italy and France, respectively). While we might hope that the more recently published management history journals would demonstrate greater diversity and variability of place, the results here are fairly consistent with their business history cousins, as Figure 5 illustrates.

When we grouped the data into six decades, from the 1950s to the 2000s, for Africa, Asia, Continental Europe (i.e., Europe minus the UK), North America and the UK, we observed some interesting changes in the representation of place over time between the three sets.[4] There are some encouraging signs, with respect to diversity, in management and business history journals. The percentage of articles relating to Asian and African locations that could be coded for place has increased steadily from around 2 per cent in the 1950s to 5 per cent in the 2000s for Asia and from 0.75 per cent to nearly 2 per cent for Africa. Correspondingly, interest in the UK has waned.

But what is starker when one compares the data is how the medicine and architecture sets show much more variability in focus over time than business. For example, architecture history papers go from next to nothing on Asia and Africa in the 1950s to 16 per cent and 4.5 per cent on these regions respectively in the 1980s, a peak which drops away again after this flourish. Medical histories interest in these two locations peaks in the 1990s (at 10 per cent) and 1960s (4.3 per cent) respectively. This would appear to indicate that medical and architecture history is more able than business history to shift historical focus so as to move with the problems or interests of the times. This relative lack of variability in business history research is something we will also see with respect to temporality in the next section.

Time

In addition to coding articles for place, we also sought to gain some appreciation of the times or ages focussed upon across our three sets of history journals and arranged these into 20-year blocks. As with place, not all articles were focussed in this way, but the vast majority (about 70 per cent overall) were, and could be coded. Whenever a broader period of time was focussed upon, we recorded the midpoint or median year.

[4] We recognize that grouping our data into continents in this regard is problematic. For example, the stories from Morocco will likely be very different from those of South Africa or Uganda. But our aim here is to illustrate in a powerful way a lack of diversity in management and business history, not to replace global homogeneity with a belief that there should be continental homogeneity.

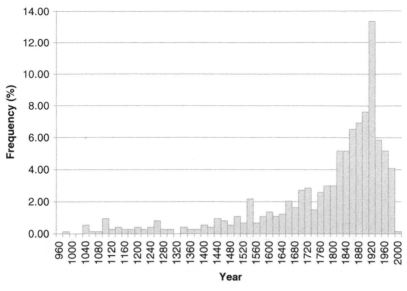

FIGURE 6 Architectural History 'Manhattan'

The bar (or 'Manhattan' skyline) charts show the frequency of dates focussed on within the journal articles for each of the three discipline sets published during the period 1950–2010 as a percentage of the total. Each has different characteristics. Architecture (Figure 6) is the most broad-ranging, with a very specific homage paid to the period 1900–20, but significant populations of articles dating back through many centuries.

Medical history (shown in Figure 7) lacks a stand-out skyscraper, but has a wide spread of significant focus of over 6 per cent representation right across the period 1800–1940 and at least 1 per cent representation all the way back to 1600.

Business history (Figure 8) is far more concentrated towards the right-hand side of the graph, with 1920–40 matching the height of architecture's tallest bar, but with a range of similarly tall edifices on either side. The periods from 1900 to 1980, in business history, each have greater representation than any single period in medical history. If we were hoping that the management history journals were broader in their emphasis, again, as with time, the patterns here are

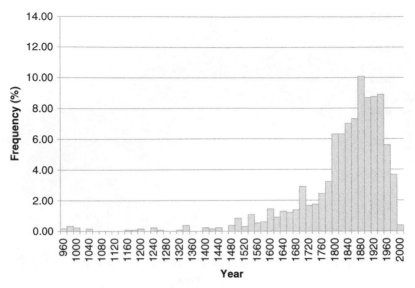

FIGURE 7 Medical History 'Manhattan'

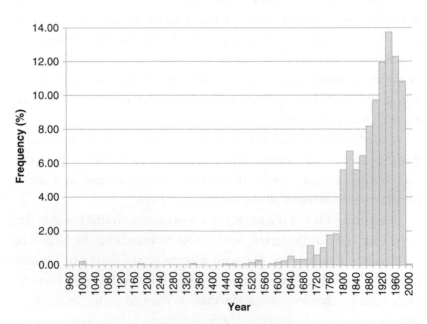

FIGURE 8 Business History 'Manhattan'

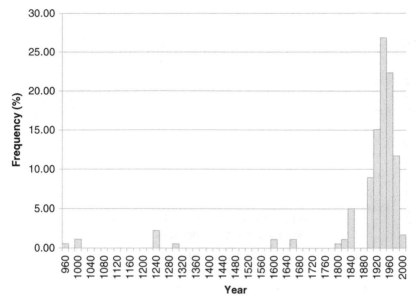

FIGURE 9 Management History 'Manhattan'

more or less the same, but with a greater intensification of bias towards sites dated 1920–60 (Figure 9).

Moreover, when we look at the average time of focus for each of our three subject sets, what falls within one standard deviation of these averages, and how these numbers change through the decades, we can interpret some interesting differences between business and architecture and medical history in terms of diversity of focus (see Figure 10).

The mean date for the 1434 Business History articles for which dates could be determined was 1879. For architecture history (n = 731) it was 1763; for medical history (n = 1308), 1791. When we removed the dates that were ascribed to articles that focussed on a broad sweep of history (e.g., 'the eighteenth century'), the averages understandably moved forward in time: business (n = 480), 1908; architecture (n = 326), 1806; medicine (n = 417), 1843.[5] Architecture and

---

[5] An interesting sidebar is just how much greater the percentage of business history journal articles relate to specific times and places (c. 80 per cent), relative to a much lower percentage in architecture and medicine (40–50 per cent) where the concerns are more often general or time/place neutral.

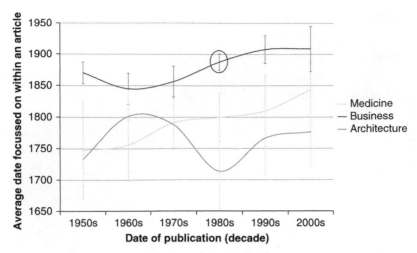

FIGURE 10 Average Date Focus within Medicine, Business and Architecture History Journals by Decade (1950–2010) with Vertical Bars Representing Single Standard Deviations

medicine show more variability of movement of the average time of focus over the decades, with a distinct shift of focus in architecture in the 1970s and medicine in the 2000s, perhaps with an emphasis shaped more by the particular concerns of the times rather than reinforcing traditional origins/sites of truth. Business has followed a steady path at a consistent distance from the past (about 100 years – or about 70 years if we adjust so as to not include those articles with rather vague dates, e.g., the seventeenth century). However, the levelling off in recent times around a mean date of 1910 would be worrying if it suggested a sedimentation and growing stagnation.

More interesting, however, may be the standard deviation results which illustrate the normal breadth of focus. Here, the standard deviations around the mean measures were two and a half times larger for medicine and architecture than for business. For business history, it was 115 years; architecture 247; medicine 261. When we removed the dates that were ascribed to articles that focussed on a broad sweep (e.g., nineteenth-century Trade Associations), the standard deviations differences were even starker: business, 47 years;

architecture, 209 years; medicine 157 years. The circle in Figure 10 (around the smallest standard deviation relating to business history writing in the 1980s) falls on the same period that most of today's major textbooks in management were consolidating into their current formats. While these texts were generally informed by books (e.g., Chandler, 1977; George, 1972; Wren 1972), these books and the text-book writers themselves were influenced by the narrow view of the field in general in creating the narrow histories that they pass on to students. These books are often now into their twelfth, thirteenth or fourteenth editions, but while nuances may shift across editions to move with the times, the key characters and events regarded as management's points of origin, and the way these are presented, have not changed.

Time and Place

Having looked at the data with respect to time and place, we then combined these dimensions, taking those articles that could be coded for both (since 1800, to enable more readily comparable graphs) and plotting the percentages for each of the three sets in bubble area graphs.

As Figure 11 indicates, Business is highly concentrated around North America between 1840 and 1860 and the UK and North America in the first 60 years of the twentieth century, although it does have representative 'dots' of interest on almost all areas of the grid.

Architecture (shown in Figure 12) has a wider range of significant interest, geographically and temporally, with more continental European focus and significant pockets of interest outside of the north western world (e.g., Africa 1820–40; South America 1840–60; Asia 1820–40).

Medicine (Figure 13) has a much broader time span of concentrated interest and a greater focus on Continental Europe than management and business history, but it demonstrates a smaller degree of interest beyond those three geographies across time than architecture. However, like business, it does cover more of the 'bases' (even if only to miniscule degrees in many cases).

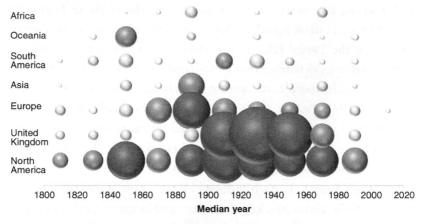

FIGURE 11 Business History Journal Time and Place

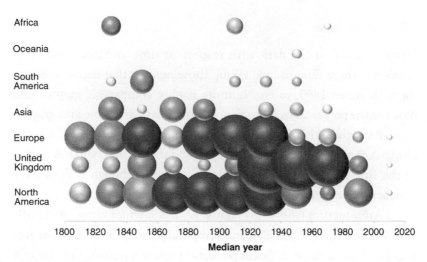

FIGURE 12 Architecture History Journal Time and Place

THE IMPLICATIONS OF CURRENT HISTORICAL
CONVENTIONS FOR MANAGEMENT'S FUTURE

We acknowledge that the study reported on above is limited. For reasons that we have explained, we have focussed on simple dimensions that could be easily coded reliably across large samples: place

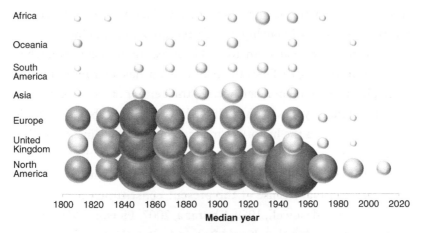

FIGURE 13 Medicine History Journal Time and Place

and time. It might be argued that diversity could be analysed by looking at disciplinary perspectives of the location that authors are based in, and we would encourage further studies that looked at these aspects. While we have not directly linked greater historical diversity to greater innovation in management thought, we believe that the arguments linking homogeneity of perspective may lead to a lack of innovation in the present, and should cause us to ponder how history may play a role in limiting perspectives of what is relevant and possible in our field. In defence of these limitations, we have investigated history not to prove current interpretations wrong, to develop causal theories of what leads to innovation or promote new truths, but to raise doubts about current norms so as to encourage greater diversity and thinking otherwise.

Early in this chapter, we outlined the premise that greater diversity of perspective can encourage greater innovation, and we linked it to current discussions about why management is not currently generating significant new theories and perspectives. We suggest that a limited view of the past may constrain perspectives of what we take management to be about in the present and subsequently could be limiting future development. We then sought to investigate the limits of the practice of management and business history writing relative to history scholarship in architecture and medicine.

So, how does management and business history compare when looked at in this light? First, the bad news: it has a far more limited geographical and temporal perspective than either of its two comparator fields of inquiry. Based on what we have outlined above, we could surmise that when the history of management and business was first taken seriously, as part of a process to legitimate the then-fledgling field in the mid-twentieth century, it embraced origins that helped legitimate and make sense of the present constitution (Cummings, 2002; Gordon and Howell, 1959; Khurana, 2007; Pierson, 1959). These origins were found in the US and Britain in the nineteenth and early twentieth centuries. Since that point, management and business history's temporal focus (unlike architecture or medicine) does not appear to have changed focus to reflect particular problems or new concerns. And, it seems now that it may be anchored on a median spot – 1900–20, as conventional histories are prone to do, unless they are challenged. There is a danger that management history may now be acting as a limit: an archive stuck in time, rather than a dynamic reflection of a vibrant field with multiple possibilities.

In reflecting on this, it is worth considering that there has not been widespread lament in the leading medical and architecture journals asking where their fields' new ideas are. It may be that their wider, more diverse and dynamic histories, and related broader view of what their boundaries could embrace, help to spur creative hybrids and other forms of innovation. However, in defence, readers may already be thinking that architectural historians, for example, would have it easier than business historians in being able to study a wider range of physical remains and plans. This is certainly true, but just as difficulty is the excuse history never accepts (Murrow, 1961), difficulty should not be an excuse for historians or management scholars. If the intent exists to study difficult or non-obvious objects or look in novel ways and adopt other perspectives, then such histories will emerge.

And this brings us to the positive news. Figure 11 also shows that business history may come from any age and location, if we choose to focus there. Specs of interest are widespread and even more so in business than architecture. Furthermore, while the management history 'Manhattan' shown in Figure 9 is similar in most respects to its business history counterpart, it does demonstrate pockets of interest prior to 1680. In addition, while the percentages are small, there are increases in articles focussing on Asia, South America and Africa.

The good news in this regard is that management's history is not atemporal. Because our view of management's past (like most history) may be shaped less by what happened as that history was forming than by present concerns as that history was written, it need not be considered immobile – as the chapters that follow will demonstrate (Cummings and Bridgman, 2011). Hence, we can reinterpret and reshape it.

While management and business history's collective memory, or perspective of the past, does appear limited when compared to other fields, what we found also points to the possible role that this history can play in broadening thinking in the future. Rather than merely teaching or implying that what is worthy of attention in management and business history happened in the UK and the US between 1800–1920, we should actively seek out, and encourage young scholars to seek out, alternative perspectives from other times and places that could be rejuvenated, or combined with thinking from other times and places to create interesting hybrids, or broaden our understanding of what the field could be about or help us to look differently at old and new management issues. New knowledge about history, we hope, will be incorporated into textbook histories that can provide new vehicles for future thinking.

There appear to be two main approaches to help promote this development: going wider than the small set of standard characters outlined in those 'chapter two' textbook histories and looking into worlds that are not influenced by modern Western industrial perspectives; and going deeper and getting more engaged with archives to gain a better understanding of the complexities of the lives and times of those claimed to be management's founders.

Going Broader: Looking at Other Worlds of Management

Diversity has been a 'hot topic' in management over the past decade. For example, Kirkman and Law's highly cited review in *Academy of Management Journal* hailed a 'real internationalization of AMJ' (2005, p.385). Such diversity, and the creativity that this would bring, has led them and others to proclaim the start of the twenty-first century as a 'golden age of international management research' (Kirkman and Law, 2005, p.379, see also Ellis and Zhan, 2011). Tempering this optimism, however, has been the observation that while international diversity has grown, mirroring the internationalization of membership of the Academy of Management, there is a homogenizing use of a Western research paradigm, 'whereby researchers inadvertently depress the development of novel ideas and theories that may prove to be useful in advancing knowledge in different national and emerging-economy contexts' (Tsui, 2007, p.1354). In other words, while knowledge development may appear more diverse, this surface diversity may in fact mask more subtle homogenizing tendencies (e.g., Bruton et al., 2005; Metz and Harzing, 2009; Meyer, 2006; Terjesen et al., 2016).

A similar process appears to be happening with regard to management history. Our own research into papers presented at the recently held first Academy of Management conference in Africa (with an aim to 'bring Africa's unique capabilities and needs to the attention of the world's organization and management scholars ...', Academy of Management, 2013), found that while a large proportion of the presentations focussed on African subject matter, they applied research techniques and theories developed in the West or did comparison studies between modern African thinking and practice and what had been found on similar dimensions in modern Western sites. Not one of the 99 presentations took as its primary focus indigenous African organizational forms or management practices and only one explicitly questioned the appropriateness of conventional theoretical foundations applied in an African setting and sought to advance an innovative perspective out of this (Mangaliso and Lewis, 2013).

While the Academy of Management in Africa initiative was certainly a step in the right direction with regard to increasing diversity, we, like Tsui and others (e.g., Decker, 2013; Li, 2012; Sundararajan, 2015; Welch et al., 2011), would encourage management scholars and educators to take different contexts seriously, to develop innovative theory and to ask novel questions inspired by a deeper contextualization, not just with regard to present empirical research, but in researching management history too.

In line with our earlier arguments with regard to creativity, it would be valuable, therefore, to combine this initiative with a real effort to find interesting and underappreciated alternative approaches to management from continents other than those enlarged on the map at the head of this chapter. For example, an exemplary study in this regard is Avner Greif's work on the coalitions formed by eleventh-century Maghribi traders from North Africa to enable them to work efficiently across borders without the legal institutions that would regulate what we today would consider a conventional market. As Greif (1993, p.526) explains:

> Expectations, implicit contractual relations, and a specific information-transmission mechanism constituted the constraints that affected an individual trader's choice of action. In particular, these constraints supported the operation of a reputation mechanism that enabled the Maghribis to overcome the commitment problem [and] reinforced the expectations on which the coalition was based, motivated traders to adhere to the implicit contracts, and led to entry and exit barriers which ensured the sustainability of the coalition.

At the time that Greif wrote this, it was customary, following the thinking of Ronald Coase, to distinguish between market and non-market institutions (like those which governed the Maghribi's practices). New forms of markets enabled by recent developments in information technology, forms that are difficult to regulate with conventional legal systems, were not known. Revisiting premodern non-market cases like that of the Maghribi provides a useful way to think innovatively about how the current rise of what we call secondary – or after – markets (Bayón, 2013), such as those operated by derivative traders, eBay, Craigslist, Amazon and AliBaba, might self-regulate, evolve and be enhanced or detracted from through the imposition of conventional market constraints (see Baumol, 1990, for a similarly insightful cross-cultural study of diverse types of entrepreneurship from different ages).[6]

Further examples of how a change in historical perspective could change future practice and scholarship could be the application of medieval, scholastic and monastic traditions to think differently about business ethics or modern knowledge-intensive firms (McGrath 2005; 2007; Wren, 2000). It had been the case that the history books used in New Zealand schools continued to promote the views of those who had first reported on the wars between the British colonial forces and the indigenous Maori, right up until the 1980s (see, e.g., Oliver, 1981, p.58ff.). The view was that the Maori had 'shewn no strategical knowledge' (Carey 1863, p.66) and that they had displayed the 'weaknesses generally associated with savage races [fighting] under no definite strategical plan and without unity of command' (Shrimpton and Mulgan, 1930). It was not until this history was questioned by others that it was discovered that the Maori had actually achieved many victories against difficult odds as a result of their 'unusual' practices that Maori approaches (loosely planned but mostly emergent) were acknowledged as worthy of further consideration (Cummings, 2002). A new generation of curious historians were then able to see that 'It is true that Maori organization was informal and unstructured. But the absence of European forms of organization does

---

[6] An inspirational project that goes wider than conventional norms in this regard is the emerging open-source African Economic History project being developed by Ewout Frankema from Wageningen University and Ellen Hillbom from the University of Lund (see www.aehnetwork.org/textbook/).

not mean that organization per se was absent' (Belich, 1986, p.130). The pride and creative dynamic that these historical re-appreciations helped promote are still being felt today. Moreover, this insight would have offered an interesting alternative view on the debates that beset strategic management in the 1990s, as to whether strategy was more truly about planning from the top or bottom-up emergence (Ansoff, 1991; Mintzberg, 1991), and which is still of interest to those who view strategy as practice or focus on the importance of micro-foundations today (Vaara and Whittington, 2012). If other civilizations had seen strategy as both planning and emergence, both big-picture and micro-foundations, could not modern strategy thinkers view it this way too?

While we certainly advocate 'going broader' in the sense we describe above, the particular focus of the remainder of this book will be 'going deeper', as we explain below.

Going Deeper: Re-engaging with the Conventional Foundations

Digitization has enabled great advances in management research. It stands to reason that more recent works are more likely to be digitized, and that those who learn to research in a digital age may be predisposed to look at what is available in this form at their desks rather than travelling further afield into original archives. However, other writers in different fields have already published work theorizing that a reducing year range of citations may lead to a narrowing of scholarship and reduction in substantive innovation (Evans, 2008).

Looking beyond the ubiquity of the internet may take researchers and educators to interesting places, and offer new insights (Decker, 2013; Schwarzkopf, 2012). For example, tracking down hard copies of data created by long-established industry associations, data that does not exist online or in electronic form, has enabled some authors to think differently about the reasons why manufacturing clusters emerge and continue to evolve even after the economic reasons have declined (Sorenson and Audia, 2000).

Similarly, looking at actual copies of *Moody's Investment Magazine* from 1911 (unavailable electronically) or the archive of the Stevens Institute in New Jersey provides us a very different view of the birth of management from modern management textbooks. F. W. Taylor's work, paramount in the minds of management historians and other scholars as the point of origin (George, 1972; Wren, 1972; Wren and Hay, 1977), is something of an afterthought in these *Moody's* pages. *Moody's*, typical of newspapers of the time, focussed far more on the legal and political setting for the 'birth' of management as we know it. Indeed, while we did not code for subject perspective in our sample of history articles, anecdotally we can say that most management and business historians look from a conventional modernist management perspective.[7] Hence, they focus on professions like engineering and economics and see management science emerging due to organizations seeking to become more efficient or needing to quickly increase production to meet demand. However, legal and political histories see developments much closer to the picture painted in the pages of *Moody's*, regarding the rise of management as coat-tailing upon Roosevelt and Pinchot's short-lived 'conservation movement' and gaining popularity only through Louis Brandeis repackaging of the ideas of F. W. Taylor and others into something that he branded 'Scientific Management' in order to win a high-profile legal case in 1910–11. Digging into the correspondence between Taylor, Brandeis and other key players behind the scenes is very insightful in this regard, and seeing conservation or sustainability as the origin of management might lead to interesting recalibrations around what it is that good management seeks to achieve. This approach forms a basis for the work presented in the third chapter of this book.

---

[7] It proved impossible to code for perspective quickly and reliably in any meaningful way. While we recognize that we do not, therefore, cover the likes of Tsui's (2007) concerns, our aim, as stated earlier, was to do what we could to raise doubts about current conventions in management and business history so as to add to the debates about the dearth of new ideas as this relates to management education.

Fruitful rethinking can also occur by considering what might be lost in translation. Recent work has begun to highlight how original work can be mistranslated or only partially translated when recast in English by Anglo writers. For example, what management students are shown to be Max Weber's contribution to their field is a snippet seized upon by modern thinkers who saw bureaucracy as a wholly negative term and subsequently painted Weber as an outmoded bureaucracy booster. This interpretation is partly enabled by the way that Talcott Parsons and others chose to translate some elements of Weber's work and not others and emphasize certain interpretations above alternatives (Clegg, 2005; Mills et al., 2014), or to translate words in ways that created different meanings. This approach for looking deeper informs our discussion in Chapter Four.

There are promising signs with regard to rethinking, deepening and broadening our views of management history and its contribution to thinking differently for the future (see, e.g., Cooke and Alcadipani, 2015; Hassard, 2012; Khurana, 2007; Rowlinson, Hassard and Decker, 2014; Usdiken and Kipping, 2014; Wadhwani and Bucheli, 2014). But to add to this emerging research agenda, we should think seriously about how we may inspire greater horizons for the next generation of management scholars, by looking for alternative historical precedents and perspectives that they can reflect upon when considering the limits of the field that they are entering into and whose future horizons they will determine. In the paragraphs below, we outline a methodology for doing this.

A METHODOLOGY FOR A NEW, DEEPER HISTORY OF MANAGEMENT

> There are three elements in my [approach]. They are (1) the refusal to accept as self-evident the things that are proposed to us; (2) the need to analyze and to know ... thus, the principle of curiosity; and (3) the principle of innovation: to seek out in our reflection those things that have never been thought or imagined.

Michel Foucault (1988, p.1–2)

In parallel with an emerging historic, or historical, turn in organization and management studies (Clark and Rowlinson, 2004), there has
also been a cultural or critical turn in management history (Rowlinson
and Delahaye, 2010; Rowlinson and Hassard, 2013). Business historians have become increasingly interested in the business aspects of
cultural industries. The work of Charles Harvey and Jon Press on
William Morris (Harvey and Press, 1991) should be noted for reaching
a much wider audience than is usual for business historians through
their contribution to a major exhibition on Morris at the Victoria and
Albert Museum in London (Harvey and Press, 1996). Business historians have also recognized the value of cultural sources such as novels
for understanding business practices, especially in relation to gender
(Maltby and Rutterford, 2006; Rutterford and Maltby, 2006). However
the cultural turn in business history goes beyond an interest in cultural industries of using cultural sources and involves the use of
concepts from cultural studies to examine the history of the corporation itself as a cultural phenomenon (Lipartito and Sicilia, 2004). Most
provocatively, Mayhew (2009) has argued that the work of economists
and business historians on the historical role of corporations can be
analysed as 'stories' and 'narratives' in the same way that novels,
journalism and popular writing on corporate power can be analysed.
Unfortunately, business historians have overlooked Mayhew's work.

The rise of Critical Management Studies (CMS), building on
work done in the area of labour process theory in the 1970s, has also
encouraged increasing openness towards rethinking history in organization studies (Braverman, 1974; Marglin, 1976 [1974]; Rowlinson and
Proctor, 1997). Drawing on Foucault for the most part, the Marxian
account for the rise of the factory and modern management was
increasingly questioned in a series of foundational texts for critical
management studies (Burrell, 1998; Clegg, 1990; Jacques, 1996). And
the increasingly critical approach to memory in organization studies
has also given rise to what could be called the deconstruction of
corporate, or rhetorical, history (Stambaugh and Trank, 2010).
Durepos and Mills (2012a; 2012b) in particular have developed

a distinctive approach to understanding how historical narratives are developed from archives that draw on Actor Network Theory, hence their term ANTi-History, which has increasingly been taken up as an approach for conducting historical research in organization studies (e.g. Bruce and Nyland, 2011).

Although each of these texts can be criticized for their cavalier treatment of historiography (Rowlinson and Carter, 2002), they have removed the strait jacket of labour process theory where the underlying rationale for all historical change in work organization is in effect known in advance. Subsequently, critical management scholars have highlighted various lacunae in the historiography of management, such as the neglect of slavery (Cooke, 2003) – which we shall investigate in more detail in Chapter Two of this book.

Our approach follows these cultural and critical leads, but it is more inspired by a Foucauldian than a Marxist perspective. Foucault (1980, p.70) wrote histories that sought to counter conventional histories which aimed at uncovering the truth of events presented as a 'progress of consciousness' that led to (or caused) a higher-level present. Foucault (1977b, p.143ff.) regarded traditional histories as legitimating the establishment and closing down of alternatives: what is to be recorded as the 'origin [becomes] the site of truth' and in a circular manner 'makes possible a field of knowledge whose function is to recover it', and such origins, rather than having an objective status, tend to be picked out and promoted because they relate to present concerns. 'In placing present needs at the origin', Foucault continues, 'the metaphysician would convince us of an obscure purpose that seeks its realization at the moment it arises', and, over time, this 'truth' then becomes 'the sort of error that cannot be refuted because it [has been] hardened into an unalterable form in the long baking process of history'.

Foucault consequently defined his type of history in this way: 'Instead of legitimating what is already known [I aim to rethink historical assumptions in order to] free thought from what it silently thinks, and so enable it to think differently' (Foucault, 1985, p.9).

Consequently, Foucault did not aim for or claim to uncover the real truth, just to do enough to raise doubts about what was promoted as the truth of the evolution of objects and subjects (e.g., Foucault, 1977a; 1978). And this is precisely the critical, cultural and creative approach to history that inspires us in its targeting of conventional assumptions about management history.

Foucault saw conventional histories as legitimating the establishment, and so he sought to write a different kind of history. He was more interested in examining the 'history of the emergence of [the establishment's] truth games' (Florence, 1984, p.314).[8] Consequently, Foucault did not seek to explain whole periods against a criterion of linear progress, but to 'define the conditions in which human beings "problematize" what they are, what they do, and the world in which they live' (1985, p.10). He tended to start with present concerns or particular problems (e.g., 'madness'), asked questions like 'why do we treat madness as we do?' and then questioned the normal responses (e.g. 'because our methods are the best suited to counter (or normalize) madness'). In this book, we adopt a similar counter-historical approach. We begin with the question 'why do management textbooks treat history as they do?' and question the normal responses: 'because it is a good representation of what actually happened' or 'because it is the most effective way to educate our students'.

Foucault spent decades developing different ways towards this aim, and his work is generally divided into a number of different phases and approaches (Burrell, 1988; Cummings and Bridgman, 2011)[9]. His early works simply sought to highlight historical inaccuracies and, through engaging in hard work of going back into the archives and re-reading often forgotten historical documents, discover the truth of how history really unfolded.

---

[8] Florence was later revealed to be Foucault writing about himself under a pseudonym.
[9] Although it should be noted that additional approaches are still being discerned as researchers and translators compile new editions of his last lectures (see Raffnsøe et al., 2016).

In his next, or 'Archaeological', phase, Foucault let go of the idea that there were historical truths to be uncovered and adopted a more structuralist approach that argued that what we considered truths were the result of prevailing paradigms or what he termed *episteme* and that these were supported and reinforced by historical understandings. His counter-histories in this period sought to reveal how these episteme worked to produce and order what we considered to be valuable knowledge.

Recognizing that archaeology offered no possibility on promoting change (all was enveloped by the structure of an *episteme*), Foucault then developed an approach called 'Genealogy'. Here, he moved away from the structuralist tendencies of archaeology and focussed instead on how micro-political webs of connection and power developed and supported the formation of truths. The development of a history that supported the current configuration was a key element of such networks, but this and all other elements that made up these formations could move and hence there was some fluidity to knowledge systems. Foucault's genealogical works were less structuralist, but they left the question: if we are all subject to power/knowledge networks, what can we do?

Richard Dreyfus and Paul Rabinow from the University of California, Berkeley helped Foucault in his later years combine archaeology and genealogy into an approach they termed 'Interpretive Analytics' (Dreyfus and Rabinow, 1983). In simple terms, this was a combination of archaeology's recognition of the role of episteme in forming knowledge, and genealogies' interest in the power networks that cut across these and both reinforces the current formation, but could also promote change as they moved. Combining the two encouraged Foucault to look at other episteme (e.g., the Ancient Greeks) as a way of showing discontinuities and how things had been different, and so could be different again if we can engage in strategies such as thinking differently about conventional histories.

Despite these different approaches, a number of counter-historical threads weave throughout Foucault's oeuvre. These can be brought together, in the interests of utility (Foucault did, after all, want his ideas to be used – Eribon, 1991; Miller, 1993), to outline more generally how a Foucauldian approach to developing a counter-history that enables us to think differently about the history of management studies, could proceed.

1. Foucault moved **from *linear time* as a model for history to *space*.**
   In this way, he sought to challenge historians who discerned gradual global evolutions in higher forms of knowledge with the notion that changes could be sudden and abrupt, only to be smoothed out later in hindsight. Hence, Foucault often began his counter-histories by juxtaposing different artefacts to depict these different 'frames'. In *The Order of Things* (1970, p.xv), a Chinese encyclopaedia's categories set against Western sensibilities illustrate 'the exotic charm of another system of thought [which is at once] the limitation of our own, the stark impossibility of thinking *that*'. In *Discipline and Punish*, Foucault (1977a) highlighted the rupture in Western views on keeping order by counter-posing a grandiose description of the public execution of the regicide Damiens with a mundane prison timetable from 30 years later. In the same works, he drew upon spatial metaphors like Bentham's model prison, the Panopticon, to depict the sudden change in the 'architecture' through which people saw the world (Foucault, 1977a). These unconventional artefacts, be they grand or low-brow, obvious or obscured and needing to be dug out of dusty archives, could open a window through which one might begin to probe an age's forgotten predispositions (Foucault, 1980, p.194).

2. Foucault (1985, p.10) did not seek to explain periods in line with a criterion of chronological progress towards higher levels of truth, but to understand why change occurs through '**defin[ing] the conditions in which human beings "problematize"** what they are, what they do, and the world in which they live' at certain points in time. He started with particular concerns or problems and asked, for example: 'why did modernity make such a problem of madness?'; and then questioned normal responses: 'because this was necessary to develop and apply the

most effective methods of curing it'. Similarly, the counter-history that follows will wonder why management becomes a major problem in the early twentieth century, question the conventional view that this was part of a gradual evolution of thinking in response to changed social and economic conditions and look again at the problems influencing the framing of thinking at this moment in time.

3. Foucault argued that these frames and problems determined and shape the objects seen. Against histories that traced the development of objects and the separate subjects that examine them, Foucault saw **object and subject as co-determining one another**. He would argue, for example, that 'Man' did not exist until the practices constituted by the rise of humanism and the *human sciences* took hold (Foucault, 1970); and that 'madness', as we conceive it, could not be conceived without the conditions that enabled *psychology*. For Foucault, this historical nominalism meant that it was the emergence of humanism in combination with the transition into modernity (an age beyond the custom of the power of the sovereign or his agents to 'do violence' in order to maintain social control) that made a problem of how control was to be upheld. This problem created the need for human sciences, which sprang forth to outline human norms and laws that should be adhered to, but these did not exist objectively or independent of the system that promoted them.

4. Rather than plotting the past in terms of its step-by-step evolution to the present, Foucault focussed on how **objects and subjects are constituted by a 'diagram' or web of relations** that spreads out from a particular problem to sustain understanding. Noujain (1987) demonstrates this dispersive, diagrammatic outlook by illustrating Foucault's key elements and relationships in the formation of psychoanalysis. The subject emerges as part of modernity's quest for bands of normality, which is sustained by latching onto already accepted scientific institutions (the modern hospital and the science of psychology). The history of psychoanalysis spoke of these links, but remained silent on how it built upon other non-scientific elements:

the confessional, a particular inheritance of Christianity, and the presence of the organizational form of asylums formerly used for interning leprosy victims.

5. Whereas conventional historians depict how some things cease (e.g., archaic methods of knowing Man) while others are constant (e.g., the object Man), Foucault's counter-histories would **overturn accepted continuities and discontinuities**. He demonstrated, for example, that Man as an object was a discontinuous and recent conception, while the new human sciences, which would 'know Man more truly', actually continued with many archaic traditions. While the 'historical tradition aims at dissolving the singular event into an ideal continuity', Foucault's histories (1977b, p.154) sought to 'transpose the relationship ordinarily established between the eruption of an event and necessary continuity', in order to 'disturb what was previously considered immobile'.

6. Finally, Foucault did not aim to uncover the real or the objective or the whole 'truth'. The aim of the counter-historian is **to raise doubts about, and alternatives to, conventional truths about the evolution** of an object in order to open things up and encourage thinking differently. Thus, while 'historians take unusual pains to erase the elements in their work which reveal their grounding in a particular time and place', Foucault's (1977b, p.90) history would be 'explicit in ... acknowledg[ing] its system of injustice. Its perception is [knowingly] slanted'.

The methods Foucault (1985, p.9ff.) employed towards his overarching aim, to free thought from what historical assumptions lead us to 'silently think and enable thinking differently', exhibited characteristics that we will draw upon. His approach was not to be comprehensive, but knowingly 'slanted' towards raising doubts about conventional histories and their basis upon assumed 'origins' (Foucault, 1977b, p.90, 144) (figure 14). He saw development stemming not from progression over a series of periods, but arising from the 'conditions in which human beings problematize' their

1. Move **from *linear time* as a model for history to *space***: juxtapose abrupt differences in different spaces rather than a smooth progression of ideas
2. Do not explain periods in line with a criterion of chronological progress, but understand why change occurs in line with **the conditions in which human beings 'problematize'** existence
3. Against histories that trace the development of objects and the separate subjects that examine them, examine how **object and subject co-determine one another.**
4. Focus on how **objects/subjects are constituted by a 'diagram' or web of relations**
5. **Overturn accepted continuities and discontinuities** in conventional historical narratives
6. Do not aim to uncover the real or the objective or the whole 'truth', just **raise doubts about, and alternatives to, conventional truths about historical evolution**

FIGURE 14 Six Counter-Historical Strategies Borrowed from Michel Foucault

existence, problematizations that became focal points for intellectual ferment (Foucault, 1985, p.10). He recognized that subjects and objects are not independent, but arise in response to these points of ferment and are sustained by relations that harden over time (e.g., Foucault, 1977b, p.144). And, to illustrate this, he would zero in on a particular point, work out from that surface to trace historical inter-relations and 'disturb' what conventional histories record as progressive continuities by bringing forgotten discontinuities to light (Foucault, 1977b, p.154).

The counter-history presented in the following chapters seeks to employ these strategies to raise doubts about our assumptions of how management studies came into being, what it responded to, what 'good' it seeks to serve, what it is fundamentally about and what it could be.[10] It overturns accepted continuities and discontinuities in its evolution, highlighting the unusual webs of relations that created and promoted its formation. It traces how the subject of management emerged in combination with the object it sought to observe, more suddenly than what we might have thought, and in response to the major problems of the ages in which it emerged.

[10] As a variation, Chapter Four's assessment of the treatment of Max Weber applies a kind of interpretative analytics, but in all other chapters use these six general elements as our method of attack.

Foucault's ideas have been applied to critiques of specific limitations in management thinking with regard to bureaucracy (Cummings and Bridgman, 2011), crisis management (Vanderbroeck, 2012) and project management (Söderlund and Lenfle, 2013). But nobody has investigated where these foundational limits have emerged from, the extent of this homogeneity relative to other similar fields or reflected upon how this may impact on innovation and creativity in the field. This is what we do in the remainder of this book.

WHAT A NEW HISTORY OF MANAGEMENT DOES

In response to our study of what management and business histories have focussed on in the past and the conventional limits associated with this, we have provided some hope and some examples of possibilities for greater and more creative engagement with history.

However, these possibilities require specific intent now, because while there are some promising signs with respect to more interest in a range of new locations, periods and angles, on current trends, it will take a long time for percentages to grow to significant levels. We will need to make an effort to think differently (to 'fill in the gaps' in Figures 8, 9 and 11) and create a more diverse archive that may inspire cross-pollination and creative thinking. This effort would, we argue, be well-rewarded. It could lead us to ask significant questions of what we consider worthy of attention in our field.

Inspired by Foucault and the emergent cultural turn in management history, our purpose here is to question that the Worldmapper result is simply a self-evident reflection of the objective reality of management history, to analyze and probe the nature of management history writing and to explore whether alternative historical vistas might inspire thinking innovatively in our field. We aim to highlight how the 'amputated reality' of management history may now be acting as a limiting 'map for modern travellers' in our field (Salvemini, 1939, p.60; Glassie, 1999, p.6).

We look again, at greater length and with a critical eye, on what has been conventionally assumed about those characters seen as the mainstays in management's evolution. We believe that decentring the way the writers and their contexts have been quickly coded, processed and subsumed into a grand historical narrative that supports conventional views of management, in order to show that their roles can be reinterpreted to inspire us in different ways, is a good first step towards rethinking management history and making it a more innovative and relevant field today. Hence, the chapters that make up the remainder of the book incorporate many of the 'primary characters' from management textbook histories noted in Table 1 and follow the chronological path on which they are presented in these conventional histories. But by looking deeper at each, what we glean from these elements is quite different from what you might have thought before, different from what is currently handed down to management studies and what currently bounds our view of where management comes from, what it is and what it can be.

In Chapter Two, Management's Formation: The Importance of the Liberal Context, we delve back into the thinking of Adam Smith and look again at the relationship between management and liberalism. This investigation leads us to conclude that we would benefit from seeing management arising not with neo-liberal economics, industrial mechanization and increasing control, but social and moral liberalism and the decline of slavery, something that conventional management histories are awkwardly silent about.

Chapter Three's investigation is titled: To What End? The Nature of Management's Classical Approach. It looks closely at the birth of management's 'classical school' and the ends that managers have traditionally sought to serve. We conclude that while the original 'good' of management is believed to be 'greater efficiency', a re-reading of the birth of management's 'classical' school and the network that popularized F. W. Taylor's ideas suggests that sustainability is management's original good, rather than a new idea that we are only now promoting.

If social and moral liberalism provides the broader context, and the manager is the key actor in management, the site where the manager acts is the organization. In The Birth of Organization Studies: Or What We Could Learn from Max Weber, Chapter Four, we re-examine the evolution of the ideas attributed to the person most often seen as this sub-field's founder. We counter conventional views by arguing that Weber's foundational insight is not that 'bureaucracy is great', but a contingency view that it and other forms of organization emerge out of specific cultural contexts: a view that should guard against the belief in general theories of organization and management.

Chapter Five focusses on the 'pulpit' from which management knowledge is generally disseminated: the formation and form of the Business School. This chapter, The Institution of the Business School, suggests that instead of aping the current form of leading business schools like Harvard, the forms that these schools could have taken if early pioneers had their way might be more inspirational today.

The Discovery of the Human Worker (Chapter Six) focusses on the character of Elton Mayo, often depicted as the first 'good guy' in the history of management. He is depicted as good because he discovered that people were humans and should be managed as humans rather than machines. But we question these conventions by asking what if the start of the good science in management studies turned out to be more bad (or at least based on bad science) than good?

Current views of management are now influenced by the way in which modern textbooks, which emerged with the exponential growth of business schools in the 1970s, arrange seminal ideas from previous decades into the 'conventional narrative'. Chapter Seven, Textbook Distortions, investigates how the form of these textbooks has reconfigured the ideas of key thinkers such as Maslow, Lewin and McGregor to make them a better fit for the accepted view of the continuous progression of management.

In Chapter Eight, The Invention of Corporate Culture, we look deeper at the formation of one of the latest 'big ideas' to have been incorporated into management's evolution. By uncovering the way in which the concept of corporate culture was stitched together by a network of shared interests and specific problems, we highlight how the perspective on culture that emerged too frequently reflects a naïve and prescriptive general theory and approach to what we would like business organizations to be (rather than what they actually are).

Finally, our concluding chapter, Rethinking Management History: New Foundations for the Future, outlines a new history for management based on thinking again and decentring assumptions about key figures and institutions, what we assume about the roles they played and how these things could be thought otherwise. The final chapter presents our view of what should replace or at least sit alongside the conventional histories of management currently presented in textbooks, in order to encourage thinking differently for the future.

To begin our counter-history, we revisit the scene that Adam Smith is assumed to have set for the study of management.

2 Management's Formation: The Importance of the Liberal Context

Management arises not with increasing order and control but increasing liberty.

Adam Smith is often listed as a pioneer in management history, but he is generally only seen through a lens that assumes efficiency is management's fundamental concern. Subsequently, Smith's treatment is limited to a few sentences on how his 'classic economics treatise' promoted the division of labour, which then required increasing control of workers administered by a growing class of professional managers. But Smith had much more to say that could influence the way we think about management that we now overlook. In fact, a Google ngram search of the terms 'efficiency' and 'management' reveals that the interest in management was higher in Smith's time than in any other period until our own age, whereas interest in efficiency only rises in the twentieth century. Interest in management in the eighteenth century was high due to a new problematization: how could liberalism and greater equality work? After an age where the ruling question was: 'Are we governing with sufficient intensity to maximize our state's power against other states?' our own liberal age begins to ask: 'Are we self-limiting the degree of government to enable optimizing mutual enrichment?' Smith was an optimist who believed that human nature left to its own devices combined with skilful management for the greater good would facilitate positive growth. Thus, Smith's real innovations were not laissez faire economics and the division of labour, but the view that liberalism is good and slavery and repression are wrong. In this way, management can be seen to emerge as we seek ways of encouraging collective effort through sympathy, persuasion and seeking mutual enrichment, and controlling people less, not more.

> By serving his own interests, as Adam Smith put it more than 200 years ago . . .
>
> George P. Mitchell perfect[ed] the technology of hydraulic fracturing [and] served the interests of society.

Joel Kurtzman, *Wall Street Journal*, 19 June, 2013

Adam Smith has been praised and blamed for many things. Smith is regarded as the self-interest above all, greed is good, rational economic man booster who promoted a right-wing neo-liberalism. He is seen as the forefather of the recessions of 1929 and 2008, a growing disparity of wealth, and even the development of fracking (Vogel Carey, 2009). This is the Adam Smith that many management students and scholars regard as a founder of their field – but is this really what he was about?

This chapter begins our counter-history of management by taking aim at two elements of the conventional history of management. The first is a dubious presence: the particular and highly simplified version of 'great economist Adam Smith' as a founding father described above. The one that supposedly argued 'the government should "let alone" the mechanisms of the market and its "invisible hand"' (Wren, 1972, p.23–24); whose 'liberal thinking formed the basis of the laissez faire doctrine' (George, 1972, p.55), who 'advocated laissez-faire capitalism . . . established the classical school [and is] the father of liberal economics' (Wren, 1972, p.23); whose major contribution was recognizing the importance and value of the 'division of labour' (Pollard, 1965, p.8ff.); the man who 'laid great stress on the division of labour and its concomitant benefits' (George, 1972, p.54). This is the Smith that is described as an important founder in management textbooks (e.g., Daft, 2015; Hitt et al., 2007; Robbins et al., 2012; Schermerhorn et al., 2014).

The second element we take aim at may be better described as an absence: that there is no mention of slavery in the history of management. We argue that this absence is partly linked to it being an inconvenient truth; and partly linked to management history's desire to see management as both a universal concern and following a continuous line of progress from the 'great' ancient civilizations,

through this simplified version of Smith, on to the 'classical management theorists' and hence through to management studies today.
Consequently, in suggesting a continuity of progress, the scene setting
that precedes Smith in the potted annals of management history outlined in textbooks include noble examples from pre-industrial settings
to build the gravity of the subject. These examples demonstrate that
great civilizations intuited the importance of the division of labour
hundreds of years before Smith apparently theorized it and the 'classical management school' claimed to make a science of it: and this
prescience enabled the pyramids, aqueducts, great walls and so on.
But no mention is made of who, exactly, built these monuments to the
advance of management. We know that they were largely built by
slaves, but this is an inconvenient fact for those seeking to promote
the value and nobility of a field.

We argue here that this absence is worse than just being evasive
and disingenuous – it undermines our field and does it a great disser-
vice. The rise of management can be seen, and should be seen, to
correspond to the decline of slavery and a new liberal morality related
to this. Not addressing slavery in our history prevents us seeing that
management comes about as a field of importance as a result of social
liberty, not economic neo-liberalism – a message far more important
than promoting a smooth, simple and noble progression to bolster an
insecure field.

This brings us back to Adam Smith. Smith's gift, his great
innovative idea, and why he should be considered a founder is not
that he promoted the division of labour and excused the selfish self-
interest that laid the groundwork for unfettered industrialization. It is
that he showed that societies work better, morally first, but by association economically too, when people are free and protected from
abuse as should be their 'sacred right'. The fundamental question his
work poses for our field is: how can we best organize when we realize
that we should not compel societies, organizations, groups and individuals, to 'follow orders or else' in ways that seek to make all parties,
individually and collectively, better off?

In this chapter, we re-examine management history in relation to Adam Smith and arrive at a series of unconventional conclusions:

- First, that Smith's key innovation is not the promotion of the division of labour as an end in itself. It is that repression, maltreatment and inequity are wrong because we all should have equal opportunities: the division of labour does not, in itself, lead to these greater goods according to Smith. It can help greatly, but it must be tempered to prevent inequities.

- Second, if we take a broader view of Smith's ideas, we can conceive of management emerging in a liberal age as slavery declines – hence management can be understood as rising not hand in hand with neo-liberal economics and increasing control, but social and moral liberalism.

- Third, we argue that Smith is not the neo-liberal economist hero he is often assumed to be.

- And, finally, that this unconventional view of management history may provide an alternative foundation for management studies as it seeks to think differently about the problems we face now.

In the pages that follow, we utilize the Foucauldian strategies outlined in Chapter One to analyse the formation and form of the conventional view of Smith as a pioneer, what this promotes as management's foundations and an alternative view that this represses. We juxtapose what Smith actually wrote with what modern interpreters of management and economic history claim that he wrote; highlight what are assumed today to be continuities of Smith's views which are, in many important respects, discontinuities; we explore how the conventional, limited view of Adam Smith emerged, the network of relations that now supports this and the subjects/objects of management and economics as we understand them; we examine the problem that Smith was actually responding to; and we critique the conventional view of Smith in order to think differently about the history and, by association, the future of management.

WHO IS THE REAL ADAM SMITH? DISCONTINUITIES AND FALSE FOUNDATIONS

> You think you are helping the economic system by your well-meaning laws and interferences. You are not. Let be. The oil of self-interest will keep the gears working in almost miraculous fashion. No one need plan. No sovereign need rule. The market will answer all things.

> The subjects of every state ought to contribute towards the support of the government, as nearly as possible, in proportion to their respective abilities; that is, in proportion to the revenue which they respectively enjoy under the protection of the state.

Which one of these quotations is Adam Smith's? Is he the promoter of *laissez faire* economics, or the advocate of a progressive tax system imposed by the State?

Despite it being closer to the view most have of Adam Smith now, and closer to the way that Smith is reported in histories of management, none of the sentences in the first quotation are Adam Smith's. The source for this quotation is *Economics* by Nobel Prize winner Paul A. Samuelson, a textbook that is now in its nineteenth edition. We learn from Samuelson that 'Like a baby, political economy was taking shape even before it was born [but] *The Wealth of Nations* (1776) of Adam Smith can be taken as providing its birthday' (Samuelson, 1980, p.639). Then, in a section titled 'Classical Economics: Smith the Prophet of Laissez Faire', Samuelson explains (1980, p.640) that: 'Smith's message said: You think you are helping the economic system by your well-meaning laws and interferences. You are not. Let be . . .' Samuelson's set up, the first-person narrative, and faux-archaic style leads the reader to believe that this is what Smith wrote. But none of these sentences are Smith's own.

It is the second quotation at the head of this section that is actually written by Smith. It is a passage from Book V of *The Wealth of Nations*. Nevertheless, the kind of interpretation that Samuelson provides is now the conventional one (Pearce and Hoover, 1995). Most economics textbooks now 'borrow heavily' from 'Samuelson's pedagogy [and] tone' (Skousen, 1997, p.137). And most popular introductory management textbooks, which were published in their first editions at around the same time as the eleventh edition of Samuelson from which the quote above was taken, follow suit (e.g., Robbins et al., 2012).

While we might assume continuity between what Smith wrote and how we report his views now, juxtaposing these two quotations enables us to begin to question the discontinuities and how they came to pass.

Why, for example, in *The Wealth of Nations*, is Smith promoting progressive taxation? Smith's view of mankind is unusual for his time. He believed that:

> The difference of natural talents in different men is, in reality, much less than we are aware of; and the very different genius which appears to distinguish men of different professions ... is not upon many occasions so much the cause, as the effect of the division of labour. The difference ... between a philosopher and a common street porter, for example, seems to arise not so much from nature, as from habit, custom, and education *(I.ii)*.[1]

While it is not easy for the State to affect habit and custom, it could tackle this inequity through investment in public education:

> The public [purse] can facilitate, can encourage, and can even impose upon almost the whole body of the people the necessity of acquiring those most essential parts of education ... The Public can facilitate this acquisition by establishing in every parish or district a little school, where children may be taught ... *(I.ii)*.

---

[1] We use Sutherland's 2014 Oxford edition of *The Wealth of Nations* and Sen's 2010 Penguin Classics edition of *The Theory of Moral Sentiments*, but give Smith's original book and chapter references to enable readers to find these passages in different editions.

And because the poorer classes have fewer resources to devote to education than the richer whom benefit more from their start in life:

> The education of the common people requires ... in a civilised and commercial society, the attention of the Public more than that of people of some rank and fortune. *(V.i, 2nd Third, article 2)*

Hence, the importance of a progressive tax where the rich pay more towards this and other important State institutions that protect people and help them feel safe to deploy their labour as they see fit, to ensure that all benefit given the tendency for a growing division of labour to lead to inequitable outcomes. This freedom, safety and protection is important because, Smith believed:

> Every man's own labour is the original foundation of all other property, so it is the most sacred and inviolable ... and to hinder him from employing this in what manner he thinks proper without injury to his neighbour is a plain violation of this most sacred property. *(I.x, Part 2)*

This sets Smith against slavery on both moral and economic grounds (an opposition that we will explore later).

This does not seem like the Adam Smith that is taught in Management or Economics. But before we investigate what Smith actually promoted, it is worth questioning some key beliefs often attributed to Smith. In this section that follows, we tackle five of these: (1) that he 'preached' *laissez faire* economics; (2) that he developed the theory that things work best when self-interest and the market are left alone and invented the metaphor of the 'invisible hand of the market' to express this; (3) that the division of labour concept (that 'classical management' authors take as a guiding light) was Smith's original insight and the pillar on which his system was based; (4) that this system created the environment for the flowering of the industrial system; and (5) that Smith must have been a free-market capitalist.

(1) Smith as a Preacher of Laissez Faire and Founder of Neo-liberalism?

In 1968, George's *History of Management Thought* explained Smith's importance succinctly (p.55): '[Smith's] thinking formed the basis for the *laissez faire* doctrine.' But this is a little muddled. The *laissez faire* doctrine preceded Smith, who then dismissed it.

Laissez faire et laissez passer (Let go and let pass) is a maxim generally attributed to Jacques Gournay (1712–1759), but more generally associated with a group of French *economistes* (sometimes termed the *physiocrats*) of which Gournay was a member (Steiner, 2003). In contrast to earlier thinkers who focussed on the ruler's wealth, gold stocks or the balance of trade, the *economistes* saw productive labour as the sole source of economic value. However, they only regarded agricultural labour as productive (industrial labour was an 'unproductive appendage' (Marx and Engels, in Sowell, 2006, p.3). The *economistes* subsequently promoted *laissez faire* trade.

While Smith knew this group's concepts well, the words *laissez faire* (or *laisser faire*) appear nowhere in Smith's vast body of work and correspondence. There are two reasons for this. The first is that it is not a term that anybody writing in English would use until much later (the 1820s, according to the Oxford English Dictionary). It is worth noting that in the first translation of *The Wealth of Nations* into French, by Duplain (in 1788), *laisser faire* does not appear, and in the later translations, it only appears on a few occasions, and then only to translate letting something go (or pass), not with respect to a free market (e.g., see the Guillaumin and Buisson translations from the mid-1800s). So it was not that Smith was using English terms to express *laissez faire*; he simply wasn't using this idea at all.

But more importantly, Smith didn't use the term *laisser faire* because he didn't advocate it. While Smith knew the *economistes*, and spent time in Paris with their leading figure François Quesnay (1694–1774), while preparing *The Wealth of Nations*, Smith only refers to 'Mr. Quesnai' once. In Book IV.ix, he offers a critique of

Quesnay and the *ecnomistes* ideas: in a group of 'speculative physicians', Smith sniffs that he is a 'very speculative physician'; and notes that the 'capital error of his system' is the notion of 'perfect liberty' as the one best way – nothing else will do, and its undervaluing of the lower classes and industry. When Quesnay used the term *laisser faire*, he meant by this that government should, after a revolution and tearing down of the old ways, completely 'let alone' the mechanisms of the market. This was not Smith's view.

In placing their faith in markets over men, Smith (IV.ix) felt that Quesnay did not consider 'that in the political body, the natural effort which every man is continuously making to better his own condition, is a principle capable of preventing and correcting, in many respects, the bad effects of a political oeconomy.' Smith believed that people achieve progress in spite of, rather than because of, the machinations of their economic masters, whatever these may be. Accordingly, Smith believed that Quesnay and associates, with their idea of wiping the slate clean and then leaving the market to work things out, lacked an understanding of human nature and the importance of pursuing policies that improved a country's institutions (Phillipson, 2011, p.196).

Despite this discontinuity between the thinking of Smith and the *economistes*, management and economic histories see Smith as continuing in the footsteps of Quesnay and the *laissez faire* boosters (Wren, 1972, p.23). And Smith is further corralled into a philosophy he did not share by posthumously being regarded as a founding father of liberal and neo-liberal economics as he was lumped together with 'antecedents'. Steiger and Roy's (2010, p.3) book *Neo-liberalism* captures a widely held view succinctly:

> Classical liberals like Adam Smith and David Ricardo preached the virtues of the 'free market' and 'laissez faire' economics. Smith is credited with creating the Scottish Enlightenment image of homo economicus – the view that people are isolated individuals whose actions reflect mostly their material self-interests. According to this view, economic and political matters are largely separable with economics claiming a superior status . . .

(2) Smith as a Promoter of 'Self-interest' and the 'Invisible Hand of the Market'?

Smith certainly did not invent the term 'invisible hand': others before him in the eighteenth century had used the expression. (Indeed, Buchan, 2006, p.2 argues that 'One could with better justice claim that Moll Flanders ... who also uses the phrase "invisible hand", is another towering contributor to the stability of international markets'). Unlike *laissez faire*, Smith did write 'invisible hand': but only three times in all his writing and once in *The Wealth of Nations.*

Smith first uses the phrase in *The History of Astronomy* (c.1758), where he writes of *the invisible hand* to which people refer to explain natural phenomena otherwise unexplainable: 'Fire burns, and water refreshes; heavy bodies descend, and lighter substances fly upwards, by the necessity of their own nature; nor was the invisible hand of Jupiter ever apprehended to be employed in those matters.' Thus far, the invisible hand is in no way a commercial mechanism. It is a circumlocution for God.

Here is its second use, from *The Theory of Moral Sentiments* (IV.i.10): 'They [the rich] are led by an invisible hand to make nearly the same distribution of the necessaries of life, which would have been made, had the earth been divided into equal portions among all its inhabitants, and thus without intending it, without knowing it, advance the interest of the society, and afford means to the multiplication of the species.' This could be the market, but more likely it would be an invisible being, the deity (e.g., the Great Superintendent, or Great Conductor, or Benevolent Nature or one of the many deistic code words that litter the book); or the imaginary impartial observer who helps individuals act morally, a key dimension of *The Theory of Moral Sentiments.*

And, finally, here is the invisible hand's single appearance in *The Wealth of Nations* (IV.ii.9): 'by directing that industry in such a manner as its produce may be of the greatest value, he intends only his own gain, and he is in this, as in many other cases, led by an invisible hand to promote an end which was no part of his intention.'

While Smith writes of *an* invisible hand in *The Theory of Moral Sentiments* and *The Wealth of Nations*, rather than *the* invisible hand in *Astronomy* – so it may not represent a deity, he does not link it to the market either: he does not specify what the invisible hand in question is. But the following interpretation of what Smith said from a prominent textbook is a good example of how the invisible hand has come to be regarded: 'According to Adam Smith, market forces allocate resources as if by an "invisible hand" – an unseen force that harnesses the pursuit of self-interest ... According to Smith, *although each individual pursues his or her self-interest, the "invisible hand" of market forces promotes the general welfare'* (McEachern, 2011, p.42 – emphasis in original). Two distant concepts in *The Wealth of Nations* are thus joined into 'the phrase that caught the imagination of economists and business people in the twentieth century' (Buchan, 2006, p.26) – the notion of the 'invisible hand' mentioned once in the 500+ pages of *The Wealth of Nations* in Book IV and 'self-interest' (from Book I). Put together, this tells economists (and management students) that self-interest is fine because the invisible hand of the market sorts things out for the greater good.

Things are not so straightforward in the original *The Wealth of Nations* though. Like *laissez faire*, Smith doesn't actually use the term self-interest. He uses the term 'self-love' instead: in one paragraph (Book I.ii), where it is revealed as 'the principle which gives occasion to the division of labour' (outlined in Book I.i):

> He will be more likely to prevail if he can interest [others'] self-love
> in his favour, and show them that it is for their own advantage to do
> for him what he requires of them ... [Thus, we should] address
> ourselves, not to [others'] humanity but to their self-love ...

Later interpreters would take self-love to be self-interest, and then take self-interest to be an immutable foundation (e.g., Stigler's, 1971, p.265 characterization of *The Wealth of Nations* as 'a stupendous palace erected on the granite of self-interest'). This interpretation leads to a far more materialistic view of what economics is about and criticisms of Smith's promotion of the 'selfishness doctrine' as 'Adam Smith's mistake' (Lux, 1991). But both interpretations may be wrong if one considers Smith's broader views, and perhaps the best way to understand what is lost here is to again consider the development of the French translation of *The Wealth of Nations*.

In all French translations prior to Garnier's (in 1805), Smith's self-love was translated as *amour-propre*. This was how the term had always been translated when the French read the works of Hobbes, Mandeville, Butler and Hume; and *amour-propre* in the works of Pascal, Voltaire and Rousseau was translated as self-love in English (Force, 2003). *Amour-propre* meant pride (and has increasingly come to mean vanity) but it also self-respect, self-regard and self-awareness. Garnier changed the conventional translation from *amour-propre* to *interet personnel* (self-interest) in response to a moral debate of the day.

It was seen to be a paradox that self-love (a vice when interpreted as selfishness) could be the cause of virtue. Writers like Mandeville had no problem with the paradox and were happy to promote self-love as both a vice and the cause of all human actions and development in his widely read *Fable of the Bees*. Smith and his mentors, Hutcheson and Hume, took a different view. Indeed, Smith's *The Theory of Moral Sentiments* (I.i.1) begins by refuting what Hume termed this 'selfish hypothesis': 'How selfish soever man may be supposed, there are evidently some principles in his nature, which interest him in the fortune of others ...' The book's moral system shows how human actions are driven by self-love and sympathy, and that the ability to put ourselves in others' shoes was a key element of our self-awareness or self-regard. This, in Smith's view, is how civilization progresses.

Debate between this view and the selfish hypothesis was prevalent in the last decades of the eighteenth century, and *amour-propre* became a hotly contested term among the *encyclopaedists* and others. In *De l'Espirit*, in a chapter entitled On the Abuse of Words,

Claude-Adrien Helvetius argued that people increasingly mistook self-love to mean pride and vanity and thereby to be a vice. Others thought the term had been corrupted by moral and religious connotations. Helvetius' solution to the confusion was a drastic one. He dispenses with the term and promotes an alternative with less baggage: *interet personnel*.

Garnier's translation is in line with this new idea. And, moreover, Garnier also translates 'invisible hand' from *The Wealth of Nations* (IV.ii) in a way that makes this seem more connected to Smith's 'first principle' than it was in the original. He translates 'he intends only his own gain' as *tout en ne cherchant que son interest personnel*. Thus both 'self-love' and 'own gain' are made one in translation: Self-interest (i.e., selfishness), promotes the division of labour, but this is made good for all by the market's invisible hand. Notions of self-regard as to one's role in society, and sympathy for others, are a long way from this view.

While it was a controversial break from the norm in Garnier's own time – discussed by the likes of Martial Desrenaudes (1802) in his review of different French translations – Garnier's interpretation found favour (it remained the standard French edition until 1995) and subsequent translations followed suit (Force, 2004). And a similar thing happened in the English-speaking world as more serious specialized economists who saw their field as separate from (and often superior to) political and moral concerns found self-love an ill-fitting term and moved towards the more understandable (to them) phrasing of 'self-interest'.

(3)   The 'Division of Labour' as Smith's Original and Central Idea?

There can be no doubt the division of labour is up front in *The Wealth of Nations* – it is the primary example discussed in Book I – but does this mean that it is Smith's central idea, his major contribution?

Perhaps the first thing to note is that the promotion of the division of labour was not new. Many of Smith's predecessors, like

Petty, Mandeville and Hume, recognized that specialization increased productivity. Even Plato (*Republic*, 370) understood the advantages produced 'when a man specializes on a single job for which he is fitted by nature and ignores all others.' Indeed, most if not all of Smith's concepts can be found scattered in numerous predecessors, but they generally left no disciples, and because Smith became economics' founder, it comes to be believed that he invented its foundational concepts (Sowell, 2006).

Second, the presentation of the division of labour in Book I.i is more the result of a structural quirk than a testament to the primacy of specialization in Smith's system. As we have already seen, Smith saw the division of labour as a result of the principle of self-love, and the proper functioning of self-love is the result of other ideas Smith had advanced in *The Theory of Moral Sentiments*: sympathy, social self-awareness and what Smith calls fellow-feeling.

Some have suggested that this unscientific back-to-front pre-sentation of evidence ahead of a theory is a practice unique to Smith's time (Buchan, 2006).[2] But Smith's structural choices can also be better understood when considering what is widely understood to have happened with the production of *The Theory of Moral Sentiments*. Smith was not writing as a researcher might today, but converting years of lectures into a book that would have an appeal broader than those familiar with his specialist subjects. This meant presenting his ideas in the light of Mandeville's popular 'selfish hypothesis', which was being widely discussed, and Rousseau's recent response against this view, which was brilliant but in Smith's mind partly misguided, even though the ideas behind *The Wealth of Nations* are more complex.

---

[2] Whether or not this is the case, Smith's approach is so far removed from good economic practice now that excuses have to be made in textbooks, lest his method (or lack of it) unsettle students. Alchain and Allen (1964, p.229) note that 'It is interesting that Smith's book did not contain a logically correct exposition', but they excuse him because it turned out to be a good thing in the end, and 'had Smith lived today', and known better, he might have labelled his method the 'don't-do-it-yourself' approach (see also Begg et al., 1984; Samuelson, 1982).

As his peers realized, Smith's political economy was deeply embedded in a system of moral philosophy, jurisprudence and politics. But most of the readership Smith sought to reach with his new book knew nothing of this. As Phillipson (2011, p.217) explains: 'The question was, how much of it did they need to know to make sense of his political economy. The answer was not much. So he made no formal attempt to explain the [background] ... His lectures were reduced to a series of strategically placed aphorisms about the ... love of improvement in determining the way that men used their labour.'

Indeed, when *The Wealth of Nations* is viewed in the context of the preparatory work laid down in his lectures on political economy at the University of Glasgow, where he preceded the technical matters relating to the division of labour with discussions on 'the natural wants and demands of mankind' and their consequences for the progress of civilization, these discussions seem 'conspicuously omitted' (Phillipson, 2011, p.271). But editorial choices, as with any book, had to be made.

Smith was, therefore, no blind advocate of the division of labour. While one might not see this if they only pick up on fragments of Smith's work, he and other intellectuals of his age that he admired, such as Kames, Ferguson and Millar, were convinced that the division of labour created specialized idiots, men 'mutilated and deformed in their faculties by making "the 17th part of a pin or the 80th part of a button"' (V.i, 2nd Third, Article 2). So while *The Wealth of Nations* begins with examples of the division of labour, it is actually about much more.

Viewed in the round, it is not that Smith is saying that the division of labour is good, it is that self-love, fellow-feeling, sociability and the communitarian behaviour that stems from these unselfish things is good – even though it takes us further from our natural or 'savage' selves, as Rousseau argued. The division of labour and related increase in social communal exchange that specialization necessitates proves that sociability is good, both morally and economically as it drives the progress of civilization, with the proviso that its negative effects should be managed effectively.

(4)   Creator of the Climate for Industrialization?

A key foundation that Smith supposedly laid for management studies, that he created the 'cultural environment for the flowering of the industrial system' (Wren, 1972, p.25), has nothing much to do with Smith. By definition, it had to be determined by others after the fact. Smith did not set out to create a cultural environment for things that happened much later. It is easy from this distance to forget, but when he wrote, industrialism was as far away as the iPad from the first automobile. Rail travel was 100 years in the future. Smith's own examples describe how transporting goods from London to Edinburgh took six weeks for the return trip in a 'broad-wheeled wagon' (I.iii). It was far cheaper to buy hand knitted socks than buy a pair whose production have been aided by anything mechanical. In this context, it is easy to see how somebody who read the whole book in the nineteenth century would brand it 'a very amusing book about old times' (Bagehot, 1876, p.273).

How is this inconvenient distance between Smith and the movement he is supposed to have laid the foundation for dealt with? Some interesting strategies are employed to mitigate the disconnection. For example: one history tells us that 'Smith was responsible for helping young James Watt find a job as an instrument maker. Watt later invented the steam engine, so in this and many other [unspecified] respects, Smith was present virtually at the birth of the Industrial Revolution, whose prophet he was destined to become' (Baumol and Blinder, 1982, p.48). Rather than just doing a common favour for somebody in a social circle that the same textbook admits was small, Smith is granted fantastical powers of foresight: he planted the seed that would lead to the creation of the symbol of a movement (the steam engine) that was beyond his imagination, but that he was destined to become the prophet of.

(5)   Smith the Free-market Capitalist?

A final misinterpretation is that Smith was right wing and pro-capitalist. Given that some economics textbooks claim that

'Capitalism is sometimes called laissez faire' (McEachern, 2009, p.42), Smith's supposed promotion of *laissez faire* leads many to assume he was also a preacher for this and big business more generally. While this may be the predisposition of some institutions which bear his name, it is not true of Smith.

Despite being a hero to many on the right, Smith expressed no political allegiances. The most political view discernible from Smith's work and life was his radical anti-poverty, anti-slavery or anti-indenture stance. His strongest conviction was likely his concern for the poorest in society, which was clearly expressed in *The Wealth of Nations* (e.g., I.iix; V.i). And his conception of a good nation was implicit in his statement that 'no society can be flourishing or happy, of which the far greater part of the members are poor and miserable' (I.vii); an idea so odd that the generation of economists after Smith mocked it. In 1798, Malthus spat in his *An Essay on the Principle of Population* (Chapter 16) that Smith confounded the 'wealth of a state' with the 'happiness of the lower classes of the people'.

Smith disliked party politics and factionalism of any kind and had good friends of all persuasions. While some have sought to remake Smith as a critic of capitalism, this has been shown to be an over-reaction to Smith's previous casting on the right wing (Kaul, 2007; Tribe, 1999). Indeed, those who have denounced latter-day Labourites who have claimed Smith as their own (most famously former UK Prime Minster Gordon Brown) are correct (e.g., Buchan, 2006). Not because Smith swung right, but because seldom has a man with so much to gain from political allegiance worked so hard to remain neutral.

THE DIAGRAM THAT SUSTAINS THE CONVENTIONAL VIEW OF ADAM SMITH

Over the past two decades, some economic historians have revisited the image of Smith captured in the five assumptions above and critiqued it (e.g., Montes, 2003; Tribe, 1999). The occasional Economics textbook has offered students a different view (e.g., Layton, et al., 2011). But it is the conventional view of Smith outlined at the head of this chapter that found its way into management textbooks and perseveres in those textbooks today.

If the foundations that Smith is said to have set down for management studies are of dubious origin, why did they, and this version of him, become and remain a starting point of most management histories? He is not like a gnostic philosopher of whom only fragments remain that could be interpreted in many ways. He wrote lucidly and we have all his published work intact – often in multiple editions that reveal his thought process with regard to how his ideas developed and could be better understood. He was not a prolific correspondent, but we have a substantial portion of his letters, especially those to his professional peers. We have multiple collections of notes taken by conscientious students who attended his lectures. Why has he been, and why does he continue to be, misinterpreted? The paragraphs below discuss how the conventional caricature of Smith emerged in response to the problems that economics and management faced as they established themselves as serious subjects, and the formation of interests that maintain this form.

We believe there are two crucial networks that help develop Smith's conventional presentation in the histories taught to management students. The first forms around management studies and business schools seeking to connect with the discipline of economics as they sought to become established as worthy new members of academia in the 1950s. The second comes as early management textbooks borrow from the first modern management histories' interpretations of economics' understanding of its heritage in the 1970s.

Management Cantilevering from Economics

A clear benefit of incorporating Smith into the story of management was that it had been 'proven' in the 1950s that economics should provide the foundation of management studies, and Smith was regarded as the Father of Economics.

The first business schools materialized in the late nineteenth century, but it would not be until the second half of the twentieth century that they would be generally accepted as part of America's academic fraternity. Playing a large part in this establishment was the formation of centralized bodies that would ensure that business schools were properly standardized and policed. By the early 1950s, the American Association of Collegiate Schools of Business (AACSB) was beginning to exert considerable influence. It now required that schools seeking membership offer instruction in the areas of economics, accounting, statistics, business law and finance (McKenna, 1989). Furthermore, two influential studies on management education were published at the end of the 1950s and sanctioned by the AASCB: Pierson's (1959) *The Education of the American Businessman*, sponsored by the Carnegie Foundation, and Gordon and Howell's (1959) *Higher Education for Business*, sponsored by Ford. The authors of both reports collaborated closely and came to the same conclusions.

Their clear message was that the gaggle of business schools, whose population had exploded after World War II, should standardize to increase the subject's credibility. 'Dozens of minor fields of specialization have been permitted to develop that never should have been introduced at all' (Gordon and Howell 1959, p.217). Subsequently, management or business studies was 'a vague, shifting, rather formless subject in which neither the foundations at the undergraduate level nor the super-structure at the graduate level can be sharply defined', and 'there is a need for a general tightening of standards in terms of the scope of the core studies' (Pierson 1959, p.233, 196). This could best be achieved through a closer and more clearly delineated association with economics, because, as Pierson put it (1959): 'Economics has traditionally provided the only theoretical framework for the study of business, and even today the two fields are so closely related they can hardly be discussed separately.'

The standardized formation of management and business curricula, promoted by the Carnegie and Ford reports, became accepted as a universal norm of what business schools should be and would be promoted by the AACSB and other institutions. While Gordon and Howell's model for development was organized around three generic disciplines, behavioural sciences and applied mathematics in addition to economics, Mosson's (1967, p.198) comparative history of management education systems written a few years later found that while '[e]conomics, psychology and sociology are all to be found in varying degrees ... the high prestige of economics – in academic circles at least – has meant that it has been the dominant discipline' (see also, McKenna 1989, p.46; Leontiades 1989, p.18). However, while Pierson and Gordon and Howell's point of view suggested to them that economics provided an obvious and universal foundation for management (the authors of both studies were economists and their reports 'bear th[at] unmistakable imprint', Leontiades 1989, p.2), it is only in the middle of the twentieth century that an association with economics provided an appropriate basis.

Locke's comprehensive study (1989, p.5) outlines the problem that business schools faced at this juncture to connect what they taught to an accepted scientific discipline: 'The gap, moreover, was hard to fill, for it was not a question of finding an existing bridge between theory and practice, one that had been shrouded in a fog of haughty academic prejudice, but of building a bridge between the two ... there was, at the outset, no discipline to teach. Science based management had to be invented.'

And such an invention would not have been aided through association with economics earlier. Even by the late nineteenth century, economics was still a marginal concern. At this time, most economists were of what is referred to as the Institutional school, which drew from Adam Smith's historical and humanistic interests. Empirical, inductive and non-theoretical in orientation, this school encouraged research into specific socio-economic contexts (Cummings, 2002). This was clearly not the stuff to gain acceptance from the mainstream scholarship of the day, which consisted of the traditional arts, the formal or pure sciences (e.g., mathematics, logic) and the empirical sciences. A historical-institutional economics was not a traditional art, nor did it replicate the form of a modem science.

However, another economics emerged towards the end of the nineteenth century. This took quite different aspects from Smith: the view of man as a rational economic being, of each individual capable of evaluating actions in terms of economic utility, and the liberal conception of each man as separate from family, class, country and custom and thus self-determining. Abstracting economic behaviour away from morality, jurisprudence and history, the neoclassical school developed a more exacting expression of Smith's assertion that the pursuit of individual self-interest produces an optimal social outcome. Further, their system mirrored that of mechanistic physics and all of their key determining factors (e. g., marginalism, utility maximisation and equilibrium) could be mathematically expressed (Bell and Kristol, 1981). While Smith's vision was Newtonian, it was only so in an analogical and qualitative sense. Smith had no pretensions to quantitative precision.

Neo-classical economics, and the views of Walras, Jevons and Pareto, isomorphic to physics and connected to other established disciplines on the 'tree of knowledge' through the common language of algebra, gained increasing acceptance as a modern science, and the institutional school more closely aligned to Smith's spirit declined, at about the same time as the first schools of business started to appear. So if economics was always the 'only theoretical framework' for business, as Pierson and others claimed, why didn't this new breed of economics align with business schools now? Because in the first decades of the twentieth century, economics spoke a language that was seen as of little relevance to business, and the majority of economists were disdainful of management studies.

Events at Wharton demonstrate how economics was unable to provide the necessary bridge that Locke wrote of at this point in time. The early Wharton professors were of two types. There were those who, in the words of one historian (Sass 1982, p.268), found 'their curricula material in the business world, not in the universities (in science)' and whose scholarship was disparaged as 'an extended form of business journalism'. Or they were teachers who came from other disciplines. Among these were economists. However, Sass (1982) and Locke (1989) note that, on the one hand, economists of the time were cool to the practical, descriptive thrust of Wharton's business programmes, let alone interested in teaching on them. On the other hand, those who did deign to teach were roundly criticized for having nothing of relevance to say to their classes. This was because neoclassicists argued that their economics should be purer, based far more on a priori logic and rational deduction than most of the other sciences that it sought to join at the academic high table:

> The science of Economics ... is in some degree peculiar, owing to the fact that its ultimate laws are known to us immediately by intuition or at any rate are furnished to us ready made by other mental or physical sciences ... [Our] method is as sure and demonstrative as that of kinematics or statics, nay, almost as self-evident as are those of Euclid. *(Jevons, 1888, p.18, 21)*

By converting economics into abstract model building in order to concentrate on general variables that could be expressed mathematically, the sort of calculi that sprang from this gave scant guidance to managers. The neoclassicists were concerned to express the mechanism of how the market as a whole worked, aspects that the manager had no direct influence over. In Locke's words (1989, p.15), the neoclassical theory of the firm was:

> Outward-looking, the entrepreneur's viewpoint inward-looking, for the theory of the firm treats the operations within the firm as a black box, an unknown, a problem that has already been solved. Because it assumes that the entrepreneur knows how to run his firm efficiently, it stops at the point where the [business person] wants analysis really to begin.

Looking back, commentators expressed surprise that: 'Even the economists in th[is] group [of traditional academic instructors] were wont to seek enlightenment more largely by speculative than by strictly scientific methods' (van Metre 1954, p.3–4). But at the time, people did not see this necessity. This passage from one commentator outlines what his contemporaries regarded as an irredeemable divide between business and economics:

> Economics and business [may] handle, to a large extent, the same material but they do not have the same spirit. Economics is a philosophical science with philosophical characteristics. Business economics is, on the other hand, an applied science. Chemistry and mechanical technology are closer in spirit to business economics than is economics. *(Schmalenbach, 1919)*

Pierson, Gordon and Howell, the AACSB and others had put forward the view that economics was the universal foundation for business studies: a view upon which management has subsequently sought to build itself. However, this idea is temporal. Only in the middle of the twentieth century, after economics 'evolved' again to become more empirical by incorporating new developments in statistics to provide substitutes for laboratory experimentation, thereby enabling it to speak a new language of probabilities and causality; and again through meshing with emerging ideas in computer engineering to promote algorithms and ratios relating to ideas like 'game theory', did it became both a valid academic foundation for management and a foundation with something useful to say to managers.

These two elements, coinciding in the middle of the twentieth century, addressed the problem of how to justify the inclusion of teaching business and management at university. It did not take long for this particular set of circumstances to become shrouded in a manner that gave it the air of a universal association. While van Metre (1954) would still recognize the transformation of economics into something that management studies could build upon as 'an unforeseen development' in the early 1950s, by 1959, Pierson would see economics as always providing these schools' 'only theoretical framework'. The link to economics and, by association Adam Smith, was a timely cantilever for supporting the rise of management studies.

Textbook Cases

While the new forms of economics that bridged across to management were a long way removed from the world of Adam Smith, they still identified him (or more correctly bits of what he wrote) as their discipline's foundation. And, by association, given that management must be based on economics, identifying Smith as a founding father for management becomes important too. It is interesting, by contrast, to note that those histories of management written prior to this convergence (e.g., Person, 1929; Urwick, 1947; Urwick and Brech, 1951; 1953) make no mention of Smith, seeing the roots of management in the development of engineering and the practices of industrialists like Babbage.

However, the next generation of management historians, those who would inform the writers of modern management textbooks, would draw out the now 'obvious' connection to Smith. In seeing Frederick Taylor and the associated 'classical' approach to management as the foundation of management studies, precedents (not just practical, but intellectual as would befit a science) were sought by this second wave of management historians in the late 1960s and 1970s. Historians like Wren, George and Pollard sought deeper roots. And in drawing this line to economics and back to the worlds of the Greeks, Romans and Chinese, as described in our introductory chapter, these management histories and early management textbooks compounded many of the reinterpretations of their counterparts in economics with regard to Adam Smith by looking back at the past through modern eyes. Hence, George (1972, p.54) can note that 'To many people, Adam Smith and economics are synonymous' and praise Smith for 'showing great insight into the evolving management function'. This contributes to the especially inaccurate view of Smith as the founder of management as well as economics that emerged with the first editions of modern management textbooks in the late 1970s.

But how do we account for the continuation of the conventional image of Smith as the *laissez faire* and division of labour advocate?

With regard to economics, some claim that more than for any other subject, history is bunk and that many economists subsequently take pride in not having read the work of those they claim as founders (O'Rourke, 2007). This may be true, but even if a modern economist did seek out *The Wealth of Nations*, it is unlikely that they would see its whole arc.

It is a book in five parts. Book V addresses the management of consequences of what has been advocated in the earlier books. It outlines the duties of government in the liberal commercial society, important focusses for public expenditure, the raising of revenue through taxation to pay for these, and the managing of public debt. Book V is a counter-weight to the commercial freedoms advocated earlier. As a consequence, Book V helps us make sense of *The Wealth of Nations* as a work in Smith's oeuvre. Smith's overarching concern was the progress of sociability, and governments had a role to play in preserving the rules of justice, equality of opportunity and the infrastructure on which sociability ultimately depended. Hence our earlier presentation of Smith's strongly held view that a progressive tax system was important (Phillipson, 2011). But Book V was trimmed out of many modern presentations of *The Wealth of Nations*. Take away this balance and it is easier to interpret Smith as the promoter of homo-economicus and material self-interest above all.

The argument used to explain the absence of Book 5 from a recent Random 'Everyman' reprint is that 'Books I-IV ... contain the whole of what Smith had to say in carrying out his aim' (Raphael, 1991, p.xxvii). Book V, the reader is assured, adds nothing of note. The 1970 Penguin edition, one of the most popular recent treatments, consists of books 1 and 2 with book 3 included only 'in order to make maximum use of the available space' (Skinner, 1970, p.7). Why fill that available space only with the earlier books? Because the Penguin volume is 'solely concerned with Smith's contribution to the principles of economics [and i]t would probably be agreed that the first two books contain the central part of Smith's work' (Skinner, 1970, p.7).

With regard to management histories, some did recalibrate their views of Smith a little in later editions. The second edition of Wren's history (1979, p.39) added a paragraph that began: 'While Smith saw the benefits of specialized labor, he foresaw its dysfunctional consequences . . .' And the fifth edition of Wren (2005, p.35) attributed other elements to Smith. But most of the original editions of modern management textbooks were written before Wren's second edition came out, and the earlier, simpler, version of Smith presented by Wren and others, and in keeping with modern economics texts like Samuelson, suited their potted histories just fine. And it still does. Consequently, to this day, Smith is presented in later editions of management textbooks in the form we have critiqued here.

THE PROBLEM THAT INSPIRED SMITH'S SYSTEM OF THOUGHT

A Problematization of Governance

As we have argued, at the time that management sought to cantilever off its status, economics had cobbled together and developed 'Smithian' fragments (*laissez faire*, the division of labour causes progress, the invisible hand of the market is for the greater good) and formed a historical view of itself that built upon these 'foundation stones'. This was justified by some on the basis that while Smith's other theories and works were rather perplexing, '*The Wealth of Nations* contains many brilliantly written passages' (Baumol and Blinder, 1982, p.48). As a result, if *The Theory of Moral Sentiments* is considered at all in management textbooks, it is in the light of the conventional interpretation of *The Wealth of Nations*, rather than the other way around (e.g., 'Smith's basic thesis was it is in an individuals' and organizations' self-interest to make ethical decisions' – Hitt et al., 2007, p.159). But what if we made the effort to look at Smith's work the other way around: as a whole, written in response to the particular problem that inspired it, and with *The Theory of Moral Sentiments* at the forefront of his endeavour?

Indeed, one of Foucault's (1977b, p.144) main critiques of conventional history was the 'presentist' way in which it would often place 'present needs at [claimed points of] origin [to] convince us of an obscure purpose that seeks its realization at the moment it arises.' Consequently, it is worth reflecting on the way we tend to see Smith as the founder of economics and responding in his work to economics problems (like how to promote the advance of industrialization) before economics and industrialization had been formed (Visker, 1995). Certainly, Smith was concerned with issues relating to the economy, but the particular problematization that spurs his work was a broader concern, and it helps us to understand Smith if we are clearer about this problem.

Smith wrote at a unique time. After centuries of royals and nobles seeking to govern, or be seen to govern, in proper conformity to moral, natural and divine laws, changes were emerging. In the sixteenth and seventeenth centuries in Europe, as the borders of nation-states became hard and fast, the problem that rulers responded to was: Am I governing with sufficient intensity, depth and attention to detail so as to bring the state to its maximum strength? And in this worldview, because economic resources were still believed to be finite, government was invoked to advance the economic interests of their own society 'at the expense of other societies' (Stuart *Works* I, p.347 in Sowell, 2006, p.360). This propagated the belief that a nation's wealth and power depended on its foreign and not its domestic trade, which built on the notion that wealth consisted in the finite store of gold, silver and other moneys. This had taken hold in Europe and reinforced old ideas that the way to increase wealth was by 'beggaring' one's neighbours (Phillipson, 2011, p.226). And this seemed to prove the value of those rulers and merchants who dealt at these international levels, rather than ordinary subjects.

But things were changing again in the eighteenth century. Serious thought and ferment were resulting in an expansion of democracy and a questioning and moving away from divine rulers. In the light of this, the concern in Smith's age was no longer 'am I ruling to the maximum,' but 'am I governing between the maximum and not enough?' (see Foucault, 2008; Hayek, 1960; Stephen, 1902).

Subsequently, debate was directed towards the idea of the self-limitation of political power. Robert Walpole, who as First Lord of the Treasury and Chancellor the Exchequer in the 1740s, was effectively Britain's first Prime Minister, sought to govern 'pragmatically', as he called it, with the aim of balancing interests in order to preserve political peace. In the following decade, the Marquis d'Argenson maxim *Pas Trop Gouverner* (Do Not Govern Too Much), and book by the same name, became popular in both France and in Britain.

In this sense, this age really was the beginning of the concept of liberalism as a system of thought: not just economic liberalism, but social and political and moral liberalism. Smith may have believed in economic liberty less than what some modern economists might like us to believe, but his system was absolutely built in response to the problematization of liberty more broadly. This was the major political and social problem of the day (and particularly in Scotland after the quelling of the Jacobite rebellion in 1746). How would things not fall into chaos, how could progress occur, without a strong ruler at the helm? This was a live question. Smith's uniquely optimistic answer was that not only will society not be damaged if we govern just enough (or at the border between too much and too little), but that it will, in fact, progress. And viewing Smith's work in response to this problem is, we argue, a better way to regard Smith.

Smith's System as a Response to the Problematization of Liberal Governance

Smith's last words were regretful: 'But I meant to have done more' (in Buchan, 2006, p.1). He had meant to do a lot more, to investigate and understand the relations between a set of interests vaster than any philosopher had dared to dream (to paraphrase Bagehot, 1876): discerning how systems of morality, society, civilization, governance and economy worked in order to comprehend how we could improve our ethical, political and material conditions. His despondency at not completing this task added to his determination that his unfinished works be destroyed at his death. Consequently, we cannot know how, exactly, he thought his system would work in total, but we do have far more to reflect on than the fragments of *The Wealth of Nations* that modern economics and management studies conventionally alight upon.

Smith's inquiries build on the work of his two great mentors Francis Hutchenson and David Hume. And his project related to the broader aims of the Scottish Enlightenment, distilling optimistic theories of sociability that explained the progress of civilization in the light of an increasing debate around liberalization. Fundamentally, Smith was positive about the human condition. Thus he examined the moral, social and material progress of humanity as opposed to 'the lamentable stories of the follies of so many of its rulers' which so many before him, including the *economistes*, had focussed upon (Phillipson, 2011, p.237). He would show that not only could liberal governance work: if combined with good management, it would encourage great progress.

Hutchenson divided philosophy into four parts: Ethics and Virtue; Private rights and Natural liberty (or Policing); Familial rights (now Political Economy or Economics); and State and Individual rights (or Politics). And Smith's first book dealt with the first of these. *The Theory of Moral Sentiments* was Smith's first attempt to gather his many years of lectures and thoughts together into a book, and it provides the ethical, philosophical, psychological and methodological foundations to Smith's later work. It begins with the already discussed assertion that at once outlines its purpose and is at odds with the view that Smith was a promoter of rational economic self-interest above all: 'How selfish soever man may be supposed, there are evidently some principles in his nature, which interest him in the fortunes of others, and render their happiness necessary to him, though he derives nothing from it, except the pleasure of seeing it.' In other words, why, if left to their own devices, are men drawn not to be selfish? Why are they sociable instead?

The answer: because of the human desire to share sentiments, and because we seek through this sharing what Smith calls 'fellow-feeling'. But given that we cannot know another's feelings directly, how do we share? We can only access other's sentiments through imagining what they are experiencing by our sensory perception of how they feel: be it joy or pain or the decisions they are facing. We achieve this by looking into our self, in other words (I.i.29): 'I judge of your sight by my sight, of your ear by my ear, of your reason by my reason, of your resentment by my resentment, of your love by my love. I neither have, nor can have, any way of judging about them.' Others do the same and we achieve mutual enrichment in this process.

How does this help us to become moral beings? Through the self-aware social practice of this simultaneous outward and inward-looking sympathy and judgement we develop in our imagination a kind 'impartial observer' viewing and judging the conduct of others and helping us choose virtuous courses of action. This impartial observer is not our conscience; it is not guilt; nor is it just the voice of God. It is driven by our sense of wanting to be understood as sociably virtuous and wanting to concur with others we admire. Hence, Smith argued: 'Man naturally desires, not only to be loved, but to be lovely: or to be that thing which is [judged by other's impartial observers] the natural and prover object of love. He naturally dreads, not only to be hated, but to be hateful; or to be that thing which is [judged] the natural and proper object of hatred' (III.i.8). These views help us understand Smith's focus on self-love in the second chapter of *The Wealth of Nations*.

Thus, Smith thought we actively and freely seek society for its own sake. While we may, in so doing, move further away from what Rousseau would see as our natural or 'noble savage' beings, we do not do it out of insecurity or weakness or vanity, but because it helps us be loved and we want to be loveable (we might use the words respected and respectable today). And through interaction with others and learning to 'humble the arrogance of [our] self-love, and [moderate] it to something that other men can go along with', we are on the path towards a virtuous life (*The Theory of Moral Sentiments*, II.ii.11). This social-civilizing process helps make us the people we would like to be, while at the same time improving society overall. And this freely given, freely sought and freely moderated mutual sympathy (rather than rulers, regulations, codes or stipulations) drives the progress of civilization.

Smith covered the first of Hutchenson's categories in *The Theory of Moral Sentiments*, and was to attempt the second with respect to policing, but for a number of reasons and after a number of delays, he instead addressed the third category in his second and (unfortunately) last book, *The Wealth of Nations*. This was not the project that Smith had envisaged after *The Theory of Moral Sentiments* or as his last, but he went at it with great gusto because focussing on political economy enabled him to show tangibly how seeking fellow-feeling, respectability and society could indeed make the world a mutually better place, materially as well as morally.

The Wealth of Nations would help assuage critics of *The Theory of Moral Sentiments* who thought it a nice idea, but without evidence and of little material consequence: the division of labour and the material progress that this can bring was the best evidence that liberal sociable exchange is not only a good thing: it explains the progress of civilization. Self-regard and sympathy created the trust necessary to enable specialization and the natural human propensity for 'truck and barter'. The division of labour developed because humans are cooperative beings who sympathize with and therefore value the endeavours of one another and will, by and large, exchange fairly if they can do so freely – a point that Smith could make at this time with reference to the case study of America at a distance from direct rule from Britain.

Clumsy and vain governments and colluding business interests may work against this progress and Smith thought this must be opposed. Indeed, in *The Wealth of Nations*, he is quite the critical management scholar in opposing prevailing big business interests in their dealings with governments of the day in this regard. Note, for example, his skewering of the way in which merchants – 'those who were supposed to understand trade' but really only 'knew perfectly how [current practices] enriched themselves' – promoted the status quo to parliaments, nobles and princes 'who were conscious to themselves that they knew nothing about the matter' (IV.i). This collusion between self-serving business interests and gullible (or self-serving) governors made 'commerce', which was in Smith's mind (IV.ii. Part 2) naturally a socializing and civilizing phenomenon not a 'bond of union and friendship,' but instead, and sadly, 'the most fertile source of discord and animosity'.

But this does not mean that Smith thought there should be no governance or *laissez faire*. Good management was required. As a set of student notes from 1764 makes clear (Phillipson, 2011, p.182ff.), he used his last year teaching at Glasgow before writing *The Wealth of Nations* to reconstruct his teaching so as to bring questions about the duties of government to the fore. He was recalibrating in order to emphasize the importance of governance in maintaining the rules of justice for fostering the sociable dispositions of its subjects. But as we have seen, Smith leaps straight into the material benefits of the division of labour for greater impact, and most readers do not get as far as Book IV and Book V where he deals with these matters.

This is a particular shame for us in management studies, because it is in book V that Smith actually writes directly about management. Indeed, the word management is used over 50 times in Book V (the division of labour is only used four times), and yet no attention is given in management history to what Smith said about it. It is in Book V (V.i, 2nd third, article 3) that he provides perhaps his sagest advice on the subject:

> For though management and persuasion are always the easiest and the safest instruments of governments, as force and violence are the worst and the most dangerous, yet such, it seems, is the natural insolence of man that he almost always disdains to use the good instrument, except when he cannot or dare not use the bad one.

This line of thinking with regard to management in the *The Wealth of Nations* may, in fact, be Smith's most original: his arguments for good management against imperialism, colonization, feudal systems and strict controls. Those practices encouraged the extension rather than the improvement of estates, and reduced tenants to a state of dependency and slavery: matters that should be as offensive to a people's sense of natural and moral justice as much as to the cause of economic efficiency.

Thus, colonization was for Smith as it was described by James Mill (in Hobson, 1965, p.51), just an elaborate government make-work project: 'a vast system of outdoor relief for the upper classes'. And while the 'work done by slaves ... appears to cost only their maintenance' Smith said, it is 'in the end the dearest of any' because it takes away from his beloved liberal sociability: a man's ability to mix and truck and barter freely (II.v). It was only man's foolish 'pride', Smith explained, which 'makes him love to domineer', rather than the economics of the situation, which explained the persistence of slavery.

Subsequently, in contrast with the view of many of Smith's claimed followers now, taxation is not the opposite of liberty or an impingement upon freedom, if collected on principles of equality, certainty and convenience, and used to protect those who may fall subject to oppression. Good management of these things and liberty should be part of the same system.

WHAT IF MANAGEMENT HISTORY TOOK THE WHOLE SMITH AS FOUNDER?

If the simplistic pastiche of Adam Smith listed in conventional histories of management as a founder is not representative of the man, what would happen if we took something closer to the complete Smith and saw in this alternative foundations for our field? And how might this enable us to, in Foucault's terms, 'think differently' about what management studies is about?

Currently, the management histories promoted in textbooks alight only on the fragments of Smith that economics claims to be founded on, the division of labour and the dingy image of Smith's pin factory case study as a precursor to the view presented of Taylorism and Scientific Management. The message to initiates is that management was founded on an evolving understanding of the efficiency gains that these industrial settings provided. Later management theorists have provided softer techniques, but the aim is still the same material gains – as efficiency is regarded as what management is fundamentally about.

However, in the light of the broader background presented here, management could instead be seen as emerging from discussions about governing and controlling things less tightly, not more. The age of liberalization and the Scottish Enlightenment problematized how things would get done, how progress would be made, without coercion, and this led to the rise of interest in good management. Consequently, for Smith, mutual improvement without coercion was what management should aim to achieve, and if we wish to regard him as a founder, this would be an interesting alternative fundamental basis for our field. It would certainly mean that management history would be less about just finding a line of continuity back to things considered precedents of the division of labour, efficiency gains and planning, directing, organizing and controlling. It would be a more inspirational basis from which to look towards the future.

As we have seen, *laissez faire* was not Smith's concept, the invisible hand was only used once in *The Wealth of Nations* (and not directly related to a free market), self-interest only emerges in translation, and the division of labour was nothing new. But what was really novel was the Smith's contention that slavery, or even the notion that a man's labour and creativity belonged to their bosses, would be detrimental to morality and mutual social and material gain. This perspective should also cause us to rethink.

That slavery should be seen as a part of management history is not new. Writers such as Cooke (2003), Esch and Roediger (2009), Hayek et al. (2010) and Crane (2013) have done an excellent job outlining the links between slavery and some management practices and pointing out the absurdity of management history's traditional silence on this. And recent critics have also outlined how even new histories, such as Khurana's *From Higher Aims to Hired Hands* (2007), focus too much on the 'higher aims' supposed in the title and too little on ignoble relations like those with the slavery system (Ruef, 2008).

What is new about our argument here is the idea that, having recognized this, we can look back to the work of Adam Smith in the round, and realize that if we take him as a point of origin for management we can see good management equated with the discontinuity of slavery and other forms of oppression. In other words, it should be impossible to think about management without thinking about slavery, as Cooke argues. Not just because there is an obvious continuity from slavery to classical management approaches, but also because we should see Smith's arguments against slavery as our field's starting point. Instead of teaching an evolutionary continuity – from the monuments built by slaves, to the promotion of the division of labour, to scientific management, to efficiency gains from subtler means – we should teach the importance of recognizing that the birth of management corresponds to the rise of social liberalism, Smith's new view of morality, and the demise of slavery. Promoting this would help students both to acknowledge the commonalities between slavery and some management techniques developed in the past (and present), and be more critical about what management should fundamentally be about.

As odd as it may sound given what we have been led to believe, actually reading Adam Smith could help us think differently about the context in which management emerged and help us define management as a less dismal enterprise, one that is about non-coercive ways of achieving progress. As a result, this view of management could lead to more sociable, and thus more civilized, futures – just as Smith would have hoped for.

3 To What End? The Nature of Management's Classical Approach

The fundamental end or 'good' of management studies is assumed to be efficiency, but it could be sustainability – if we look at history differently.

Conventional management histories employ an efficiency-obsessed F. W. Taylor as a hero/anti-hero, a noble but flawed leader of the rise of management studies whose simplistic views must be overcome. Subsequently, the conventional narrative informs us that management studies began when a highly mechanistic worldview was applied to work and organization, but since then we have developed a better, more humane understanding, culminating in recent ideas about ethics and sustainability. Looking more deeply at how Taylor's ideas took hold upsets this flow. It enables us to see that Taylor's Scientific Management only captured the wider imagination, and thereby gave birth to management as a subject of serious interest through its connection to a specific political problem: Theodore Roosevelt and his deputy Gifford Pinchot's quest to promote 'conservation' after decades of laissez faire expansion in North America. How might management be different if we believed that its founding and fundamental end was not mechanistic efficiency, but rather, in Pinchot's words: 'the wisest use of resources for the benefit of the greatest number of people for the longest possible time'?

What is good is something that comes through innovation. The good does not exist ... in an atemporal sky, with people who would be like the Astrologers of the Good, whose job is to determine what is the favorable nature of the stars. The good is defined by us, it is practiced, it is invented. And this is a collective work.

Michel Foucault (1988, p.13)

For a quarter of a century, we have tried the approach of polite incremental change, attempting to bend the physical needs of the planet to our economic models need for constant growth and new profit making opportunities. The results have been disastrous, leaving us in a great deal more danger than when the experiment began.

Naomi Klein (2015, p.26)

What is the 'good' that management theorizing aims to advance? Traditionally, this good has been seen to be efficiency: how to grow outputs, usually financial outputs, per inputs. This makes sense, given the lens that conventional management history provides us. Management precursors such as the Egyptians, Chinese and Romans were important because they developed efficient ways of planning, directing, organizing and controlling. Adam Smith is a key foundation stone because he theorized the importance of the division of labour and *laissez faire* economics in enabling greater efficiency, and this promoted the development of industrialization and mechanization: the context in which modern organizations emerged. Management studies' 'classical school' is labelled as such because those categorized as belonging to it sought to develop more pointed theories that advanced the division of labour and efficiency within organizations. And the reason they did this? We teach our students that it was done to address the universal problem of efficiency. Thus, we come to understand that what management studies is fundamentally about, the 'good' it seeks to advance, is efficient performance in this regard.

People do not talk as openly about seeking to serve efficiency in management as they did in the past, and, as we outlined in Chapter One, management histories in recent textbook editions now show that thinking has evolved to include modern perspectives like sustainability. However, given the way that new developments are added on to the list of ideas categorized in management textbooks as they cycle through new editions, there is, we believe, a danger that in addressing sustainability as 'the new big idea' it will be seen as the latest tool to be employed as an overlay upon the fundamentals of management, before eventually being buried in the sequence as other new approaches supersede it. In other words, sustainability becomes merely part of the 'polite incremental change' that goes nowhere much, which recent books like Naomi Klein's, cited at the start of this section, complain about.

Klein and others argue that we need to fundamentally change the way we do things and completely move away from old management thinking: that sustainability and other related goods are 'now in conflict with the fundamental imperative at the heart of our economic system: grow or die' (Klein, 2015, p.21). We suggest instead that we may advance fundamental change by moving back to management studies' foundations. That the 'good' conventionally regarded as the fundamental heart of management was in fact invented, defined and practiced by us. But we have defined it this way for so long that it now seems objectively true and immutable. Looking again at the so-called birth of management studies can reveal a different kind of problem and a new good that key players were seeking to address in their promotion of the subject.

While Klein may suggest that the forces of capitalism and the environment have never clashed before in the way they are clashing now, in fact they have – over a hundred years ago. And it was this clash that led to the popularization and establishment of management studies. The problem was how to curb *laissez faire* economic development in the United States without losing political popularity. The good appealed to, and in fact invented for the purpose, was 'conservation'. But we have forgotten this.

Appreciating what we have forgotten in this regard can help us put management theorizing on a fundamentally different footing, one less likely to see sustainability filed away when the next big idea in management takes its place. Rather than management history being a big part of the problem, taking a deeper look at management history may be a more effective solution than distancing ourselves from it.

In our previous chapter, we argued that management studies took an extremely limited set of insights from Adam Smith, and that serious thinking about management should be seen to emerge not as we seek increased division of labour and industrialization, but when we better appreciate the sacred right of freedom and want to organize and advance societies in ways that have mutually beneficial outcomes. In this chapter, we similarly apply Foucauldian counter-historical strategies (juxtaposing quotations to expose discontinuities where we would assume continuity to be the case; looking at how particular problematizations promoted the development of new objects and subjects; looking again at the webs of relations that developed and sustained these formations) to show management's 'classical period', F. W. Taylor and the foundational aim or good that we ascribe to management studies in a different light.

THE NAME OF THE GAME IS EFFICIENCY:
THE CONVENTIONAL VIEW OF TAYLOR'S
PLACE IN THE HISTORY OF MANAGEMENT

We outlined the development of management as it is portrayed in management textbooks in Chapter One. While there are other important figures in the story, Adam Smith, Max Weber, Elton Mayo and so on, the figure to whom most attention is devoted is always F. W. Taylor. The key document is his *Principles of Scientific Management*. The key date, if one is provided, is 1911: 'If one had to pinpoint the year that modern management theory was born, one could make a strong case for 1911 ... this was the year that Frederick W Taylor's *Principles of Scientific Management* was published' (Robbins, 1994, p.41).

While we are told of an important continuity in management history, an arc that takes us from the noble ancients to the father of economics and on to Taylor at the head of the classical school of management, Taylor's appearance is also marked out as a significant departure: a great illumination. As Peter Drucker put in his book, *Management* (1973/2008, p.1), while the roots of management go back over 200 years, management 'as a discipline' is a 'product of the twentieth century'. And because it was Taylor 'who first popularized the word "management"' it is he who marks the birth of the discipline.[1]

W. J. Duncan is more emotive than most, but this quote from his *Great Ideas in Management* (1989, p.2) illustrates the perspective promoted by this view:

> We certainly could begin [this story] in the fourteenth century with Machiavelli [and] no doubt we could learn much from Moses, perhaps Jethro and maybe even old 'Nick'. But to take management back that far [would] be an illusion, a myth, a fairy tale. Of course there were managers and organizations, and some people understood management processes and leadership. But there was no discipline management ... Management as a discipline began when people started systematizing it, codifying it, and developing prescriptions for how to manage it better. Eventually, theories that could be taught and learned emerged. That was the beginning of management.

This is what Taylor did: he developed management theories. And he did this, according to the story that Duncan, Drucker and others promote, to advance the cause of, and need for, greater efficiency of performance. This is the birth of management studies proper.

---

[1] Drucker (Drucker and Maciariello, 1973/2003, p.12) goes on further to say that while Adam Smith is a forebear of management, 'management did not exist when [he] did his work', which seems a little unfair seeing as Smith uses the word management over 50 times in *The Wealth of Nations*. Indeed, Drucker (Drucker and Maciariello, 1973/2008, p.12–13) – perhaps management's most popular author ever – compounded the misconceptions about Smith that we highlighted in the previous chapter by writing that, to Smith, 'the economy was impersonal and governed by objective economic forces'.

This origin narrative relates to management emerging as the economic and social conditions arose that both enabled greater efficiency and fuelled a demand for greater efficiency. A typical example of how the discontinuity that is Taylor is inserted into a narrative of continuity follows:

> We can see early examples of management practice in the
> construction of the pyramids and in the arsenal of Venice. [One key]
> historical event [after these] was the publication of Adam Smith's
> *The Wealth of Nations*, in which he argued the benefits of division
> of labour (job specialization). Another was the Industrial
> Revolution, where it became more economical to manufacture in
> factories than at home. Managers were needed to manage these
> factories, and these managers needed formal management theories
> to guide them. [This led to the rise of] Frederick W. Taylor, known
> as the 'father' of scientific management. [He] studied manual work
> using scientific principles – that is, guidelines for improving
> production efficiency. *(Robbins et al., 2014, p.67)*

This perspective builds upon and reinforces earlier interpretations. For example:

> Scientific management was the first approach to emerge in the
> history of management theory. Its most fundamental feature was
> a concern with efficiency ... This form of management developed in
> response to a pressing need in the United States to increase
> productivity in the early twentieth century when there was
> a shortage of skilled labor. *(Pearce and Robinson, 1989, p.32)*

> In the early part of the twentieth century, as railroads opened up in the
> western portion of the US and the nation's population rapidly grew ...
> the demand for manufactured products was great. New manufacturing
> plants were built, attracting waves of new immigrants ... The earliest
> attempts to study behavior in organizations came out of a desire of
> industrial efficiency experts [like Taylor] to improve worker
> productivity. *(Greenberg and Baron, 1997, p.9ff.)*

While Taylor may be derided in some quarters now for his extremely mechanistic worldview, he is still regarded as foundational: 'It is fashionable today to look down on Taylor [but] his approach to work is still the basic foundation' (Drucker, 1973/2008, p.14); 'To denounce Taylor's work for ignoring the intricacies of modern motivational thought is much like attacking Sir Isaac Newton because he failed to invent non-Euclidean geometry or discover the theory of relativity' (Bedeian, 1986, p.40). While our understanding may have superseded his, so the story goes, Taylor's *Scientific Management* is still the key point of origin in the conventional narrative of management history and the field today stands on its shoulders.

Wrapped up in this historical understanding are beliefs and practices about the basic or fundamental 'good' of management studies. In other words, what are we studying or theorizing to achieve? If for the normal sciences, the aim is to get closer to an understanding of how things work; for medicine, the preservation and improvement of physiological life; and for architecture, the creation of better living environments, what is it for management? Historians like Williamson and Chandler were certain that organizations emerged and persevered because the visible hand of management made them more efficient than markets. Drucker's seminal book, *The Concept of the Corporation* (1946/1964: 44), stated that management and organization must be 'measured by the yardstick of efficiency'. In the 1960s and 70s, Harold Koontz (1961) built his efforts to order management theory around this: 'increasing efficiency' was the 'goal of all managers' and, he claimed, it should also be the reason for developing management theory (Koontz and O'Donnell 1974, p.7). As Luther Gulick (in Gross 1964, p.120), succinctly put it, for management: 'whether public or private, the basic "good" is efficiency'. Kinicki and Williams (2009, p.42) begin their textbook chapter on management history with a 'major question: If the name of the game is to manage work more efficiently, what can the classical viewpoint teach me?'

As this mechanistic view moved out of step with attempts to promote a more humanistic outlook it has faded from the foreground in some fora, but other related financial measures of performance have risen and indeed an ever-increasing amount of theorizing in the field has been related, directly or indirectly, to achieving increases in end variable financial returns or outputs relative to inputs (March and Sutton, 1997). Indeed, philosopher Alasdair Macintyre (1984) developed a term to express the rationality associated with this management worldview: a circular 'bureaucratic rationality', where efficiency is both the end aimed for *and* the means to achieve this end.

This rationality was dominant in the twentieth century and is still seen by many as a loop that entraps development (Cunliffe, 2009; Kavanagh, 2013). For example, Gary Hamel (2007, p.12ff.) claims that: 'as managers we are captives of a paradigm that places the pursuit of efficiency ahead of every other goal. This is hardly surprising, since modern management was invented to solve the problem of inefficiency'. Hamel's brief history of how this came to be illustrates the field's historical assumptions. He attributes management's invention to two men: Taylor – the self-centred mechanistic inventor of scientific management driven only by efficiency, and Weber, whom Hamel derides for 'saluting' bureaucracy in his 'anthem' to it. We will, in Chapter Four, show this view of Weber to be a modern misconception (Cummings and Bridgman, 2011; Mills, Weatherbee and Durepos, 2013), but in this chapter, we want to shine a light back into the forces that led to scientific management becoming what it became, and how Taylor and this origin of management came into view *in situ* at that key moment of 1911. Rather than a history that shows a continuous progress to the present in hindsight, and the past in the light of this perception of progress, we zero in to look at the political reasons, discontinuities and problematizations associated with that claimed point of origin as they were occurring.

A COUNTER-HISTORY OF THE ORIGIN OF MANAGEMENT
STUDIES

The Particularly Modern Good of Efficiency

The two quotations above are both translations of the same passage
from Aristotle's *Metaphysics*. The first is from Smith and Ross'
Oxford translation of 1908 (the same time that Taylor was thinking
deeply about how to promote his ideas). The second is from the first
page of *Functions of the Executive* by Chester Barnard published in
1938: 'the most influential book in the entire field of management ...
since Taylor's *Scientific Management*' (Koontz 1980, p.51; cf. George
1972). The translation Barnard uses is Tredennick's from 1935.

> We must consider also in which of the two ways the nature of the universe
> contains the good or the highest good, whether as something separate and
> by itself, or as the order of the parts. Probably in both ways, as an army
> does. For the good is found in the order and the leader, and more in the
> later; for he does not depend on the order but it depends on him.
>
> Aristotle's *Metaphysics* (XII, 1075a)

> For the efficiency of an army consists partly in the order and partly in the
> general; but chiefly in the latter, because he does not depend upon the order,
> but the order depends upon him.
>
> Aristotle's *Metaphysics* (XII, 1075a)

This opening quotation of *Functions*, cast with the authority of
Aristotle, serves to show how important effective management is to
organizations of any sort, and imply the desired end towards which
Barnard's view of management is set: efficiency. But what strikes upon
the juxtaposition of the two quotations is the lack of the word efficiency in the 1908 translation. Barnard's excerpt starts part way into
the passage, turning 'For the efficiency ...' into the beginning of
a sentence (so we do not see that Aristotle was using relations between
a general and an army as an analogy to describe how the world is given
form). But the word efficiency is Tredennick's translation. For anyone
familiar with Ancient Greek, the 1930s version may seem strange.
The Greeks did not have a word to equate with efficiency as we read it
now, and nor did the English language until the end of the nineteenth

century. More recent translations do not use the word, returning to phrasing similar to Smith and Ross. But in 1938, and indeed through all but the decades on the edges of the twentieth century, the idea that efficiency is the greatest overarching good, or the ultimate cause of form (for it is in this sense that Aristotle is referring to 'good'), becomes possible and even appears natural. It had become taken for granted, or 'silently thought'.

However, at the point that management studies is said to have begun, efficiency was not yet held in this regard. While Taylor and his contemporaries were seriously investigating mechanistic efficiency as a means to an end, the loop of bureaucratic rationality had not yet closed. Efficiency was not yet widely viewed as *the* end or aim in itself. But because management history understands its subject with hindsight, it looks back through the twentieth century 'lens' of efficiency and often appears to assume, paradoxically, that Taylor both *caused* what Haber (1964: 52) and other mid-century historians called the 'veritable flood of efficiency' that hit post–1911 (where 'efficient and good came closer to meaning the same thing in these years than in any other period of history', Haber, 1964, p.ix), and *was caused by it*. It sees Taylor's work in terms of its furthering efficiency, mechanistic thinking, industrialization and little else. We argue that by returning to the moments where these early management ideas were formed, where Smith and Ross's view was more reflective of the mainstream than Tredennick and Barnard's, we might see history differently.

In doing so, our most surprising discovery is that the thing that we assume to be the opposite of, or furthest point away from, management's materialistic-mechanical starting point: sustainability (or conservation in the language of Taylor's time): may in fact be a cause of it. While this may be interesting in itself, the motive for highlighting this is not to show current views of management's progress to be ill-founded. We believe that by charting a different historical point of origin for management, we can think beyond 'bureaucratic rationality' and determine a different aim or 'basic good' for management theorizing.

A Problem, a Network Coalescing around a Solution and the Rise of Management Studies

Michel Foucault (1977a) argued that human science subjects did not emerge independently, as a more scientific view was applied to enable us to see more of the objective truth. Rather, they, and their object, the 'normal human-being', emerged as discipline was made a problem following the demise of traditional modes of controlling society through violence or its threat. The political 'solution' was the development of scientific laws of normality that would enable 'deviants' to be dealt with: disciplined and punished. In this counter-history, we posit that management studies, as we know it, emerged not as a smarter gaze was applied to understand the objective laws of management, but in response to a unique problematization in the years that preceded 1911. The problem was how to control the development of big business, which was regarded by many to be 'running amok' in the United States. The solution was the 'conservation movement'. This created the space for the first theories of management to enter mainstream consciousness. The paragraphs that follow outline how this happened.

Roosevelt, Pinchot and the Problem of Controlling the 'Special Interests'

Theodore Roosevelt had form as an opponent of big business. So much so that a plan was devised by big business interests and their links in the Republican Party to lessen his influence by lining him up to be William McKinley's vice presidential running-mate. Then as now, the position carried minimal influence. But the plan did not account for McKinley's assassination on 14 September 1901. Roosevelt thus became President at a pivotal moment: a transition from The Gilded Age to The Progressive Era, when 'the nation suddenly "woke up" to attend, in its own fashion, to the stress and distress of an industrial civilization' (Fink 2001, p.1). His agenda put him on a collision course with the 'heroes' of the Gilded Age's rapid industrial expansion (Carnegie, Morgan, DuPont) and what were called their 'special interests'.

In his second annual message to Congress on 3 December 1902, Roosevelt outlined the problem that inspired his presidency and the Progressive Era:

> No country has ever occupied a higher plane of material well-being than ours. [This] is due to no sudden or accidental causes, but to the play of the economic forces in this country. [While] the conditions have favored the growth of so much that was good, they have also favored somewhat the growth of what was evil. [Our] industrial development must not be checked, but side by side with it should go such progressive regulation as will diminish the evils [and] regulat[e] the combinations of capital which are, or may become, injurious to the public.

As a small subset of this agenda, Roosevelt's statements about the need for the conservation of forests have led him to be called 'our earliest and most passionate environmentalist' (Donald 2007, p.164). But the influence of this subset would grow as it came to provide a language that would help Roosevelt counter those that began to organize against him.

His greatest ally in this fight was Gifford Pinchot. Pinchot was ostensibly just the head of the Forestry Bureau, but his influence was far wider. Roosevelt (1914, p.409ff.) came to regard him as standing 'first' among his staff. And it was Pinchot's initiative that turned the tide when it looked like Roosevelt's attempts to take on the special interests might peter out. By the end of 1906, influential business interests in the West and conservatives in the East were organizing against Roosevelt's attempts to curb the industrial growth that, in their minds, was a key part of the 'American Dream'. Faced with the prospect of losing influence, Roosevelt intensified his 'anti-special interests' agenda (Harbaugh, 1967).

Pinchot's (1937, p.262ff.) breakthrough, the idea which in his words 'put the stone at the end of the club', was the invention of a 'conservation movement' in early 1907:

The idea was that all these natural resources which we had been dealing with as if they were in watertight compartments actually constituted one united problem ... We had been dealing with [it] piecemeal, and ... not attacking the problem in a united battalion. The idea was so new that it did not even have a name ... Finally Overton Price suggested that we should call it 'conservation' and the President said 'O.K.' So we called it the conservation movement.

In the face of mounting opposition to his progressive agenda, Roosevelt had populated his administration with experts and had increasingly looked to scientists and members of the emerging new 'professions', like engineering, to help make cases for a variety of initiatives towards greater controls. However, these men were more difficult for the general public to relate to than the big business rhetoric they were utilized to oppose (Andrews, 2006). Realizing that the message had to be sold more effectively, Pinchot sought to engage the 'bully pulpit' and 'unleash ... a veritable crusade of enthusiasm for conservation' in order that 'a movement peculiar to federal scientists and planners [might become] deeply rooted in the minds of the public at large' (Hays 1959, p.122).

Pinchot (1910, p.23) defined conservation in emotive terms 'To make our country a permanent and prosperous home for our children and our children's children'; and in more measured detail: 'The first principle of conservation is development, the use of ... natural resources ... for the benefit of the people who live here now ... In the second place, conservation stands for the prevention of waste ... [And third] natural resources must be developed and preserved for the benefit of the many, and not merely the profit of a few ... Conservation means the greatest good for the greatest number for the longest time'. These definitions provided Roosevelt and his technocrats a unified aim they could direct themselves towards. Conservation became a powerful combination of applied common sense, science and humanity that any small businessman, farmer or householder could understand (see Pinchot, 1910, p.80). This was the utility of conservation as a line of argument. As Roosevelt put it:

All this is simply good common sense. The underlying principle of conservation has been described as the application of common sense to common problems for the common good. If the description is correct, then conservation is the great fundamental basis for national efficiency. *(Presidential 'Special Message' of 22 January 1909)*

As Samuel Haber's (1964, p.xii) study of this period observes, the ideas of big business were so intertwined with American patriotism that they 'could not with ease be attacked frontally, they could [only] be outflanked'. How could any business person who had the America's best interests at heart oppose conservation so put?

The new language of conservation was showcased at the Conference on the Conservation of Natural Resources in May 1908, which propelled conservation to the forefront of public consciousness. The driving force behind it was Pinchot, without whom the Conference 'neither would or could have been called' (Roosevelt in McGee, 1909, p.10). For the first time in US history, all Governors were summoned to the White House to discuss one issue. This was deemed necessary because, as Roosevelt (in McGee, 1909, p.3ff.) explained, the question of conservation, 'the gravest problem of to-day', had become 'so vital'. In the opening address, James Hill outlined what was seen to be at stake (McGee, 1909, p.64ff.):

Of all the sinful wasters of man's inheritance of earth ... the very worst are the people of America ... Either [we] seize the reins of government with a strong hand, or [the] republic will be as fearfully plundered and laid waste by barbarians in the twentieth century as the Roman Empire of in the fifth ... [T]he principles of conservation of national resources ... must be heartily accepted by all, as the first condition, not only of continued material prosperity, but also of the perpetuation of free institutions and a government by the people ... If this patriotic gospel is to make headway, it must be by just such organized missionary work as is to-day begun.

Pinchot (1937, p.263) was very pleased with the Conference's impact: 'I know of no similar instance, where a great new idea was introduced to the public in so short a time. At the beginning of the week hardly anyone knew what conservation meant, and by the end everybody knew'.

While the seeds of the conservation movement may have been planted as a particular project relating to forestlands, it became Roosevelt and his supporters' way to address the largest problem of the age. As Roosevelt claimed in one of his last Presidential messages (on 22 January 1909): 'The policy of conservation is perhaps the most typical example of the general policies which this Government has made peculiarly its own during the opening years of the present century'; and as mid-century historians would reflect:

> The broader significance of the conservation movement stemmed
> from the role it played in the transformation of a decentralized,
> nontechnical, loosely organized society, where waste and
> inefficiency ran rampant, into a highly organized, technical,
> and centrally planned and directed social organization which could
> meet a complex world with efficiency and purpose. *(Hays 1969, p.2)*

The stage was set for the emergence of management studies.

The People's Lawyer

Once Roosevelt's term ended, the conservation agenda became vulnerable. But Pinchot was determined to keep up the fight. The main event that kept the conservation movement in the media after Taft became president was the Pinchot–Ballinger legal case of 1910; and in particular, the representation of Pinchot's side by the so-called 'people's lawyer', a Progressive lawyer from Boston named Louis D. Brandeis.

On the surface, what came to be known as Pinchot–Ballinger controversy was not really about Pinchot or conservation. It was about Louis Galvis, an employee of Taft's new Secretary of the Interior Richard Ballinger, who informed Taft of what he saw as Ballinger's improprieties in selling public lands to private interests. Fired for whistleblowing, Galvis took his story to *Collier's Magazine*, who published it and was subsequently taken to court by Ballinger on behalf of the Taft government. Pinchot, who believed that Taft and

Ballinger were soft-peddling on conservation issues, seized the opportunity to fight Galvis' corner.

Collier's hired Brandeis to represent them. While his 'people's lawyer' moniker related to his being *for* the interests of ordinary people *against* the special interests of big business, it also reflected his ability to skilfully market the causes he was representing through the media to get public opinion onside. In consultation with Pinchot, Brandeis saw an opportunity to do this by making the case into a public seminar on conservation. Big business, in collusion with secretive and self-serving government bureaucrats, were seeking to do down an ordinary hard-working man (Galvis) who wanted what was best for the future of his fellow Americans.

A letter from Brandeis to his mother (1 March 1910: Urofsky and Levy, 1972, p.325) provides an insight into his strategy: 'The unfitness of Mr Ballinger is being made more and more apparent ... Meanwhile the people are led to think about conservation, are learning what it means; and the investigation must prove a very helpful education'. By the end of the case, Brandeis had succeeded in making it a debate about the goodness of conservation and its connection to a new American Dream. His (1914, p.xlv) closing argument in the Ballinger case began: 'This investigation has been referred to as a struggle for conservation, a struggle against special interests. It is that: but it is far more. In its essence, it is the struggle for democracy, the struggle of the small man against the overpowering influence of the big'.

It worked. Galvis and *Collier's Magazine* were cleared, but, more importantly for Pinchot and Brandeis, the case 'did indeed result in centring public attention on the vital need of immediate and effective conservation programmes' (Strum, 1989, p.138; cf. Pollack 1956, p.240ff.). Pinchot (1937, p.264) was exceedingly pleased with how the case had 'nailed down in the minds of the American people what this conservation business was all about'. And through it, according to legal historians (Urofsky and Levy 1972, p.xvii), Brandeis 'emerged as a major spokesman for the preservation and orderly development of natural resources'.

1910 was a big year for Brandeis. After Pinchot–Ballinger, he worked with Pinchot's brother Amos for the National Conservation Association on a high-profile piece of labour arbitration, and then the case that led to the rise of management as a field of general importance.

The legal case for which *Scientific Management* was created was commonly referred to as the Eastern Rate Case (ERC). In 1910, Eastern Rail Road Company submitted an application to the Interstate Commerce Commission seeking permission for increasing freight rates. Brandeis represented shippers who were opposed to the rate increase. Brandeis claimed he had 'no thought of introducing the question of scientific management' as the case began (Brandeis in Drury, 1915, p.17). This is not surprising, given that scientific management did not yet exist. While the ideas that would be gathered under this banner had been forming for years, and the two words occurred together in Taylor's *Shop Management* in 1903 ('fortuitously' and without the intention of naming anything, according to Drury, 1915, p.16), scientific management had not yet been named. The term was, in fact, developed by Brandeis for the specific purpose of winning the ERC.

Under pressure for being seen as anti-enterprise, Roosevelt and Pinchot had sought to use an alternative business-relatable language to counter the conventional *laissez faire* views of big business, and now Brandeis would do likewise. Partway into the hearing, having been surprised by the operational ignorance of the railroad company executives in the witness box, he decided to develop a new argument; reduce waste through new production practices and the rates can stay as they are and the railroads' bottom-line could even grow. Win-win, Brandeis would argue. How could any good business person disagree?

But like Roosevelt, he knew this message would look better backed by men of science, or at least men sounding scientific. He decided to gather a set of production consultants to act as witnesses to make the railway men look out-dated. And, like Pinchot, knowing the importance of gathering testimony under a banner that could be recalled and admired by pressmen and the public alike, he made this a key consideration at the gathering. He knew Harrington Emerson and through him, assembled a group including Frank Gilbreth and Henry Gantt to discuss the case. The consultants suggested that one person they were all happy to associate their own ideas with was F. W. Taylor. And after discussing alternatives including Functional Management, Taylor System, Shop Management, and Efficiency, they agreed that the best name for this given Brandeis' aims was 'Scientific Management' (Copley, 1923, p.372; Drury 1915; Nadworny, 1955).

When Brandeis subsequently made contact with Taylor to discuss the case and his potential involvement, he found Taylor less than enthusiastic. He did not particularly like the term scientific management (while he did use the term after Brandeis made it popular, 'he continued to cherish a certain distaste for it': Copley, 1923, p.372) and unusually for Taylor, who generally took every opportunity to promote his ideas and give advice, he declined Brandeis' request to testify on the grounds that knew little about railroads and, just in case that excuse did not pass, because he had prior commitments (Nelson, 1980). However, a later letter to a friend suggests a more downcast reason. Taylor thought Brandeis' proposed use of his ideas would 'be so indefinite and vague that it will not be possible to seriously influence [the inquiry]' (Taylor to Dodge, Stevens Archive, 8 November 1910: 098J008).

While it may seem surprising in hindsight that Taylor would react in this way, his jaded response is understandable given the state he was in. Taylor had retired from his work at the Midvale Steel Factory in 1907 to devote time to promoting his ideas to a wider audience. With his personal assistant M. L. Cooke, he sought to take on teaching and speaking assignments and provided guided tours and talks for anybody who would listen. But by 1910, he was becoming frustrated that his system had not become as popular as he had hoped and even the professional body that he had once been the president of, the American Society of Mechanical Engineers (ASME), was shunning his work. As Robert Kent (1932, p.39) reminded readers on the twentieth anniversary of the Taylor Society, Taylor's system at this time 'was not making very great progress ... In fact ... it was being ignored'.[2] But Taylor's disposition changed after Brandeis' invocation of scientific management achieved the desired media reaction. The front-page headline in the *New York Times* on 21 November, as his 'expert witnesses' began to take the stand read: RAILROADS COULD SAVE $1,000,000 A DAY: Brandeis says Scientific Management Would Do It. Soon Taylor (in Copley, 1923, p.369) was writing excitedly to a supporter who had been travelling abroad, that 'A very extraordinary thing has happened through a Boston lawyer'.

The Marketing of Scientific Management

Taylor became increasingly enthusiastic as a range of popular publications sought comment from the man cited by Brandeis' expert witnesses. While Brandeis had wanted Taylor to appear, the fact that he did not turned out well. The experts' appeal to a mysterious unknown guru added to the buzz surrounding the ERC. Unbeknown to Taylor, Brandeis carefully orchestrated the subsequent media interest (Brandeis, 1914, p.xlv).

Now engaged, Taylor sought Brandeis' advice about how to deal with the press. On 7 December, Brandeis allayed Taylor's uncertainty by saying that: 'there ought [not] be the slightest conflict between the different magazine writers; indeed I should think that ... the more people who wrote about it and the more magazines that treated it, the better' (Brandeis to Taylor, 1910, Stevens Archive, 098J022). Brandeis was happy to encourage many to report on Taylor in general terms, but he also realized the value of granting a longer exclusive to one widely read national magazine, and he steered Taylor towards *American Magazine*.

American Magazine had a wide readership (Taylor had preferred the more high-brow *Atlantic Monthly*). The editor, Ray Stannard Baker, was a fellow progressive whom Brandeis knew he

---

[2] The Taylor Society was also inspired by Brandeis' intervention. During the discussion with Brandeis about creating a seemingly unified management movement, Gilbreth claimed that such a movement needed a Society.

could trust to put a wholly positive spin on the foundation of the legal argument he was laying out in the ERC. And Baker had also agreed to publish a 'companion piece' on Brandeis' good works titled *Brandeis: A Remarkable Record of Unselfish Work Done in the Public Interest*. Here the author would explain (Poole, 1911, p.490) that 'Mr. Brandeis's activity not only had the effect of concentrating public attention upon the [ERC] case and the real issues involved, but also of creating widespread and unusual interest in the question of scientific management'.

On 3 December, Brandeis (in Urofsky and Levy, 1972, p.390) wrote Baker that Taylor was now 'entirely in accord with us at to the desirability of publishing in the *American Magazine*, in preference to all others ... he will be glad to aid you in any way'. Indeed, the extent of Brandeis' orchestration of the campaign is indicated later in this letter where he begrudgingly accepts that Baker is not going to publish the Brandeis and Taylor articles as quickly as Brandeis – who was keen to keep up the momentum during the ERC – had wished.

Over the next few weeks, Taylor worked in close contact with Baker on the article draft. It was based on one developed a few years prior as a pamphlet to capture Taylor's thinking. Taylor had submitted this to the ASME, who kept deferring a decision on whether they would publish it, adding to Taylor's professional frustration at this point (Cummings, 2002; Wrege and Stotka, 1978). The *American Magazine* article and supporting editorial would become a lengthy three-part exposition of Taylor and scientific management across March, April and May issues. Finally, Taylor had a pulpit from which to spread his gospel. And while the content of the article was not new, its framing, and in particular, the end towards which it aimed, was.

While Taylor and Baker crafted the articles, Brandeis won the ERC. His use of the new language of efficiency and scientific management appeared to take the railroad executives by surprise. Indeed, some exchanges indicate that they did not understand what Brandeis meant exactly by 'efficiency', the terminology was that new. One exasperated Railroad Company witness huffed to Brandeis that 'you say efficiency I say economy' (Mason, 1946, p.324). Indeed, despite later writers seeing efficiency as a fundamental or universal good, this sense of the word was actually still being invented in 1911.[3] The ICC ruled in favour of Brandeis and 'the people', and the railroads had to withdraw their rate increases.

Brandeis' nous and the ensuing interest in Taylor helped keep the conservation flame alive and sparked a crusade for greater efficiency and management in all affairs: 'an efficiency craze' hit America like a 'flash flood' and '[e]fficient and good' would subsequently go on to become 'closer to meaning the same thing in these years than in any other period of history' (Haber, 1964, p.52, 10). However, it is important to recall that this interest was not the cause of scientific management – it took off in the years *after* the ERC was won. And despite later writers seeing Taylor as a booster of all things efficiency, he actually thought the 'efficiency craze' and 'societies' that sprang up to further it to be misguided. As he wrote to somebody seeking his endorsement for such a society (in Copley, 1923, p.387): 'I hardly know what to say ... All the world, of course, wants efficiency now [but] this is not a sufficient basis for a group of men to get together'. But whatever the consequences of the ERC, Taylor acknowledged in a letter that it was Brandeis who had 'w[oken] up the whole country' to management as a subject. Indeed, he continued: 'I have rarely seen a new movement started with such momentum as you have given this one' (Stevens Archive, 9 January 1911, TP98 J).

[3] In these years, qualifying nouns were often used to express this particular sense of the word. For example, *Seldes'* (1917) article *'American Efficiency in England'* demonstrates the extent to which production efficiency was still a foreign concept in Europe; Hoover refers to 'Taylorism efficiency' at a conference in 1921; and when Roosevelt used efficiency in an 11 March 1895 letter, he clearly meant it in a different way to the sense he would imply when advocating scientific management 18 years later: 'I do not give a snap for a good man who can't fight and hold his own in the world. A citizen has got to be decent of course. That is the first requisite; but the second, and just as important, is that he shall be efficient, and he can't be efficient unless he is manly. (Walter Camp Papers, Reel 15, Yale University, New Haven, CT).

What Inspired the Origin of Management Studies

Despite the conventional understanding of management's formation now being bereft of Brandeis, his contribution was widely credited as it happened, and not just by Taylor. After losing the ERC, Railway President Daniel Willard told the *New York Times* that 'As I see it, there is only one thing for us to do – to put into effect the Brandeis greater efficiency system' (New York Times, 24 February 1911). And another journalist quotes a key (unnamed) supporter of Taylor as saying 'By a single stroke Brandeis created a greater advance in scientific management than would otherwise have come in the next quarter of a century' (Poole, 1911, p.490).

Early histories of management also gave Brandeis primary status. The first sentence of Drury's *Scientific Management: A History and Criticism* (1915, p.15), begins: 'The significance which has come to be associated with the words scientific management may be traced to an event which occurred in the later part of 1910 ... [This was the ERC]. It happened that Louis Brandeis ... assumed the leading position among the 15–20 attorneys lined up against the proposed advances'. Copley's analysis is similar (1923, p.369ff.).

And having acknowledged Brandeis thus, both Drury and Copley ask the obvious follow-up question: what drove Brandeis to reconfigure his strategy in the ERC so as to spark the birth of modern management? Both were close enough to the primary source to ask the question directly, but they received varying answers. To Drury (1915, p.17), Brandeis said that he visited a client who owned a shoe factory and was as impressed by its operations as he was unimpressed with the railroads' practices. This caused him to further investigate current best practice in production. In a footnote in Drury, Brandeis also claims that he was aware of Taylor's *Shop Management* when it came out and with Emerson's work, but 'these had wholly dropped from his mind' before the case.

But in response to Copley, Brandeis' story had shifted (1923, p.370–1). Brandeis attributes the cause to remembering 'discussions which I had on the subject of efficiency with Mr. Harrington Emerson ... I also had in mind, among other things, a pamphlet on Shop Management by Mr. Taylor'. These are reasonable answers to give to authors writing from the perspective of a history of management, but their differences might make one wonder how accurate Brandeis' recollections are.

A lawyer is not likely to answer questions about his thought processes in presenting a case by saying he was influenced by other cases he had been working on, but there is evidence that Brandeis saw the invocation of Taylor as part of a broader campaign, related to 'his interest in all forms of conservation, or as he put it, the elimination of waste' (Dilliard, 1941, p.32). Brandeis' friend Max Lerner reflected (1939, p.80) that Brandeis' 'studies in connection with the Ballinger investigation' influenced his subsequent cases. For example, as he moved from Ballinger to the ERC, he was involved as a mediator in a dispute between garment factory owners and unions. Lerner claimed that Ballinger 'had given him some notion of how the natural resources of the country were disposed of. But here, among the Jewish garment workers in New York, he found human resources that equally called for conservation'. According to Strum (1989, p.168ff.), Brandeis 'saw scientific management as a way of achieving conservation: of machines, of capital, and above all, of labour'. She goes on to claim that: 'His particular approach [in the ERC] appears to have been affected by his involvement in Pinchot–Ballinger and the whole question of land conservation'.

Brandeis' personal correspondence is also revealing. It shows how diligent he was in keeping the Pinchot brothers in the loop throughout the ERC, and to impress upon them the connections between the causes. On 14 November 1910, Brandeis (in Urofsky and Levy, 1972, p.386) wrote to Amos: 'The time is come when you and Gifford ought to get into the railroad efficiency fight, as the greatest field for immediate conservation, and to set to work all the conservation organizations for our support'. On 17 December, Gifford sent Brandeis a letter of congratulations for having 'broken' the ERC with his efficiency argument. Brandeis replied (in Urofsky and Levy, 1972, p.396), 'I thank you for your congratulations. You have so thoroughly trained the American mind to conservation that this new form as presented in railroad efficiency has found a relatively easy path'. Brandeis also encouraged Rudolph Gaar Leeds, editor of the *Indianapolis Sun* (9 November 1910 in Urofsky and Levy, 1972, p.383), to send a reporter to the ERC hearings by explaining the significance of the case thus: 'Of all the social economic movements with which I have been associated none seems to me to equal this in importance and its hopefulness ... and I feel sure there is no field of conservation which is more important than this. It is conservation which will enure to the benefit of the present as well as future generations'.

In keeping, the first line of the first book published with scientific management in the title ran as follows: 'The efficiency movement, of which scientific management is an important factor, expresses a new philosophy that conceives of conservation as the central motive in the conduct of industry'. The book, published in May 1911, was *Scientific Management and Railroads* by Louis Brandeis' (1911, p.4).

Indeed, while it may seem far-fetched today to think of conservation as the inspiration that caused management studies and the good that it sought to serve to take flight, the evidence is there not only in the first line of the first book on scientific management, but also the first line of another: Taylor's *Principles of Scientific Management* (which was developed from the *American Magazine* articles). While many have critically analysed the content of what is now seen as management's founding document, its initial framing and aim are generally overlooked: 'President Roosevelt, in his address to the Governors at the White House, prophetically remarked that 'The conservation of our national resources is only preliminary to the larger question of national efficiency' (Taylor, 1911, p.1).

Roosevelt did not say this exactly. What he said (in McGee, 1909, p.12) as he sought to connect conservation to America's future was 'Finally, let us remember that the conservation of our natural resources ... is yet but part of another and greater problem to which this Nation is not yet awake ... the problem of National efficiency, the patriotic duty of insuring the safety and continuance of the Nation'. So, while Roosevelt meant something different than Taylor by efficiency here, he had mixed and matched the term loosely. And Taylor's interpretation, while skewing the emphasis, was in keeping with Roosevelt's views and increasingly (thanks to Roosevelt, Pinchot and Brandeis) emerging popular opinion.[4]

Taylor may have jumbled Roosevelt's words, but their placement in *The Principles* was no accident. Taylor told a friend in January 1911 that the articles for Baker were 'by far the most difficult piece of writing I have ever undertaken. I have had to write and rewrite it eight or ten times to get it into the form which I thought people would be interested in reading' (Taylor to Crozier 11 April, Stevens Archive, 1911 TP185B). Subsequently, while the content of *Principles* is similar to that expounded in Taylor's (1903) *Shop Management* (Cummings, 2002), there are some significant changes that link the content to the issues of the day. The naming of the approach scientific management and subsequent allusion to science; the greater use of practical examples; efficiency and its derivatives being used more than twice as often in *Principles*; becoming 'more efficient' being referred to as a measure of progress; and of course, the ends of conservation and reducing waste are nowhere to be found in *Shop Management*. Taylor's comment to a friend in the middle of 1911, that: 'The interest now taken in scientific management is almost comparable to that which was aroused in the conservation of our natural resources by Roosevelt' (Taylor in Urwick, 1956, p.60) shows how pleased he was that his work was finally gaining

---

[4] Indeed, an annotated draft of principles in the archives of the Stevens Institute of Technology's Taylor archive shows how Taylor misquoted Roosevelt in multiple ways. When his statement was repeated in the second paragraph of page 1, they wrote the 'large question of national efficiency' rather than the 'larger question'. We are grateful to archivist Leah Loscutoff and her team at the Institute for their help in this regard.

popularity, how much of a big deal conservation was at this juncture, and the value of associating his work with Roosevelt and Pinchot's conservation initiative.

It is not surprising then that Taylor would title an address he gave to the Philadelphia Club just as he was finalizing the *American Magazine* articles, The Conservation of Human Effort; or that magazines of the day would outline his approach in articles titled The Conservation of Human Effort (Orcutt, 1911); and The Conservation of the Worker (Cotter 1913). Or that a contemporary of Taylor's, Clarence Bertrand Thompson (1917, p.286), would note that 'Mr Taylor in his treatise on the subject used the title 'The Art of Management' while others in speaking of Mr Taylor's work refer to it as the "Conservation of Human Effort"'. Or that Harlow Person's (1929, p.25ff.) comprehensive assessment of *Scientific Management's* place in management history, would describe how: 'In contrast to the general attitude of opportunism set by the earlier frontier conditions appeared a new attitude ... [It was a] new attitude which enabled scientific management to become [a] dominant force'. He then explained that the number one of ten contrasts that were 'components' of this new attitude, from which *Scientific Management* sprang, is 'Conservation versus waste'. Or that a 1917 review places Taylor's work in a broader development thus (Thompson, 1917, p.172):

> the obstacles to the development of scientific management betray
> their smallness and transitoriness in comparison with the greatness
> and permanence of the forces with which its progress is allied ... Its
> close relationship to the movement for the conservation of all
> resources has been pointed out and its far-reaching consequences as
> an agency for the conservation of human effort have struck forcibly
> the popular imagination.

Or that W. D. Hemmerly, in a letter of commiseration to Taylor's son after Taylor had passed away, would write (28 August, 1915 to Kempton Taylor, Stevens Archive, 014N001) that: 'it is due to [Taylor's] kind interest in me that I have been as successful as I have in such work as I have undertaken so far in my attempts to spread his gospel of conservation'.

Roosevelt's Reinforcement

Theodore Roosevelt, who had first issued the call for conservation, was pleased with scientific management's emergence. He did not comment publicly on the ERC, but his response to a complaint on the outcome to financier Henry Lee Higginson ('The present unsatisfactory condition in railroad affairs is due ninety-five percent to the misconduct, the shortsightedness, and the folly of the big railroad men themselves' – Perry, 1921, p.435) is a good indicator that Brandeis' victory was, for him, a 'signal moment in an emerging pragmatic progressivism' (Donald, 2007, p.188). Indeed, so arresting was the continued buzz around conservation and efficiency playing out in Pinchot–Ballinger and the ERC that Roosevelt parlayed the new language into a key theme in speeches to define what progressivism meant as he launched the Progressives as a third party against the Republicans and Democrats. Roosevelt now related Progressivism to what he termed a New Nationalism. Roosevelt struggled to define what this actually meant, but his clearest invocations incorporated the new ideas of conservation and efficiency: 'The supreme political task of our day, the indispensable condition of national efficiency and national welfare, is to drive special interests out of public life'; 'National efficiency has many factors. It is the necessary result of the principles of conservation widely applied'; 'Conservation has become a great moral issue in becoming a patriotic duty'; 'Conservation is the road to national efficiency'; and '100 per cent American, 100 per cent Efficient' (see, for example, Roosevelt's New Nationalism speech of 31 August in Osawatomie, Kansas and his speech of 6 September 1910 in St Paul).

Roosevelt wrote an article for *The Magazine of Business* towards the end of 1911 titled 'Scientific management is the application of the conservation principles to production', where he claimed that 'The time, health and vitality of our people are as well worth conserving, at least, as our forests, minerals, and lands'. This was widely quoted in publications as diverse as *American Country Girl*, *Journal of Industrial and Engineering Chemistry* and *American Poultry Advocate*. He also provided an endorsement to be printed at the head of Gilbreth's *The Scientific Management Primer*, published on the crest of the wave of public enthusiasm for management following the ERC in early 1912 (Gilbreth, 1912, p.2):

> Scientific management is the application of the conservation principle to production. It does not just concern itself with the ownership of our natural resources. But in the factories where it is in force it guards these stores of raw materials from loss and misuse ... We couldn't ask more from a patriotic motive.

While it is hard to imagine such a prominent politician in a similar situation endorsing another management book, we can see why Roosevelt did so with this book at this moment. Conservation, efficiency and scientific management gave Roosevelt's hard-to-define third-way political movement purpose: both an end to be aspired to and a means to that end (greater efficiency through approaches like scientific management).

A Counter-historical Summary

Historians looking back at the emergence of new technical professions like engineering and figures like Taylor have defined the early years of the twentieth century in America an age of efficiency. Hence, it is easy now to miss that this was also 'an age of conservation', that conservation was 'the slogan of the day' (Bodenstar, 1918, p.12, 337), and that its problematization that led to its creation resulted in great intellectual ferment.[5] But the influence of conservation and how it precedes the growth of management studies is more obvious when one looks at

---

[5] A wave of conservation 'best-sellers' followed the Governors' Conference, including Van Hise's *Conservation of Natural Resources in the United States* (1908); Cronau's *Our Wasteful Nation* (1908); Gregory's *Checking the Waste: A Study in Conservation* (1911); and Russell's *Natural Resources and National Wealth* (1911).

contemporary writing. For example, reporting on these themes in *Moody's Magazine* (the self-described 'monthly review for investors, bankers and men of affairs') in the first six months of 1911 makes interesting reading.

Prominent in the January issue's *Financial Book World* section (Moody's, 1911, p.70–1) is a review of Van Hise's *Conservation of Natural Resources in the United States*. The reader is reminded that 'Magazines and newspapers have been filled with conservation for the past three years'. And the book praised as a 'practical presentation of the conservation problem . . . which is at present one of our paramount issues'. Van Hise is described as 'well fitted to speak upon the subject' due to being 'one of the delegates to the White House conference on conservation and a member of the National Conservation Commission appointed by President Roosevelt'. In February (1911, p. 140–1), Pinchot's *The Fight for Conservation* is reviewed in the same section: 'Conservation, the meaning of which was practically unknown in 1907, has become a household word, says Mr. Pinchot. He might have added that Pinchot too, has become a household word'. As the review adds: 'the attitude toward conservation of any man in public or private life [now] indicates his stand in the fight for public rights'. In March (1911, p.150ff.), the lead item in the editorial is the ERC result. The biggest feature is a collection of opinion pieces on the case, including contributions from Brandeis and star-witness Emerson. Emerson claims it a victory for 'a new and very simple science – namely a high order of common sense applied to every minute operation'. April (1911, p.231) begins with a letter to Moody's from the President of the New York Central Railway Lines Company, refuting claims by ERC commentators in the previous issue. May (1911, p.331) contains a large article by the Director of the Bureau of Railway News and Statistics, who takes issue with figures referred to in the March issue and with the basis of the ICC's report on the ERC. Also in this issue is a review of Brandeis' book *Scientific Management and the Railroads*, which is praised for 'explain[ing] in the most concise and clearest text we have seen what efficiency engineering, or scientific management, is' (1911, p.362–3). Finally, the June issue (1911, p.440) reviews *Principles of Scientific Management*. And here we are told that 'Of making of books on scientific management there is no end since Mr. Brandeis gave the subject such spectacular advertising in the railroad rate cases, and the general reader may be growing bored by having scientific management stare him in the face so constantly'. But it is worth reading, because '[Taylor] is a man who for thirty years has been working out a business system of which few readers ... had even heard before the consul for the shippers told the railroads about it publically'.

Upon reading such a counter-history, it is reasonable to conclude that a young lawyer, an innovative forester and the twenty-sixth President of the United States played crucial roles in giving life to management studies in addition to F. W. Taylor, and that what united them was the association of good management with conservation.

WHY CONVENTIONAL MANAGEMENT HISTORY DOESN'T REGARD CONSERVATION

If the link between conservation and the creation and acceptance of scientific management as the original management theory of general consequence was once seen so clearly, why do we not see it now? The Conservation Movement burned brightly, but faded fast. Nobody worked the bully pulpit like Roosevelt and once he and Pinchot left the spotlight, the movement declined. Conservation Congresses served as forums for debate until 1915, but were soon undermined by internal squabbling. Brandeis went on to great things (he became the first Jewish Justice of the Supreme Court in 1916), and his crowning achievements were in the field of law. While he maintained an interest in management, it was not his profession. He had little interest in becoming a leader in the field, and unlike Taylor, he did not have a group of management consultant 'followers' who had an interest in seeing his reputation furthered.

Those who wrote the history of management in the 1940s and 1950s, like Urwick and Brech, looked backwards for antecedents of what management had come to be in their own time. Many Taylorites were still active and Urwick wrote in hagiographic style, drawing a continuity of progress back from them, to Taylor; then, ironically, to the barons of the industrial revolution that Roosevelt and the conservation movement opposed. Management historians were more likely to examine the works of management professionals rather than law or politics and contextual socio-political factors were sifted out of the narrative. This was the baton passed to the writers of the management histories that informed the management textbook industry in the 1970s and 1980s, when the first editions of many of today's most popular texts were drafted (Cummings and Bridgman, 2011; Grant and Mills, 2013). The most influential historians in this regard, as Chapter One outlined, were George, Chandler and Wren.

George's (1968) *History of Management Thought* starts with a continuum of major contributions to management, with Taylor's contribution significantly larger than any other of the 93 names. Networking management to the most noble of influences, Diocletian, Thomas Jefferson and Jesus are seen as contributors, but not Roosevelt, Pinchot and Brandeis.

Chandler does not see Roosevelt, Pinchot, Brandeis or conservation as important. And a summary of his and Wren's viewpoints may be best expressed in Chandler's (1973, p.393) review of Wren's first (1972) edition of *The Evolution of Management Thought* (currently in its eighth edition). Wren 'might have produced a more penetrating analysis if he had focussed on the changing nature of the private business enterprise in the United States ... from a small shop to a giant corporation', as these were 'the most critical determinants of the ways in which management thought evolved'. In other words, Wren would have done better if he had seen history as he saw it, but if one is to focus on men rather than economic changes, Chandler does agree with Wren's choice of Taylor as a 'central figure'.

Wren does not discuss conservation, although he mentions Roosevelt and the ERC briefly as background influences. However, in recent years, Wren's history has altered its tone further towards the 'great man' approach that sees Taylor as the protagonist in the birth of management. Until the third edition of *Evolution*, we are told that:

> Great national concern [that] was voiced by President Theodore Roosevelt and others over the depletion of America's resources ... Taylor who had for three decades fought against the misuse of both physical and human resources, *found himself* as a result of the railroad hearings *the man of the hour. (1972, p.141*, emphasis added)

This analysis was backed up with a two-part summary diagram: the first a timeline of the key actors; the second charting the social, economic and political backdrop. The political column lists 'conservation of natural resources' between 'congressional investigations' and 'progressivism' (1972, p.271). But, by the fourth 1992 edition, the second part of the diagram is gone and the quotation reproduced above is subtly changed so as to end: 'Taylor who had for three decades fought against the misuse of both physical and human resources, *gained a wide audience as a result of the railroad hearings*'. Written this way, Taylor is no longer just 'the man of the hour', fortunate to be in the spotlight at that point in time, but 'the man'.

Relatedly, Wren's earlier editions describe Brandeis as a minor contributor in furthering management thought (1972, p.182–3), but by the fourth edition, this and references to books by and about Brandeis have disappeared. Brandeis fades and Taylor becomes increasingly established as the man who made management. The zeroing on Taylor may have been influenced by a survey undertaken by Wren (Wren and Hay, 1977) that sought to investigate differences between management historians, business historians and general members of the Academy over who they regarded as the most influential historical figures. It found widespread disparity between those names that populated the top twenty for the three groups. The one common denominator: Taylor was clearly number one in all three sets. A further factor may be that Brandeis' correspondence (which we found to be so revealing) was not published until 1974, so even if the early management historians had wished to look deeper at Brandeis and his motives, they would not have had this resource.

Indeed, adherence to the 'Taylor was the man' story occurs even in books that are critical of accepted management conventions. Braverman (1974) follows Chandler's marks, while more recent texts like Fulop and Linstead (1999, p.210ff.) take Taylor and *Scientific Management* (which they label 'his own particular brand' of management 'for which he coined the term') as a starting point, seeing him as a continuation of the industrial revolution and the factory system. Morgan's unconventional *Images of Organization* (2006) uniquely provides a historical perspective as a general backbone, but the narrative is the same: management theory begins as Taylor and his followers employ a mechanistic gaze, it then evolves increasingly organic as that initial point of origin is built upon. Monin's (2012) critique, seemingly unaware of the network of relationships we have described in this chapter, takes to task Taylor's audacity and opportunism in seeking to legitimate his work via Roosevelt and his noble cause (Monin, 2012, p.92ff.).

But while it may be hard to align the characterization of Taylor today with conservation, the association was not far-fetched in his own day and it seems hard to claim to know from this distance that Taylor was anything but sincere in seeing his work as related to conservation. For example, Hughes' (2004, p.200) broad historical sweep in *American Genesis* claims that: 'Taylor rightly associated his scientific management with the broader conservation movement that had attracted national interest and support during FDR's term as president', as they and he did share many of the same principles. The archive at the Stevens Institute also reveals that Taylor was a member of the National Conservation Association established by Pinchot, and for Taylor and his peers, the connection between the two movements would have been clear.

Shenhav (2002) does paint a different history, one that dispels the paradoxical convention that Taylor single-handedly made management which was also a smooth progression of earlier 'industrial' thinking and practices. 'It is only in relation to other factors in the management movement that Taylorism can be understood in a contextual and historical perspective', he claims (2002, p.35). But unlike our focus on how the popularization of management is greatly aided by a network of political, legal, media and marketing forces of the moment, Shenhav traces the causes to the hard-fought growth and gradual continuity of engineering as a profession and the spread of machine efficiency as the measure of goodness.

Under Chandler and others' influence, the histories of management that aspiring managers encounter have taken increasing efficiency as a key criterion for inclusion, but, perhaps pressed for space, and a desire for an easy to follow story, they have been more enamoured by Wren and George's approach of stringing together the biographies of great men. Given this, whether the approach is conventional or critical, it is not surprising that as the history of management has looked backward, Roosevelt, Pinchot and Brandeis are not seen and what Taylor is said to have initiated and spread is not the gospel of conservation but, as Wren (1972, p.147ff.) phrases it, 'the gospel of efficiency'.

ALTERNATIVE FOUNDATIONS AND DIFFERENT THEORETICAL AIMS FOR MANAGEMENT STUDIES

> For management, whether public or private, the basic 'good' is efficiency.
>
> Luther Gulick (in Gross 1964, p.120)

> [R]esources must be developed and preserved for the benefit of the many, and not merely the profit of a few ... the greatest good for the greatest number for the longest time.
>
> Gifford Pinchot (1910, p.23)

The efficiency-obsessed F.W. Taylor, *The Principles of Scientific Management*, the spread of the factory system, the increasing

influence of the industrial revolution, modern economics and individual materialism, a mechanistic engineering mindset: these are conventionally seen as the causes of the birth of management studies.
This view has corresponded with an often unspoken belief that management's rationality was bureaucratic rationality, to use MacIntyre's
(1981) term, where efficiency was both the overarching end and the
means to achieve it.

It is not easy to free ourselves from this set of assumptions,
because, as Kanigel (1997, p.7) says about *Scientific Management's*
legacy, it now 'so permeates ... modern life that we no longer realize
it's there'. But what if we did think differently about management
studies' historical constitution and nature? The idea that the rampant
development of big business was the problem, conservation the solution, and that management studies leapt into consciousness as a result
of the ensuing intellectual ferment of this particular setting, seems
far-fetched now. But when one gets closer to what was being written at
the time of that 'point of origin', one may be encouraged to see
management differently. And the effort could be fruitful.

It has been said that management studies is a particularly
American profession. Our study confirms that to be true, but not in
the way we thought. More than the professionalization of engineering
societies and other forms of knowledge, population growth, immigra-
tion, and industrialization, what is truly different about the context in
which management studies emerged, what is uniquely American, is
the speed of the rise of big business and conservation movement as
a political response to this. This did not occur as a major concern: the
problem of the day, anywhere else. In this respect, management studies may be an American gift. But it could have been received and
utilized differently with a different historical perspective on what it
was about.

What if Roosevelt, Pinchot and Brandeis were taught as management pioneers? What if we recognized management becoming
a subject of wide interest as a result of awakening to the perils of big
business interests or capitalism run amok? What if we saw it as a break

from relentless march of industrialization rather than another step in its continuity? What if recent interest in sustainability was not as far away from classical management as it could be, but bringing us back to where management began? In keeping, what if the aim, or the basic good, of management, was conservation: to seek to ensure the greatest good for the greatest number for the longest time? Or what if this was the aim towards which management theorizing was directed?

Management studies in general could also be changed. In recent decades, it has been overtaken in people's minds as a desirable subject by the seemingly more high-minded ideals of leadership, entrepreneurship and innovation. But what if it could move beyond a belief that its purpose was subservient to the 'good' of efficiency towards a more noble aim? (Indeed it is this subservience to a 'means posing as an end' – efficiency – that leads MacIntyre and other scholars to claim that management can never really be a craft or a profession – c.f. Kavanagh, 2013). Pinchot, in a debate held while the Pinchot–Ballinger case was ongoing, said in response to Ballinger's claim that as a good government bureaucrat, he had discharged his duties completely within the law: 'An institution or a law is a means, not an end, a means to be used for the public good, and to be inter-preted for the public good' (Pinchot, 1947, p.417–8). And, given the way that we have configured the good of management, we too allow managers the defence of acting according to the 'laws of management', rather than engaging in debate about what those so-called laws should be serving other than greater efficiency.

These are unsettling questions and ideas, difficult debates, and the potential outcomes would be difficult to operationalize. (Pinchot's 'good' is much more difficult to express mathematically than increas-ing efficiency or annual 'return on investment' – but not impossible). We do not have the space to explore them further here, and in any event, we are not the best people to do so; innovation in this respect (as described in the quotation by Michel Foucault as the head of this chapter) should be a collective work. But we hope that by encouraging rethinking the historical development of, and by association, the foundational nature of management and management studies, as we have done in this chapter and the previous chapter, we may spur critical thinking about what management is here to serve. What if the origin, good and aim of management studies was defined and practiced as conservation: or what we might today call sustainability?

4 The Birth of Organization Science: Or What We Could Learn from Max Weber

Weber's foundational insight is not that bureaucracy is great, but a contingency view that modes of organizing reflect specific contexts.

If the manager is the actor in management studies, the organization is his or her domain. The conventional history of management deploys the character of Max Weber as a pioneer in organization science in two ways. First, as a serious and renowned thinker whose interest in the things that management took itself to be about added credence to the emerging field. Second, as the avid promoter of bureaucracy – the support of which has come to be seen as wrong-headed as more decentralized or organic forms of organization have come to the fore. However, if we explore more of what Weber wrote, rather than just what his later interpreters chose to translate and management textbook writers chose to distil, we find a far more complex figure. Weber could see why and how bureaucracy would come to be the dominant organizational form in the early decades of the twentieth century and its advantages in this context, but he was troubled by what its dominance would mean for humanity. This chapter explores what a more rounded Weberian view of human organization would mean for our understanding of management's past and future.

> Max Weber, a German sociologist, lawyer and social historian, showed how management itself could be more efficient and consistent in his book *The Theory of Social and Economic Organizations*. The ideal model for management, according to Weber, is the bureaucracy approach.

Bateman and Snell, *Management* (2009, p.45)

In keeping with the antipathy towards history that we noted in Chapter One, some management textbooks do not cover history at all, while others package it into an appendix (like Bateman and Snell, 2009, quoted above). But all those that include a history of management somewhere in their pages promote the importance of Max Weber. If Taylor is the father of management studies, Weber is the father of organization science[1]. The quotation from Bateman and Snell is typical of the way in which Weber is perceived. Its unwitting inaccuracies with respect to the man will appear strange to those who have studied Weber, but this simplified 'straw-man' version of Max Weber fits well into the evolutionary narrative of management history into which he is slotted. In a nutshell, this goes:

1 Increasing division of labour and industrialization provides the context for a concern with greater efficiency.
2 Taylor and the 'classical school' are the first to generate explicit theories aimed at making workers more efficient.
3 Weber promotes bureaucracy as the best (i.e., most efficient) form of organization within which work should be done. He is thus, the first organization scientist and his work is where organization studies begins.

In this way, Weber is often hailed and dismissed at once. His standing as a serious academic from an older discipline who undertook a study of organization adds gravitas to management studies and organization science as these newer disciplines establish themselves. At the same time, management histories can show that despite being a great academic, Weber got it wrong: that we (later management and

[1] This chapter draws from Cummings, S., & Bridgman, T. (2011). The Relevant Past: Why the History of Management Should Be Critical for our Future. *Academy of Management Learning & Education, 10*(1), 77–93.

organization scholars) are cleverer and our theories have led us closer to the truth about organizations. For example:

> According to Max Weber, bureaucracies are the ideal organizational form. [This] contrasts with more modern approaches to organizational design that claim that different forms of organizational structure may be more or less appropriate under different situations. *(Greenberg and Baron, 2003, p.11)*

Thus, we have another addition to the conventional management history narrative of noble roots laid down by great thinkers (the giants on whose shoulders we stand) *and* the progressive evolution that more modern thinkers have provided since.

This chapter investigates the increasingly twisted portrayals of Max Weber as this narrative is developed and maintained in management textbooks, as these texts move through various editions from the 1970s to the present day. It argues that the increasing intensity of Weber's misrepresentation does us few favours. If we and our students were aware of the depth of Weber's insights, and how far in advance they are of things that we are told they are lesser than (like the 'plug and play' version of corporate culture invented and promoted since the 1980s – see Chapter Eight for more on this), management theorizing today could be greatly advanced.

That Weber has been misrepresented in management studies has been noted on a number of occasions (Aldrich, 1979; Hill, 1981; Jackson and Morgan, 1982; Clegg, 1992): Richard Weiss, for example, claimed that the misguided portrayal of Weber as 'the most influential proponent of the bureaucratic model' (Zey-Ferrell, 1979, p.48), was due to 'mistranslation' (Weiss, 1983, p.242). We, however, are not setting out to describe the mistranslation or over-simplification of Weber, or anyone or anything else for that matter. We are more concerned to understand why and how a wrong-headed configuration of Weber continues, and in some cases intensifies in best-selling management textbooks to this day, and to examine the process or system that shapes and maintains such a 'straw-man'. And, we examine the effects of not questioning the presentation of historical figures like Weber in textbooks as these are fed to the next generation of management thinkers in their formative stages. We highlight Weber to illustrate once more why improving the ability of an aspiring manager to critically evaluate how history and historical figures may be misrepresented and misappropriated will greatly improve their ability to be creative, encouraging less bounded and more substantial developments in management theory and practice for the future.

If multiple editions of management textbooks are our data in this chapter, Michel Foucault's 'counter-historical' phases or approaches (outlined in Chapter One) provide us with the lenses to analyse them. We begin our analysis by invoking Foucault's 'early works' to firstly uncover the flaws in the treatment of Weber as a historical figure in management textbooks. What we uncover raises further questions. Consequently, we draw upon Foucauldian 'archaeology' to try and understand how the paradigm that prevailed in the United States in the middle of the twentieth century reconfigured Weber in ways that allow statements like those by Bateman and Snell and Greenberg and Baron (cited earlier) to pass as the truth. We then use Foucauldian 'genealogy' to interrogate the contents of a popular management textbook as it has shifted through nine editions since Weber's archaeological reconfiguration.[2] We will begin this genealogy by juxtaposing statements about Weber from three editions of the same textbook. This will lead us into a broader discussion of what aspects of these representations of Weber have been continuous and which have been adapted and changed over the 25 years and nine editions of this text. Having done this, we will explore the networks of power that may on the one hand sustain the continuity of this version of Weber and at once subtly reinterpret this 'strawman' to suit the times in which each edition emerges.

Reflecting the above organization of Foucault's approaches, our analysis of Weber's historical presentation in management textbooks is arranged in three parts:

[2] We define the field of 'management textbooks' broadly to include related subject areas such as organizational behaviour, operations management and strategy.

1 an application of the thinking of his 'early works' to *question the truth* of this presentation;

2 an approach closer to his archaeological period to investigate how this questionable truth was *shaped by a particular episteme;* and

3 that of his genealogical inquiries to draw out *the power relations that sustained and subtly shift* this strawman.

HOW MANAGEMENT STUDIES DISTORTS WEBER'S INSIGHTS

Those management textbooks that do cover the ideas of Max Weber as part of the history of their field, generally present him as belonging to 'the classical school'. Here, he and other figures (most commonly Frederick Taylor) appear as an early stepping stone towards the field's present heights. Like all stepping stones, they exist on the pathway to something else: namely, in this instance, the better views of management that have been developed since. In this manner, history enables us to see *gravitas:* through a continuity of great thinkers applying their minds to the problem of management; and a *cutting edge:* through a discontinuity in the form of a series of advances beyond 'classical' views (Cummings, 2002). In their presentations of history, these textbooks draw upon a number of histories of management that emerged in the middle of the twentieth century as the subject was attempting to legitimate itself as a worthy field of inquiry. Histories like those written by Mooney and Reiley (1931/1947), George (1968), and Wren (1972) traced, for the first time, a continuity and progression from great or 'noble' civilizations and thinkers like the Egyptians, Romans and Greeks; Plato, Jesus, Benjamin Franklin and Thomas Edison, on to great management thinkers of their own times, such as Drucker, Fielder, Vroom, Locke, March and Simon.

In this historical scheme, Weber is cast as an inventor and leading supporter of bureaucracy as the ideal or one best way of organization and a whole-hearted supporter of mechanistic efficiency. He is generally described as a classical organization theorist or management expert and a booster of Taylorism. His major contribution to the field is often dated at 1947.

Two of the world's best-selling introductory management texts inform us that Weber 'considered the ideal organization to be a bureaucracy' (Stoner, Freeman and Gilbert, 1995), and that bureaucracy is 'his ideal type' (Robbins and Coulter 2002, p.37). Among other leading texts, Robbins and Mukerji's (1990, p.42–3) treatment of Weber in *Managing Organizations: New Challenges and Perspectives* provides a good summary of the prevailing view. At the end of a chapter titled 'The Evolution of Management Thought', a review question asks students to 'Define Weber's ideal organization'. They are expected to have learnt that Weber's 'ideal organization' exhibits bureaucratic principles. The best-selling management book of the past three decades, *In Search of Excellence* (Peters and Waterman, 1982, p.5), confirms that Weber 'pooh-poohed charismatic leadership and doted on bureaucracy; its rule-driven, impersonal form, he said, was the only way to assure long-term survival'.

In works that optimistically portray the progress of management, Weber's 'love of bureaucracy' leads to complaints that he 'went too far in advocating a machine-like organization' (Dale, 1967, p.12); that he did not pay 'attention to the human factor in organizational design' (Schwartz, 1980, p.19); or that he paid 'repeated homage' to the outmoded 'Taylor system' (Gerth and Mills, 1954, p.261; Gross, 1964). In pessimistic works (e.g., Ritzer, 1996), Weber appears as a promoter and forerunner to the evils of de-humanization. Elsewhere, Weber is cast as an 'organizational theorist' (DuBrin, 1984; Wren, 1994); a 'management expert' whose 'main concern [was] the nature of bureaucracies' (Clutterbuck and Crainer, 1990, p.18); or an 'organizational designer'. Schwartz (1980, p.19) describes Weber as providing 'six guidelines for organization design' which are Weber's six elements required for a bureaucracy to function effectively. In these ways, Weber is seen as both a pioneer whose intellect lends weight to the fledgling field and a problem to be overcome and dismissed as wrong-headed, old-fashioned or one-dimensional as the subsequent advance (i.e., discontinuity) of management thinking is traced.

However, a critical appreciation of history can, without too much effort, show these historical representations to be false. They conceal rather than reveal the truth. Weber was a lawyer, a historian, economist, philosopher, political scientist, and a sociologist, but he was not an organization or management expert. Such fields did not exist in his world. He never actually designed an organization. His effort was to attain a diagnosis, not a prognosis of his society, and bureaucracy, while a serious concern, was not his main concern – his vision was much broader (MacRae, 1974). Further, it is unclear whether Weber was even familiar with Taylor's work. He did visit America in 1904, but Taylor was only known to a very small circle of supporters in the first decade of the twentieth century and did not become widely known until 1911 in the US and some years later abroad (Cummings, 2002). In any event, perhaps through a desire to promote simple and coherent chunks of linear progress, Weber is quite wrongly tarred with the same brush as Taylor, a very different character. Indeed, the criticism that Weber over-emphasised efficiency comes despite the fact that the modern sense of efficiency as the ratio of inputs over outputs was a term foreign to Weber's German tongue at the time he wrote (Albrow, 1970).

Weber's use of the term 'ideal' also confuses management writers. Weber's 'ideal types' were not in any sense good or noble or a best-case scenario. He used the term to indicate a model or measure against which societal development might be compared: 'ideal', in his language, meant 'not fully exemplified in reality'. Hence, Weber conceived of three ideal types of authority: traditional, charismatic and rational-legal, each of which sponsored different or competing forms of organization. In his political analysis, Weber makes it clear that a best-case scenario might be a charismatic or innovative organization in tandem with a bureaucratic organization. He even examined how traditional monarchies or aristocracies could work well. One could claim the modern contingency approach to organization to actually be a continuation of Weber's thinking.

Moreover, Weber was *entirely pessimistic* about the advance of bureaucracy. History for Weber was 'an eternal struggle between bureaucratic rationalization and charismatic invention' (Allen, 2004, p.108). He despaired at bureaucracy's inexorable rise, driving the spirit and humanity out of life (Allen, 2004; MacRae, 1974). Weber (1948, p.337, 214) was sure that bureaucratic organization was 'always, from a formal technical point of view, the most rational type', but it exhibited only a 'technical superiority over other forms'. This made it an obvious form only because of the particular nature of his times: the manifestation of a 'victorious capitalism' resting on 'mechanical foundations' where the '"objective" discharge of business primarily means a discharge of business according to calculable rules and without regard for persons' (Weber, 1930, p.181–2; 1948, p.215). Weber yearned for 'charismatic figures', not bureaucrats (Allen, 2004, p.108), as this passage makes clear:

> Rational calculation [and bureaucratic logic] reduces every worker to a cog in this bureaucratic machine ... It is horrible to think that the world could one day be filled with nothing but those little cogs, little men clinging to little jobs and striving toward bigger ones – a state of affairs ... playing an ever increasing part in the spirit of our present administrative systems, and especially of its offspring, the students. This passion for bureaucracy is enough to drive one to despair ... the great question is therefore not how we can promote and hasten it, but what can we oppose to this machinery in order to keep a portion of mankind free from [the] supreme mastery of the bureaucratic way of life. *(Max Weber, 1909, in Mayer, 1943, p. 127–8)*

A final notable falsehood is the dating of Weber's major contribution to management or organization theory at 1947. This is most starkly presented in a 'timeline of milestones', complete with photographs of the 'key contributors', on the inside front cover of *Behavior in Organizations* (Greenberg and Baron, 1993). This line of portraits begins with Taylor 1911; Mayo 1927–1932; Weber 1947; and Stogdill 1951. Although no references are provided, there are similarities between this and C. S. George's 'Management Continuum', first published in 1968. A condensed list of George's key figures is listed below: 350 BC Plato, 20 AD Jesus Christ, 1525 Machiavelli, 1776 Adam Smith, 1785 Thomas Jefferson, 1900 F. W. Taylor, 1927 Elton Mayo, and 1947 Max Weber.

That Weber had been dead for 27 years makes 1947 seem an unusual choice. But when one recognizes that 1947 was the year Talcott Parsons' American translation of selections of Weber's *Wirtschaft and Gesellschaft* ('Work and Society') appeared, and one begins to investigate the episteme within which Parsons was operating, reasons behind the creation of management textbooks' version of Weber starts to be revealed.

HOW DIFFERENT PERIODS PROMOTE PARTICULAR TRUTHS ABOUT WEBER

The analysis in the previous section begs the question as to how this picture of Weber comes to pass. A Foucauldian archaeological approach helps to explain this, with reference to the specific set of views and values or episteme that emerged in the United States in the middle of the twentieth century. In doing so, we shall see that 1947 is in fact an accurate dating of Weber's entry into the annals of management history. Prior to 1947, Weber, as management studies knows him, did not exist. Indeed, the first and only management teaching textbook to predate 1947, Burleigh B. Gardner's (1945) *Human Relations in Industry*, while focussed extensively on organization and efficiency, makes no mention of Weber. He was still being created by a very particular episteme and a peculiarly effective individual within that episteme: Talcott Parsons.

Wirtschaft and Gesellschaft was left unfinished on Weber's death. As it was planned to connect elements of Weber's other schemes, one can say that his whole corpus was incomplete. So, in

MacRae's (1974, p.14) words, to consult Weber is often 'somewhat like divination, like using a Tarot pack or the I Cheng'. Hence, Marianne Weber's (1975) biography positions Weber as a great humanist and champion of good causes. Shils (1987) saw Weber as a free market liberal prophetic in warning *against* bureaucracy. Bell (1960) and Lipset (1969) hailed Weber's view that the reconciliation between opposing forces was the desired end. Bendix (1966) claims Weber's work belongs to the intellectual heritage of European liberalism (a point discussed by most Weberian scholars, with one notable exception: Parsons). For Gerth and Mills (1948), Weber's works were romantic tragedies representing 'humanist and cultural liberalism rather than economic liberalism'. But, of all of the writers to interpret Weber, Parsons would be the most influential in the episteme when many of the management textbooks that our students still use were issued in their first editions (Allen, 2004).

Parsons discovered Weber in the 1920s while studying in Germany. He wrote a brilliant doctoral thesis on him, and began an English translation of Weber's essay, *The Protestant Ethic and the Spirit of Capitalism* (1930). He returned to America and took up a position at Harvard, keen to help establish and add backbone to the fledgling field of sociology in the United States. He was also, quite naturally, keen to see the field develop in the way that he thought best, and to build his own reputation. Weber was an excellent conduit for all of these aims, but to create the type of sociology that Parsons sought required the invention of a unifying order over and above Weber's unfinished or disparate theses. Indeed, Parsons' quest for a unifying logic that could explain the fundamental essences beneath social and organizational diversity, and thus explain all things, is completely in keeping with what many in the new human sciences like sociology and ecology were seeking and offering in the middle of the twentieth century (Lyotard, 1984, p.50–1).

In the late 1930s, Parsons' mission led him to undertake a translation of Weber's *Wirtschaft and Gesellschaft*. But it is important to remember that his translation, titled *The Theory of Social and*

Economic Organization, was in fact a translation of some of *Wirtschaft*, with particular attention paid to the sections that interested him in their relation to building bases for the fledgling science of sociology: namely, those on bureaucracy and the notion of the ideal type (Mayhew, 1982). Much, including Weber's own introduction to *Wirtschaft*, was left out. Indeed, most of Weber's extensive writing on religion, law and politics was not translated for many years hence.

In the years following World War II, the Parsonian interpretation took hold and spread out. New sociologists and intellectuals from many other fields were drawn to Parsons' Weber: a value-free social scientist with a system above political conflicts whose triumphant rational-legal mode of authority and its bureaucratic instrument offered both rationale and hope for a more certain world. And Weber's adoption by the intelligentsia in this period after the War was further aided by Parsons' downplaying of Weber's pessimism, bleakness, and emphasis on unequal power relations with regard to rational-legal authority and bureaucracy (Allen, 2004; Clegg, 1992; MacRae, 1974).

Why would Parsons want to be positive about the power of rational authority and bureaucracy? It may have something to do with how Parsons, both a patriot and an internationalist, interpreted America's emerging role in the new episteme that would mark a shift in power from the old world to the new. This view would seem exceedingly prescient and hopeful after the Dionysian carnage that the War had wrought. Parsons saw the American paradigm in relation to the European one as analogous to that between Greece and Rome. In notes made for a lecture at Harvard in 1933 (1933, p.5–6) he outlined the similarities:

> Culturally, like the Romans, we [Americans] are not creative, our genius is 'practical' ... We like the Romans, are fairly receptive to art and taste, and to ideas, tho we do not create them. The unity of our culture is rather that of economic-legal institutions, than the type of basic 'consensus' which always seem to be involved in

> a creative culture ... [However] ... there seems a fair possibility we
> may help create a social framework within which European culture
> can have a fairly long life.

Thus, Parsons saw the United States as an emerging exemplar of
a rational-legal, and increasingly bureaucratic, society. While such
a society would not in itself promote creativity (as Weber had pointed
out), Parsons thought that such a society was extremely good.
It provided the best chance for European culture to survive, spread
and be refined, much as the Romans had done with Greek culture.
This was an optimism clung to by many during a period when intellectuals were removing themselves from Europe and entering the US.
Parsons believed that the emergence of America as a centre of power,
with its flourishing economic-bureaucratic society, would prove
Weber's pessimism about bureaucratization wrong (Wearne, 1989).

Parsons also justified making Weber less pessimistic by pointing
out that Weber used his 'ideal types' in two ways: as a methodological
device, a useful measuring stick to help him analyse societies; and as
a means of describing what he had unearthed to be the case about
a society. 'That Weber called both ideal types without distinguishing
them' Parsons (1929, p.33) noted 'leads to serious confusion,
a confusion which is especially marked in his analysis of capitalism'.
He then argued that Weber confused his rational-legal-bureaucratic
ideal with something that could happen. If he had remembered that
such an ideal type could never be, and realized that within a world
where the rational-legal view dominated, creativity and spirit would
still exist, perhaps even prosper, he might have been more optimistic.
And, 'if this error is corrected the absolute domination of the process
of rationalization over the whole social process' that Weber had predicted and which had caused his angst 'falls to the ground' (Parsons
1929, p.49). Parsons' translation would correct the 'error' of Weber's
pessimism. The most obvious example of how this was done is his
translation of Weber's use of *herrschaft*, which generally means 'domination'. Parsons' translated it as 'leadership'.

Many beyond the mainstream of management studies are critical of Parsons' interpretation. Tribe (1988, p.8) connects this 'construction' of Weber to 'the "agenda setting" activities of Parsons and his associates'. According to Wearne (1989, p.43), 'Weber became the personification of the mores for Parsons' social scientific enterprise'. While MacRae (1974, p.88), a little more sympathetically, argues that Parsons 'extracted and elaborated something latent, a systematic sociology of great range and power … This system … is at once an invention and a discovery. But it is not, I think, all that there is in Weber'. However, when management scholars began to systematically trace the development of management in the episteme that pervaded America in the 1950s as part of a campaign to establish management as a serious university-worthy discipline (Khurana, 2007), they latched on to Parsons' re-discovered great thinker who had concerned himself with organization and looked no further (Clegg, 1990). They subsequently distilled from Parsons' interpretation a Weber who contributed to the development of the fledgling field of management by defining and championing bureaucracy (George, 1968; Wren, 1972).

Further refinement of this strawman occurred as the early management textbooks borrowed from Parsons' interpretations. However, this view of Weber is not all-encompassed by the episteme we have described in this section. Indeed, if one can find a book that draws on a range of translations of Weber, and a wider range of Weber's writings than is generally the case, from 'left-field' as it were, one will find a different, more rounded Weber (e.g., Clegg et al., 2008, p.485–527; 654). So, while Weber is influenced by the episteme described here, he can be otherwise. Our next section undertakes a genealogical analysis that traces Weber's malleability as he is subtly shaped and changed in different contexts as management studies sees itself as evolving.

HOW THE WEBER WE THINK WE KNOW IS SHAPED BY A DEVELOPING NETWORK

The key question, then, is not 'Did bureaucracy ever catch on?' but rather 'Is it as effective as Weber contended?' The answer, unfortunately, appears to be mixed ... [While] it is hard to question the positive effects of [some bureaucratic] principles ... bureaucracy also extracts important costs.

Baron and Greenberg, *Behavior in Organizations* (2nd ed., 1986)

Weber['s] ... classical organization theory has fallen into disfavor in large part because it is insensitive to human needs and not suited to a changing environment. Unfortunately, the 'ideal' form of an organization, according to Weber, did not take into account the realities of the world in which it operates.

Greenberg and Baron, *Behavior in Organizations* (4th ed., 1993)

Weber's universal view of bureaucratic structure contrasts with the more modern approaches to organization design, which claim that different forms of organizational structure may be more appropriate to different situations. Also, because bureaucracies draw sharp lines between the people who make decisions (managers) and those who carry them out (workers), they are not popular today. After all, contemporary employees prefer to have more equal opportunities to make decisions ...

Greenberg and Baron, *Behavior in Organizations* (9th ed., 2008)

While an archaeological critique enabled us to understand why a peculiar view of Weber may have emerged in management textbooks, its main weakness is that its stringent view of the episteme tends not to allow for or explain movement of this view. As the quotations above demonstrate, while the idiosyncratic interpretation of Weber that we have pointed to in our previous sections continues to thrive, there is also considerable room for reinterpretations.

In this section, we explain why this happens, through the application of a genealogical approach to analyse the presentation of Weber in nine editions of a popular management textbook over a 25-year period. From archaeology, we draw upon the notion that the episteme in which management textbooks as a genre emerge enables and encourages statements that promote this strawman version of Weber. Unlike archaeology, however, a genealogical approach allows us to highlight the relationships and interests that sustain these interpretations of Weber in management texts and how the nature of this network leads to some subtle changes over time.

Through this lens, the construction of the Weber strawman can be seen to make the contemporary study of management both possible and progressive. It makes it possible by providing a historical foundation on which subsequent research can be layered, a foundation that has hardened through a series of interpretations that have built upon each other. This sedimentation of knowledge makes the enterprise of management research appear to both be based on noble foundations and continually advancing. However, our genealogical analysis also reveals that the Weber strawman remains contingent and that his theorizing, as well as his contribution to history, depends on the prevailing power-knowledge relations of the day. When these shift, so too does Weber, in a way that promotes the progressive or 'cutting-edge' nature of contemporary thought, as the quotations juxtaposed at the head of this section reveal. In 1993, Weber was the naïve organization theorist who failed to recognize that change and human needs would count against bureaucracy. By 2008, he had become a naïve organization theorist who advocated a universal view and an authoritarian style of management, thereby failing to foresee that contingency theory was the way forward and that employees would demand participation in decision-making.

Through a genealogical critique, we can trace these processes of sedimentation and reactivation to demonstrate how the foundations of management knowledge provide a base on which knowledge can accumulate, whilst also being sufficiently malleable to demonstrate the relevance and superiority of contemporary thinking on the subject. In this section, we do this through an analysis of a popular management textbook, 'Behavior in Organizations: Understanding and Managing the Human Side of Work'. We surveyed a range of management textbooks which revealed a similar treatment of Weber, where he is positioned as 'sincerely believing' in 'his model' or 'his theory' of an ideal organization, views which have subsequently been surpassed by 'today's managers' who believe that it 'takes away the employee's creativity' and a contingency approach that takes us beyond the Weber's belief in 'universally applicable' management practices (Robbins, 1997, p.548; Robbins and Coulter, 2005, p.30–6; Robbins et al., 2006, p.48–51). Following our survey of various textbooks, we chose to use *Behavior in Organizations* as an illustrative case of this broader phenomenon. This book was particularly well-suited to examining how Weber's depiction, something we might assume to be solid, may shift over time. It has been through nine editions over 27 years, has had the same authorial team, is still being widely prescribed, and has described Weber's contribution in eight of its nine editions in the main body of its text (as opposed to appendices or footnotes). In analysing the editions, we sought to identify elements of continuity and discontinuity. The key findings with regard to the discontinuities are summarized in Table 4. Having identified what stayed the same and what changed, we then offer some explanations for why this might be.

The most striking continuity across all nine editions of the text is the Parsons-inspired interpretation of Weber.[3] While the entry in the first edition cites Gerth and Mills' 1948 translation of *Essays in Sociology*, the other editions have the Henderson and Parsons' translation of *Theory of Social and Economic Organization* (1947) as their source.[4] In this Parsonian interpretation, elements of the narrative remain constant – Weber believed bureaucracy was the one best way to efficiently organize work, in the same way that Taylor believed that scientific management was the best way to perform a task. There is also continuity in the critique of Weber for lacking the complexity of mind to recognize that contingency approaches are best. Throughout all editions, we are told that bureaucracies are not as efficient as Weber maintained, making them neither an ideal nor perfect organizational form. Finally, there is continuity in the ongoing value ascribed to Weber's contribution. Whilst his supposed ideal bureaucracy is unrealistic in today's business environment, the theory of bureaucracy

---

[3] There is no mention of Weber in the text of the third edition, although he continued to feature in the timeline inside the front and back covers.

[4] In the fourth edition, this is erroneously cited as a 1921 publication and this error remains uncorrected in all subsequent editions.

Table 4 *Weber's Development across Multiple Editions of a Textbook*

Edition	Description of Weber	Characteristics of the ideal bureaucracy	Weber's view of bureaucracy	Critique of bureaucracy
1 (1983)	Sociologist	Specialization Hierarchy Abstract rules Impersonality Qualifications and promotion on merit	Most efficient design, should be adopted as widely as possible. Bureaucracy consistent with trend in Western civilization towards rationality.	Some bureaucracies efficient but not all. Thwarts upward communication. Rules become ends. Stifles personal growth. Not the ideal form in all situations.
2 (1986)	Sociologist	Specialization Hierarchy Rules Impersonality Hiring by qualifications promotion by merit Written records	Weber appalled by inefficiency, waste and corruption. Ideal form which all organizations should strive for.	Negative association with 'red tape'. Useful for large organizations. Produces rigidities. Thwarts upward communication. Over-reliance on rules. Reduces motivation. Not the ideal form in all situations.
3 (1990)	*Weber not mentioned*			

	Description	Characteristics	One best way	Criticisms
4 (1993)	Classical organizational theorist, sociologist, organizational scholar	Formal rules and regulations Impersonal treatment Division of labour Hierarchical structure Authority structure Lifelong career commitment rationality	One best way to organize work, just as scientific management provides a one best way to perform jobs. A universal view of structure.	Negative association with 'red tape'. Not all bureaucracies inefficient and unproductive. Insensitive to human needs and changing environment. Based on Theory X assumptions.
5 (1995)	Classical organizational theorist, sociologist, organizational scholar hierarchical structure	Formal rules and regulations Impersonal treatment Division of labour Authority structure Lifelong career commitment rationality	One best way to organize work, just as scientific management provides a one best way to perform jobs. A universal view of structure.	Negative association with 'red tape'. Insensitive to human needs and changing environment. Based on Theory X assumptions.
6 (1997)	Classical organizational theorist, sociologist,	Formal rules and regulations Impersonal treatment Division of labour	One best way to organize work, just as scientific management provides a one best way to perform	Negative association with 'red tape'. Insensitive to human needs and

Table 4 (cont.)

Edition	Description of Weber	Characteristics of the ideal bureaucracy	Weber's view of bureaucracy	Critique of bureaucracy
	organizational scholar	Hierarchical structure Authority structure Lifelong career commitment rationality	jobs. A universal view of structure.	changing environment. Based on Theory X assumptions.
7 (2000)	Classical organizational theorist, sociologist, organizational scholar	Formal rules and regulations Impersonal treatment Division of labour Hierarchical structure Authority structure Lifelong career commitment Rationality	One best way to organize work, just as scientific management provides a one best way to perform jobs. A universal view of structure.	Negative association with 'red tape'. Insensitive to human needs and changing environment. Based on Theory X assumptions.
8 (2003)	Classical organizational theorist, sociologist,	Formal rules and regulations Impersonal treatment Division of labour	Hierarchy of authority where higher ranks issue orders and lower ranks carry them out.	Bureaucracies unpopular today because employees prefer equal opportunities. Insensitive to human needs and

organizational scholar	Hierarchical structure Authority structure Lifelong career commitment Rationality	A universal view of structure.	changing environment. Based on Theory X assumptions.
9 (2008) classical organizational theorist, sociologist organizational scholar	Formal rules and regulations Impersonal treatment Division of labour Hierarchical structure Authority structure Lifelong career commitment Rationality	Hierarchy of authority where higher ranks issue orders. A universal view of structure.	Bureaucracies unpopular today because employees prefer equal opportunities. Insensitive to human needs and changing environment. Based on Theory X assumptions.

contains valuable elements which have subsequently been built upon by other scholars. This has the effect of solidifying management's position as a worthy 'new science'.

Descriptions of Weber as a management thinker play an important role in the narrative of management history. For management to constitute a field of study, it requires a history, which in turn requires early management thinkers. Critical analysis of *Behavior in Organizations* usefully demonstrates this writing of history and its gradual sedimentation. In the first edition, Weber is a 'sociologist' (1983, p.510). By edition four (1993), however, he is also a 'classical organizational theorist' (p.16) and an 'organizational scholar' (p.596). These last two subject positions are productive of organizational studies (or management) as fields of study, distinct, say, from psychology or sociology. 'Classical organizational theorist' also has the effect of adding depth to the historical narrative, by locating Weber within a group of supposed like-minded theorists from which we have subsequently moved on. By viewing editions of the text as layers of interpretations, we can see how Weber as an 'organizational theorist' becomes the 'truth', despite this interpretation being factually erroneous, as highlighted earlier in the chapter.

Another continuous feature in the presentation of Weber across the nine editions of is the inclusion of the characteristics of Weber's 'ideal bureaucracy'. However, there are subtle differences in the presentation of these characteristics in editions one and two compared with edition four onwards. In the first edition, there are five characteristics, but from the fourth edition onwards, there are seven, even though the first edition states that 'Weber was quite precise. He felt that in its ideal form, bureaucracy was characterized by five major factors' (1983, p.510).[5]

In addition to a change in the number of characteristics, there is a shift in their ordering in the fourth edition. Whereas the first two editions began with 'specialization' (which became 'division of labour'

---

[5] In the first edition, rationality was not included as one of the five characteristics, although it was listed separately as an underlying theme.

in the fourth edition onwards), in the fourth and all consequent editions, the first feature of the ideal bureaucracy is 'formal rules and regulations'. This characteristic was previously called 'abstract rules' (first edition) and 'rules' (second edition). As well as the change in label, there are changes in the description of this characteristic:

Edition 1   'All tasks would be carried out in accordance with a consistent system of abstract rules' *(1983, p.510)*

Edition 2   'Activities should be carried out in accordance with rules and standard operating procedures' *(1986, p.439)*

Edition 4   'Written guidelines are used to control all employees' behaviors' *(1993, p.17)*

It would be a step too far to label this as a misrepresentation of Weber. But by modifying the description of the characteristics of the ideal bureaucracy, readers of the text are more likely to draw a negative impression of the value of rules and regulations. What was in the first edition a system for delivering consistency, which could be interpreted in a positive light, becomes, by the fourth edition, the more sinister control of all behaviour. Elevating it to the first characteristic of bureaucracy suggests that it was the most important feature of the ideal bureaucracy. These could be considered to be minor changes, but they have the effect of reinterpreting Weber in a way that reflects the concerns of the time, namely, the stifling effects of bureaucratic rules expressed in the common association of bureaucracies with 'red tape'.

Another illustration of the reinterpretation of Weber appears in edition eight, and is repeated in the ninth edition, where the references to 'red tape' disappear and a new theme gains prominence. 'Because bureaucracies draw sharp lines between the people who make decisions (managers) and those who carry them out (workers), they are not particularly popular today. After all, contemporary employees prefer to have more equal opportunities to make decisions than bureaucracies permit' (2003, p.11).

This passage is of interest for several reasons. First, is the language used – 'workers' in bureaucracies become 'employees' in today's organizations. Second, is the assumption that it is only 'workers' who receive orders in bureaucracies, which is odd given that bureaucracies are associated with multiple layers of managers receiving orders from other managers. Third, is the emphasis on 'equal opportunities' demanded by today's employees in contrast to bureaucracies, in which workers are forced to follow orders. This conveniently ignores the fact that most contemporary organizations are bureaucratic, to some degree.

Again, the changes here are subtle, but they construct a view of Weber using a binary logic in which the past is positioned as inferior to the enlightened or evolved thinking of the present day, whatever that might be. Throughout the nine editions of the text studied, there is a subtle but significant development of the historical narrative to reflect contemporary concerns. First, it was that Weber did not realize the cost of bureaucracy would likely outweigh the financial benefits. Then he did not see that people were much more 'theory Y' than 'theory X'. Later, when it was contingency theory that required a counter position, Weber was led into the discussion as the advocate of a universal approach to structure.

By 2005, it may have been the concern for empowerment and participatory styles of management that encouraged the construction of Weber as the promoter of an authoritarian style of management. It is an example of the 'historical presentism' that Foucault (1977b, p.148) describes in Language, Counter-memory and Practice: 'In placing present needs at the origin, the metaphysician [or historian, seeks to] convince us of an obscure purpose that seeks its realization at the moment it arises'.

The overriding feature revealed by this critical analysis of the nine editions of Behavior in Organizations is the way in which Weber's work is progressively reduced and simplified and its evaluation becomes increasingly negative. In the first edition, Weber's view of bureaucracy is placed within the context of his observation of 'a shift toward rationality in *all* spheres of life (politics, religion, economics, etc.)' (1983, p.510, emphasis in original). In the second edition, it is explained that Weber's writings were a response to organizations that, at the turn of the twentieth century, were characterized by 'inefficiency, waste and corruption' (1986, p.438). In these early editions of the text, there is a balanced evaluation of the pros and cons of bureaucracy, being well-suited to some organizations but not others. From the fourth edition onwards, the location of Weber within a particular historical context gradually disappears. Students are given no indication of the changing nature of organization that Weber experienced during his lifetime and the benefits that a bureaucratic mode of thinking had brought, such as promotion being based on merit rather than family connections. It might not be a coincidence that this characteristic of the ideal bureaucracy appeared in the first two editions of the text, but not from the fourth edition onwards, being replaced by 'impersonal treatment', which carries a more negative connotation. Throughout subsequent editions of the text, the evaluation of bureaucracy theory becomes increasingly negative. By the ninth edition, the best that can be said is that 'contemporary OB owes a great deal to Weber for his many pioneering ideas' (p.15).

The construction of the strawman Weber is an ongoing process comprising processes of sedimentation of prior interpretations and a reactivation and reconstruction of Weber based on popular concerns of the present, such as the demand for autonomy and responsibility. By reconstituting Weber as the stepping stone from which we have progressed to a more enlightened view of management, management texts are able to lay claim to being at the cutting-edge of management thought, our encounter with the past relevant only in so far as it demonstrates the value and superiority of contemporary ideas. Paradoxically, this rewriting of the historical narrative surrounding Weber's work occurs within the context of a reduced interest on the part of textbook authors in interrogating history, based on an assumption, articulated by Robbins (1997) that students are not interested in the historical evolution of management knowledge. It is this representation of history which leads us to conclude that history remains important to authors of popular mainstream management textbooks, if only for the purpose of constructing the 'bad old days' with which to compare today's liberated state of affairs. History and Weber's part in it is not an objective account of past events. It is written for the present and we can expect it to be rewritten again for future generations of students, in such a way that connects to the issues of the day.

WHAT WE COULD LEARN FROM A DEEPER UNDERSTANDING OF MAX WEBER

Perhaps we should begin this conclusion by asking 'does any of this (or indeed any of the history reported on in the preceding chapters) really matter?' If we share best-selling management textbook author Stephen Robbins' assessment of history, the answer is 'no'. In his textbook *Managing Today*, history is relegated to the appendix, 'where faculty can assign it and students can read it when, or if, they wish' (1997, p.xvii). On this reasoning, any representation of Weber matters little, so long as students know that flatter, more flexible organizations work and that bureaucracy does not; that contingency theory is best; deciding that employees should make their own decisions works, but making decisions for them does not, and so on.

However, if we believe that management studies and organization science are more diverse and more complicated than this; or if we believe that what we see as 'the best way' changes over time; or if we believe that it is not the latest theories that run organizations, but managers making judgements about the relative merits of different ideas and how these might be interpreted, then a critical appreciation of history should be of interest and will be of great use to students. To illustrate, we can start by outlining a number of ways in which students' self-awareness and judgment might be improved by thinking about Weber and his misrepresentation.

First, for students to see that a great figure like Weber struggled with the pros and cons of bureaucracy would be a better way of initiating them into our field and its long-standing complexities, than presenting him or other historical figures as simpletons. This would provide students with greater confidence to realize that there really is no one best way, not even for 'great thinkers', and that they, like all good managers, must always assess contexts and the strengths and weaknesses of the available options before taking action.

Second, instead of ruling out 'Weberian bureaucracy' as completely bad or outmoded, recognizing this interpretation to be an oversimplification can reveal a number of intelligent possibilities. For example, recognizing that fashionable flat hierarchies are not a revolutionary discontinuity, that they are, after all, hierarchies, and that the longevity of this form indicates that it has some strengths, should help students to develop ways to make bureaucracies more human or egalitarian instead of unwittingly dismissing them wholesale. As Harold Leavitt (whose 85 years gave him an extremely broad point of view) put it, 'the intensity with which we struggle against hierarchies [ultimately] only serves to highlight their durability' (Leavitt and Kaufmann, 2003, p.98). Indeed, it should be recognized that a major strength of a bureaucracy is the way its impersonality can engender fairness and prevent discrimination (Du Gay, 2000). A more rounded appreciation of Weber could encourage a better appreciation that organizations can contain both bureaucratic and non-bureaucratic elements based on a clear understanding of the potential strengths and weaknesses of the form.

Third, while culture has become a recent concern for managers (to be discussed in more detail in Chapter Eight) we might, ironically, learn more about it from reading Weber than more modern culture gurus like Peters and Waterman who mocked what they saw as his love of bureaucracy. We might come to understand the Max Weber who believed that contemporary institutions and their management could only be understood by knowing how they and the social-political cultures within which they lived had developed in peculiar ways over time (not the person described in most management textbooks).[6] In effect, Weber's work promotes the contingency approach that management history sees as being an advance on Weber's simplistic views, a contingency approach that says not that bureaucracy is the one best way, but that different cultures sponsor different best ways, or organizational forms that fit prevailing currents. An approach that is an advance on the contingency approach that is believed to have superseded Weber: an approach that recognizes that managers cannot just simply decide to plug in one organizational approach or another, but must work dexterously with and within the cultural networks in play. Indeed, Khurana (2007, p.15) claims that the apparent originality of his thesis in his *From Higher Aims to Hired Hands* is largely due to a lack of awareness in management circles of an approach which recognizes the relationship between economic institutions and social norms, an approach that Khurana traces back to Weber.

Fourth, on becoming aware of Weber's broader views, a management scholar or practitioner might begin to think critically about why he has been depicted in such a crude and expedient way. It may be human nature to put people in boxes, to see simple categories and continuities and progress and certain one best ways, when in actual fact, the world of organizations is more complex and nuanced, but the case of Weber should alert us to the complexities involved in making good managerial judgements while working against such predilections to over-simplicity. Hence, this critical historical perspective can help breed greater self-awareness with regard to where a student might place themselves on a spectrum of views about

---

[6] We are conscious of not falling into the trap of creating our own strawman by treating 'management textbooks' as a homogenous entity with respect to Weber's portrayal. It is pleasing to see the growth of other 'critical' textbooks that provide a more informed treatment of Weber (e.g., Clegg et al., 2008; Jackson and Carter, 2000; Knights and Willmott, 2007; Linstead et al., 2004; Thompson and McHugh, 2001).

bureaucracy, or under what conditions they might see bureaucracy as a good approach. Such self-awareness can work against a herd mentality that can drive phenomenon from blindly employing 'best practice' in strategy development to the global financial crisis (Fox, 2008; Nattermann, 2000). With such awareness, a manager who makes the excuse that they were only following what others were doing becomes clearly disingenuous.

Finally, thinking critically about the way management history is related to the present should help us once again to see history's worth as a relevant repository of useful events and ideas with which to approach present issues, rather than a long-gone irrelevancy best skipped over to so as to narrow our gaze on present heights. Organizational design can be greatly aided by looking seriously at what clever minds attempted in the past. For example, General Motors, in the 2010s, may seem like an abject failure from which little inspiration may be drawn, until one recalls the managerial innovations of Alfred Sloan and how these changed the world nine decades ago (Bilton and Cummings, 2010); the GFC seems less daunting, and less of a cause for hyperbole, when seen in the light of a hundred years of crises.

Armed with a less 'black and white' understanding of the foundations of organization science, we might also be able to engage in broader, more generative, discussions about new organizational forms with a better understanding of substantial continuity and divergence over time (Palmer et al., 2007). For example, we may be more motivated to see what might be beyond contingency theory were we to recognize that Weber had arrived at a conclusion that was in advance of this 100 years ago. Or that interesting blends could be built from bureaucratic and non-bureaucratic elements, or that information technology may have advanced to a point where the strengths that Weber attributed to bureaucracy might be achieved while incurring the weaknesses to lessening degrees. Or, that there may be forms that pre-date bureaucracy, which retro-active forces could discover and reinvent. Or, that forms exist beyond the binary logic of bureaucratic/non-bureaucratic.

While the creative possibilities that we have outlined here relate directly to the case of Weber, we have used Weber only as an example of what we believe to be a much broader phenomenon in the presentation of the progress of history in management texts. Other similarly simplistic binary interpretations of progression in organization science include centralization (old and bad) and decentralization (new and good); management (old and bad) and leadership (new and good); stability (old and bad) and change (new and good); and planning (old and bad) and emergent strategies (new and good). Many textbooks in the 1990s were sure that decentralization was 'the way of the future' and that centralization was dead (Cummings, 1995). Later on, 'Leaders' became those confident of their ability, willing to take risks and the people that make things happen, while 'Managers' were those threatened by change, bothered by uncertainty and preferring the status quo (Campling et al., 2008). This simplistic thinking compliments dominant assumptions within the mainstream about organizational change – that (paradoxically) change is the only constant, that change is inherently good and stability dangerous, and that change must be embraced by all and will lead to success. And, at the same time, some works have set up planning as 'old-hat', dull and outmoded in contrast to a more advanced approach to strategy that is oriented towards emergence and the vagaries of culture.

We should not allow simplistic historical interpretations like these should to set hard and fast, and recognizing that we can shift them can be liberating: it can inspire us to be more 'retro-active' in order to recreate what we see as historically important and thus think differently in the present and for the future. These are issues that we shall return to in later chapters of this book.

A critical awareness of Weber, and other historical foundations, could inspire young scholars towards projects that reinvestigate the past, to spark radical questioning in the present and to change our field in positive ways for the future. If we believe that innovation is important, it may be that encouraging those concerned with management and organization to think about the representation of the historical evolution of our field is just as important as reflecting on the latest trends and 'what works now'.

5　The Institution of the Business School

Instead of aping the current form of business schools like Harvard, reflecting on the form that business schools could have taken might lead to greater innovation.

While the emergence of the Business School is not covered in most histories of management, its formation promotes particular forms of management knowledge. It is, therefore, key in the development of management studies. Events since the 1940s have narrowed the view of what a good business school should be and do, and the idea that Harvard is the original and best school in the business promoted this process. But Harvard did not spring 'fully formed' as the model that we associate with it now and business schools more generally today. Its development was contested and it could have turned out differently. However, this contest and these alternative potential pathways are overlooked in favour of a smooth evolution where the present is but a continuity of the past. One of the most interesting but forgotten relationships in this regard is that between HBS Dean Wallace Donham and philosopher A.N. Whitehead. Together, these two discussed, articulated and advanced a very different view of what a business school could be: one with a new type of pedagogy that would not only inspire business people, but rejuvenate Western learning and society. Since then, this dream has been diminished and a limiting binary discourse has emerged: one where HBS is both criticized for being overly managerialist and action-oriented, and at once admired and aped. Understanding how this has happened can help us think again about what a business school could be and do.

Economics has traditionally provided the only theoretical framework for the study of business, and even today the two fields are so closely related they can hardly be discussed separately.

Pierson, *Education of the American Businessman* (1959).

Mathematics, geometry and drawing, book-keeping and penmanship, correspondence and the correct use of the English language, geography, technology, law, economy, history and biography, modern languages. Ten subject areas, to be studied as equal parts.

General Robert E. Lee's suggested curriculum for a 'Students' Business School' at Washington University (1869).

This chapter presents a counter-history of the formation and form of business schools.[1] Hence its focus moves away from our approach of looking deeper at the characters that conventional management histories and textbooks identify as the main players in the development of management. Curiously, perhaps, management textbook histories almost always make no mention of the development of business schools. But, given our emphasis on developing alternative views of management's historical development to promote innovation, we agree with Porter and McKibbin's assessment in *Management Education: Drift or Thrust into the 21st Century* (1988): 'Whatever else can be said about the American collegiate business school, one thing is certain: It is the mechanism for bringing about any change in business education. If innovations are to be made, it will be through the business schools'.

Business schools are where most people have (for the past 30 years) learned about management, so investigating the emergence of their form and the formation and promoting a rethinking of these through revisiting conventional history, are an important part of our project to think differently about management. While we agree with

---

[1] This chapter takes some elements from Bridgman, T., Cummings, S. and McLaughlin, C. (2016). Re-stating the Case: How Revisiting the Development of the Case Method Can Help Us Think Differently about the Future of the Business School. *Academy of Management Learning & Education*, 15(4): 724-41.

Porter and McKibbin's assessment of the relationship between business schools and innovation, we don't agree with their approach. Porter and McKibbin's report was the first AACSB sponsored follow-up on the 1959 reports by Pierson and by Gordon and Howell about the state of management education. While it suggested some changes around the margins, it did not question, and indeed supported, those reports views' that business schools should be standardized and fundamentally founded on economics. In effect then, Porter and McKibbin's report, despite recognizing the role that business schools would play in promoting or repressing innovation, promoted the idea that economics was 'the only foundation', thereby promoting an innovation-repressing homogeneity.

In Chapter Two, we outlined how the view of Adam Smith as a founder of economics, and a precursor of management, was based on a way of conceiving of economics (or an episteme to use Foucault's term), that was particular to the middle of the twentieth century. This was the kind of economics that those concerned with setting business schools on a solid foundation could see as providing the only theoretical framework for business and management, ever.

Hence, when historians (or those interested in using history to justify their ideas about how things should be) looked back, they identified Wharton as the first business school. It could be seen to fit, in embryo, with what a business school with this kind of economics at its core should look like. C. S. George (1972, p.85) was clear that Wharton was the first and 'for seventeen years, in fact, the only' business school; and Wren (1972, p.128) too names Joseph Wharton as 'founder of the first school of business'. (He also points out an interesting link in the network of the conventional formation: that it was Wharton who gave F. W. Taylor a big break, employing him to work as a consultant at his Bethlehem Steel Company and supporting his approaches against the views of his co-owners.)

Even though we do not recognize them through the narrow lens which supports the prevailing view in the middle of the twentieth century, there were schools conceived to teach management or business or commerce before Wharton. For example, few people know that General Robert E. Lee founded a business school after the Civil War. Much to people's surprise, Lee took the job of chancellor of Washington College – now Washington and Lee University – and took a particular interest in what he termed 'practical education' (Lee Jr., 1905; Freeman, 1935). On 8 January 1869, on behalf of a committee focussed on increasing practical education initiatives, he presented a report to Washington College's Board of Trustees proposing a plan for a school of business. In the report, a curriculum of ten subjects 'to be studied in equal parts' was described (Marsh, 1926, p.657).[2] That curriculum is reproduced in the second quotation at the head of this chapter.[3] Ruef (2008) outlines a number of schools that were established in the antebellum period, which even modern historians now overlook, and similarly had curricula very different to the prescriptions of 1959 reports of Pierson and Gordon and Howell (1959).

Earlier schools of commerce in Portugal and Scotland (both established around the same time as those countries attained their own respective diplomatic, economic and intellectual heights: 1500 and 1770) incorporated graphical subjects such as cartography and geometry, like Lee's curriculum. While they may seem unusual to us, they made sense to them, likely influenced by an association with similarly stochastic disciplines or practices, military leadership and international relations (Boyd, 1961; Grant, 1876; Rodrigues et. al., 2004), rather than recognizing that the science of economics must be their core.

[2] The authors would like to thank C. Vaughan-Stanley, librarian at Washington and Lee University, for helping to unearth the documents that outline Lee's work towards a business school. Even beyond business history, this portion of Lee's life has slipped out of the fabric of modern understanding. Douglas Freeman's (1935) four-volume *R.E. Lee*, the only source that details Lee's last years, was widely read in 1935 when it won the Pulitzer Prize. But it is now published in a one-volume abridged version with Lee's university life removed. Other works that describe Lee's business school are hard to find, but include Lee Jr., (1905) and Riley (1922).

[3] The proposal was approved, but Lee became seriously ill just a few weeks later and never recovered. The College subsequently failed to raise the necessary funds, and Washington's business school did not come to pass.

Following the argument we developed in Chapter One, looking at how these schools from other times, *episteme*, or parts of the map, did things differently would likely be a good spur to innovation. While they may force us to discuss uncomfortable associations (e.g., the antebellum schools' relationships with supporters of slavery; the links to military thinking), at least their difference from today's norms could stimulate debate and substantive change rather than incremental sameness. But as we have explained, while we would encourage others to look wider in this way, our tactic here is different. It is to look deeper at those moments conventionally identified as key to the emergence of business schools and reveal forgotten complexities that might help us think differently about our field.

Our particular target in this regard is the institution of Harvard Business School (HBS) and the pedagogical approach that most associate with it, and which, by association with Harvard's pre-eminence, has become management's pedagogy: the Case Method. While Wharton may be acknowledged to be the first business school, there is no doubt that Harvard, established in 1908, has, for 100 years, been the most prestigious. It is the school that most others aspire to be, and to teach like (Contardo and Wensley, 2004).

In this chapter, we first outline the conventional view of the Harvard Case Method and how its form has been supported by HBS down through the decades. We then re-examine this in a counter-history that highlights discontinuities, in contrast to the continuities promoted by the conventional history. In so doing, we are able to show that the Case Method is an *invented tradition*, a set of practices, normally governed by overtly or tacitly accepted rules and of a ritual or symbolic nature, which seeks to inculcate certain values and norms of behaviour by repetition, which automatically implies continuity with the past (Hobsbawm, 1983a:1). According to this view, traditions which are claimed are often not what they appear, being constructions of a 'suitable historic past' (1983, p.1). Such invented traditions have the effect of establishing social cohesion, legitimating institutions and authority relations; and inculcating beliefs and values. They also shape present and future practice by developing conventions, which become established as 'best practice' that is passed onto new practitioners.

We explore the invented tradition of the Harvard Case Method by juxtaposing against the conventional historical narrative, problems that confronted many of the key players at Harvard in the 1920s and 1930s, which are no longer recognized in HBS's history, and the network that formed around these alternative views. While this network did not result in major changes in the institution or its pedagogy, our counter-history certainly highlights the 'possibility of thinking otherwise', to use Foucault's term. And it is this thinking differently about what a business school could be and how managers and management academics, as a result, might be encouraged to think and do differently, that we wish to emphasize here.

THE CONVENTIONAL HISTORY OF THE HARVARD CASE METHOD: CLARITY OF PURPOSE, REFINEMENT, EVOLUTION

> How can we state the aims of the school? ... giving the student training for practice in dealing with business problems. This requires practice in 1) Ascertaining facts; 2) appraising and sorting facts; 3) stating business problems in a business way; 4) analyzing business problems; 5) reaching definite conclusions; 6) presenting such conclusions orally and in writing.

> Memorandum from Dean Donham outlining his vision for HBS in 1920 (in Copeland, 1958, p.77)

> The case method "asks not how a man may be trained to know, but how a man may be trained to act."

> Dewing (1931, p.2)

Histories of the HBS case method (for example, Copeland, 1958; Garvin, 2003; Grandon Gill, 2011; Merseth, 1991; Mesney, 2013) follow a narrow channel – starting with the business school's adaptation of the approach to legal education at Harvard.[4] In 1870, Christopher Columbus Langdell, Dean of the Harvard Law School, felt law would be best studied through the derivation of general principles

---

[4] Cruikshank's (1987) *A Delicate Experiment* is a notable exception.

from numerous examples, so he took the radical step of refusing to give a lecture, instead asking a surprised student to 'state the case' (Cruikshank, 1987, p.74). An interested observer of the law school's experiment was Edwin Gay, who would become the first Dean of Harvard's business school when it was established in 1908.

Despite Gay's enthusiasm for the 'problem method', as he called it, uptake was slow, because unlike in law, there was no corpus of cases available to work with and the school lacked the financial resources needed to employ researchers to produce them (Copeland, 1958). Following Gay's decision to resign his deanship in 1919, Harvard President Lawrence Lowell, formerly a professor in the Department of Government, approached his former protégé, Wallace Donham, whom Lowell had funded through Harvard Law School, to replace him. Upon graduating, Donham worked in banking, specializing in corporate restructuring and achieving some notoriety as a court-appointed receiver for the troubled Bay State Street Railway Company between 1917 and 1919. The electricity street railway sector was rationalizing in the face of increased competition (from the private motor car) and higher labour and materials costs. Donham kept several thousand streetcar workers on the job throughout the war, with the railway union giving him a silver clock in recognition of his efforts (Cruikshank, 1987).

Donham accepted Lowell's offer of the deanship. He was excited by the opportunity to strengthen HBS and was keen to establish himself as an authority in the fledgling field of labour relations. Donham was familiar with the case-based approach of Harvard Law School and moved quickly to secure its future as HBS's primary pedagogical method. He convinced marketing professor Melvin Copeland to produce a 'problem' book rather than a standard textbook (Copeland, 1958; Cruikshank, 1987). And, at his first faculty meeting in 1919, Donham outlined a plan to expand the Bureau of Business Research, which would be tasked with producing cases (he preferred this term over 'problems') for use in the classroom. After discussions with President Lowell and members of faculty, Donham prepared his memorandum (cited at the start head of this section), which outlined his vision for the school.

HBS's place as the single most influential institution in the history of business education is often associated with the unwavering clarity of purpose from these historical origins to the present day, that the principal objective of a business education is to learn how to solve business problems and its consistent commitment to how this objective can best be achieved: through the Case Method of teaching. Despite the many environmental changes business schools have encountered through the years, history tells us that the Case Method has remained true: 'modern cases retain the same basic features described by Donham' (Garvin, 2003, p.60). Thus, conventional accounts of the history of the Case Method at HBS draw a straight line from what is picked out as the first articulation of the Case Method in 1920 to today, a consensus passed down through the years in a way that is indicative of it always having been so.

The Case Method 'asks not how a man may be trained to know, but how a man may be trained to act' (Dewing, 1931, p.2). Students take real-life situations and 'help managers learn how to determine what the real problem is and to ask the right questions' (Hammond, 1976, p.2). Through an analytical process, a set of recommendations are developed for solving the problem. The magic of the Case Method is not that there is a right answer (Delves Broughton, 2008) – it is not about students looking in the back of the book to see if they have arrived at the right solution (Gragg, 1940) – it is that there must be *an* answer, arrived at by the careful weighing up of the facts of the case (Copeland, 1958).

Anteby (2013) provides us with a valuable insight into the 'inner workings' (p.140) of current Case Method practice at HBS in *Manufacturing Morals*, an ethnographic account of how faculty and students are socialized to focus on solving cases in a business-like manner (i.e., focussing on the 'facts' in a 'business way' as Donham put it in 1920), and subsequently avoiding the discussion or promotion of value and moral positions. Case teaching is highly choreographed, a 'well-oiled collective apparatus', Anteby explains (2013, p.53), with teaching notes providing intricate details of which questions to ask when, and what boards should look like at the end of teaching sessions. Whilst faculty are free, in theory, to teach as they wish, this is discouraged by organizational routines. In particular, 'preaching – of specific conclusions or any moral viewpoint – is seen as an ineffective mode of instruction. If anything, preaching in silence is the norm at the School' (2013, p.69).

In recent years, following corporate scandals and the global financial crisis, some have criticized this 'Harvard approach'. Attention has focussed on the shortcomings of today's business graduates, with the HBS Case Method seen as contributing to a narrow, instrumental, amoral, managerial perspective on business. It has been criticized for constructing mythical, heroic portrayals of leadership (Chetkovich and Kirp, 2001; Collinson and Tourish, 2015); privileging senior management views (Mintzberg, 2004) and managerialism (Contardo and Wensley, 2004); leading students towards predetermined answers (Currie and Tempest, 2008); focussing on the solving of problems rather than the framing and definition of problems (Chia, 2005); excluding the voice of women, the poor (Kweder, 2014) and labour (Starkey and Tiratsoo, 2007); neglecting the interests and influence of other stakeholders (Bridgman, 2010; Starkey and Tempest, 2009) and containing a flawed logic of translatability from one context to others (Grey, 2004). Its pervasive influence on business education globally is also seen as a concern: for example, Liang and Wang (2004) warn Chinese case writers against 'blindly following the case writing approach of the Harvard Business School' (p.411), viewing HBS cases as undersocialized, treating organizations as 'a mere tool for profits, while neglecting their social nature' (p.404). At the heart of these criticisms of the Case Method is its emphasis on action and application, the way it locates students in the position of the manager, requiring them to prescribe solutions and actions, rather than thoughtfulness and a broader view.

And yet, despite these criticisms, and despite the flux and transformation which has characterized many other areas of business education, supporters of the Case Method can point to its endurance and how it has grown in strength. For Harvard faculty like David Garvin and other Case Method 'evangelists' (Garvin, 2003, p.56), its raison d'être, the emphasis on action and business application, is the cause of its longevity and continued success. It is still a key part of the HBS ethos, an ethos that many (if not most) business schools seek to mimic. It seems that 100 years of history is hard to shift. Like it, criticize it, or defend it against those criticisms, it is what it is. Except that it isn't.

A COUNTER-HISTORY OF THE HARVARD CASE METHOD:
BREADTH OF PERSPECTIVE, CONTESTATION, REVOLUTION

> We are not ex cathedra laying down the law about business and the way it must be done; we are not trying to put these men in leading strings and control their opinions; we are not endeavoring to prevent them from **thinking** and to keep them from having a basis on which to **think for themselves**. On the contrary, everything that we are doing is intended to have exactly the opposite effect. We are trying to give them the basis for sane **thought** and independent thought and we are stimulating this **thought** as much as possible.

> Dean Donham to Howard Elliott, 27 April 1921 (Baker Library Historical Collection – emphasis added)

> 'We need in business and politics administrators who are able not only to handle their specialized problems well, but also to see things in wide relations and do their part in maintaining society's stability and equilibrium'.

> Donham (1933, p.420)

The emergence of the Case Method is not the solid straight line from Dean Donham's conception in 1920, through Dewing, Hammond and others, to Anteby's criticisms 95 years later. In the 1920s and 1930s, Donham and several of his contemporaries faced new problems and began to rethink what the Case Method, and by association, business schools, could be. Our histories could record statements like the two from Donham above. Their emphasis on thinking independently and deeply highlights an important and largely forgotten discontinuity and should make us think again about how settled Donham's views were in this period.

These ideas, and the many that surrounded it in the debates of this period in the 1920s and early 1930s, which sought to fundamentally rethink assumptions about how we teach and what we teach and which run counter to the conventional view, have been glossed over in histories of the Case Method and of HBS as an institution. But placing Donham's three quotations together, inserting his second quotation with its emphasis on reflective thought rather than merely acting in accordance with current or general best practice, paints a very different picture of the development of the Case Method. It indicates that there may have been contestation rather than consensus and a continuity of ideas and practice.

With the centennial of the Case Method upon us, we thought it timely to look back and explore its formation, as well as to examine how these events have been recorded in history. Our objective is to revisit the tradition of the Case Method in a more substantial way; to construct a counter-history that highlights events and characters from the past that have been forgotten or ignored by the conventional history; and to counter the view shared by Anteby and the critics and defenders of the Case Method, that it is as it ever was. What we found surprised us.

Not only does the alternative narrative of the past that we unearthed disrupt the binary of good/evil which enslaves contemporary debates about the Case Method, and the associated binary of thought/action that both sides appeal to (for the Case Method boosters the focus on action is what makes it great; for critics the focus on action ahead of thought is a negative), it can inspire us to think differently about current concerns with the relevance, legitimacy and impact of business schools. Especially when we consider the parallels in the turbulent macro-economic environment of the Great Depression era and today, which has brought questions of the future of capitalism and relations between government and society to the fore (Henisz, 2011; Marens, 2010; Mills, Weatherbee, Foster and Helms Mills, 2015).

As we started researching the origins of the Case Method, a process which included visits to the Baker Library at HBS and The Harvard University Archives,[5] we soon became aware of a much more diverse and interesting past. What is understood to be the Case Method today is what Donham articulated in his 1920 memo, but missing from the conventional history is the story of how his thinking, and those of others at Harvard, shifted as the United States became gripped by social and economic crisis – conditions not dissimilar, it could be argued, to the present. In this section, we focus on a series of 'critical moments' during Donham's deanship that shed new light on the past and which have the potential to stimulate new thinking on the challenges facing business schools today. These events coalesce around his relationships with Robert Fechner, Ordway Tead and Alfred Whitehead. Three men conventionally viewed as marginal characters in the histories of the HBS Case Method, but whose contributions deserve greater consideration.

Fechner and Donham: A Broader Perspective to Understand Organized Labour

As noted earlier, historical accounts of the HBS Case Method see the cultivation of a managerial mindset as an integral and enduring feature, with students required to slip into 'the shoes of the managers' (Hammond, 2009, p.1). Yet, an incident early in Donham's tenure as Dean, at a time when the Case Method was taking shape, suggests that taking the position of organized labour was part of the promise Donham saw for it. And he was prepared to stand up to those who challenged him.

---

[5] We are grateful to the staff of the Baker Library Historical Collection at Harvard Business School, as well as Harvard University Archives for assisting us during our visits.

The sharp deflationary recession of 1919–20 provoked wide-spread industrial unrest. On the HBS programme were first-year courses in Industrial Management, Labor Technique and a second-year course in Labor Problems. The written form that we associate with the Case Method today had not established itself at HBS at this time. Rather, courses could include a series of 'walking cases' (Cruikshank, 1987, p.71), with local people connected with business invited in to present their 'problems' to the class. Donham himself would teach, presenting cases from his experience of the railways. Others included Ordway Tead, who would speak about his experience in conducting labour audits, and local industrialist F. C. Hood, who operated a rubber factory in Watertown, Massachusetts (Donham to Hood, 10 February 1921, Baker Library Historical Collection). Donham had learnt from his time at the Bay State Street Railway Company the importance of understanding the views of unions, so he hired Robert Fechner, an influential labour leader with the International Association of American Machinists, a union affiliated to the American Federation of Labor.

Fechner's appointment raised the ire of F. C. Hood, who wrote to Donham in January 1921 with his concerns about the teaching of labour and its potential negative effect on the endowment fund. Hood noted that 'Some of the boys in the Business School told me that they were saturated with the union labor standpoint' (Hood to Donham, 28 January 1921, Baker Library Historical Collection). Hood also relayed his concerns to Howard Elliott, a Harvard graduate, chief executive and endowment seeker for HBS. Elliott wrote to Donham in April 1921 questioning whether it was 'a wise thing' to have Fechner lecturing 'young men of impressionable age' and 'sowing the seeds of social unrest' (Elliott to Donham, 21 April 1921, Baker Library Historical Collection). Donham rejected the accusation, describing Fechner's appointment as 'exceedingly constructive', since labour issues had been ignored previously and providing this perspective enabled students to think critically (as per the quotation from

Donham with which we disturbed the conventional narrative at the head of this counter-history).

> We are not ex cathedra laying down the law about business and the way it must be done; we are not trying to put these men in leading strings and control their opinions; we are not endeavoring to prevent them from thinking and to keep them from having a basis on which to think for themselves. On the contrary, everything that we are doing is intended to have exactly the opposite effect. We are trying to give them the basis for sane thought and independent thought and we are stimulating this thought as much as possible. (Donham to Elliott, 27 April 1921, Baker Library Historical Collection)

Howard Elliott was not reassured by Donham's letter, pointing to the 'great deal of talk about the alleged radicalism and socialism of the atmosphere at Harvard' (Elliott to Donham, 30 April 1921, Baker Library Historical Collection). Correspondence between Donham and Hood continued throughout 1922 and 1923. In December of 1923, Hood wrote to Donham inquiring whether Fechner taught using cases and, if so, requesting to see them (Hood to Donham, 21 December 1923, Baker Library Historical Collection). Donham replied that 'from my standpoint Fechner himself is a very definite application of the case system' (Donham to Hood, 4 January 1924, Baker Library Historical Collection). Hood penned an angry response:

> The thought of any department of Harvard having professors who are socialists or Bolshevists or labor unionists is abhorrent to me, especially in these days when some of the very foundations of our Government are being attacked ... I do not agree that Fechnor (sic) is a "definite application of the case system", or how an instructor can be a "case". (Hood to Donham, 11 January 1924, Baker Library Historical Collection)

The Fechner incident is mentioned in Cruikshank's history of HBS, but is missing from other accounts. More significantly for the purposes of this paper, Donham's openness to the voice of unions, based on his experiences of the railways and the rapidly shifting context of the day, is not part of the conventional history of the origins of the HBS Case Method. It challenges the story of a single-minded and enduring cultivation of a managerial worldview.

Tead and Donham: Contesting the Values Underpinning 'Rational' Managerial Actions

The conventional account of the HBS Case Method gives primacy, as we have seen, to the cultivation of judgement through discussion of real life business problems. Donham's 1920 memorandum outlining the Case Method is the epitome of a rational decision-making process – identify the problem (or problems), analyse the causes and take action to resolve them. Case Method advocates see this as a strength, while critics highlight its failure to acknowledge the value-laden nature of managerial decision-making. As Grey (2004, p.180) notes:

> [V]alues are inscribed, but rarely acknowledged, in any and every management or accounting technique. For in acting upon other people and on the world, management has consequences, both good and bad, and so managers, regardless of whether they like it, and realize it, are in the domain of values.

Whilst the Case Method, with its emphasis on action and its blindness to values, is seen as anathema to a critical management education, when it was forming at HBS, contesting the values underpinning managerial actions was actually seen as part of its promise.

A central character in this thread is Ordway Tead who, as noted earlier, taught with Donham and Fechner on the courses in Labor Technique and Labor Problems at HBS during the 1920s, in addition to lecturing at Columbia University. Tead campaigned for democratization of the workplace through regulation to create tripartite management structures that would dilute employer power and give workers and consumers an effective voice (Nyland and McLeod, 2007). Like Grey above, Tead (1960, 1964) regarded management and administration as moral arenas because of the consequences of decisions and actions taken, meaning any study of business and administration without an explicit consideration of values was an impoverished one. Faculty should reflect on their stance on moral issues that arose in their subjects, and should actively consider the wider political, economic and cultural significance of their material (Tead, 1964).

Tead was excited by the possibilities for the Case Method developing at HBS, describing it as 'an exceedingly provocative method of instruction' (1921, p.363) for requiring students' minds to be active, critical and creative. This overcame the limitation of the lecture method, which merely required students to absorb the ideas of others. Like many of his contemporaries, Tead saw value in the application of psychology to industrial issues. However, he also knew that, armed with this knowledge of human behaviour, 'exploitation of corporate groups by clever leaders' was a real possibility (1933, p.4). In the second edition of his book, *Human Nature and Management*, Tead added an appendix of questions and case problems. The objective was the 'stimulation of clear thinking and cultivation of a broad, liberal, and humane attitude of attack on problems of human relations' (1933, p.309). In one case, he described a billings department manager who started posting on the number of billings achieved by workers each week. Output increased sharply, but there had been no study by management to determine a reasonable level of output. One question assigned to the case was 'How can the danger of exploitation due to the use of techniques suggested by psychological knowledge be minimized? What is exploitation?' (1933, p.310).

While Tead was well-respected and his writing was influential at this time, he appears as a marginal figure in contemporary management history. There has been some attempt to recover his contribution to management thought (O'Connor, 2001), but his writing on pedagogy has received scant attention. On the potential he saw for the Case Method to explore the relationship between values and actions, there is silence. This aspect of the Case Method's past is not recorded in its history.

Whitehead and Donham: A Revolution in Academia Led by Practically Informed and Philosophically Guided Schools of Business

Much more prominence is given to English philosopher Alfred North Whitehead, who joined Harvard's Philosophy Department in 1924 and stayed there until his retirement in 1937. In their book on the Case Method, Barnes, Christensen and Hansen (1994, p.5) note that HBS 'owes a great deal to the intellectual gifts' of Whitehead, who had an enduring interest in education, being heavily involved in administrative activities during his tenure at University of London.

Whitehead rejected any distinction between abstract and practical knowledge and one of the reasons for the shift to Harvard was to allow him the space to consider this nexus. He believed 'education is not merely an appeal to the abstract intelligence. Purposeful activity, intellectual activity, and the immediate sense of worth-while achievement, should be conjoined in a unity of experience' (Whitehead 1933, p.444). Whitehead imagined business schools as an exemplar for his revolutionary vision of the university, but for this combination of imagination and action to be fully realized, there needed to be freedom of thought, stimulated by a diversity of opinions and perspectives.

Whitehead's advocacy was useful for Donham and HBS, which was under attack from Veblen (1918), who saw no place for the business school in universities, and by Flexner (1930), who studied 15 case volumes at HBS and found 'not the faintest glimmer of social, ethical, philosophic, historic or cultural interest' in them (p.132). Whitehead's (1928) paper, 'Universities and their Function', was initially an address to the AACSB. Donham asked Whitehead if the address could be reprinted in a publication celebrating the completion of a building project at HBS. Whitehead initially agreed, but wrote to Donham the following day retracting his acceptance, saying he wanted to try Atlantic Monthly first:

After a night's reflection over the project, I am sure that it will
impair a possible utility which I have very much at heart.
The reference to the Business Schools – which is exactly the sort of
illustration wanted for my argument – is really subordinate to the
general purpose of 'putting over' a way of conceiving the nature of
university work in general. *(Whitehead to Donham, 7 May 1927,
Baker Library Historical Collection)*

While Whitehead is celebrated in histories of HBS for providing
Donham with legitimacy for the business school, as well as
a justification for the action-orientation of the Case Method, curiously absent are other, relevant aspects of both his thinking and his
relationship with Donham. Like Tead, Whitehead was concerned
about how an obsession with 'material things and of capital' (1925,
p.284) had become divorced from the active consideration of values,
which were 'politely bowed to, and then handed over to the clergy to
be kept for Sundays' (p.284). What was needed, Whitehead believed,
was 'to strengthen habits of concrete appreciation of the individual
facts in their full interplay of emergent values' (p.277), rather than
the traditional approach of studying abstract ideas divorced of values.
In other words, Whitehead thought that the kind of business school
that Donham was developing could provide a guide for other parts of
universities, where the binary of thinking/acting had tipped too far
towards abstract theorizing and away from ethics, application and
action and the valuable reflection that could result in combining
both.

Whitehead's view of the business school and the university was
undoubtedly shaped by the dramatic changes within society at the
time. He was dismayed by the speed with which industrialization had
developed, as well as its form – mass production and the specialization
of knowledge (1925). Whitehead saw successful societies as being
based on routine, which created stability. This was under threat
because of the rapid advancement of scientific technologies.
In a lecture given to HBS, which appeared as the introduction of

Donham's (1931) book, *Business Adrift*, and was later reprinted in his own book, *Adventures of Ideas* (1933), Whitehead called on business schools to develop foresight amongst their students, to enable them to understand and predict social change – the antithesis of short-sightedness which Whitehead saw as symptomatic of his Age: 'Such a reflective power is essentially a philosophic habit: it is the survey of society from the standpoint of generality' (xxvi–xxvii). What he advocated was not a study of business *in* society, but a study *of* society, based on a philosophic outlook, in which business plays an important part. 'We must not fall into the fallacy of thinking of the business world in abstraction from the rest of the community. The business world is one main part of the very community which is the subject-matter of our study' (xxvii). This idea of foresight extended beyond the 'notion of enlightened self-interest', which had become popular during the 1920s, as capitalists such as J. D. Rockefeller responded to rising labour unrest.

Donham and Whitehead developed a close relationship, meeting regularly on Saturday afternoons for lengthy discussions (Cruikshank, 1987)[6]. In the foreword to *Business Adrift*, Donham acknowledged the influence of Whitehead's thinking – 'his essay summarizes and states, more clearly than I possibly could, the philosophical concepts on which my thinking is based (viii). Donham accepted Whitehead's identification of constant change as the major threat facing Western civilization and saw the United States' descent into economic crisis as evidence that this threat was becoming reality. Donham called on business to maintain employment in the face of falling demand (something he had learnt from his times in the railways). He advocated cutting working hours while leaving wages at existing levels, in the hope that undiminished purchasing power combined with additional leisure time would stimulate demand. Local newspaper *The Harvard Crimson* commented: 'These ideas are not new, but they have hitherto been considered

---

[6] We found little in the Harvard archives as a result of Whitehead's preference for conversations over correspondence (Hendley, 2002).

radical, indeed socialistic, and it is a surprising indication of the progress of the times to hear them from the Dean of a Harvard graduate school' (21 September 1932). A review of *Business Adrift* in *Time* magazine (1931, p.46) concluded that 'beneath all the learning at Harvard Business School there is a philosophical undercurrent, the ingredient most recommended by Dean Donham to his countrymen'.

Like Whitehead, Donham was highly critical of the emphasis on specialization in business and law education. Indeed, he also became aware of the limitations of the narrow approach to the Case Method he had promoted just years earlier. Business education had become preoccupied with solving problems in organizations. 'We need in business and politics administrators who are able not only to handle their specialized problems well, but also to see things in wide relations and do their part in maintaining society's stability and equilibrium' (Donham, 1933, p.420).

In the histories of HBS and its Case Method, the contribution of Whitehead is noteworthy for what is left out. Barnes et al. (1994) credit Whitehead's lasting legacy of action-oriented learning, but say nothing of his ideas about consideration of values or business as a sociological study. McNair's (1954) collection of papers on the Case Method makes no mention of Whitehead at all.

Accounts of Donham's contribution are also partial. Copeland's (1958) institutional history of HBS devotes a whole chapter to him, but makes no mention of his writing on the state of US capitalism in the 1920s and 1930s, despite Whitehead crediting Donham for helping to 'avert the disaster of an American social revolution' (1942, p.235). Donham's normative stance was seen, in retrospect, to be 'confusing' (Cruikshank, 1987, p.187) and has been forgotten by histories of HBS and the Case Method.

HOW POST–WWII DEVELOPMENTS GLOSSED OVER THE INNOVATIONS OF THE 1930S

There is no rationale or philosophy of business capable of justification apart from a considered philosophy of life. And until all the teachers in

> schools of business perceive this profound and necessary truth, the meth-
> ods of instruction, including the provocative case method, will remain
> thin and inconclusive. There has to be a confronting and examining of the
> reasons why business functions, of the meaning of its functioning, and of
> its human purpose in a democratic society. *(Tead, 1953, p.106)*

The business school environment after World War II was a very different place to that experienced by Tead, Donham and Whitehead in
the interwar period. There were continuing challenges to the legitimacy of business schools, but the challenges were of a different form.
The crisis of the Great Depression had passed, capitalism was stabi-
lized and the demand for business schools to address pressing social
issues dissipated. Business schools were now under pressure to
improve their academic standing through the development of
a systematic, scientific body of knowledge (Gordon and Howell,
1959; Pierson, 1959), whilst preserving the ideal of management as
a profession that had been the mission of business schools since their
inception (Khurana, 2007). For Herbert Simon, the pursuit of 'pure
science' (1967, p.6) was entirely 'relevant' for a professional school
committed to training future managers – prefiguring a debate that
would resurface with intensity nearly 50 years later (Bennis and
O'Toole, 2005; Ghoshal, 2005; Pfeffer and Fong, 2002).

Originally, Donham (1922) had hoped the Case Method would
satisfy this demand for new knowledge by developing general principles though a process of inductive empiricism, but by the 1950s, this
was seen as a failed project. While recognizing the foundational importance of economics, supporters of the Case Method were now keen to
promote management and business as a different branch from pure
science by emphasizing its training function, thus narrowing the
understanding of what the Case Method was, or could be. Fritz
Roethlisberger, a central figure in the growth of human relations at
HBS, put it thus:

> Although related, we assumed there were two kinds of knowledge
> that needed to be different. One is the kind of knowledge that is
> associated with the scientist who is seeking to make verifiable

propositions about a certain class of phenomena. The other is a kind of knowledge that is associated with the practitioner of a skill in relation to a class of phenomena. *(Roethlisberger, 1954, p.8)*

The practitioner, said Roethlisberger, was like a skilful carpenter, who knew what wood to use in certain situations, compared with wood scientists, who understood the composition of woods. HBS decided it was better equipped to train carpenters than create wood theorists (Barnes et al., 1994). At this time, the narrow, managerialist interpretation of the Case Method that could be taken from Donham's 1920 memo fitted well with the ideological underpinnings of human relations which had transformed the HBS curriculum, being democratic (students participate in class rather than being 'told what to think'); individual (every situation is treated differently and stereotypes and categorizations are avoided); and co-operative (students have a common goal to analyse the case and learn from each other) (Ronken, 1953). Kenneth Andrews' (1953) edited book *The Case Method of Teaching Human Relations and Administration*, dedicated to Donham, contained contributions from HBS faculty involved in teaching and researching human relations. In a chapter by Harriet Ronken, 'What one student learned', Ronken tells the story of Allen Price, a student who held left-wing views and was resistant to the Case Method: 'he went outside the case; he told stories from his own experience; he reported newspaper articles on topics like "unions" ... he appealed to anything that he thought would give him grounds for an opinion except the case' (1953, p.49–50). Over time, however, he learnt to engage with the complexity of the individual cases, started to consider his own psychological processes and shifted from thinking in stereotypes about 'union members' and 'capitalists' to seeking to understand 'real people' (p.62).

The failure to realize the promise of a critically reflexive Case Method was a disappointment for Tead. The quotation at the head of this section comes from Tead's review of Andrews' edited volume. While Tead remained supportive of the Case Method, he was 'also for far more which it curiously ignores' (Tead, 1953, p.106). In his eyes, it had become an 'educational gadget'. Developments after WWII were largely technical ones, such as parabola-shaped classrooms and positioning lecturers below their students, rather than overlooking them from a raised platform, as had been the situation before (Barnes et al., 1994). For Tead (1953), business cases had become problem-solving exercises underpinned by the unscrutinized values of profit maximization and logistic feasibility. It was a pity, he said 'that there is no longer an Alfred North Whitehead to help lead the technicians out of the bleak wilderness of techniques discussed without benefit of some philosophy' (106).

RECONSTRUCTING THE HISTORY OF MANAGEMENT PEDAGOGY TO INSPIRE FUTURE INNOVATION

Histories of the Case Method and of HBS itself do not see the debates and complexities that we have highlighted here. Discussions about the status of management as a profession are more than a century old (Cruikshank, 1987; Khurana, 2007) and continue to the present day. Typically, however, these give little consideration to the promise of the Case Method, which is seen as delivering a practical training in business administration based on decision-making, whilst other parts of the curriculum and programme, such as developing courses on social responsibility and business ethics, cultivate the values of business as a profession.

Indeed, critical scholars have not seen much to celebrate in this history of HBS or its Case Method. Donham is typically portrayed by them as a realist who knew that capitalism was teetering and saw that emphasizing the social aspects of business was a way to retain managerial autonomy (O'Connor, 1999; Yogev, 2001). After all, his exemplars of enlightened self-interest were Rockefeller and Carnegie who 'harmonized' their economic and social obligations (Donham, 1927, p.407) – hardly a challenge to the establishment.

Our purpose here is not to dismiss these interpretations, but to construct an alternative narrative. The dramatically shifting context of the 1920s and 1930s provided fertile ground for the germination of a range of radically different ways of thinking about business education. Donham's interactions with Fechner, Tead and Whitehead suggest that irrespective of his initial motivations, his actions went beyond political expediency. The controversy surrounding Fechner suggests a genuine determination on the part of Donham to have the voice of organized labour represented. Tead saw the possibilities for the Case Method to provide a deep, critical reflection on the use and potential abuse of knowledge about management, informed by the explicit consideration of values. And Donham's friendship with Whitehead significantly shifted his thinking about business and its sociological function and led to his interventions in national political debate. It also gave him a new perspective on the limitations of the Case Method in its conventional form, and possibilities for how it could be reshaped. Revisiting these events with a different lens can provide a useful spur for thinking differently now: both about the Case Method itself and the challenges facing business schools in the twenty-first century.

This is not to imply that the Case Method or HBS's approach to educating their students has been static. Advocates have recognized that whilst it remains a valuable approach, management education must respond to the challenges of globalization, innovation, creativity and technological change (Datar et al., 2010). There is now more attention given to experiential learning, often conducted internationally, and exposing students to business situations that are less structured and problem-focussed than cases, often by way of simulations. Harvard Business Publishing now produces 'brief cases' (5–8 pages in contrast to the traditional 30 pages), multimedia cases and online simulations, in addition to its regular cases. But despite this, the Case Method and assumptions about its purpose remain central to the teaching of students at HBS, as well as being a key part of the HBS brand, and, by association, those other institutions who seek to be like Harvard. Harvard Business Publishing continues to produce books on the Case Method (Andersen and Schiano, 2014; Ellet, 2007) and supplementary products such as on-line tutorials for students, as well as resources for teachers, including face-to-face seminars hosted by universities around the globe. The business of Case Method teaching remains as vital for HBS as ever before.

While there has been incremental change, we argue that a deeper rethinking of history can inspire more fundamental shifts. We outline four specific areas for innovation inspired by the Case Method's forgotten past below.

Thinking Deeply about Labour Relations, Rather than Dismissing Them as Irrelevant, Unfashionable or Not Our Business

In providing teaching on labour relations in the early 1920s, the express purpose was to expose students to 'real-world' problems and to get them to understand these 'problems' from the perspective of labour, rather than examine them from just the perspective of capital. Donham fought hard to resist the pressure exerted by F. C. Hood over his appointment of Fechner, which left him open to accusations of fermenting communist beliefs amongst the study body. Donham rejected the accusation that including the voice of organized labour was 'dangerous', highlighting the value of gaining a genuine understanding of this perspective. Additionally, Tead was an advocate of increasing worker voice and workplace democracy through collective bargaining and strong trade unions.

In the current context, organized labour has been in decline over a long period. Trade unions do, however, remain an influential actor in many countries, particularly at the macro level in serving on tripartite committees, lobbying government on industrial relations reforms or working with MNCs, NGOs and international bodies on framework agreements aimed at improving working conditions in supply chains. Despite this, the rights of workers to freedom of association and collective bargaining through trade unions (Principle 3 of the United Nations Global Compact) have largely been airbrushed out of business school curriculums. Industrial Relations departments have been forced to rename themselves as Human Resource Management departments or are subsumed under the broader umbrella of organization studies. Similarly, unions rarely appear in HBS case studies (Anteby, 2013) and, indeed, are largely absent among the writings of critical management scholars; they have become something of a 'missing subject' within the business school (Bridgman and McLaughlin, 2012). We might also extend the lesson of Donham's defence of the inclusion of organized labour to other stakeholders, who had less of a presence in the 1920s and 1930s, and who may be impacted by management decisions and may not share the same managerial perspective, such as non-unionized workers, particularly those marginalized in atypical and insecure employment, local communities and NGOs. Here, we are not envisioning the classic 'stakeholder perspective', where students consider the interests of other stakeholders and take them into account in making a decision, but rather their perspective might be analysed as part of a deeper and more critical thinking around the impact of business on its stakeholders and on society (Starkey and Tempest, 2009).

Stimulating Processes of Critical Reflection – Cases Are an Opportunity to Think about How We Think

We could also strive to realize the vision Tead had for using the Case Method to develop more thoughtful practice through assessing critically the assumptions underpinning managerial actions and the impact of those actions on others (Cunliffe, 2004). As the Case Method became sedimented after World War II, it became wedded to the ideological positioning of human relations. Notable in Andrews' (1953) volume is that while a number of the contributors talk about the importance of challenging preconceptions and assumptions, this critical questioning is narrowly confined within the managerialist worldview of human relations as a subject. Tead had in mind a far more radical questioning, which required an in-depth understanding of the advancements in industrial psychology but with an awareness of its exploitative effects, especially if applied instrumentally in organizations. It is a study 'of' management rather than 'for' management, an aim shared by critical management educators. These issues remain as relevant today as they were nearly a century ago, given what we know about the poor treatment of workers in MNC supply chains, the growth of zero-hour contracts (which shift many of the risks in employment from the employer to the employee), exploitation of local communities and the impacts of business on climate change, to name but a few examples.

Against the Narrowing Tendencies of 'Decision Forcing' and Taking Real Action – Addressing the Global Challenges of Our Age

Undoubtedly, there has been a surge of interest in business ethics in the wake of the financial crisis, in the hope that future business leaders might act more ethically (Currie, Knights and Starkey, 2010). This implies that unethical conduct is the result of morally deficient managers, rather than a product of the broader system (Bridgman, 2010). For both Tead and Whitehead, business was a part of a wider society and needed to be examined as part of that society, and this influenced Donham in his concern about the direction of US capitalism and what he saw as an increasing fragmentation of the fabric of society. Taking inspiration from his approach calls, we argue, for an analysis which integrates individual managerial behaviour with a range of social, political and ideological factors.

To do this requires challenging the dominance of the decision-forcing case – the structuring technique that places students in the 'shoes' of a character in the case, usually a manager, needing to make a decision to solve a business problem. Decision-forcing cases dominate because of 'the conviction among teachers in the professions that the essence of professional skill is the ability to make decisions under trying circumstances' (Lynn, 1999, p.107). This has the effect of socializing students into a managerial worldview by requiring them to don an ideological 'hat' by making decisions based on criteria of efficiency, productivity and profitability (Wensley, 2011).

The decision-forcing case overlooks the way in which individual managerial decisions are shaped by the structures of global capitalism, where the demands of institutional investors and the fluidity of capital markets incentivize managers to make short-term decisions. As Thompson (2003, 2013) notes in his 'disconnected capitalism thesis', individual managers and firms may wish to act responsibly towards their stakeholders, but they are unable to keep their side of the bargain; such is the pressure from global finance. We would suggest that, in the spirit of Donham and Whitehead, the Case Method might be re-envisaged to elicit a deeper critique of modern day capitalism and its impact on society, that students would be challenged with deeper questions about the relationship between business and society, such as: 'do corporations have too much power and influence?', 'what role should the state play in regulating business?' or 'is contemporary capitalism part of the problem when it comes to the issues of our age, such as climate change?' (McLaughlin, 2013; McLaughlin and Prothero, 2014). Case studies could play an important role in critically engaging students with the global challenges we face in building a more inclusive, ethical and sustainable society.

Recognizing that the Formation and Form of What We Consider a Business School Should Be Is Shaped by the Environment and Politics in Which It Emerged

A fourth and final idea that we believe our counter-history of the emergence of business schools and the Harvard Case Method highlights is also a Weberian lesson (see Chapter Four): that the form of the business school today is not fundamentally related to an objective understanding of what management is. Rather, it is influenced by the problems and concerns and cultural mores of the times when the key players involved sought to shape things. Hence, much as Barley and Kunda (1992) identified different 'surges' of discourse in management theorizing depending on prevailing socio-economic conditions and trends, when we look again at the history of schools like HBS, we can see a contestation and swings of opinion based on the political, economic and cultural conditions of the day. For example, there is little doubt that economic recession and public opinion regarding managers and business-people caused pause for thought about what a business school should be and do. Hence, it could do so again. The idea that economics or the Case Method approach promoted by history are 'the only theoretical framework' or the 'best way of educating managers' are not facts no matter how much they are stated as such. They are value judgments.

Those who wrote the history of business schools in the middle of the twentieth century 'placed present needs as origins', to use Foucault's term. This is why they picked out schools that had a basis in economics and the Case Method as key. There is nothing stopping people today placing our present needs as origins, selecting other elements from the past that they think would make for a better kind of business school. Recognizing this can free our thinking. If there is no foundational reason why business schools are shaped the way they are, then we can ask: what should a business school be and do now to reflect the context, the aims, and the kinds of organization we want now?

RE-STATING THE CASE

> I hope that the umbilical cord that intravenously feeds the past, present and future with the sustaining power of the status quo, can be cut in order to allow for new births.
>
> Jenkins (2003, p.18)

There is a growing awareness that business education has reached a crossroads (Datar et al., 2010). During and in the immediate aftermath of the financial crisis, pressure grew for change. Dominic Barton (2011), global managing director of McKinsey and Company, warned ominously of the potential for 'the social contract between the capitalist system and the citizenry [to] truly rupture, with unpredictable but severely damaging results' (p.86). In a tone eerily similar to Donham's *Business Adrift*, Barton said business leaders face a stark choice – either they reform capitalism, 'the greatest engine of prosperity ever devised' (p.86), or stand by and watch as government takes control.

But there are now signs that the impetus for change is receding. As the financial crisis eased, there have been calls for a return to 'business as usual'. Robert Simons (2013), who teaches a 'Designing Winning Organizations' course at HBS, blames new courses on business ethics and corporate social responsibility for a decline in the competitiveness of US industry. For Simons, business schools have lost focus on their historical mission – 'the business of business is teaching business. And successful businesses require an over-riding focus on the tough choices needed to prevail in competitive markets' (p.31). Simons sees the Case Method as salvation, because of the way it trains future managers to 'make tough, consequential choices' (p.12).

We have been here before, of course. As Jacques (1996) notes, the default mode of business education throughout its history has been pragmatism. The 'business hero, real or fictional, has been the "man [sic] of action"' (p.7), who makes courageous decisions under uncertainty to improve the bottom line. During times of relative stability, this pragmatism enables a focus on solving problems. However, during times of crisis, the problem-solving approach becomes a problem itself, because it is more concerned with making assumptions rather than examining them. 'Paradoxically, during times such as these, "pragmatic" approaches to problem-solving are obstacles to solving concrete problems while questioning basic values and assumptions – philosophy – is pragmatic' (p.7).

This critical questioning was exactly the response of Donham, Tead and Whitehead to the economic turbulence of the 1920s and 1930s. In our present time of arguably unprecedented economic, social and environmental crises, we need to heed this lesson that a narrow focus on solving business problems risks costing business schools their legitimacy. The difficulty, however, is that our ability to learn from this past is limited by the histories that we have. As critical historian Keith Jenkins notes, social formations attempt to reproduce themselves in a stable condition 'so that all potentially destabilizing and dangerous excesses are either absorbed or rigorously excluded' (2003, p.17). Continuity is desired to maintain a controllable connection between the past, present and future. In the economic crises of the 1920s and 1930s, there was no history of the Case Method or the business school, allowing a fluidity about what these could be. Now we have a 100-year history of tradition and supposed continuity of thinking to fall back on, to seek reassurance that we have been through tough times before and the Case Method has seen us right. The 'invented tradition' of the Case Method makes creative, innovative thinking about the present and the future more difficult.

While our particular focus has been a reflection on the development of the Case Method, the relations between Donham, Whitehead, Tead, Hood and Fechner were about much more than this. They were about the form of business education and its relation to society in general, and in the case of Whitehead, about the very nature of knowledge and education. Then, as now, case teaching and pedagogy in general are connected. However, today our view of both may be narrowing the other. When one looks at recent HBS advertising (see below), one likely associates it with a narrow view of conventional case teaching, and either thinks it great because Harvard is preeminent and has a wonderful historical lineage, or thinks it is terrible because it is an overly simplistic approach spread far and wide due to Harvard's pre-eminence. Our radical suggestion is that Harvard itself is not the problem stifling development. Rather it is our limited understanding of its, and our, past.

From our position more than 80 years beyond the Great Depression, we wonder what those looking to learn the lessons of the global financial crisis will glean from its history in 80 years from now. That will likely depend on what happens next – whether the events of the past decade were a temporary loss of confidence in capitalism, with 'business as usual' restored, or signal the early stages of a deep crisis which will precipitate a larger upheaval (Galbraith,

FIGURE 15 Banner Advertising Harvard Business School at Harvard
Business School c. 2014
Source: Photograph by S. Cummings (reproduced with permission)

2014). This level of uncertainty gives the present more than a passing
resemblance to the past (figure 15).

Anteby (2014) believes it is time for HBS to stop 'preaching in
silence' – 'When there is copious evidence that some corporate behaviours are egregiously immoral and millions of people are now facing
radically reduced living conditions because of the actions of a few,
silence can no longer be the answer'. We share his sentiments, but not

his belief that normative silence has been the way at HBS since the inception of the Case Method a century ago. HBS and the Case Method have a past that has not been a feature of their histories. Substantive innovation, of the counter-history inspired kind we have presented here, requires the 'umbilical cord' of history to be cut and re-routed back through the thoughts of those who faced questions about the legitimacy of business schools in the 1930s. By 're-stating the case', we aim to stimulate new thinking about the state of business pedagogy, education, and the aims we are seeking to serve, as managers and educators, today and for the future.

6   The Discovery of the Human Worker

What if the start of 'good science' in management studies turned out to be a backward step?

After the presentation of the 'classical' or mechanistic influences on management, Elton Mayo's research is presented as evidence for a kinder, gentler and more scientific type of management. But what if the research on which his 'human relations' school was founded was not all that it seems? How would the good guys turning out to be not so good change our view of management's history and change our agenda for management studies for the future? This chapter brings into focus the wider factors influencing Mayo's research. It deconstructs and critiques a habitual revelatory narrative in textbooks, one where Western Electric – an authoritarian, bureaucratic corporation, ignorant of human factors – is enlightened and turned around by the arrival of behavioural scientists from Harvard and their 'discovery' of human relations at work. Our anti-revelatory analysis offers a wider canvas on which to portray the host corporation and the famous series of organizational investigations conducted therein. In so doing, we describe not only how Mayo constructed a narrative for explaining the findings from Hawthorne that appealed to his social networks, their right-wing politics and maintained the status quo, but also diminished and set back the field of management.

> Although critics attacked the research procedures, the analysis of the findings and the conclusions, it is of little importance from a historical perspective whether the Hawthorne Studies were academically sound or their conclusions justified. What *is* important is that they stimulated an interest in human behaviour in organizations.
>
> Robbins et al., *Management* (2015, p.54)
>
> As scholars now look back, the Hawthorne Studies are criticised for poor research design, weak empirical support for the conclusions drawn and the tendency of researchers to overgeneralize their findings. Yet the significance of these studies as a turning point in the evolution of management thought remains intact.
>
> Schermerhorn et al., *Management* (2014, p.43)

The Hawthorne Studies, 1924–32 (see Roethlisberger and Dickson, 1939), are the largest, best-known and most influential investigations in the history of management research.[1] They are associated primarily with HBS professor Elton Mayo and the research team he joined and then led at the Western Electric Company's Hawthorne Works, Cicero, Illinois in 1928. These studies, and the Hawthorne Effect theory that they 'discovered', revolutionized management. Or so the story goes.

The Hawthorne Effect theory claims that 'workers' improved performance . . . is due to special attention received from their supervisor' (Adair, 2003, p.452). (Wikipedia defines it for the masses as 'a type of reactivity in which individuals modify or improve an aspect of their behaviour in response to their awareness of being observed'.) The upshot taken from the Hawthorne Effect is that if you show human interest in people, they are both happier and more productive at work. This is seen a revolutionary advance upon Scientific Management's view that people would be more productive if efficient systems were designed that enabled both owners/managers and workers to earn more money. As Wren (1972, p.299) puts it, 'the Mayoists downgraded the lure of money' and from this point, 'social relations' came to be regarded as paramount.

---

[1] This chapter draws from elements of Hassard, J. S. (2012). Rethinking the Hawthorne Studies: The Western Electric Research in Its Social, Political and Historical Context. *Human Relations*, 65(11), 1431–61.

The conventional historical narrative with regard to Hawthorne, promoted in most textbooks until quite recently (and many to this day), was that Mayo and his team made this breakthrough scientific 'discovery': a discovery upon which the so-called 'human relations' school of management was founded (as reflected in research accounts by, e.g., Mayo, 1933, 1935, 1945; Roethlisberger, 1941; and Roethlisberger and Dickson, 1939). The conventional narrative says that this revelation brought about a 'paradigm-shift' in management. A shift away from the simplistic, mechanistic and dubious science of Taylorism, Scientific Management and Weberian Machine Bureaucracy, and towards good science with more noble aims that showed that people were not attachable and detachable automatons or cogs in a machine (e.g., Luthans, 2010; Rollinson, 2008; Smith, 2007). For many decades, results from the Studies have formed a bastion of the 'human relations' approach, through producing theory and evidence that challenged and rejected the assumptions and principles of Taylorism.

'Scholars generally agree', writes Robbins et al. (2015, p.53) that: 'The Hawthorne Studies had a dramatic effect on management beliefs about the role of people in organizations and led to a new emphasis on the human behaviour factor in managing organizations'. Davidson et al.'s (2009, p.47), introductory textbook, also called *Management*, employs Wren's history to back this idea up. Overviewing the evolution of management thought, Wren observed: 'The outcome of the Hawthorne research was a call for a different mix of managerial skills [than the technical skills promoted by earlier approaches]. A different and new paradigm of management thought was called for.'

Davidson et al. cite the fourth or 1994 edition of Wren's *Evolution of Management Thought* as the reference for this claim (Wren, 1994, p.247). But a couple of pages further on from where they take this quotation, one can read how the history surrounding Mayo and Hawthorne was changing. Wren's history was beginning to reflect new research (in particular, Charles Wrege's work, such as *Fact and Fallacies of Hawthorne: A Historical Analysis of the Hawthorne Illumination Tests and The Hawthorne Studies*, in 1986). This research cast doubt on the objectivity and validity of the school and theory upon which the dramatic 'new paradigm' was based, research not available when Wren wrote the first edition of his book.

What is interesting, however, is the way that the history of management as presented in textbooks is adjusted in the light of the Hawthorne Studies being discredited by those textbook authors who are fully aware of this discrediting.

Some are bluntly honest. The quotations at the head of this chapter concede that the research procedures, the analysis of the findings and the conclusions of the Hawthorne researchers have been attacked; and note their poor research design, weak empirical support for the conclusions drawn and the tendency of researchers to overgeneralize findings. There is a wealth of evidence that Schermerhorn and Robbins point to that has made this plain over the past few decades (e.g., Carey, 1967; Franke and Kaul, 1978; Jones, 1990; 1992; Rice, 1982; Sonnenfeld, 1985; Yunker, 1993).

Samson and Daft's textbook (2015, p.55) acknowledges a similar set of research and goes even further, noting that: 'To be historically accurate, money was probably the best explanation for increases in output [in the Hawthorne Studies] but at the time experimenters believed the explanation was human relations.'

To be clear, this is a remarkable turnaround. Recall that Hawthorne's revelation was that human relations were more important than money. But it has turned out, and these textbooks start to acknowledge, that not only is Mayo and his associates' research poorly conceived, the actual findings back up those of the management theorists that history tells us were superseded by Hawthorne.

But then, having acknowledged this, a choice is made. Rather than rethinking history in the light of these new facts, it is decided, in likely the only histories of management that most management students will ever read, that historical accuracy is not that important. Mayo and Hawthorne are still important because they are a 'turning point' and 'advance in the evolution of management'; they stimulated a new interest, a new paradigm, based on the discovery that 'Man is a human being – even in industry' (Whyte 1959, p.3) and gave birth to the 'human side' of work (Greenberg and Baron 1995, p.17). In the binary world that conventional management history promotes, the old mechanistic, grubby money way was bad and the new human relations way was good. This is a view that persists in the minds of even unconventional and critical authors, who refer to management's traditional 'dichotomies of control versus commitment, Taylor versus Mayo, formal versus informal, mechanistic verses organic' (Parker, 1992, p.651; see also Alvesson, 1995, p.1061–2) and Mayo as moving beyond a 'narrow Taylorist perspective' (Morgan, 2006, p.35). And despite inaccuracy, this historical narrative is to be maintained.

Yet, in the light of the previous chapters in this book, this conventional narrative of Hawthorne as an advance only appears so because of the extremely simplistic way that Mayo's perceived predecessors are portrayed. Focussing on human behaviour with respect to work and management was nothing new. As the following pages will show, it is a moot point whether Mayo's 'humanism' is on a par with Taylor, and it is certainly less than that exhibited in Weber's or Smith's writings.

To our way of thinking, as we will explain in this chapter, The Hawthorne Studies represent a step backwards. Not only was social man less at the centre of his research than Smith's or Weber's, Mayo came to Hawthorne empowered from Harvard and 'in alliance with Dean Donham's desire to address social and industrial issues [to help] define a new curriculum focus' (Anteby and Khurana, 2007). But Mayo's gaze turned out to be narrowly managerialist.

The two-step approach of acknowledging the 'issues' with Hawthorne but still giving them pride of place in management's history leads to continuity issues (e.g., Robbins et al.'s (2015) textbook still notes – as it had done in earlier editions – that the Hawthorne experiments were 'set up ... like any good scientific experiment' (p.52) before acknowledging two pages later that 'research procedures' were dubious). Nevertheless, the idea that the history of management could be presented to young initiates as anything other than an evolutionary series of advances is unconscionable. That the Hawthorne Studies could be de-evolutionary goes against the meta-narrative of all conventional management histories, that of progress through standing on the shoulders of previous 'giants' like Mayo.

On the contrary, we will argue in our conclusion to this chapter that recognizing and promoting Hawthorne and Mayo as a devolution could be liberating.

LOOKING AGAIN AT THE FORMATION OF THE HAWTHORNE STORIES

As will already be clear from this chapter's introductory paragraphs, our counter-history here aims to overturn a number of commonly assumed discontinuities with regard to the Human Relations School.

- Where management histories promote Mayo and Hawthorne as more scientific than Taylorism, we question this. While Scientific Management was not actually very scientific, the Hawthorne studies were highly flawed in their operation. But recall that it wasn't Taylor that sought to label his work scientific (see Chapter Three) – he initially tried to resist this terminology. It seems that Mayo had no such qualms.

- While management histories promote Hawthorne as representing the discovery of the importance of human relations, our counter-history has already shown that Smith put human relations at the centre of his system two centuries earlier (see Chapter Two) and Weber tried to encourage people to recognize the importance of human constructs like culture and socio-political environments (see Chapter Four).

- Whereas Mayo is often regarded as the antithesis of, a break from and advance upon Taylor in modern management textbooks, we would point out that recent research suggests that scientific management – as established in the 'Taylor system' (see Kanigel, 1997) – while certainly involving time study and wage incentives, was in fact more of an all-embracing programme – one that continued to evolve throughout the

1920s and 1930s (see Nyland, 1996; Nyland and Heenan, 2005).[2] Additionally, although Human Relations is recurrently defined and explained as a *successor* movement to scientific management, in American industry, the term actually predates the work of Elton Mayo and the Harvard Group (see Bruce, 2006). Indeed, earlier historians, writing before the Taylor/Mayo dichotomy got set in the conventional textbook sequencing of progressive steps, saw Mayo as a continuation of Taylor: almost peas from the same pod. As Wren exclaims (1972, p.298ff.): 'it is amazing to note the high degree of similarity of goals between the two men'. Neither questioned the aim or the 'logic of efficiency' which by Mayo's time had become, for most, the fundamental aim of management. Wren (1972, p.275–99) shows how Taylor and Mayo were 'strikingly similar' in their quest to 'reduce obstacles' or 'impediments' to efficiency. By Wren's third edition of *Evolution of Management Thought* in 1987, however, the subsection on the similarities between Taylor and Mayo had been dropped.

• While Hawthorne is seen as broadening management's agenda, we shall show how what was advanced by Mayo's team was narrower than the scope that Dean Donham and his network were seeking to develop and promote at Harvard in this period, which included the voices of multiple stakeholders (see Chapter Five).

We shall reinforce these counter-historical over-turnings further in the remainder of this chapter, but we shall do so by focussing on one particular espoused historical discontinuity. This is the idea that Mayo and his team came to Hawthorne and found a typically dismal old-fashioned organization and turned it around into something truly progressive and more productive, in the process 'proving' that their 'new' theory could be generally applied to make any organization better.

---

[2] On this issue, we would also draw attention to the evolution of a continuing scientific management tradition at Hawthorne in the 1920s and 1930s (notably under the guidance of Henry Fleetwood Albright, Western Electric's 'champion of scientific engineering') and how the company helped 'export scientific management to Japan' (see Adams and Butler, 1999, p.76–80).

In targeting this we shall, by association, raise further doubt about the espoused discontinuities listed in the bullet points above. We will also highlight how the problem that Mayo and his team were responding to was as much 'how to continue to stay in the good books with our sponsors' as 'how to advance our scientific understanding of work and management'. Relatedly, we explore how rather than objectively revealing more about the object of the study, the subject and object of the study shaped or co-created one another. But primarily, in a Foucauldian spirit, we look deeper at the networks of relations and contextual elements that shaped the formation of the Hawthorne Studies.

Although the Hawthorne Studies are well-known, the context in which these ergonomic, psychological and sociological investigations were conducted is less so. Indeed, it has remained an essentially anonymous actor in the main research accounts subsequently produced. While organizational scholars have focussed persistently on the various phases that comprised the investigations, they have given far less consideration to a range of social and political factors that shaped the host enterprise and its workforce at this time. It is argued that to achieve a more grounded and balanced narrative on Hawthorne, one that takes account of the circumstances of the setting in which the investigations were conducted, greater attention needs to be paid to contextual issues related to the firm's strategy, management and culture.

The principal counter-historical question this chapter asks, therefore, is *was Western Electric the kind of enterprise that many management historians assume it to be around the time of the Hawthorne Studies?* This is answered by considering two contextual issues and examining networks related to these: on the one hand, the nature of the company's corporate context – through analysis of its industrial reputation and business philosophy; and on the other, the firm's cultural context – through examination of its social organization and communal experience. As a result of these inquiries, we find that by the early 1920s, rather than being an unexceptional firm, Western Electric had developed into one possessing a distinctive corporate profile and singular corporate culture. In particular, prior to the arrival of Elton Mayo, at face value, it was already a 'progressive' company espousing many 'human relations' style philosophies, although not for the reasons ascribed by mainstream management theory. With this knowledge, we offer not only fresh insights into the history of the Hawthorne Works, but new interpretations of the Harvard-influenced research conducted therein.

The reminder of this chapter is subsequently developed in three phases. The first outlines the case for considering contextual research as a means to better understand the Hawthorne Studies. The second addresses the task of developing this kind of research, presenting two cases relevant to understanding the character and climate of the organization in the early decades of its history. The third phase sees findings from these accounts discussed as part of a contextually-informed approach to interrogating historical assumptions in management studies.

DECONSTRUCTING HABITUAL NARRATIVES
AND DEVELOPING CONTEXTUAL ACCOUNTS

> The investigators never undertook a systematic study of the social organization of the company, and it is therefore impossible to characterize it in detail or entirely accurately.

Roethlisberger and Dickson (1939, p.538)

In organization and management theory, a major criticism of research on the Hawthorne Studies is that it represents 'closed-system' analysis. In other words, as the focus is upon explaining a handful of social science investigations, the research base tells us relatively little about the culture or climate within which the host organization operated (see Burrell and Morgan, 1979; Katz and Kahn, 1966; Scott, 2003). Indeed, even where respected scholars suggest they are studying, more holistically, the 'origins' of the Hawthorne Studies (e.g., Wrege, 1976), the analysis is confined largely to technical issues relating to the investigations themselves.

A corollary of closed-system investigation is that in the majority of studies on Hawthorne, the host organization is treated as a commonplace location for conducting research in industry. The Hawthorne Works is portrayed as an unexceptional site from which results can be generalized, a seemingly representative organization in case-study terms. The inference is that while the experimental site is ordinary, the empirical results – regarding group dynamics, informal organization, management style, work satisfaction, etc. – are extraordinary.

In contrast, the counter-historical analysis developed here is concerned not so much with revisiting the various phases of the Hawthorne investigations (see Bramel and Friend, 1981; Carey, 1967; Franke and Kaul, 1978; Greenwood et al., 1983; Landsberger, 1958; Pitcher, 1981; Wrege, 1976; Wren and Bedeian, 2009; and Yorks and Whitsett, 1985 for this) as defining the character of Western Electric as a corporate actor and employer (see Adams and Butler, 1999; Fagen, 1975, 1978; Gillespie, 1991; Wachholz, 2005). It is argued that when the company's reputation for scientific and technological innovation is considered alongside, for example, its paternalism, anti-unionism and singular cultural legacy, the Hawthorne Works emerges as a very particular location for conducting management and organizational research.

This chapter therefore relates to a body of literature that has sought to identify wider contextual factors influencing the Studies and in particular Elton Mayo's Harvard-based research group at this time (e.g., Bruce and Nyland, 2011; Gillespie, 1991; Nyland and Bruce, 2012; O'Connor, 1999; Smith, 1998; Wrege, 1976; Wren, 1985; Wren and Bedeian, 2009; Wren and Greenwood, 1998): Amongst other things, such research has served to deconstruct and critique an habitual *revelatory* narrative in textbooks on organization and management theory; one where Western Electric – an authoritarian, bureaucratic corporation, ignorant of human factors – is enlightened following the arrival of behavioural scientists from Harvard and their 'discovery' of human relations at work.

Among research that has developed an anti-revelatory approach, the work by Richard Gillespie (1991) has been seminal. Gillespie questions just *how* revelatory the findings from the various Hawthorne investigations were. He focusses not so much on the technical specifics of the experimental phases as on broader issues related to them, such as methodological insights revealed in the personal communications of the Hawthorne researchers. Gillespie argues for example that when the initial (pre-Harvard) Illumination Experiments commenced at Hawthorne in November 1924, both superintendents (e.g., George Pennock, Clarence Stoll) and researchers (e.g., Homer Hibarger, Charles E. Snow) alike were *already* aware that 'human factors could influence production and thereby interfere with the experimental results'. As a result, they 'did all they could to minimize this effect' (p.42). In contrast to the standard narrative of contemporary textbooks in organizational behaviour, Gillespie argues that the researchers were aware of a range of wider social-psychological influences on the experiments – such as the 'Hawthorne Effect' (French, 1950, p.82) – from the day the Studies began. Thus, such forces did not have to be 'discovered'. Recent research has noted, similarly, that when Mayo and the Harvard Group initially published their findings, industrial commentators such as Mary B. Gilson suggested that they had not actually 'discovered' anything that was not already widely known in American industry (see Gilson, 1940; Nyland and Bruce, 2012; Wrege and Greenwood, 1982).

With regard to the Harvard-influenced research, Gillespie also assesses the context in which the scientific discourse of the Mayo Group was produced. In the process, he questions the degree of intellectual integrity that the Hawthorne Studies narrative possessed. Gillespie suggests that the seemingly 'logical and unambiguous' narrative of 'scientific discovery' in Roethlisberger and Dickson (1939) was actually 'constructed' in the face of 'disagreements between the researchers over interpretation and meaning' (p.175). He describes how 'the factory site' for this evidential 'production process' was not so much 'the Hawthorne plant of Western Electric', but rather 'Elton

Mayo's Industrial Research Department at Harvard Business School' (p.175). In other words, as presented in *Management and the Worker* (Roethlisberger and Dickson, 1939), the narrative developed by Mayo's research group emerged as much from internal politics at Harvard as scientific evidence from Hawthorne.

A kindred line of analysis, but focussing on a wider set of contextual influences, is found in network-based research by O'Connor (1999) and Bruce and Nyland (2011). Both studies adopt an anti-revelatory or deconstructive stance through suggesting that Mayo's social networks and right-wing politics influenced the kinds of evidence claimed for by the Harvard Group. O'Connor's work, for example, documents the influence of Mayo's political ideology on the early development of the Human Relations School (HRS) at HBS. Identifying relationships between key members of the HBS-HRS social network – notably Wallace Donham, Dean of HBS, 1919–42; Beardsley Ruml, Director of the Laura Spelman Rockefeller Memorial fund (which funded Mayo's research); John D. Rockefeller Jr. (who backed Mayo's research amidst concerns over labour relations in his industrial empire: see Bottom, 2006); and Mayo himself – O'Connor (1999: p.117) describes how the HRS and HBS achieved success by 'positioning themselves as solutions to pressing social, economic, and political issues of the period between World War I and the New Deal'. She argues ultimately that this network facilitated 'the powerful alignment of the HRS and the HBS agendas in relationship to national, corporate and research agendas of the day' (p.117). Mayo's political ideology was successful in that it 'convinced business leaders that his agenda would solve their worries' (p.129) with this network of influence extending to the executives of the Western Electric Company. O'Connor's contribution can be summarized in the argument that: 'Scholars often note that Mayo entered the Hawthorne studies when they were already in progress. They note less that Mayo entered them at a time when his own ideas about politics and psychology were fully formed' (p.125) (see also Bourke, 1982).

Similarly Bruce and Nyland (2011) develop a network-based explanation of contextual forces influencing the work of Mayo and the Harvard Group, one underpinned by actor-network theory (see Latour, 2005). Their research complements O'Connor's (1999) through challenging the orthodox view that the HRS emerged in the interwar years 'as a response to the alleged inhumanity and simplistic innovation the Scientific Management tradition was striving to develop within the workplace'. In contrast, Bruce and Nyland argue that the HRS was in fact a 'right-wing and decidedly undemocratic innovation that was developed in response to the demand from organized labour that workers be ceded an active and significant part in management decision-making'. They describe how Mayo and the HRS were able to 'translate the prevailing context and in so doing create a forum in which powerful actors came to agree that the Human Relations school was an innovation worth building and defending'. Whereas O'Connor's analysis of the politics of achieving legitimacy focusses primarily on the relationship between the HRS and the HBS, for Bruce and Nyland (2011), it is the link between Mayo's work and the interests of key industrialists, notably John D. Rockefeller, Jr., that is critical. They illustrate how 'the meta-narrative regarding SM [scientific management] and HRS became the received wisdom' and in the process how 'conservative, anti-liberal segments of the American business community, seeking a return to the managerial hegemony they believed they enjoyed in the pre–New Deal era, stood to gain' (p.384). Ultimately, they question the extent to which 'Mayo's interpretation of the Hawthorne experiments was more reflective of his pre-formed personal views than of the actual empirical results', with such ideological predispositions serving to 'shade Roethlisberger and Dickson's "official" account' (p.385).

This chapter is directed similarly at promoting contextually-informed research on Hawthorne. The analytical trajectory is, however, different to that of Gillespie (1991), O'Connor (1999) and Bruce and Nyland (2011). Rather than focus on Elton Mayo and those connected to him, our investigation focusses instead on the reputation and culture of the host corporation in the period prior to and encompassing the Hawthorne Studies.

The emphasis is placed, primarily, on developing a concept of 'prior context', or considering the 'parts that immediately precede' an event or era and which serve to 'clarify its meaning' (Oxford Compact English Dictionary, 1996, p.212). We wish to acknowledge a number of excellent contributions that identify ideological and political factors relevant to our understanding of the Hawthorne Studies (e.g., Bendix, 1956; Gillespie, 1991; Rose, 1970), and other commendable accounts that explain important social networks linked to Hawthorne and the Harvard Group (see, e.g., Bruce and Nyland, 2011; Nyland and Bruce, 2012; O'Connor, 1999), as much as the Harvard-based offerings which first disseminated the Hawthorne findings (e.g., Mayo, 1933; Whitehead, 1938; Roethlisberger and Dickson, 1939 – quoted at the beginning of this section). The charge of contextual omission can be levelled at a major reanalysis of the Studies – Landsberger (1958) – as well as the principal biographical work linked to them, Trahair's (1984) study of Mayo. Even in Gillespie's (1991) analytically more rounded study of Hawthorne, contextual analysis is frequently restricted to details of factory organization, industrial relations systems and personnel policies. The broader industrial reputation and cultural character of the Works are factors not extensively explored. The present research, therefore, aims to resolve this problem by redirecting organization studies away from the well-documented *logic* of research at Hawthorne towards the less-familiar *context*. We do this not to specify direct causal links between contextual factors and events in a firm's history, but rather to describe, qualitatively, the culture, atmosphere and environment in which certain organizational factors emerged and were developed. Put simply, the objective is to provide a broader historical perspective on the company than is characteristically offered in the normative closed-system treatment of Hawthorne in management and organization studies.

TWO CONTEXTUAL CASES

To address this central objective, we develop two historical case accounts relevant to understanding, respectively, the corporate and cultural character of the enterprise.

The first case (the 'neglected corporate context') assesses the industrial reputation and corporate philosophy of the early Western Electric Company. In so doing, it draws information mainly from secondary sources, in the form of company histories and studies of American capitalism. The case is also informed by evidence from primary sources: for example, advertisements, catalogues, manuals and photographs. These were consulted during two visits to the Hawthorne Works Museum (Morton College, Cicero) in 2010. During these visits, assistance in locating materials was provided by the Docent of the Museum, a former Hawthorne Works manager. In addition, primary sources from the Western Electric and Hawthorne Studies collections at Baker Library, HBS, were consulted during a visit in 2011.

The second case (the 'neglected cultural context') focusses on the communal experience of Hawthorne employees and specifically the symbolic impact of a tragic event on the workforce and local community. The case is informed by a range of primary and secondary sources. Those of most significance were again made available by the Hawthorne Works Museum, and included internal company documents (letters, memos, notices, etc.), volumes of *Western Electric News* (1912–33), plus other in-company publications (e.g., *Hawthorne Microphone* and *Western Electric Magazine*). Assistance in their collection was again provided by the docent. Other materials consulted in developing this case include academic studies in maritime economics, research by Chicago local history societies, internet sites, and documents from the Baker Library collections.

Methodologically, these case accounts adopt respectively two approaches to historical research: 'historical deconstruction' and 'ethnographic history' (see Hassard and Rowlinson, 2010). They also reflect, principally, two sociological registers – macro and micro.

The first case focusses predominantly on the macro-level context of the firm, and notably issues of socio-economic and political environment. The analysis reflects 'historical deconstruction' in the emphasis placed on 'puncturing popular historical myths rather than in sustaining them' (Hassard and Rowlinson, 2010, p.9). In the first case, this underpins explanation of the distinctive character and profile of the Western Electric Company. As a research strategy, historical deconstruction ranges from straightforward debunking through to subtle appreciation of how histories are constructed (Evans, 1997). In management history, Charles Wrege is generally regarded as its foremost proponent (see Wrege and Greenwood, 1991; Wrege and Perroni, 1974).

The second case adopts a predominantly micro-level perspective and focusses on communal and symbolic factors influencing Western Electric at this time, notably the impact of a major tragedy on its management and workforce. This research reflects 'ethnographic history' through its concern with cultural events and their meaning/interpretation. Examples of ethnographic history in management and organization studies can be found in Childs' (2002) account of the management of slavery in the St John d'el Rey Mining Company, Brazil, and McKinlay's (2002) analysis of banking careers in Scotland before World War I. Ethnographic history is informed primarily by formal sources – such as board minutes, ledgers, annual reports, etc. – but can also draw upon informal materials, such as cartoons and doodles in McKinlay's work.[3]

Case A: The Neglected Corporate Context: The Bell System, Welfare Capitalism, and the Progressive Era

As the Company grows it must be more human – not less so.

Extract from: Policy #10, Employee Relations Policies, Hawthorne Works, Western Electric Company (May, 1924)

---

[3] Although these case accounts are directed at different historical ends, there are however instances of thematic overlap in their analysis. For example, certain issues of reputation and philosophy inform the case on 'cultural context', while themes of culture and symbolism inform the case on 'corporate context'. This is a largely inevitable bi-product of conducting qualitative historical research, where the emphasis is placed on broad issues of interpretation and meaning rather than the narrow control of variables (Green and Troup, 1999; Hassard and Rowlinson, 2010).

One of the reasons why the failure to consider contextual forces relating to the Hawthorne Works represents an oversight is that the Western Electric Company was a significant corporation in American industrial expansion. When management students first encounter the Hawthorne Studies, given they have probably never heard of Western Electric and receive little feeling for the company in available resources, it is understandable for them to assume this is an enterprise of marginal significance. Nothing could be further from the truth; Western Electric is important because it is woven deeply into the fabric of American industrial history.[4]

But just *how* prominent was the Western Electric Company? Before we examine a specific event that brought the firm to the world's attention, we assess its general corporate profile in the early decades of its history. To establish this, we trace landmark events and developments from the time the company joins the Bell System in 1881 up to the start of the Hawthorne investigations in 1924.

Western Electric and the Bell System. In accounting for the formative history of Western Electric, the year 1881 stands out, for this is when the inventor and patentee of the telephone, Alexander Graham Bell, purchased a controlling interest in the Western Electric Company of Chicago (Fagen, 1975). At this point, Western Electric officially joined the Bell 'System'.

The economic motivation was that since winning a legal battle over a patent with Western Union, Bell had experienced problems in meeting market demand. In particular, he had trouble in coordinating the activities of his three existing licensee manufacturers in

---

[4] Like other iconic manufacturers of the late nineteenth and early twentieth century, Western Electric was emblematic of the technical inventiveness, pioneering spirit and commercial power of the United States. Symbolically, nothing reflects this better than the corporation's masthead logo and trademark of the period – *The Genius of Electricity* (or *'Golden Boy'*). Designed in 1916 by Evelyn Longman, to symbolize the telephone as a modern messenger, this Mercurial figure sees a naked, muscular, white male, wrapped in thick electrical cable, grasping three bolts of lightning, and standing aloft a modest globe, the American corporation as capitalist god (Hawthorne Works Museum, 2010).

Baltimore, Chicago and Cincinnati (Brookes, 1976). Bell sought a single manufacturer with the capability for handling mass demand and found it in Western Electric, which at the time was America's largest manufacturer of electrical products (Reich, 1985). Western Electric thus became the exclusive manufacturer of telephones in the US for the American Bell Telephone Company, which in 1899 would become AT&T (Fagen, 1975).

As his original telephone patent was due to expire in 1894, Bell proposed to source inventions and patents increasingly from outside concerns in order to bolster the company's innovative capacities (Reich, 1985). This strategic decision would see Western Electric's engineering departments initially forced to concentrate on 'adaptation and improvement' rather than 'invention and creation' (Adams and Butler, 1999). In 1907, however, a significant change of policy saw proposals to develop a 'research branch' of Western Electric, a move which would usher in a period of major technological breakthroughs for the firm (Israel, 1992). Notable among them was development of the high vacuum tube in 1913, which basically brought with it the 'electronic age', with Western Electric emphasising the fact in advertisements depicting, for example, 'My Electrical Home' (Hawthorne Works Museum, 2010). Another signal development during this period saw the expanding research operation at Hawthorne create technology that would make transcontinental telephony a reality, from 1914 (Brookes, 1976).

The Hawthorne Works, Welfare Capitalism and AT&T. In terms of the evolution of the Hawthorne Works itself, on 14 September 1902, Western Electric purchased 113 acres of prairie land west of Chicago (Whyte, 1977). Three years later, founder and still president, Enos Barton, advocated relocating the company's main manufacturing facility from downtown Chicago to this rural setting near the small town of Hawthorne, later incorporated into Cicero (see Kay, 2000).

The Hawthorne plant, which officially opened in 1907, soon developed a reputation within American industry as a champion of 'welfare capitalism', or the practice of businesses providing welfare-like services to employees (Jacoby, 1997). Under welfare capitalism, companies would typically offer workers higher pay and superior non-monetary compensation (such as health care, housing, and pensions, plus possibly social clubs, sports facilities, and in-house training) than what was available from other firms in the industry (Brandes, 1976). However, there was a price to be paid, for much of the strategic thinking behind it was that higher levels of compensation and welfare would act as a bulwark against the rise of organized labour. In the case of Hawthorne, the provision of such welfare policies and practices was writ large. The Works became virtually a city in its own right – containing a hospital, power plant, fire brigade and evening school (the 'Hawthorne University'), as well as a gymnasium, running track, baseball team, greenhouse, brass band, magazine and an annual pageant, which ran until 1980. Many events were run by the Hawthorne Club, which organized dances, concerts, sports, parties and the annual picnic (Hawthorne Works Museum, 2010).

By 1914, the Hawthorne Works had expanded to become Western Electric's sole manufacturing site, having absorbed the company's other facilities in New York and Chicago (Fagen, 1975). Despite later opening smaller plants in other locations, from this point on, as Whyte (1977, p.23) suggests, 'the story of Hawthorne is practically the story of Western Electric'. A year later, the Western Electric Manufacturing Company was incorporated in New York as a wholly owned subsidiary of AT&T, under the name Western Electric Company, Inc. At this time, in locations where AT&T subsidiaries provided the local service – which was the vast majority (Fagen, 1975) – all components and connected devices of the 'public switched telephone network' were manufactured by Western Electric (Brookes, 1976).

Complement, Community and Culture. In terms of the size and composition of workforce, by 1917, 25,000 people were employed at the expanding Hawthorne Works, with a large percentage being local residents of Czech, Hungarian or Polish origin (mostly first or second generation immigrants). As aerial photographs of the period suggest, the plant dwarfed Cicero itself, whose population in 1910 was 15,000 (Kay, 2000). The firm held a virtual monopoly in its industry, which some commentators suggest served to buttress its sense of social unity (Adams and Butler, 1999).

Although many Hawthorne employees commuted to work from Chicago or suburbs such as Berwyn, LaGrange, Morton Park, Oak Park and Riverside, a large percentage of the workforce resided within a mile or so of the Works (Whyte, 1977). Local historical societies suggest that as Hawthorne employees were frequently 'neighbours at home as well as co-workers', this fostered a 'family culture' in which ethnicity, in particular, was 'a common denominator that helped galvanize relationships among employees' (Wachholz, 2005, p.24–6). Indeed, most Hawthorne employees experienced a common work-life pattern, living within a 15-minute walk of the plant and residing in rows of workers' 'cottages' at a rent of $15–20 per month (Wachholz, 2005). Even when employees resided further afield, 'life experiences were common' (Lindberg, 1997, p.17), with the working day bounded by the cheap commute on the streetcar – the '5 cent "El" ride' (Whyte, 1977, p.22).

Another distinguishing feature of this communal profile was that Western Electric employed a relatively large percentage of women workers (even before women's suffrage). Although having no significant role in managerial or supervisory work, there were women operatives in most manufacturing areas of the plant, and notably those sections where 'delicacy of touch', and 'carefulness', was valued for performing intricate tasks, such as coil winding (Wachholz, 2005, p.26). A feature of early company picnics was of a large group of Hawthorne women workers (known colloquially as the 'window smashers') marching and wearing 'Votes for Women' sashes (Adams and Butler, 1999, p.94).

Under the company philosophy of welfare capitalism, a Women's Club was opened in late 1912, one year after the Men's. Wachholz (2005, p.26) suggests that the Women's Club allowed women to participate in Hawthorne's wider welfare activities – such as education programmes, entertainment, and sports – this including roles in the organization of employee picnics (see later). The Hawthorne plant was indeed the 'social center' (Whyte, 1977, p.22) for the surrounding community, and its clubs were 'enormously popular' among 'the large number of young men and women and those who lived in the working-class suburbs adjacent to the works' (Gillespie, 1991, p.19).

The 'Progressive' Era. In terms of the political and ideological context, this was the time of the Progressive Era presidencies of Roosevelt, Taft and Wilson, an era characterized by social activism and the movement's desire to moderate the excesses of corporate capitalism (Glad, 1966). Noted for its antitrust sentiments, stress on efficiency and faith in experts, the Progressive Movement emphasized above all the 'welfare of the individual' (Buenker et al., 1986).

Reflecting such ideology, during August 1912 Magnus Alexander, (President of General Electric) sent the text of a speech he had given to the American Academy of Political and Social Science to Theodore Vail (President of AT&T) in which he drew 'particular attention' to the potential for creating a 'Department of Applied Economics, which might be more properly be called a Department of Applied Psychology' (Adams and Butler, 1999, p.89). In Alexander's words, the goal of such a department would be to 'apply the same scientific, calculated and sagacious study to the *human needs* in industry that are now applied everywhere to the engineering, selling, financial and purchasing requirements' (Adams and Butler 1999, p.89; emphasis added). In September 1912, Vail's associate, Walter Allen, suggested (with perhaps an element of cynicism) that establishing such departments within the Bell System would, 'benefit the companies in their general public relations by convincing the public that the management has really at heart the *human side* of the business and is striving to better conditions in industry' (Adams and Butler 1999, p.89–90; emphasis added).

In any event, the following year, AT&T announced the creation of the Bell System 'Benefit and Insurance Plan'. Although implementation of employee welfare plans had commenced in 1906 – with a modest pension scheme aimed at 'help(ing) the company attract and retain workers and discourage them from striking' – the introduction of a welfare plan throughout the Bell System was useful in that it assisted the corporation in convincing its political masters that Bell (a virtual monopoly) was 'socially responsible' (Gillespie 1991, p.8). Whether or not the motives of corporations practicing such welfare capitalism were genuinely 'progressive' remains moot (see Ebbinghaus and Manow, 2001; Hicks, 1999; Tone, 1997). What is certain, however, is that by the early 1920s, Western Electric's Hawthorne Works was an archetypal 'modern manor' (Jacoby, 1997).

Expansion, Innovation and Profile. In the period preceding the Hawthorne Studies, Western Electric was also one of the major distributors of electrical equipment in America (Fagen, 1975). In line with the huge expansion of demand for such goods, the company even supplied a wide range of items manufactured by other firms. This saw distribution not only of standard equipment for the home – such as refrigerators, sewing machines, electric fans, vacuum cleaners, etc. – but also of less standard items, such as electric toys (Hawthorne Works Museum, 2010).

Around the start of the Hawthorne investigations (late 1924), Western Electric had a catalogue approaching 1300 pages and rivalled General Electric and Westinghouse as a manufacturer and distributor (Fagen, 1975). With a workforce of over 30,000 employees (Kay, 2000), the company had expanded its initial welfare capitalist practices and was recognized (according to local history and in-company sources) as a provider of above-average wages, good working conditions, and valued fringe benefits (Hawthorne Works Museum, 2010; Wachholz, 2005; Whyte, 1977). It promoted, paternalistically, 'an informal cradle to grave covenant between employer and employee' (Adams and Butler, 1999, p.98). Arguably the major plank of the Bell System by the mid-1920s, Western Electric was a corporation of 'high public profile'; one that had applied 'the new personnel policies to an extent unsurpassed by any other company' (Gillespie, 1991, p.17).

Finally, shortly after the Hawthorne investigations commenced, a restructuring exercise by AT&T, in 1925, saw the founding of Bell Telephone Laboratories, Inc. This body absorbed much of the research and development work previously carried out by Western Electric's engineering department (Reich, 1985). 'Bell Labs', as it became known, would be owned 50:50 by Western Electric and AT&T, with this reorganization establishing institutional responsibilities which lasted until the 1980s. At this time, the Bell System largely functioned thus: Bell Labs designed the network; Western Electric manufactured the telephones, cables, transmission equipment, switching equipment, and installed the phones; the Operating Companies billed the customers; and AT&T ran the long-distance network (Fagen, 1978; Page, 1941). Ultimately, Western Electric and Bell Labs would invent the loudspeaker, bring sound to motion pictures, win a Nobel Prize for the invention of the transistor and introduce systems of mobile communications which would culminate in the cellular telephone (Fagen 1975, 1978; Hawthorne Works Museum, 2010; Israel, 1992).

During its formative history, therefore, and notably the period immediately preceding and encompassing the start of the Hawthorne Studies, the Western Electric Company had achieved significant corporate profile, developing a reputation for technological innovation and mass manufacturing capability. In addition, it was a signally paternalistic enterprise and major sponsor of welfare capitalism, with such policies and practices facilitating an image that it was a 'progressive' employer.

Case B: The Neglected Cultural Context: The Eastland Disaster, Communal Experience and Organizational Symbolism

> We are the victims of a disaster so awful that the world has stood aghast at its horrors, even in this year of horrors.
>
> H. B. Thayer, President, Western Electric Company; Western Electric News, (1915a: 1)

The second case account of neglected context concerns social organization and communal experience. Specifically, we develop an ethnographic perspective to document the impact of a tragic event on the Hawthorne plant, its workforce and the local community. More than any other, this incident serves to define the character and constitution of the Works in the period preceding the Hawthorne investigations.

This case revolves around a tragedy – the *SS Eastland* disaster – on the Chicago River during the Hawthorne Works Employees' Annual Picnic of July 1915, an event not discussed or referenced in any of the primary research accounts of the Hawthorne Studies (e.g., Mayo, 1933; Roethlisberger and Dickson, 1939; Whitehead, 1938). This was, however, the most notable event in the formative history of the Works, one that brought Western Electric to the world's attention. While the incident had a profound effect on 'Chicago's developing social fabric' (Bonansinga, 2004, p.240) and served to 'scar the collective memory of the metropolitan area' (Hilton, 1995, p.234), it was however a largely 'neighbourhood affair', with the main impact being on the 'communities near the Hawthorne plant, Berwyn and Cicero' (Adams and Butler, 1999, p.90). In what follows, details of the disaster are presented alongside discussion of how it affected the workforce and local community. The case also assesses how Western Electric symbolically managed the aftermath, with this issue being considered further in the Analysis and Discussion section.

The Hawthorne Works Picnic and its Expansion. The history of the 'Hawthorne Works Employees' Fifth Annual Picnic' is that on 24 July 1915, the Western Electric Employees' Association chartered five Great Lakes passenger steamers to carry almost 7,000 employees, their relatives and friends on a four-hour excursion from Chicago to Michigan City, Indiana. This had been an annual event since 1911 and was considered *the* social outing of the year for a young workforce of predominantly immigrant origin engaged in repetitive telephone assembly work (*Western Electric News*, 1915b).

The number of employees attending the annual picnic began to increase significantly from 1913. Following attendance by approximately 3,500 for the first two years, in 1913, it increased to over 6,000. The main reason was that the picnic shifted its focus from inviting the immediate family of employees to members of the extended family (*Western Electric News*, 1915b). In a rather gendered statement, Hawthorne publicity for the 1914 picnic declared, for example: 'Bring along her mother and her sister and her sister's youngsters. Make a family party of it' (Hawthorne Works Museum, 2010). This expansion, however, brought with it the need to provide additional transport capacity, and in being a maritime outing, to charter an additional vessel for the voyage across Lake Michigan. For the 1914 excursion, therefore, an extra ship was hired, the *SS Eastland* (*Western Electric News*, 1915b).

One year later, the 1915 picnic was organized by the newly formed Hawthorne Club (or Western Electric Employees' Association) which had been created from the merger of the Men's and Women's clubs in April (Whyte, 1977). For the 1915 event, the Hawthorne Club established a formal structure for organizing the event. This saw employees encouraged to take part in various aspects of the process, joining committees such as: 'Program, Judges, Prizes, Beach, Dancing, Tug-of-War, Central, Honorary, General, Amusement, Picnic, Transportation, Tickets, Photographic, Reception, Grounds, Publicity, Music, Athletics, and Races' (Wachholz, 2005, p.28). The destination for the 1915 picnic was Washington Park, Michigan City, which offered a range of facilities appropriate to the event, including a baseball park, roller coaster, electric merry-go-round, dancing pavilion, bowling alley, amusement park, bathing beach and picnic grounds (Wachholz, 2005). The outing was arranged such that, after disembarking at Michigan City, passengers would partake of a 'pot-luck' picnic and then engage in various activities organized by the committees. Although the Hawthorne plant normally operated for six days a week, it was closed for the Saturday of these annual festivities, always the last in July (*Western Electric News*, 1915b).

The SS Eastland. The background to the tragedy of the 1915 Works Picnic was a series of events relating to the aforementioned *SS*

Eastland. In wake of the 1912 sinking of the *RMS Titanic*, the LaFollette Seamen's Act (1915) was passed mandating 'lifeboats for all'. In the case of Great Lakes passenger ships, this would see additional lifeboats and rafts fitted, despite advice that this could cause some vessels stability problems. Indeed, for at least one of the steamers hired for the event, the *Eastland*, a boat that sat relatively high in the water, this would make her potentially unstable (Hilton, 1995).[5]

On the morning of Saturday, 25 July 1915, Hawthorne Works employees and their families boarded the *Eastland* on the south bank of the Chicago River, downtown between Clark and Lasalle Streets (*Western Electric News*, 1915b and c). People had not been allocated to specific ships and there were no passenger lists. The *Eastland* was scheduled to be the first vessel to depart and by around seven o'clock, 2,752 passengers had boarded (Hilton, 1995). With many passengers initially standing on the wharf side to wave to friends, but subsequently moving to the river side to observe the view, the *Eastland* began to list initially towards the wharf and then the river (*Western Electric News*, 1915c). Attempts to stabilize the vessel by adding water to the ballast tanks failed to remedy the problem (Hilton, 1995).

During the next quarter of an hour, possibly due to passengers wishing to observe a canoe race, an additional number moved to the river side (Bonansinga, 2004). One suggestion is that this caused further listing and allowed water to pour in from portholes on the main deck, causing furniture and passengers to slide (*Western Electric*

---

[5] The *Eastland*, a large luxury vessel known as the 'Speed Queen of the Lakes', was suspected of possessing design flaws which made her susceptible to listing (Bonansinga, 2004). In particular, the centre of gravity was unduly high, making the boat potentially top-heavy when passengers gathered on the upper decks (Hilton, 1995). An incident of overcrowding in July 1903 saw the *Eastland* list and water flow up one of her gangplanks. Although the problem was resolved, a further case of listing occurred in 1906, this time resulting in formal complaints being registered against the owners (Hilton, 1995). In an attempt to correct *Eastland*'s listing tendencies, its licensed capacity was reduced several times: from 3,300 passengers down to 2,800, then 2,400, and finally 1,125. However just three weeks before the 1915 Hawthorne Works picnic, inspectors increased the capacity to 2,500 (Hilton, 1995).

News, 1915c). (Counter-arguments, however, question elements of this scenario: see Hilton 1995, p.234–5.) In any event, ten minutes after the gangplank had been drawn in and when the *Eastland* began to push off from Clark Street dock, the vessel lurched, rolled and capsized, resting on the river bottom, which was only twenty feet beneath the surface (Hilton, 1995). Given that a large number of passengers had already moved below decks ('It had begun to drizzle ... and the mothers had taken their children inside': *Western Electric News*, 1915d, p.20) hundreds became trapped due to the sudden capsizing of the vessel. Despite an immediate response by the tugboat *Kenosha* and the fact that the vessel was still partially tied to its mooring, 841 passengers (mainly women and children) and four crew members perished, the death toll including 22 whole families. This represented the greatest loss of life in Chicago's history, America's worst maritime disaster, and for Western Electric, 'the greatest tragedy that has ever befallen organized industry' (*Western Electric News*, 1915e, p.16).

Impact, Aftermath and Symbolism. In the days following the tragedy, Western Electric made little effort to operate the Hawthorne plant (*Western Electric News*, 1915b). On Monday 27th, a few hundred employees turned up for work followed by a few thousand on Tuesday. By the end of Tuesday 28th, Western Electric had turned away around 800 local residents offering to fill the jobs of victims (Adams and Butler, 1999). Wednesday 29th saw the day of the greatest number of funerals and was declared an official day of mourning by the company; the main entrance gates were draped in black. All but very essential employees were excused from work in order to attend the many services held in Illinois and cities across the United States. *En masse*, Western Electric's senior management team attended a special memorial service in Chicago (*Western Electric News*, 1915b).

Historians have described the impact of the incident on the Chicago metropolitan area (Hilton, 1995) and in particular on the western suburbs around Cicero (Kay, 2000; Wachholz, 2005). Within the Hawthorne plant itself, 'survivor stories' (*Western Electric News*,

1915c) recounted acts of heroism performed by the crews of the *Kenosha* and freighter *Schuylkill*, the Coast Guard, frogmen and divers, doctors and nurses, members of the public and Hawthorne employees themselves. In accounting for the tragedy in the *Western Electric News*, however, the company suggested, rather paternalistically, that it did not wish to 'single out any individual for personal mention' as this could be 'unfair to the rest' (1915b, p.8). As survivors of the *Eastland* continued to work at Hawthorne for several decades, this preserved the disaster in the company's oral history (Whyte, 1977). Indeed, the last known survivor of the *Eastland*, Libby Hruby, daughter of a Czech immigrant employee, died locally in Berwyn as late as 6 November 2004 (Archiver.rootsweb.ancestry.com, 2011).

Sources also describe the role Western Electric played in the relief effort (see Hilton, 1995; Wachholz, 2005; *Western Electric News*, 1915b). Meeting with officials of the City and the Red Cross at City Hall the following morning, the company's senior executives agreed to raise $200,000 within 48 hours. In addition, Western Electric offered a $100,000 subsidy to the relief initiative. Ultimately, both figures were over-subscribed. Of the corporation's initial subsidy, $75,806 was spent on funeral expenses (Hilton, 1995). Wider action saw Western Electric make its medical, nursing and welfare staffs available to survivors and the families of victims, with treatment being offered at either the Hawthorne plant or by way of house calls (*Western Electric News*, 1915b, d, and f).

In early August 1915, Alexander Graham Bell, who had been retired from the telephone business for a number of years, but still held considerable stock in AT&T and Western Electric, accompanied his wife Mabel on a visit to the Hawthorne Works (Inficad.com, 2011). During the visit, the Bells reputedly stopped at each work station, shook hands with employees and discussed the disaster and how it had affected them. Sources suggest that Mabel Bell took details of employees who had perished together with the names and addresses of family members affected by the tragedy. These individuals subsequently received notes of condolence and personal gifts from the Bells (Inficad.com, 2011). This visit was followed by a period of recruitment in which Western Electric adopted a policy of favouring victims' relatives when assessing employment applications (Adams and Butler, 1999).

Although more passengers perished on the *Eastland* (841) than the *Titanic* (832), after initial media coverage, the event began to fade from national attention. Among the possible reasons are that the incident was overshadowed by the more global news coverage of World War I or that the City of Chicago did not want negative media coverage and so suppressed the incident (Hilton, 1995). Another possible explanation, however, is that as those who perished were predominantly working class immigrants – mainly women and children – they represented actors with relatively little 'voice'. Unlike the *Titanic*, the *Eastland* did not claim the wealthy or famous, nor did any of Western Electric's executives perish.

In the years that followed the tragedy, there appears a subtle change of register in what might be called the social emphasis of the firm. One example is that from 1918, Western Electric started to make a series of 'industrials' – short films about the nature of the business. As Wrege (2008, p.2) has noted, several of these films (e.g., *People and Productivity* and *A Square Deal for His Wife*) were markedly 'people oriented' and appear socially enlightened for the time.[6] Indeed this was a period in which Western seemed keener than ever to emphasize its 'Square Deal Policy' for employees – a policy in which 'practices have been worked out to make things convenient and pleasant for every member of the great Western Electric family' (Albright, 1917, p.29). Another subtle change around this time saw the sub-title of *Western Electric News* change from: 'Produced Once a Month for the Employees' to 'The Employees' Magazine'.

In the early decades of Western Electric's history, therefore, the *Eastland* tragedy served to bring sociological profile to an organization that already possessed a significant industrial reputation. Above all,

---

[6] Wrege (2008) suggests that a decade or so later, Western Electric policy changed to making predominantly business-oriented (or 'promotional') films.

the event served to galvanize the workforce, bring clarity to social and organizational relations and make overt a range of cultural and symbolic forces within the enterprise. These are factors that have yet to be fully accounted for in historical readings of Hawthorne.

REANALYSING HAWTHORNE

These twin cases offer contextual information relevant to understanding the character and culture of Western Electric's Hawthorne Works during the early decades of the twentieth century. In terms of organizational research, they identify neglected 'actors' in the company's 'network of meaning' (see Bruce and Nyland, 2011; Mills and Durepos, 2010). The first case illustrates how Western Electric had developed a distinctive corporate and industrial profile, and the second, how the social and cultural awareness of its workforce was impacted by a major human tragedy. Taken together, they counter the traditional practice of explaining organizational behaviour at Hawthorne within a contextual vacuum.

Corporate Philosophy and Reputation

Through initially analysing corporate philosophy and reputation, it has been argued that during the early twentieth century, Western Electric was a prominent employer. We have illustrated how this decidedly paternalistic company, a major player in the Bell System, possessed 'high public profile'. In addition to its transcendent reputation for technical innovation, we note how, from its opening in 1907, the Hawthorne facility had a considerable reputation for promoting welfare policies and practices. Describing a photograph of the Hawthorne Club track and field meet of 1927, Gillespie (1991, p.20) suggests this represents 'welfare capitalism at its peak'; this picture was taken less than a year before Elton Mayo first entered the Works. An organization renowned for technological advances and possessing state-of-the-art facilities, in the years preceding the Hawthorne investigations, the Western Electric Company was also known for practicing the 'new personnel policies', for which its standing was apparently 'unsurpassed'. In addition, it was avowedly anti-union and deployed a range of measures (overt and covert) for combating the combination of workers.

It can be argued, however, that such a corporate style was not only the result of 'strategic choice' (Child 1972), but also determined by industrial and sectoral 'contingencies' (Burns and Stalker, 1961, Lawrence and Lorsch 1967). Although many American corporations of the early twentieth century received prominence for promoting apparently 'progressive' employment practices, this was nowhere more evident than for 'science-based firms such as those in the electrical manufacturing industry' (Adams and Butler, 1999, p.97). As Jacoby (1997, p.20) suggests, in many high technology companies of the period, forms of welfare-influenced organization, incorporating an emphasis on 'progressive' forms of employment, had gained 'the aura of technological inevitability'.

Likewise, reflecting Walter Allen's 'applied psychology' proposals for Bell companies a decade earlier, psychologist Robert Yerkes (1922, p.56–7) in a speech to the National Research Council outlined the shift in personnel research from 'things that are worked with, to the worker; from the machinery of industry, to the man who made, owns, or operates it'. Yerkes' speech suggests that employee psychology and well-being were on the personnel research agenda years before Mayo exploited his significant Rockefeller support at Hawthorne. This resonates with Gilson's (1940, p.98) review of Roethlisberger and Dickson (1939), which suggests that the Hawthorne Studies 'operated at the kindergarten stage of industrial knowledge', in that it they had 'consumed years to discover' notions that 'should have been clear at the outset if the investigators had acquainted themselves with the experiences of others'.

Further, Bendix (1956, p.311) notes how, in the years preceding the Hawthorne investigations, many managers had 'anticipated Mayo with regard to a reassessment of the motivations of workers', and indeed that during the early 1920s, 'several writers had pointed out that it was wrong to think workers were only interested in money'.

Bendix comments on how many of Mayo's sentiments appear to have been rehearsed in the earlier 'Open-shop' campaign, which like Mayo tended ideologically to 'neglect ... trades unions and their role in industry'. Indeed, Bendix argues that employees involved with the campaign directed their attentions to 'introducing many measures designed to forestall [unions] by satisfying the demands of workers in line with managerial objectives', the campaign thus reflecting many of the motives of welfare capitalism.

In her critique of *Management and the Worker*, Gilson (1940, p.100–1) similarly draws attention to the failure of Roethlisberger and Dickson (1939) (and thus the Hawthorne research team as a whole) to discuss the issue of labour unions. She argues that in 'six hundred pages describing the Western Electric experiment, costing thousands of dollars, and supported by some of the wealthiest groups in the country, no reference is made to organized labour except a short statement, unindexed, that it was so seldom mentioned by any workers that it was not considered sufficiently important to discuss'. Gilson adds that the deployment of internal spies by Hawthorne's management – designed to identify labour activists amidst industrial uncertainty from the late 1920s – may be one of the reasons why in the twenty thousand-plus interviews of the plant-wide Interview Program (1928–30) workers were reported to have 'criticised the company in no instance'. She suggests 'we know of no instance where spies have been employed without some fear of unionism'. Indeed, the 1937 [US Senate] Committee on Education and Labor noted how from 1933 to 1936, Western Electric spent $25,825.76 on such espionage (see Gilson, 1940, p.100).

Such factors may provide explanation for why founder Enos Barton and the early directors of the Western Electric Company put so much effort into establishing welfare capitalism at Hawthorne – to shore up a particular form of liberal political economy by appearing to create 'capitalism with a human face'. Although in terms of American industry as a whole, Western Electric's seemingly enlightened organizational practices were perhaps atypical (c.f. the early working conditions and industrial relations climate at Ford's Highland Park and

Rouge plants), they were nevertheless taking place in an ideological climate where such deliberate paternalism was not completely unheard of. This perhaps suggests a hypothesis for management history to explore: that Western Electric's highly paternalistic climate provided a particularly congenial environment for Mayo and his colleagues to conduct their research (see Whitehead, 1938, p.13, on this point).[7]

Indeed, in May 1924, six months prior to the start of the Illumination experiments and four years before any Harvard involvement, the Hawthorne personnel function had issued to employees responsible for 'directing the work of others' a statement of the company's Employee Relations Policies, commonly referred to as the 'Ten Commandments'. Completing a list of similar homilies, the last exhorts managers and supervisors to: '*Carry on the daily work in a spirit of friendliness. As the Company grows it must be more human – not less so*' (Extract from: Policy # 10, Employee Relations Policies, Hawthorne Works, Western Electric Company, May 1924: emphasis in original).

By the mid-1920s, therefore, if 'social man' (Mayo, 1933; see also Dingley, 1997; Rose, 1970) had not yet been discovered in *theory* at the Hawthorne Works, for a range of ideological and commercial motives, Western Electric's management was already minded to meet his 'human relations' needs in *practice*. Politically, it can be argued that Mayo – well-known as an anti-union academic (Bendix, 1956; Trahair, 1984) and someone 'shrewdly tuned in to what he believed his benefactor [John D. Rockefeller Jr.] wanted to hear' (Bruce and Nyland, 2011, p.391) – was readily disposed towards Western Electric's strategic paternalism. Contrary to the orthodox narrative of management

---

[7] This should not be read, however, as characterizing Hawthorne as a 'workers' paradise' at this time. Apart from the use of in-house spies, there is evidence for example of the company making restrooms uncomfortable (i.e., lack of heating in winter; lack of ventilation in summer) so that employees would return to work quicker (Charles Wrege: personal communication). This perhaps resonates with the image of the industrial restroom as portrayed in Charlie Chaplin's film *Modern Times*. The local nickname for the plant, after all, was the 'Bohemian Bastille'!

and organization studies, which suggests a theoretical and practical paradigm-shift in the wake of behavioural experimentation, the impression from this research is that Mayo and his team *did not so much turn the sociological tide at Hawthorne as swim briskly with it.* Indeed, Roethlisberger and Dickson (1939, p.540), in a rare reference to Western Electric's cultural evolution suggest that 'perhaps the secret of this company's favourable history of industrial relations lies in the fact that it possesses a remarkable number of social processes by means of which the individual is integrated or identified with the collective whole'. They go on to acknowledge that 'a large number of these integrating factors were to be found in the activities sponsored by the Hawthorne Club' (Roethlisberger and Dickson, 1939, p.540), a key arm of Western Electric's welfare capitalism and a strategic bulwark against unionization.

It can be argued further that the union of Western Electric and Elton Mayo's Harvard Group – brokered by the influential network of John D. Rockefeller Jr. – was to prove a genuinely symbiotic one. Both would profit significantly from the reputation the Hawthorne Studies were to bring. Whilst Mayo and his colleagues, through their long-term access to and involvement with Western Electric, could bask in the glory of discovering a new management model, 'social man', the corporation could build on its reputation for progressive polices and employee welfare through the profile gained from a wealth of publications (three books and 33 articles by the Harvard Group between 1929 and 1939) on humanistic 'discoveries' at Hawthorne. Indeed, one of the original reasons why Western Electric executives had approached HBS for assistance with the Hawthorne Studies programme was that personnel director T. K. Stevenson had been impressed by Mayo as a 'communicator', following a talk he had given on 'What Psychology Can Do for Industry in the Next Ten Years' to an executive lunch at the Harvard Club in October 1927 (Trahair 1984, p.208).

Thus while evidence suggests that Western Electric was undoubtedly 'scientifically' managed in the period prior to the Hawthorne investigations (see Adams and Butler, 1999, p.78–80), this is not the whole story, for the company also emphasized, for a number of reasons, 'human relations' style philosophies through its strategic paternalism and welfare capitalism. Before Elton Mayo's time at the plant, the Hawthorne Works was already providing many of the classic ingredients of a human relations approach to workforce management – through media for satisfying social needs (e.g., social clubs, sports teams), providing facilities for personal development (e.g., the 'Hawthorne University') and devising policies for making the organization 'more human' (e.g., the 'Ten Commandments'). The narratives of contemporary textbooks on management and organization fail to take such factors into account. Sociologically, although Braverman's (1974) well-known suggestion is that the Human Relations School functioned as the 'maintenance crew' for Scientific Management – psychologically oiling its exploitative economic wheels – another evolutionary explanation is that the doctrine of 'human relations' ultimately functioned as a *modernizing agent for welfare capitalism*. For many industrialists, the appeal of the Human Relations School's constellation of job-based development and enrichment practices possibly lay in providing a watered-down well-being for firms not or no longer willing to support the full menu of welfare capitalist services in order to avoid labour turnover and unionization.

Cultural Experience and Identity

If the first case illustrated macro themes of corporate reputation and philosophy, the second focussed mainly on micro issues of cultural experience and identity. Specifically, the latter case described the impact of a major tragedy on Western Electric, its workers and the local community. In so doing, the case has not only offered insights into the habitus or life-world of Western Electric's employees, but also the symbolism of how the company handled the aftermath of a traumatic event.

To appreciate the cultural context of the Hawthorne Works at this time, an argument is made for revealing, ethnographically, the impact of critical incidents such as *Eastland* on the corporation's social fabric. This case suggests that the essence of organizational relationships is often revealed during moments of social crisis (Erikson, 1976). In contrast to so-called orthodox or mainstream analyses of Hawthorne in organization studies, which focus primarily on empirical data and their evaluation, this research highlights factors and forces whose influence extends beyond the work of Elton Mayo and the Harvard Group.

In making this argument, a focus of investigation has been the character of those working-class communities that bordered the Hawthorne plant and provided the mainstay of its labour force. This has been explored in relation to what, for Western Electric, was the most notorious event in its history – the tragedy of the Works Fifth Annual Picnic, which crystallized issues of social organization and communal experience. In the wake of this tragedy, the well-publicized relief actions of Western Electric and the high-profile visit by the Bells appeared to place the symbolic accent even more firmly on paternalism and welfare.

We have shown how the *Eastland* disaster and its aftermath were consumed primarily by Hawthorne's largely ethnic working communities. At the turn of the twentieth century, one-fourth of America's labour force was foreign-born, including half of all unskilled workers (Jacoby, 1985). When early social scientists at the University of Chicago, such as Jane Addams and Florence Kelley, conducted their 'social surveys', they found astounding cultural variety in the neighbourhoods of Chicago (see Elshtain, 2002; Sklar, 1995). It was such ethnically diverse communities that came together to chase the utopianism of the 'American dream'.

Hawthorne represented a similar social experiment. Sociologically, it reflected the co-existence of cultural groups facing what Mary Parker Follett called the 'dynamics of integration' (see O'Connor, 2011). For example, the establishment of the Hawthorne Evening School saw Western Electric incorporate an education programme for immigrant workers that had previously taken place at Jane Addams' settlement complex, Hull House (near Western's earlier

Clinton Street facility). From around the turn of the century, this arrangement had seen Hull House submit monthly accounts to Enos Barton, with the system reflecting 'a primitive form of welfare capitalism' (Adams and Butler, 1999, p.95). Indeed, Western Electric's provident funds, together with the development of the Hawthorne Club's educational and recreational programmes, 'essentially institutionalised the paternalism of Enos Barton ... at Hawthorne' (p.96).

A key contextual factor highlighted by the *Eastland* tragedy, therefore, is the cultural experience of the Hawthorne workforce, an issue that brings into focus the values, goals and motives of ethnic communities. Hawthorne comprised a diverse workforce, but its distinctive social and organizational history engendered a heightened sense of solidarity. Kai Erikson's famous remark that in the face of major disasters (such as *Eastland*) it is 'the *community* that cushions pain ... represents morality and serves as the repository for old traditions' (1976, p.193, emphasis in original) appears to fit Hawthorne well. The research presented here suggests that crucial to understanding the cultural fabric of the Works is comprehension of the demographic character and communal experience of its workforce, or what Roethlisberger and Dickson (1939, p.538) refer to as its 'social organization'.

For ethnographic history, appreciation of the social organization of the Hawthorne plant requires awareness of the cultural preferences of ethnic communities at this time. A good starting point is the anthropological and sociological literature on 'ethnic Chicago' (see Lindberg, 1997). If we take, for example, the sizeable Czech community at Hawthorne, we find that in the Chicago of the early twentieth century, it was residing in what was now the world's third largest Czech city (after Prague and Vienna), one that, by the 1920s, boasted four Czech-language newspapers (Cozine, 2005). Politically, Czechs tended to support the Democrats, with this support peaking on the election of Anton Cermak, a Czech immigrant, as the Democratic mayor of Chicago in 1931 (Gotfried, 1962). Socio-economically, the Czech community in Chicago had established its own network of institutions, including savings and loan associations, mutual benefit societies, and fraternal organizations (Lindberg, 1997). More prosaically, such first and second generation immigrants (and notably working women) provided regular support for family networks in their country of ethnic origin (Baker Library, 2011). Hogan (1978) and Weiss (1981), suggest that transplanted peasant culture – which emphasized family collectivism, religious devotion and attitudes towards the value of money – affected workplace relations at sites like Hawthorne. Above all, in terms of personal preferences, this literature suggests that 'by the 1910s and 1920s', Czech workers in Chicago 'earned more and worked at a wider range of occupations', with an important corollary for this research being that 'as operatives at Western Electric', their energies were 'devoted more to ethnic and neighbourhood organizations than to radical or unionist activity' (Cozine, 2005, p.153).

Hypotheses arising from this excursion into 'social organization' include that in the economically more buoyant period of the mid-1920s – encompassing the early Hawthorne investigations (i.e., the Illumination Experiments and the initial Relay Assembly Test Room studies) – such ethnic communities not only possessed a familial orientation, but were also relatively quiescent as an industrial workforce (cf. Carey, 1967). A further suggestion from the 'ethnic Chicago' literature is that this was more significant in the case of women workers, for whom Hawthorne, given the nature of its assembly operations, was a major local employer (Lindberg, 1997; cf. Bramel and Friend, 1981; see also Locke, 1982). Such hypotheses provide grounds for ethnographic history to reinterpret the orthodox narrative of studies such as the Relay Assembly Test Room, where issues such as gender and ethnicity are rarely accounted for in the explanations of organizational behaviour textbooks.

The notional quiescence of ethnic groups at Hawthorne in the 1910s and 1920s, however can be contrasted with the image of Hawthorne workers that emerges from the later, more sociologically oriented, Bank Wiring Room investigation of the early 1930s. One contextual explanation for why the men of the Bank Wiring Room established a 'negative group dynamic' (as opposed to a positive or quiescent one) is that this was a natural reaction to the timing of the study. Simply put, the research coincided with a sharp rise in unemployment during the early years of the Great Depression (see Garraty, 1986); Western Electric was making large-scale redundancies and workers wished to preserve their jobs, a contextual factor of which the Harvard Group, although aware, was keen to downplay. Despite 13 of the 14 operators being in 'very poor financial condition' and that the group as a whole 'speculated endlessly on when the depression would end', Roethlisberger and Dickson (1939, p.531) maintain that the Bank Wiring Room study 'was not a "depression story"', a position that seems implausible when all factors are considered. When discussing 'the effects of the depression', Roethlisberger and Dickson's defence of their primarily psychological analysis of 'cliques' and 'output restriction' – a central plank of the Hawthorne Studies narrative – appears flimsy.[8]

Similarly, taking their lead unquestioningly from *Management and the Worker*, organizational behaviour textbooks ignore the dramatic shrinkage of the American economy during the 'hard years' of the Depression and how this was so critically experienced at Western (where sales fell from a high of $411 million in 1929 to less than $70 million in 1933: Adams and Butler, 1999, p.222). The 1930s was in fact the only decade of the twentieth century in which the number of telephones per head of population fell (Fagen, 1978). In contrast to some forms of hypothesized corporate enlightenment emerging at Hawthorne in wake of Harvard Group investigations, there is

---

[8] With regard to the Bank Wiring Room, despite *Management and the Worker* offering sociological analyses of the 'output situation' (chapter XVIII), 'supervisory situation' (chapter XIX) and 'internal organization of the group' (chapter XXI), the case material in these chapters is mostly lacking in contextual insight. Although some exceptions can be found in the more discursive sections of the 'interemployee relations' chapter (chapter XX, see, e.g., p.460–2), as Roethlisberger and Dickson (p.459) rightly caution: 'In this chapter, only the descriptive material pertaining to the relations which existed among the fourteen operators will be presented'. In other words, the research was to remain 'closed-system'.

evidence to the contrary – of increased workplace control throughout the 1930s, notably through AT&T executives pressurising Western's management over productivity. Indeed, throughout the early decades of the twentieth century, the influence of AT&T should not be understated, for as Charles Wrege has suggested (personal communication), Western Electric had 'no real autonomy' at this time and functioned primarily as a 'ward' of AT&T. Danielian (1939), for example, notes how the 1935–37 investigation of the telephone industry by the Federal Communications Commission revealed within AT&T divisions significant work intensification alongside widespread redundancies and a preference for hiring on a part-time basis. Charles Wrege (personal communication) has argued similarly that his personal conversations with Bell operatives who were employed around this time revealed a 'human touch' within the System, but only on the part of the workers themselves, who (reminiscent of the Bank Wiring Room subjects) would 'stall the work as long as possible so that the operators could be kept on longer'. This represents another instance of where context-based research serves to question, qualify or even contradict textbook explanations of organizational behaviour at Hawthorne.

This form of analysis can also be extended to the last of the three main Harvard-influenced phases of the Hawthorne investigations – the Interview Programme. While many of the sections of *Management and the Worker* devoted to the Programme involve a more sociological style of analysis (see Roethlisberger and Dickson, p.189ff.), and notably those which describe 'non-directive' research, once again, the explanatory focus is almost exclusively on *internal* issues of organization. This is witnessed for example in explanations of 'complaints and personal equilibrium' (chapter XIV), 'attitudes within the supervisory organization' (chapter XV) and (the rather unconvincing chapter on) 'complaints and social equilibrium' (chapter XVI). It can be argued that a stronger emphasis on contextual forces would have yielded more perceptive, critical and compelling information from investigations that, despite focussing on 'the relations existing between work effectiveness and personal situations' (p.315), did so predominantly from the Harvard Group's preferred 'psychopathological' perspective. A number of other contextual factors, such as the company's overt anti-unionism and covert forms of surveillance, undoubtedly skewed the results of the Interview Program, a mass exercise that reported virtually 'no criticism of the company'.[9] Again, this line of analysis puts in new (contextual) light research by the Harvard Group that is so regularly and unquestioningly recounted in organizational behaviour textbooks.

Contextual Research by the Harvard Group?

Finally, in this discussion of wider influences on the corporate and cultural shaping of Western Electric, we must qualify our 'neglected context' thesis by acknowledging that at one stage during the Hawthorne investigations, there was a desire expressed to break with a closed-system experimental approach and account for the effects of external forces on the firm and its workforce. This relates principally to a proposed anthropological study of local communities in correspondence between Mark Putnam and W. Lloyd Warner. In May 1930, Mayo sent Warner (a Harvard anthropologist) to Hawthorne with a letter of introduction to Putnam (Chief of Hawthorne's Industrial Research Division), a visit made in response to a suggestion by William Dickson (Chief of Hawthorne's Employee Relations Research Department) that 'social relationships' also be studied at Hawthorne. Impressed with Warner's anthropological per-spective, Putnam became convinced that 'the next research should be of the home and social life of Hawthorne workers', a view supported by Dickson (Gillespie, 1991, p.155). This appeared

---

[9] It would be a mistake to consider that things were exclusively 'rosy' at Hawthorne in the pre-Depression period. As Charles Wrege (personal communication) for example has pointed out, under Hawthorne's 'Extra Incentive Earnings Plan' (1925), higher piecework earnings had the drawback that if the workers, as a 'gang', earned $100, it had to be split with the 'Gang Boss' and the 'Section Chief': 75 per cent for the workers, 25 per cent for the supervisors. The foreman and the assistant foreman were not *legally* entitled to this distribution, but following 'Hawthorne ethics', they demanded their 'cut'. Wrege thus suggests that Hawthorne at this time was not necessarily the 'nirvana' that official company statements described.

a natural progression, given that in the 'non-directive' research of the Interview Program, a range of 'life experiences' related to the employee's 'social situation' were hypothesized as influencing work attitudes (see Roethlisberger and Dickson, p.201–5; 270–91).

Two factors, however, served to prevent such contextual research from being realized at Hawthorne. The first was a *volte face* by Warner himself, who when more familiar with Cicero (and no doubt its notorious resident, Al Capone), decided its communities had become 'too disintegrated' (Gillespie, 1991; Jacoby, 1986); Warner opted instead to study the more 'stable' community of Newburyport, Connecticut (see Warner and Lunt, 1941). The second was opposition primarily from Fritz Roethlisberger to the research direction Warner wished to take, which represented a significant shift from the established psychopathological approach of the Harvard researchers (see Gillespie, 1991, p.157; Roethlisberger and Dickson, p.313–5). With the possibility of researching the local community abandoned, Warner focussed instead on internal factory research at Hawthorne, and on providing the research model for the Bank Wiring Room, albeit a study which ultimately downplayed the importance of significant contextual influences on the experimental setting.[10]

This, then, was the nearest the Harvard Group would come to undertaking contextual research in the Hawthorne Studies

---

[10] Although not leading to formal anthropological research on Hawthorne's local communities, Warner's influence certainly extended to other Harvard Group 'latecomers'. Notable here is Warner's relationship with the social anthropologist Burleigh B. Gardner and especially the latter's development of the nondirective interviewing method (see Jacoby, 1986: 613–9). As a graduate student at Harvard in the early 1930s, Gardner attended seminars conducted by Mayo and Lawrence Henderson, and later joined a team of student interviewers hired by Warner for his 'Yankee City' (Newburyport) project and related studies. Subsequently, through Warner, Gardner obtained a job in Western Electric's new 'employee counseling program', which used nondirective interviewing for therapeutic purposes. After working at Western Electric for five years, Gardner wrote *Human Relations in Industry* (1945), a book based on his experiences. Warner's influence on Gardner is perhaps reflected in the greater sensitivity the book displays towards social class, ethnicity, and the world outside the workplace, especially the reasons why workers join unions, this representing a notable political departure from Mayo and methodological departure from the Hawthorne Studies programme.

programme. In the final section of *Management and the Worker* (Part V), within a discussion of the 'social organization of the plant', Roethlisberger and Dickson (1939, p.554–8) make fleeting references to the influence of the 'foreign element' and its 'value system' (p.556) and how human sentiments 'do not exist in a social vacuum' (p.558). But such wider social and cultural issues never received formal investigation in the Hawthorne Studies, despite Roethlisberger and Dickson (1939) initially noting, for example, the large percentage of 'Czechoslovakians' (p.6) at Hawthorne, or later offering an assurance that 'did not go by unheard' (p.272). Despite the ethnic background of five of the six initial members of the Relay Assembly Test Room being Central European (p.23: the sixth member was Norwegian) and only three of the 14 members of the Bank Wiring Room being ethnically 'American' (p.404: the modal ethnic group was 'Bohemian'), as Roethlisberger and Dickson (p.538) ultimately admit: 'The investigators never undertook a systematic study of the social organization of the company, and it is therefore impossible to characterize it in detail or entirely accurately'. This is despite that fact that one of the defining models in *Management and the Worker* – Figure 32: 'Scheme for Interpreting Complaints Involving Social Interrelationships of Employees' – presents the 'Social Organization of [the] Company' as one of the key influences on 'Satisfaction or Dissatisfaction' (p.375).

For the Hawthorne Studies, therefore, additional evidence from such contextual analysis could and should have been woven into those areas of the Harvard Group's research seeking sociological explanation of workplace attitudes and behaviour. This would have offered deeper insights into why, for example, the women of the Relay Assembly Test Room appeared so 'integrated' (Roethlisberger and Dickson, 1939, p.540), the men of the Bank Wiring Room seemed 'antagonistic' towards one another (Roethlisberger and Dickson, 1939, p.519) and the subjects of the Interview Program 'criticized the company in no instance' (Gilson, 1940, p.101).

HAWTHORNE: A STEP FORWARD IN MANAGEMENT STUDIES, OR THE START OF A SLIPPERY SLOPE?

> Smithers, don't you see ... *a happy worker is a busy worker.*

> C. Montgomery (Mr.) Burns (*The Simpsons*, 'Simpson and Delilah', s02e02)

The aim of this chapter has been to provide contextual insights to help us think differently about one of the most famous moments in the history of management research, The Hawthorne Studies. We have sought to deconstruct, in a Foucauldian manner, aspects of those hegemonic narratives so regularly embraced in explanations of the Hawthorne Studies in conventional management histories, in particular, the popular yet flawed narrative of discontinuity that in the wake of the Harvard Group investigations, an 'engineering' culture reflective of 'scientific management' was replaced at Western Electric by one of sociological 'enlightenment' under 'human relations' management.

In contrast, drawing initially upon research into welfare capitalism, it has been argued that not only were American industrialists aware of social and psychological issues in the workplace prior to Elton Mayo's arrival at Hawthorne in 1928, but also that Western Electric, for a range of ideological and commercial reasons, had promoted elements of a 'human relations' philosophy prior to any so-called enlightenment stemming from Mayoite interventions. For a range of motives, welfare capitalism at the Hawthorne Works had sponsored forms of employee well-being long before any social-psychological or social-system constructs were hypothesized for interpreting the behaviour of its workforce. Popular narratives in organization studies (see Etzioni, 1964, for one of the earliest and best-known) that situate the Hawthorne Studies as a decisive or 'pivotal' (Thompson and McHugh, 1990, p.76) turn from 'hard' scientific to 'soft' human relations management are remiss in that they overlook the impact of a range of economic, ideological, and political forces on the cultural shaping of major American industrial corporations at this time.

Such forces were often directed at resolving, through strategically determined welfare capitalism and hard-edged corporate paternalism, the problems of an increasingly hostile industrial relations climate. It was felt, in particular, that such 'progressive' practices may allow large American firms to 'avoid the dreaded unionism' (Witte, 1954, p.15), or else the threat of high labour turnover, which could reduce company profits significantly. In the pre-Depression era, company loyalty (especially among semi-skilled workers) was a valuable asset, and Western Electric was keen to cultivate it. In the same year as the *Eastland* disaster, 1915, for example, the company instigated a system of 'service pins' for long-term employees, in a move that suggested 'rewards for output had been supplemented with rewards for loyalty' (Adams and Butler, 1999, p.96).

On the other hand, we have noted that the economic downturn of the 1930s saw AT&T put increased commercial pressure on Western Electric and other Bell System divisions, with the result that a tougher work environment ensued (Danielian, 1939). Contrary to the folklore sometimes peddled in management textbooks (e.g., that an alienating corporate culture, pre-Mayo, was transformed into a munificent one, post-Mayo), evidence suggests that the reverse was likely true at Western, where a relatively benevolent climate in the 1920s became harsher during the 1930s. In other words, our research here suggests that the influences acting upon the organization and management at this time were many and varied, with organizational philosophies being far more subtle and complex than many 'models of management' in contemporary textbooks suggest.

More than this, we believe that the increasing doubt that ours' and others' findings have provided through deeper historical engagement with Hawthorne, should raise serious questions with regard to the validity of the Studies' findings and the degree to which these constitute a theoretical 'advance' or discontinuity with the past. And we argue that this should encourage us to rethink it and Mayo's place in the management histories that we encourage students to read and base their understanding on.

We question the idea that an event whose main historical contribution is defined by people outside of management studies as being that it showed 'how easily research results could be distorted' (Adair, 2003, p.453), is a good foundation stone. Furthermore, allowing the idea that the Hawthorne Studies (which *The Simpsons* can employ to poke fun at the banality of modern management) is a scientific advance upon thinkers like Smith and Weber creates a very low bar for later advances to get over. As such, this historical narrative allows the overly simplistic interpretations that follow (like the 'discovery' that good organizations have always had strong corporate cultures – see Chapter Eight) to appear like further progress.

Rather than brushing off the historical inaccuracies that we are increasingly aware of and continuing with the conventional script as management textbooks appear prone to, we argue that recognizing these inaccuracies and rewriting management history accordingly could be liberating. It could encourage scholars to seek broader perspectives and more nuanced theorizing, and to not settle for the view that the discovery of a general theory that 'a happy worker is a busy worker' was a significant breakthrough in the history of our field.

Indeed, we will argue in our final chapter that making Mayo and Hawthorne a cautionary tale in management history and moving straight from the likes of Taylor and Weber to the social psychologists of the next generation in looking for the next 'advance', could make for a more inspiring history. But for this to work, we would first need to redress the 'dumbing down' of these theorists' ideas into simplistic models in management textbooks. It is this dumbing down – of theorists like Maslow, Lewin and McGregor – that our next chapter's counter-history examines.

7 Textbook Distortions: How Management Textbooks Process History and Limit Future Thinking

Current views of management may be limited by the way textbooks arrange 'seminal ideas' into the conventional historical narrative.

The 1970s saw the emergence of the modern management textbook, divided into stratified chapters and sections, and illustrated in ways conducive to modern forms of lecturing large cohorts of students. Into these textbooks, management ideas from previous decades were distilled into digestible blocks and 'placed in context' by a history describing how these blocks built upon one another. In so doing, however, many research ideas were twisted and compromised. In order to illustrate how such distillations and simplifications emerged, this chapter looks firstly at how the ideas of Kurt Lewin were reconfigured to fit into this management textbook narrative. It then looks at how a number of Lewin's contemporaries and antecedents, which make up the later parts of the conventional management textbook history, are similarly processed, filed and stunted. In this regard, we pay particular attention to the work of Abraham Maslow and Douglas McGregor, whose theories of motivation have come to be seen as foundational for our field. How might the development of management studies be different if we understood and communicated ideas such as theirs differently?

> Kurt Lewin introduced two ideas about change that have been very influential since the 1940s ... [one] was a model of the change process ... unfreezing the old behavior; moving to a new level of behavior; and refreezing the behavior at the new level.
>
> What the fifth (1990, p.81) edition of *Organizational Development* by French and Bell records about Lewin and CATS
>
> [...]
>
> What the early (1973–83) editions of *Organizational Development* record about Lewin and CATS (i.e., nothing)

Kurt Lewin's 'changing as three steps', or CATS (Figure 16), is regarded as the classic or fundamental approach to managing change.[1] Initiates to the sub-field of change management are generally shown a progress of consciousness that begins with CATS as a key foundation, the first and now 'classic' theory, and culminates in the current 'state of the art'. Lewin has been criticized by scholars for over-simplifying the change process and has been defended by others against such charges. It seems that everybody in the management literature accepts CATS' pre-eminence as a foundation upon which the field of change management is built.

FIGURE 16 Change as Three Steps

But as the quotations above illustrate, prior to the early 1980s Lewin's CATS was largely unseen. Somehow, by the end of the 1980s, despite the fact that this formation was anomalous to what Lewin actually wrote or likely intended for the idea, CATS was the basis of our understanding of a fast-growing field: change management.

In this chapter, we present a counter-history of the presentation of post–World War II management theories in management textbooks. While we might assume that these would be the same as, or a continuation of, how they were presented by the theorists who developed them, the counter-history presented here shows them to be distorted, largely by the form of the modern management textbook.

---

[1] This chapter draws on elements of Cummings, S., Bridgman, T. & Brown, K. (2016). Unfreezing Change as Three Steps: Rethinking Kurt Lewin's Legacy for Change Management. *Human Relations*, 69(1): 33–60.

We show how CATS takes shape and develops into something far more than its author might ever have anticipated. We examine how Lewin moves from a minor figure, into a grand founder whose application of science enabled the discovery of the fundamentals of change management, to the well-meaning simpleton who must be improved upon. We argue that CATS was not as significant in Lewin's writing as both his critics and supporters have either assumed or would have us believe. This so-called foundation of change management has less to do with what Lewin actually wrote and more to do with others' making.

We find similar processes at play when we examine Abraham Maslow's contribution to the management sub-field of motivation – his 'hierarchy of needs' theory (HON). Maslow is an 'iconic figure in the history of management ideas' (Cooke et al., 2005, p.133). Like Lewin, Maslow was a psychologist rather than a management theorist, as is commonly portrayed in management textbooks. Like Lewin, Maslow's ideas were brought into the field of management by others, whose interpretations are mistakenly attributed to him. And, like Lewin, Maslow has been criticized for his simplistic theorizing. As we shall outline later in the chapter, not only is the textbook representation of Maslow's theory of motivation far from what he actually wrote, but he was aware of the criticisms that others might make of his work, if they interpreted it narrowly, rather than in the way he intended it.

As a final illustration of the way in which later figures defined as key on the 'management continuum' are dumbed-down in this way, we look at one of the key interpreters of Maslow, Douglas McGregor and his theorizing about the assumptions managers hold about workers. Lewin's CATS, Maslow's HON and McGregor's Theory X and Y (XY) have taken on a life of their own beyond what their authors intended. All three of these examples show, in surprising ways, just how mobile and subject to reinterpretation key theories in the history of management are.

In our endeavour here, we do something that management theorists now seldom do; we go back and look at what Lewin and Maslow and McGregor actually wrote. We find that what is known of these ideas today is largely a reconstruction by others. We do so using the lens of 'interpretive analytics' (Dreyfus and Rabinow, 1983), which we outlined in our introductory chapter. Interpretive analytics combined Foucault's archaeological and genealogical approaches. Archaeology studies the effects of episteme, an archaeological strata or: 'world-view[s] ... which impose ... norms and postulates, a general stage of reason [and] a certain structure of thought' (Foucault 1976a, p.191) on the development of knowledge objects, the 'conditions of possibility' for acceptable knowledge at particular times (1970, p.xxii). Genealogy, on the other hand, traces the networks of relations that procreate knowledge's formation over time. The archaeological side of interpretive analytics 'deals with the *system's enveloping discourse* ... The genealogical side of analysis, by way of contrast, deals with series of *effective formation* of discourse' (Foucault, in Dreyfus and Rabinow 1983, p.105; see also Foucault 1985, p.12, our emphasis).

We draw on this approach in this chapter to show how a number of mid-20th century management theories take on their modern form and develop into something different from what their authors intended. We explore the episteme particular to the 1970s and 1980s that made possible and structured the forms of truth that we see in management textbooks today. Beyond this, we analyse the reduplication, continued formation and hardening of the historical view of these theories up until, through and beyond the 1980s and the development and continuity of many questionable interpretations that help maintain today's belief in them as noble, necessary, but overly simplistic foundations upon which we have built but moved beyond.

THE DEVELOPMENT OF A THEORY MOULDER

An archaeological view can help us explain how Lewin, Maslow, and McGregor's research is cut into the 'classic models' that are attributed to them today. The 'conditions of possibility' for these versions of CATS, HON and XY fit with particular problems, viewpoints and values that framed the development of management textbooks, and management as a field in general, around the year 1980. Whilst they are now common features of the landscape of management education, comprehensive textbooks that supply all the materials necessary for a university course in management, divided into sub-field segments that could be matched to a particular lecture on a topic – e.g., managing change, human resource management and leadership – did not exist much before 1980. Many, if not most, of the best-selling textbooks are later editions (often the twelfth, thirteenth or fourteenth editions) of the originals created at this time.

In the paragraphs to follow, we examine five inter-connected epistemic conditions that promoted the development of the modern form of management textbooks and the classic models that these textbooks promoted as key foundation stones in the continuum of management. These are: a desire to be relevant, to appear scientific, to have historical provenance, to find enough content to fill the sub-headings and a desire or will to provide solutions.

1   Will-to-Relevance: Growing Associations of Business Academics Concerned to Have Impact

Initially, many in the Academy who studied and taught management were critical of the kind of 'pop-management' that began to emerge towards the end of the 1970s. Edgar Schein, in a *Sloan Management Review* article reviewing two early pop-management books, *Theory Z* and *The Art of Japanese Management* (1981, p.58; 62; 63), noted that 'neither book refers to the growing literature', that their arguments were supported by a 'meagre data base' and their 'quick fix . . . prescriptions' were 'glib', 'superficial' and 'naïve'.

Gradually, however, the Academy began to fear its own irrelevancy in the eyes of the growing audience of managers wanting actionable knowledge. For example, in 1985, a special Academy of Management symposium devoted to organizational change was held. Its publicity materials noted that executives were wrestling with the challenge of keeping organizations competitive and that 'an examination of what these executives and their organizations were doing would probably reveal that, in fact, many of the things being tried were consistent with research and theory in organizational behaviour' (Pfeffer, 1987, p.31). The highlights of this symposium were published in the first issue of *The Academy of Management Executive*, a new 'linking endeavor' between academics and practitioners (Burke, 1987, p.5). One paper, incidentally, related Lewin's 'classic theory of change' to a Harvard-style case of a practitioner's experience (Beer, 1987, p.52). Others distilled their research insights into simple linear diagrams (Barnes, 1987; Beck, 1987).

2   Will-to-Science: A Desire to Present Knowledge in a Scientific-looking Package

Many of the best-known and best-selling management textbooks of today were first published in the late 1970s and early 1980s (e.g., Baron, 1983; Cummings and Worley, 1975 (first edition written by Huse); Robbins, 1979; Wheelen and Hunger, 1983). But in the 1980s, later editions took on the appearance that is familiar to us today.

One change in their form in these early years mirrored the new presentation of pop-management and 'bridging' journals like *The Executive* – the insertion of more simple frameworks and diagrams of steps or levels to be followed. These translations of knowledge into diagrams were supported by changes in publishing technology, but looking back at the transition that these books make, it is clear that something more is happening. The diagrams were excellent tools for making teaching to increasingly large groups of management students easier (in the next decade, slide packs associated with texts would start to be promoted). And, at the same time, these general models made the subject look more scientific; classification schemes aide memoires not unlike a Periodic Table or map of the solar system. This was, to borrow a pop-management phrase, a 'win-win'. Relevance to a growing consti- tuency of managers was important, but so was maintaining and pro- moting the idea that management was a serious science.

This will-to-science in management studies can be linked to two major reviews which we have described earlier in this book. These were carried out at the end of the 1950s, prompted by mass expansion in US business education and the perceived threat to academic standards. In addition to its advocating economic science as core, the Carnegie Foundation's Report argued that business schools must pursue the development of a 'systematic body of knowledge of substantial intellectual content ... in the form of 'a set of business sciences' (Gordon and Howell, 1959, p.71–2). Similarly, The Ford Foundation's report claimed that 'the need is not for any kind of research ... but for research which meets high scientific standards' (Pierson, 1959, xv). While these views became widely shared over the next two decades, some stakeholders were beginning to question the impact of this scientific drive on business education. A 1980 study by Professors Hunger and Wheelen (who would soon write perhaps the most successful strategic management textbook – now in its thirteenth edition) found that 'Most [respondents] took the stance that schools have gone too far with quantitative methods [and] modelling [and] felt it was time to return to the teaching of more practical skills and techniques' (Hunger and Wheelen, 1980, p.29). Frameworks provided the ideal vehicle towards this aim, one that still looked like scientific language was being deployed.

In change management, for example, one can discern this desire to appear more scientific gathering strength in the 1970s, through frameworks and particularly prescriptive 'n-stage models'. For example, Greiner's (1972, p.41) article, *Evolution and Revolution as Organizations Grow*, begins by claiming that 'To date, research on organizational development has been largely empirical, and scholars have not attempted to create a model'. In response, Greiner showed in a set of diagrams that organizations move through a 'series of developmental phases'. Then, in order to better arm managers, he (1972, p.46–7) outlines 'specific management actions', 'solutions' and 'explicit guidelines for managers' (see Tushman, 1974 for a similar approach).

This will to present knowledge in generic frameworks or step-by-step general prescriptions, when combined with the other main development in 1980s management texts chapters containing clearly articulated sub-fields covering discrete but connected bodies of knowledge, each with their own historical provenance, saw the form of the modern management textbook take shape. This was a form that listed ideas and frameworks in chronological order progressing from early foundations to the latest thinking.

3 Will-to-History: A Worthy Academic Provenance Is Good for Each Member of the 'Set of Business Sciences'

In the modern age, outlining academic provenance is a useful way to seek a field's place at the table of legitimate subjects (Tsoukas and Cummings, 1997). To further its inclusion as a worthy member of the university fraternity, a history was needed of how change management or motivation or human resource management had evolved from serious scholarship on long-standing issues and not just the opportunistic and instrumental concerns of 1980s. This was also something desirable in the minds of students, managers and consultants.

For a sub-field like change management, for example, that sought to map or retrospectively graft itself onto 'fractally distinct' but related subjects like psychology and sociology (Abbott, 2001, p.11ff), Lewin, the social psychologist, was a perfect intellectual 'father'. The idea that one of the twentieth century's most innovative social scientists, with an outstanding track record of theory development based on solid experimentation and lengthy empirical observation, who the first and best thinkers directly concerned with organizational development and change based their theorizing and practice upon, was embraced.

4 Will-to-Fill: Multiple Sub-field Chapters of an Equivalent Length and Structure Need to be Filled with Content

Building repositories for management knowledge that had drawers for each of its set of sub-sciences meant that these drawers needed to be filled with exhibits that were relevant, scientific-looking and in an order that demonstrated their historical provenance. Hence, having management textbooks with chapters meant that the chapters needed to appear naturally to have equivalent content. Rather than just being concerned to report the history of management in general, each sub-field needed historical precedents and foundations too. The work of the likes of Lewin and Maslow were useful because, even though they did not class themselves as management scholars, their research could be related to the management concerns of the day. Useful also was the theoretical contribution from Mayo's research, now firmly ensconced on the continuum of management (see Chapter Six), that a happy worker is a productive worker. Theories about what made workers happy were now needed.

In this respect, organizational change, the sub-field which Lewin would be the founder of, also benefitted from a space created by the decline of 'organizational development'. Pioneers from that existing sub-field that dealt with organization change might have been at the forefront of the new textbook chapters that dealt with this issue. However, a widening group of academics, consultants, publishers and managers interested in change criticized OD for being preoccupied with ineffectual ideas. OD practitioners typically adopted the role of 'facilitator' or 'process consultant' – roles which were divorced from strategy, technology and operations (Marshak and Heracleous, 2004; Worren et al., 1999).

This perceived 'gap' encouraged the emergence of 'a rival, more business-oriented approach referred to as change management' (Marshak and Heracleous, 2004, p.1050). The transition is captured by Palmer et al. (2009), who analysed articles in the two sub-fields published between 1980 and 2006. OD's dominance was total in 1980, but by 1993, Change Management, with its scientific looking frameworks and intervention solutions, had completely surpassed it. Indeed, the sixth 1995 edition of *Organizational Development* (the text quoted at the head of this chapter) would be the last. While OD had to move with the times in retrofitting Lewin's CATS into its line-up, this was not enough to overcome the fact that, very quickly, the sub-field appeared old-fashioned. It did not fit the episteme.

5   The Will-to-Sell-Solutions: American Industry and Management Consultancies Seek to Compete Differently

Around 1980, a new phenomenon occurred: pop-management. Demand was fuelled by a growing group made anxious by their own status mobility, the rise of Japan's business culture and the comparative decline of US industry. An enlarged managerial class, eager for the knowledge that would help them climb the ladders of the new knowledge economy, turned books like *Theory Z* (Ouchi, 1981), *The Art of Japanese Management* (Pascale and Athos, 1981) and *In Search of Excellence* (Peters and Waterman, 1982) into best-sellers.

Supply was fuelled by management consultancies. McKinsey & Co moved to head off its rapidly growing competitor Boston Consulting Group (whose revenues in the late 1970s were growing rapidly, aided by popular new frameworks like the BCG matrix) by developing saleable knowledge through linking up with academics such as Tony Athos at HBS. From this marriage came the McKinsey's Seven-S model, which borrowed the form of a model developed by Athos' Harvard colleague, J. P. Kotter (1978). McKinsey's approach demonstrated the potential of academics and consultants coming together to develop memorable and applicable 'truths' for managers seemingly backed by 'university quality' research. (We shall come back to this new development in our next chapter on the creation of corporate culture).

The effective conditions we have outlined above form a prism through which the ideas of the likes of Lewin, Maslow and McGregor are refracted in the early 1980s. But before, within and beyond, there is some to-ing and fro-ing as their ideas are utilized, developed, promoted and maintained by networks of interested individuals and institutions. Starting with CATS, in the pages that follow, we illustrate just how mobile the ideas that we might assume to be continuous are in management. In later parts of the chapter, we look similarly (but in less detail) at the examples of HON and XY to illustrate that Lewin's treatment is not a 'one-off' event.

FORMATION 1: CHANGE AS THREE STEPS

Students of change management, and management generally, are informed that Lewin was a great scientist with a keen interest in management, that discovering CATS was one of his greatest endeavours and that his episodic and simplistic approach to managing change has subsequently been built upon and surpassed. However, the more that we looked at the history of CATS, the more the anomalies between the accepted view of today and what Lewin actually wrote came into view.

Our first observation was that referencing of Lewin's work in this regard is unusually lax. A footnote to an article by Schein (1996) on Lewin and CATS explains that: 'I have deliberately avoided giving specific references to Lewin's work because it is his basic philosophy and concepts that have influenced me, and these run through all of his work as well as the work of so many others who have founded the field of group dynamics and organization development' (Schein, 1996, p.27). This explanation of the unusual practice of writing a paper about a theorist who has been a great influence without making any references to his work, despite referencing the work of others who have been less influential, encouraged us to look further. Most who write about CATS, if they cite it at all, cite 'Lewin, 1951', *Field Theory in Social Science*. This is not a book written by Lewin, but an 'edited compilation of his scattered papers' (Shea, 1951, p.65) published four years after his death in 1947. *Field Theory* was edited by Dorwin Cartwright as a second companion volume to an earlier collection of Lewin's works compiled by Kurt Lewin's widow with a foreword by Gordon Allport (Lewin, 1948).

Normally in academic writing, providing a name and date reference without a page number implies that the idea, example or concept referred to is a key aspect of the book or article. Of the nearly ten thousand citations to 'Lewin, 1951' listed on Google Scholar, none of the first hundred (that is, the most highly cited of those who cite Lewin) provide a page reference. But despite this, mention of CATS in *Field Theory* is devilishly difficult to find. It is the subject of just two short paragraphs (131 words) in a 338-page book (1951, p.228).[2]

As one reviewer of the day makes clear, Lewin 1951 contains 'nothing, other than the editor's introduction, that has not been published before' (Lindzey, 1952, p.132). The fragment that would be developed into the CATS model is from an article published in 1947 titled 'Frontiers in Group Dynamics': the first article of the first issue of *Human Relations* (Lewin, 1947a). It is buried there in the twenty-fourth of twenty-five sub-sections in a thirty-seven-page article. Unlike the other points made in *Field Theory* or the 1947 article, no empirical evidence is provided or graphical illustration given of CATS, and unlike Lewin's other writings, the idea is not well-integrated with other elements (Lewin, 1947a, p.34ff.). It is merely described as a way that 'planned social change may be thought of' (Lewin, 1947a, p.36; 1951, p.231), an example explaining (in an abstract way) the group dynamics of social change and the advantages of group versus individual decision-making. It appears almost as an afterthought, or at least not fully thought out, given that the CATS metaphor of 'unfreezing' and 'freezing' seems to contradict Lewin's more detailed empirically-based theorizing of 'quasi-equilibrium', which is explained in considerable depth in *Field Theory* and argues that groups are in a continual process of adaptation, rather than a steady or frozen state. Apart from these few words published in 1947 (a few months after Lewin's death), we could find no other provenance for CATS in his work, unusual for a man lauded for his thorough experimentation and desire to base social psychology on firm empirical foundations.

A book edited by Newcomb and Hartley contains a chapter claimed to be 'one of the last articles to come from the pen of Kurt Lewin' (Newcomb and Hartley 1947, p.v). It combines some ideas from the *Human Relations* article, but gives a little more prominence

---

[2] While it is relatively common for page references not to be included when referring to books this old, it is unusual for page references to almost never be provided. By contrast to Lewin and CATS, more than 20 per cent of the academic articles that refer to Lewin's concept of 'topology' via Lewin (1951) do provide page references.

to CATS, labelling it a 'Three-Step Procedure' and attempting to link it to some empirical evidence. However, this evidence seems completely disconnected from the 'procedure'. The chapter begins (Lewin, 1947b, p.265) by explaining that 'The following experiments on group decision have been conducted during the last four years. They are not in a state that permits definite conclusions.' None of the other chapters are framed in such a tentative manner. And the editors acknowledge that the book went to press after Lewin's death (Lewin, 1947b, p.282–3). All of this suggests that Lewin may not have had the chance to fully revise the paper or that elements might have been finished by the editors.

Despite the lack of emphasis on CATS in Lewin's own writing, the impression is that Lewin gave great thought to CATS. Lewin's recent defenders see CATS as one of his four main 'interrelated elements' (Burnes and Cooke, 2012, p.1397) that Lewin 'saw ... as an interrelated whole' (Burnes, 2004, p.981); or one of 'Lewin's four elements' (Edward and Montessori, 2011, p.8). But there seems no evidence for this. Having searched Lewin's publications written or translated into English (67 articles, book chapters and books), the Lewin archives at the University of Iowa and the archives at the Tavistock Institute in London where *Human Relations* was based, we can find no other Lewinian origin for CATS.[3]

Moreover, CATS was not regarded as significant when Lewin was alive or even in the period after his death. Tributes after Lewin's death acknowledge many important contributions, such as action research, field theory and his concept of topology. But Alfred Marrow (1947) does not mention CATS, nor does Dennis Likert, in the same issue of *Human Relations* in which Lewin's 1947 article appears. Ronald Lippitt's (1947) obituary reviews ten major contributions and CATS is not one of them. None of the many reviews of

---

[3] We appreciate the efforts of the library staff and undergraduate research assistant Jooyi Park at the University of Iowa and Juliet Scott and her staff at the Tavistock Institute for their assistance with this research. We would also like to thank the exhaustive efforts of our research assistant at Victoria University, Katherine Given.

'Lewin, 1951' mention it as a significant contribution (e.g., Kuhn, 1951; Lasswell, 1952; Lindzey, 1952; Shea, 1951; Smith, 1951), and neither does Cartwright's extensive introduction to the volume. Papers on the contribution of Lewin to management thought presented by his daughter Miriam Lewin Papanek (1973) and William B. Wolf (1973) at the Academy of Management conference do not refer to CATS. Twenty-two years after Marrow wrote his obituary, his 300-page biography of Lewin does make brief mention of CATS as a way that Lewin had 'considered the change process' shortly before his death, but notes that Lewin had 'recognized that problems of inducing change would require significantly more research than had yet been carried out' (1969, p.223). Even a three-volume retrospective on the Tavistock Institute, which refers extensively to Lewin's work and the way he inspired other researchers, is silent on CATS (Trist and Murray, 1990; 1993; 1997).

A few writers cite Lewin's chapter in Newcomb and Hartley when referring to CATS. A significant number cite the 1947 *Human Relations* article. But far more cite *'Field Theory* 1951'. And it is unlikely that many who cite Lewin now read his words; a lack of connection that may explain some interesting fictions. The most significant may be the invention of the word 'refreezing' as the full-stop at the end of what would become change management's foundational framework – a term that implies that frozen is an organization's natural state until an agent intervenes and zaps it (as later textbooks promoting Lewin's 'classic model' would say 'refreezing the new change makes it permanent', Robbins, 1991, p.646).

Lewin never wrote 'refreezing' anywhere. As far as we can ascertain, the re-phrasing of Lewin's 'freezing' to 'refreezing' happened first in a 1950 conference paper by Lewin's former student Leon Festinger (Festinger and Coyle, 1950; reprinted in Festinger 1980, p.14). Festinger said that: 'To Lewin, life was not static; it was changing, dynamic, fluid. Lewin's unfreezing-stabilizing-refreezing concept of change continues to be highly relevant today.' It is worth noting that Festinger's first sentence seems to contradict the second, or at least to contradict later interpretations of Lewin as the developer of a model that deals in static, or at least clearly delineated, steps. Furthermore, Festinger misrepresents other elements; Lewin's 'moving' is transposed into 'stabilizing', which shows how open to interpretation Lewin's nascent thinking was in this 'preparadigmatic' period (Becher and Trowler, 2001, p.33).

Other disconnected interpretations include Stephen Covey noting the influence of 'Kirk Lewin' on his thinking about change (Covey, 2004, p.325) and citations for articles titled 'The ABCs of Change Management' and 'Frontiers in Group Mechanics', both claimed to have been written by Lewin and published in 1947.[4] On further investigation, despite these articles being cited in respected academic books and articles (in Bidanda et al., 1999, p.417 and Kraft et al., 2008 and 2009) and sounding like something the modern conception of change management's founding father might have written (anyone simple enough to reduce all change to an ice cube might write about change being as easy or mechanical as ABC), they do not actually exist.

Scholars like Clegg (et al., 2005, p.376) and Child (2005, p.293) have critiqued Lewin's work for being too simple or mechanistic for modern environments or unable to 'represent the reality of change' (Tsoukas and Chia, 2002, p.570). Indeed, in recent years, this has become something of a chorus, with a number of writers (e.g., Palmer and Dunford, 2008; Stacey, 2007; Weick and Quinn, 1999) associating 'classical 'episodic' views' (Badham et al., 2012, p.189) or 'stage models, such as Lewin's (1951) classic' (Tsoukas and Chia, 2002, p.570), with the 'classical Lewinian unfreeze-movement-refreeze formula, which had guided OD work from its inception', but which was now inappropriate 'for the rapid pace of change at the beginning of the twenty-first century' (Marshak and Heracleous, 2004, p.1051).

However, once again, these prosecutions seem unrelated to what Lewin actually wrote. Lewin never presented CATS in a linear

---

[4] The references are to Lewin, K. (1947). The ABCs of change management, *Training & Development Journal*, March, 5–41; and Lewin, K. Frontiers in group mechanics. In: Cartwright, D. (ed.) *Field theory*. Harper, New York (1947).

diagrammatic form and he did not list it as bullet points. Lewin was adamant that group dynamics must not be seen in simplistic or static terms and believed that groups were never in a steady state, seeing them instead as being in continuous movement, albeit having periods of relative stability or 'quasi-stationary equilibria' (1951, p.199). Lewin never said his idea was a model that could be used by a change agent. He did, however, do significant research and published highly respected articles that argued *against* Taylor's mechanistic approach (Lewin, 1920; Marrow, 1969, p.14ff.).

Perhaps the view of Lewin as a simplistic thinker emerges from his presentation in management textbooks, where the major output of his life-work appears to be a rudimentary three-step model developed as a guide for managerial interventions. But it is hard to imagine that anybody with Lewin's background would hold such a simplistically ordered worldview. He studied philosophy and psychology. He worked at the Psychological Institute at the University of Berlin until 1933 and devoted himself to establishing a Psychological Institute at the Hebrew University in Jerusalem after leaving the growing anti-Semitic chaos of Germany. His first major article contrasted Aristotle and Galileo (Lewin, 1931), and 'undoubtedly one of the last pieces of such creative work from the pen of Kurt Lewin ... mailed to the editor on 3 January 1947' (Schilpp, 1949, p.xvi-xvii), was a piece on the philosophy of Ernst Cassirer (Lewin, 1949). Lewin fled to the US in 1933 to the School of Home Economics at Cornell University where he studied the behaviour of children. From 1935 to 1945, he was at the Iowa Child Welfare Research Station at the University of Iowa. While in Iowa, Lewin listed his title as 'Professor of Child Psychology'. But despite a highly dexterous mind and growing up amid real chaos and change, he is demeaned by modern texts that smugly claim that his CATS 'has become obsolete [because] it applies to a world of certainty and predictability [where it] was developed. [I]t reflects the environment of those times [which] has little resemblance to today's environment of constant and chaotic change' (Robbins and Judge, 2009, p.625–8).

CATS is claimed to be one of Lewin's most important pieces of work, a cornerstone, which it was not. Lewin is claimed to have developed a three-step model to guide change agents, which he did not. Lewin is assumed to have given us the terms unfreeze-change-refreeze, which is only 33 per cent right. Lewin is consequently dismissed as a simpleton, which is clearly not the case. In light of these anomalies, we sought to investigate how Lewin's CATS developed into such a seminal foundation.

Genealogical Formation Leading up to the Early Management Textbook Prism

The early seeds of this formation may be discerned in the reception afforded CATS in the work of two key interpreters in the small but growing field of management studies, Ronald Lippitt and Edgar Schein in the 1950s and 1960s.

Ronald Lippitt was Lewin's PhD student. Despite not regarding CATS as worthy of mention in his 1947 tribute to Lewin after his death, Lippitt remembers how important it was a decade later. Lippitt explicitly and frequently cites what he calls Lewin's 'three phase' model (Lippitt et al., 1958, p.129) as the basis for his seven-phase model (see Figure 17), designed to be used by what are termed, in a new turn of phrase, 'change agents' in the book *Dynamics of Planned Change*. The focus on the model to be used by change agents starts to turn Lewin's thinking about change into an instrument.

It is not known why or how Lippitt and his co-authors came back to Lewin's idea (despite dedicating the book to Lewin, they only cite his 1947 *Human Relations* article and a 1943 study on food habits), but it was useful to claim Lewin, the venerated master, as a foundation. Particularly as commentators of the day noted, it was not clear what else the model of Lippitt et al. is based on. Even though the preparadigmatic nature of management studies allowed for bolder interpretations than we might expect today, eyebrows were raised in related fields. A review of the book in a psychiatry journal claims that the 'influence of Kurt Lewin is obvious but

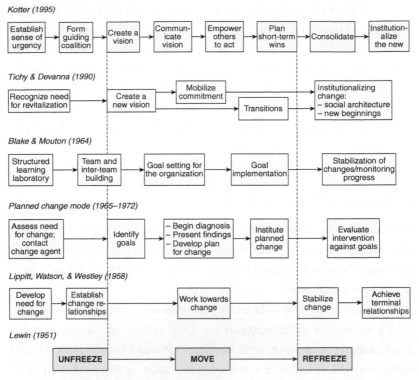

FIGURE 17 The Accretion of Theories of Change Management
Source: *Recreating Strategy* (Cummings 2002)

liberally combined with any current school of psychotherapy' (Senft, 1960, p.316). Another in *American Sociological Review* notes that: 'since the authors have not attempted to test any one set of hypotheses, many more questions are raised than answered' (Brotman, 1958, p.342).

Not long after Lippitt's work was published, other fragments emerged that would reinforce what we now consider to be the basis of change management. The first record we can find of 'refreezing' being used in a management context was by Schein in a 1961 article 'Management Development as a Process of Influence'. Schein, who cites the 1947 *Human Relations* article, also describes the three elements as 'phases'. Although he does not cite Lippitt in his first interpretations of CATS, by 1965 in a more considered work with Warren Bennis, Lippitt et al.'s work is widely acknowledged, particularly with respect to furthering our knowledge of what Schein and Bennis term 'change agentry' (1965, p.206).

Now connected to Lippitt's, Schein's interpretation loads the emphasis further towards CATS as an intervention tool, calling the steps 'phases of influence' (Schein, 1961, p.62). As significant as the transposition from freezing to refreezing in this regard is Schein's switching out of Lewin's 'moving' for 'changing'. Together, these reinterpretations move CATS from a way change may be observed to a lever for a change agent. Schein also back-fills the three-phase (unfreezing-changing-refreezing) model with Kelman's (1958) 'mechanisms of attitude change' to create some supporting subheads under the three-phase headings. In later publications, including one titled 'The Mechanisms of Change', Schein creates tables that list his development of Lewin's idea with more clarity. In so doing, CATS becomes a basis for a seven-stage 'Model of attitude change' (Schein and Bennis, 1965, p.275 – see Figure 17; and a seven-stage approach to process consulting (Schein, 1969).

While Schein originally acknowledged that what he had developed was a 'derivation of the change model developed by Lewin' (1961, p.62), later works will attribute more authority to Lewin. By 1965, CATS will be described as 'what Lewin described as the stages of change' (Schein and Bennis, 1965, p.275). By 1985, 'Lewinian change theory' (Schein, 1985, p.309). By 1992, what Lewin found to be 'the fundamental assumptions underlying any change in a human system' (Schein 1992, p.298). It is these formations, rather than what Lewin actually wrote, that will enable the criticism that Lewin and his model is too instrumental, too simplistic and mechanistic for the complexities of the modern world.

While Schein and Lippitt had good reason to invoke Lewin and develop his sketchy idea, another less directed element would later fill in the background to the emerging freezing/refreezing metaphorical model. The Tavistock Institute, Europe's leading think-tank on the fledgling field of management, was greatly influenced by Lewin, but, independent of him, launched a major research project on resistance to change that would influence British management thinking for many years. This was The Glacier Project, named for the company that had agreed to be the subject of the study, the Glacier Steel Company. One might think that if Lewin's CATS had been seen as a big deal at this time, a link between a great man's model that spoke of unfreezing/refreezing and a project on resistance to change called Glacier would be made much of. But not yet. Long-time Lewin fan and project leader Eliot Jacques' (1951) book on the project doesn't mention CATS.

In later years, these disparate elements – Lippitt and Schein's interpretations and the glacial freezing/unfreezing imagery – would accumulate into the historical narrative we accept today. But up until the late 1970s, the idea of CATS as a foundational theory authored by the great Kurt Lewin had little influence on the mainstream of management education. In fact, the first comprehensive histories of management either do not mention Lewin at all (George, 1968), or mention him but only in relation concepts other than CATS (Wren, 1972). While Gordon Lippitt's book, *Visualizing Change* (1973), refers to Lewin liberally and is replete with drawings, these are not in the linear-episodic form that we now associate with CATS. The first edition of *Organizational Behaviour: Concepts and Controversies*, by Stephen Robbins (1979) – typical of the new form of comprehensive management textbooks which still guide teaching today – does not mention Lewin in the main text. However, a new perspective was emerging. Robbins' chapter on organizational development states that: 'In very general terms, planned change can be described as consisting of three stages: unfreezing, changing and refreezing' (Robbins, 1979, p.377). A footnote to this statement cites 'Lewin, 1951'. But the lack of a page reference and Robbins' arrangement of the terms suggests some other influence. Much more would be made of CATS though, by the end of the 1980s and beyond.

*Genealogical Formation Leading up beyond the Early
Management Textbook Prism*

The new form of CATS made possible by the conditions described
above was in a nascent state throughout the 1980s, but throughout
this decade and beyond, the formation that sustained this truth was
maintained, hardened and was subtly developed. As we have said
throughout this book, given most management initiates only encounter a history of management in introductory courses and textbooks,
these books may provide the best insight into the conventional view
of management's origins. In order to gauge how different authors and
texts enable and sustain this form and formation of CATS, we
focussed our attention on top-selling textbooks that had been through
multiple editions, such as Kreitner and Kinicki's *Organizational
Behaviour*, Greenberg and Baron's *Behavior in Organizations* and
Schermerhorn et al.'s *Management in Organizations*. In order to illustrate the developments we observed, we present here an analysis of
Robbins' *Organizational Behaviour*, first published in 1979 and now
in its seventeenth edition (2015). Robbins' presentation is typical of
that in other mainstream textbooks, but we focus on it here because of
its ubiquity, and because its longevity and consistency of authorship
means its narrative begins prior to the epistemic conditions described
in the previous section, continuing right through to the present day.
It is 'the best-selling organizational behaviour textbook, not only in
the U.S.A. but also internationally' (Robbins et al., 2009, p.iii).

We noted earlier the lack of attention paid to Lewin in the first
edition of Robbins in 1979. But, reflecting the enveloping episteme
outlined in our brief archaeology above, things developed through the
1980s and beyond. The second edition of Robbins, published in 1983,
is retitled *Organizational Behaviour: Concepts, Controversies and
Applications* (underlining added), but the text in the second edition
touching on CATS is the same as the first. However, by the third
edition in 1986, 'Resistance to Change' which was previously
reviewed in a few short paragraphs after the mention that 'change

can be described as consisting of three stages: unfreezing, changing and refreezing' has become a sub-section in its own right. This is placed before another new sub-section titled 'The Change Process' (1986, p.457ff.). This begins: 'When resistance to change is seen as dysfunctional, what actions can be taken? Reducing resistance to change can be best understood by considering the complexity inherent in the change process.' Accompanying the text is a new diagram showing a linear progression from unfreezing, to movement and refreezing (in the form presented at the start of this chapter in Figure 16). The text is now not just describing stages by which change may occur, but a way of solving (i.e., better managing) resistance to change. A footnote further on in the text links to 'Lewin, 1951', but the figure is not attributed or linked to Lewin in any way. (Kreitner and Kinicki attempt to draw firmer links, but those who follow them may be disappointed. Their footnote invites readers to go to Lewin (1951) 'for a full description of Lewin's change model'.).

The fourth edition (1989) is the same as the third, apart from new margin summary points that provide definitions of Unfreezing and Refreezing. However, a new section, 'The OD Consultation Process', explains how 'The unfreezing-movement-refreezing of planned change' can be 'elaborated upon to orient it more specifically to the needs of the OD practitioner or consultant' (1989, p.534). This elaboration of Lewin is now supported by references to Burke's *Organization Development*. Burke, the founding editor of *The Academy of Management Executive*, quoted in our Archaeology section, glowingly describes Lewin as 'the theorist among theorists' (Burke, 1982, p.30), and uses the similarities between Lewin's and Ronald Lippitt's model of planned change to claim an underlying fundamental or generic approach to change on which he bases his development. In this edition of Robbins, an additional reference to Kolb and Frohman (1970b) appears to provide a stronger link back to Lewin. But while Kolb and Frohman's seven-stage framework, which Robbins copies and adapts, looks useful for consultants, neither it or the cited MIT Working Paper on which is it based (Kolb and Frohman,

1970a) make any mention of Lewin or CATS. Instead, they claim their framework was based on Lippitt et al. and Schein. Perhaps in the pre-paradigmatic 1970s they did not see the link to Lewin, or the need to find a link to a deeper foundation.

By 1991's fifth edition, change management's self-supporting view of Lewin's CATS has been created. While the characterization of Lewin is now significantly different from the first edition, the reference is unchanged 'Lewin, 1951' (no page reference given). There are two other innovations in the fifth edition: review/discussion questions at the end of the chapter, including '8. How does Lewin's three-step model of change deal with resistance to change?' (1991, p.653); and a section called Point-Counterpoint (1991, p.651), where old theories, like 'Lewin's three-step model' are contrasted with more recent, complex (i.e., better) thinking. Lewin is now being given a second role. He is now both a noble founder and an overly simplistic man whose thinking has been surpassed in our increasingly complex world.

In the sixth edition, 'Lewin's Three-Step Model' is given a new introduction: the heading 'Approaches to Managing Organizational Change', followed by 'Now we turn to several popular approaches to managing change. Specifically, we'll discuss Lewin's classic three-step model of the change process and present the action research model' (1993, p.676). By 1993, CATS has become the 'classic' in a line-up of approaches managers can use to manage change. The linear three-stage diagram that first appeared in 1986 without title or attri-bution is now boldly titled 'Lewin's Classic Three-Step Model of the Change Process'. Curiously, while Lewin spent a large portion of his life working on action research, and little-to-none on CATS, no refer-ence at all is made to Lewin's work in Robbins' pages on action research.

Then, from this point on, subsequent editions follow the pattern set in the sixth with two gradual developments. The list of 'Approaches to Managing Organizational Change' grows longer (by the mid-2000s there is a list of four: 'Lewin's classic', action research, organizational development, and 'Kotter's eight-step plan' (Robbins and Judge, 2009, p.625–8). And the Point-Counterpoint staged debate becomes more pointed, with the two opposing sides (old/bad versus new/better) lined up against each other on the same page. The anti–'Lewinian/CATS' counterpoint is clear that Lewin's approach 'has become obsolete. It applies to a world of certainty and predictability ... and it reflects the environment of those times. It treats change as occasional disturbance in an otherwise peaceful world. However, this paradigm has little resemblance to today's environment of constant and chaotic change' (Robbins, 2001, p.574). This development of Lewin certainly takes us a long way from the actuality of Lewin's life and work. But this foundation myth will dovetail well with, and mutually support, developments in the annals of management history more broadly, which chart the field's general progression from the noble but simple towards today's great heights.

As described earlier, the first editions of Wren's *Evolution of Management Thought* (1972; 1979; 1987) make no mention of Lewin's views on change, describing instead Lewin's work on group dynamics, topology and field theory. But the fourth edition in 1994 inserts a new paragraph into this discussion telling us that 'Lewin viewed change behaviour as a three-step procedure' (Wren, 1994, p.279), despite it jarring with Lewin's contributions expressed earlier in Wren's chapter: how 'a group was never in a steady state of equilibrium but was in a continuous process of mutual adaptation ... with continuous movement and change' (Wren, 1972, p.324; 2009, p.336). This is supported by a correctly attributed quotation from Lewin's chapter in the Newcomb and Hartley book of 1947, and an explanation that 'Lewin's three-step procedure provided a foundation for future action research and organizational change and development techniques' (Wren, 1994, p.279). The sixth edition of Wren (2009, p.441) further expands on Lewin's contribution and the work of 'his disciples' and notes how later experts like Argyris and Schön 'echoed Kurt Lewin'.

Robbins and Wren are not lone voices. They are part of a wider self-reinforcing network, and this is what makes it difficult to see behind this formation and think otherwise. Conventional and critical textbooks, history books and articles relate and reinforce the current accepted form of 'Lewin's CATS'. Another recent textbook provides a good example with which to conclude. The Asia-Pacific edition of *Organizational Change Development and Transformation* (Waddell et al., 2014), begins its second chapter, 'Understanding Change', with a sub-section on 'Lewin's change model': 'One of the early fundamental models of planned change was provided by Kurt Lewin' (p.33). This opening statement is footnoted 'Lewin, 1951'. No other reference to Lewin is provided in the book, but there are references to the work of Schein and Lippitt. French and Bell's link to Lewin in their *Organizational Development* described in our archaeology section also comes not from Lewin's work directly, but through Schein's 'improvements' (Lewin's 'model' is illustrated by a table by Schein from his 1969 book, *Process Consultation*, which breaks Lewin's consideration into steps and sub-steps); and Lippitt et al.'s (1958) 'modifications' (which 'lays out the logical steps involved in OD consulting'). Like Robbins' fourth edition onwards, French and Bell's fifth edition (1995) notes the further 'developments' by Kolb and Frohman, and Burke. And these ideas are reconfirmed in the later book of organized seminal readings, *Organizational Development and Transformation* (French et al., 2005: see p.105–6).

CATS has come a long way. It has become a vehicle by which, as Whitley describes (1984), an academic field seeks to promote, paradoxically, innovations that follow collectively agreed fundamental concepts. Indeed, the fragment of 'Lewin's Three Steps' has become a solid foundation and inspiration for further development by many. As Figure 17 seeks to illustrate, when the epistemic conditions of the 1980s were receptive to 'truths' presented as scientifically grounded, practically useful and related to worthy academic provenance, the emerging sub-field of change management provided these by looking back and patterning the interpreted fragments of Lewin, Lippitt et al., Schein and Bennis, Kolb and Frohman and others, into a foundation.

Moving forward within the enveloping episteme that helped form CATS as we tend to think of it today, this heritage helps to inspire, directly and perhaps subconsciously too, other 'n-step guides for change' (Collins, 1998, p.83), often crossing back over into other sub-fields or popular themes of the day. For example, Nadler and Tushman's (1989) 'Principles for Managing Reorientation' and Kotter's (1995) '8 Steps of Leading Change' innovate while staying true to the Lewinian fundamentals. By the mid-1990s, management consultancy-driven lists of 'principles' like those in 'Better Change: Best Practices for Transforming Your Organization', by the Price Waterhouse Change Integration Team (1995) also fit with the para-meters while going into greater detail (there are 15 best practice principles), proudly claiming that 'the science of managing change and implementing serious improvements in large organizations is evolving rapidly' (1995, p.vi). And as other topics such as leadership and learning are problematized and become popular concerns, approaches like Tichy and Devanna's (1986) 'Three-Act Model of Transformational Leadership', and Schein's 'Model of Change/ Learning' (2010) can also claim Lewinian heritage.

Moreover, one can trace an interesting spiral of influence and inference in the work of Kotter in particular. Recall it was Kotter's framework that prefigured that first McKinsey model that helped to create the environment within which the diagramming of Lewin's CATS came to pass. There is an interesting reinforcing circle in Kotter's recent pop-management books – *Our Iceberg is Melting*, 2006, and *The Heart of Change*, 2002 – with their use of the iceberg metaphors and penguin motifs. Whether these are attributable to the author or other employees of the publishers, they are so resonant of the ice imagery attributed to Lewin that it adds further mass to the network that promotes CATS' foundational status, for better and for worse, or, we might say, for nobler and simpler.

Through this analysis of the form and formation of CATS, we may observe how it has grown from a brief aside, to a useful fragment to buttress others' emerging ideas, to a way change might be thought of, to a fundamental underpinning, to an overly simplistic model which we have advanced beyond; from something that one might observe in a social group, to a tool for consultants and other change agents to instigate, manage resistance, and make change happen. In short, we argue that CATS has become far more fundamental and instrumental than Lewin ever intended it to be. And while the reinterpretation of Lewin's musing and subsequent facsimiles have produced knowledge by providing confidence in a fledgling sub-field; a historical foundation on which subsequent research can be layered; an appearance of both noble foundations and continual advancement, it is a solid foundation only in the sense that it has hardened through a series of interpretations that have built upon each other, and this sedimentation may now repress other ways of seeing or organizing thinking about change. This has encouraged the sort of simplistic n-step thinking that attracted attention away from teaching its binary other, namely process thinking about change. Something that the vast majority of Lewin's work, and indeed the field of OD before change management took precedence, could have promoted.

But this formation, development and re-formation of CATS is not an isolated case in the annals of management theory. In the next section, we observe similar dynamics at play in the representation of another idea that has come to be regarded as another important foundation stone of management thought.

FORMATION 2: BUILDING MASLOW'S PYRAMID

A staple of introductory courses in management is the topic of motivation. This makes sense in the light of the fact that Mayo's theory that a cared-for worker is a more productive worker; if this is true, then understanding how workers are motivated will be extremely helpful for future managers. Typically the first theory of motivation presented to students, (and, in our experience, the one students are best able to recall) is Abraham Maslow's hierarchy of needs (figure 18).

Kenrick et al. (2010, p.292), citing 'Abraham Maslow's classic 1943 *Psychological Review* paper' (Maslow, 1943), note that 'the powerful image of a pyramid of need ... has been one of the most cognitively contagious ideas in the behavioral sciences'. Maslow's

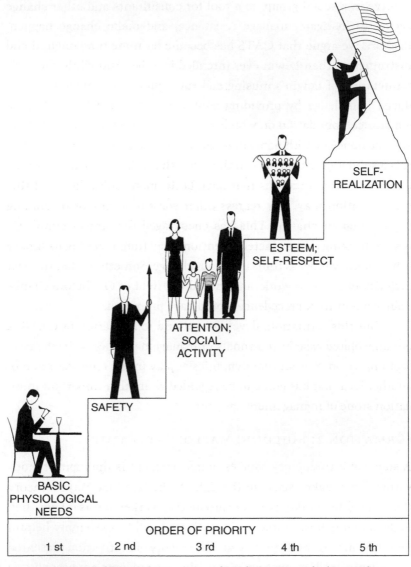

FIGURE 18 An Early Rendition of Maslow's Hierarchy/Pyramid
Source: *Human Relations at Work* (Davis 1957, p.41)

triangular construction legitimates the field of organization behaviour through its insight that managers should design work in a way that allows their employees to satisfy their 'higher order' needs. It is used to demonstrate that providing stimulating, challenging work leads to satisfied workers, increased commitment and higher levels of organizational performance.

As far we are can tell, Maslow never presented his work in the form of a pyramid or triangle, as it is almost universally depicted in management texts. Just as in our analysis of Lewin and CATS, we need to look at other actors and networks to explain Maslow's influence on management studies. Maslow's HON theory first appears in 1957 in a textbook by Davis, an article in *Administrative Science Quarterly* by Pellegrin and Coates and an article by Douglas McGregor based on an address he gave at Massachusetts Institute of Technology (Davis, 1957; McGregor 1957; Pellegrin and Coates, 1957). It is McGregor's representation that we focus on here, since he is credited most for popularizing Maslow's needs theory within management education in his 1960 book, *The Human Side of Enterprise*, which became a best-seller (Ballard, 2006; Cooke and Mills, 2008; Haire, 1969). The book 'catalysed Maslow's growing impact on business theorists and executives, and brought him fame' (Hoffman, 1999, p.251).

McGregor introduces the hierarchy of needs in a chapter on Theory X, the set of negative assumptions about human nature which McGregor argues is a traditional but outdated approach to management. Maslow's 1954 book, *Motivation and Personality*, is one of 11 references listed by McGregor at the end of the chapter. Maslow, like the ten other authors, is not named within the body of the chapter – this is a popular management book after all, and filling the text with citations would likely not appeal to his audience.

McGregor's description of HON is striking for two reasons. First, he uses very similar phrasing to Maslow. For example, McGregor's 'man is a wanting animal' (p.36) closely resembles Maslow's 'man is a perpetually wanting animal' (p.370). McGregor's 'Man lives by bread alone, when there is no bread' (p.36) appears to copy Maslow's 'It is quite true that man lives by bread alone – when there is no bread' (p.375).

The second striking feature of McGregor's interpretation is that it contains many of the misrepresentations of Maslow which have subsequently appeared in management textbooks. Table 5 presents the labels associated with HON in Maslow's original 1943 paper, three editions of *Motivation and Personality*, as well as McGregor's description and a selection of top-selling management textbooks. In *Motivation and Personality* (1954, 1970, 1987), Maslow added 'belong-ingness' to 'love' as the description of the third needs level, but he did not use the label 'social', which is typically used in modern textbooks. McGregor's influence is not obvious in the references these textbooks use, but as was the case with Lewin, there is reason to question the accuracy of the referencing. Robbins et al. (2016, p.175) have a figure presenting HON as a triangle, with the third level being 'social' needs. Their source is Maslow 1987 – which uses neither the triangle nor that label. Bateman and Snell (2009, p.482) cite Maslow (1943) as their source. Their labels are 'social' and 'ego' needs – neither of which were used in that paper and both of which, we argue, have McGregor (1960) as their likely origin.

Further evidence of McGregor's influence on the interpretation of Maslow's theory surrounds one of the most popular criticisms of the hierarchy of needs – the simplistic view that people are motivated to satisfy only one need at the time, that needs must be fully satisfied before they move to a higher level need and therefore that a satisfied need is no longer a motivator of behaviour. As McGregor (1960, p.39, emphasis in original) summarizes: 'The man whose lower-level needs are satisfied is not motivated to satisfy *those* needs. For practical purposes they exist no longer.'

If we look at what Maslow actually wrote, he is very clear that while this is one possible interpretation of his theory, it would be a 'false impression' (1943, p.388). In explaining his need categories, he acknowledges that the examples he uses are extreme. For instance, while he says a starving man will be overwhelmed by the

Table 5 *The Development of Maslow's Five Elements of Motivation*

Maslow (1943)	Maslow (1954, 1970, 1987)	McGregor (1960)	Bateman & Snell (2009)	Schermerhorn et al. (2014); Robbins et al. (2015); Robbins et al. (2016)	Hitt et al. (2007); Davidson et al. (2009)
physiological	physiological	physiological	physiological	physiological	physiological
safety	safety	safety	safety	safety	security
love	belongingness and love	social	social	social	belongingness
esteem	esteem	ego	ego	esteem	esteem
self-actualization	self-actualization	self-fulfilment	self-actualization	self-actualization	self-actualization

physiological need to satisfy his hunger, and 'such a man may fairly be said to live by bread alone' (p.374), he is quick to point out that such extreme situations are rare in a normal, peaceful society: 'In actual fact, most members of our society who are normal, are partially satisfied in all their basic needs and partially unsatisfied in all their basic needs are the same time'. (p.388)

Therefore, contrary to McGregor's interpretation, which is reproduced in many textbooks, Maslow is clear that 'any behaviour tends to be determined by several or *all* of the basic needs simultaneously rather than by only one of them' (1943, p.390, emphasis in original). To illustrate his point, he offers the example of a person who is satisfied 85 per cent physiological, 70 per cent safety, 50 per cent love, 40 per cent self-esteem and 10 per cent self-actualization. Davis, along with McGregor, is credited for bringing Maslow into management thinking (Cooke and Mills, 2008) and offers an interpretation of needs theory more in keeping with Maslow's formulation. He talks about the five needs as priorities, with some dominant depending on the situation. He talks of needs being 'reasonably satisfied' and 'reasonably achieved' (1962, p.24) – never in absolute terms, as interpreted by McGregor.

Another common critique of HON which appears both in textbooks, as well as in scholarly journals (Wahba and Bridwell, 1976), is its lack of supporting empirical evidence. Students on introductory management courses could be forgiven for thinking that Maslow claimed supporting empirical evidence where there was none, or worse, that he was not interested in research.

> Members of the human relations movement, unsubstantiated by research, uniformly believed in the importance of employee satisfaction ... For the most part, the people associated with this movement – Abraham Maslow and Douglas McGregor – were individuals whose views were shaped more by their personal philosophies than by substantive research evidence ... On the other hand, some OB researchers relied on the scientific method for the

study of organisational behaviour. These behavioural science theorists engaged in objective research of human behaviour in organisations. They carefully attempted to keep their personal beliefs out of their work. *(Robbins et al., 2015, p.54)*

Certainly, it would be fair to level this criticism at McGregor's portrayal of HON in *The Human Side of Enterprise.* In fairness to McGregor, he never claimed to be doing justice to the complexities of Maslow's theory. McGregor acknowledged that his 'generalizations about motivation are somewhat oversimplified' (p.36), but for him, they were a means to an end – shaping management practice.

But while McGregor wrote for an audience beyond the academy, Maslow *was* committed to scientific endeavour. Maslow acknowledges in his 1943 paper that his theorizing 'derives most directly ... from clinical experience' (p.371); however, he also traces its intellectual lineage to James, Dewey, Wertheimer, Goldstein, Freud and Adler, as well as Gestalt psychology. As can be seen below, the importance of scientific evidence is what drove him to articulate his theory of motivation.

It is far easier to perceive and to criticize the aspects in motivation theory than to remedy them. Mostly this is because of the very serious lack of sound data in this area. I conceive this lack of sound facts to be due primarily to the absence of a valid theory of motivation. The present theory then must be considered to be a suggested program or framework for future research and must stand or fall, not so much on facts available or evidence presented, as upon researches yet to be done, researches suggested perhaps, by the questions raised in the paper. *(1943, p.371)*

When HON first appeared in management studies, it *was* seen to be supported by empirical evidence: [it] 'has been accepted as being in "striking harmony" with current research findings dealing with worker motivation and morale' (Pellegrin and Coates, 1957, p.515). It is also interesting to note that while Maslow and McGregor are criticized by Robbins et al. (2015) for the lack of empirical support provided for their theorizing, no such criticism is levelled at Lewin for CATS.

If, as seems to be the case, that McGregor's reconstruction of HON is the origin of its representation in management textbooks, it is not surprising that the theory has attracted the criticism it has. The critique is in many respects a critique of McGregor's interpretation of Maslow, without acknowledging McGregor's role as the conduit. As we saw with the case of Lewin and CATS, in textbook production such misrepresentations become layered upon each other and harden over time.

FORMATION 3: MCGREGOR'S BINARY THEORY — THEORY X OR THEORY Y?

Ironically perhaps, our final illustration of how foundation stones on the continuum of management history come to be recast by the form of the modern management textbook and the possibilities afforded by the state of management in the early 1980s concerns McGregor himself. The misrepresentation of McGregor's work is perhaps the most unfortunate of the three we have analysed in this chapter, since unlike Lewin and Maslow, his ideas were not buried in hard-to-find academic journal articles published in the 1940s. *The Human Side of Enterprise* is widely available today and its key ideas are expressed in a style which makes them easy to understand, and therefore seemingly difficult to confuse.

Nevertheless, the standard textbook portrayal of McGregor's contribution focusses exclusively on his description of Theory X and Theory Y as assumptions that managers make about workers. Theory X managers, we are told, assume workers are lazy, dislike work and need to be coerced, whilst Theory Y managers have a more optimistic view of human nature, seeing workers as desiring recognition, responsibility and challenge – the higher-level needs identified by Maslow. McGregor is then represented as advocating Theory Y, on the grounds that a more satisfied and committed worker is a more productive worker.

That is actually a reasonably fair portrayal of McGregor's views of X and Y discussed in *The Human Side of Enterprise*. However, like has been the case with Lewin and Maslow, it is a very selective appropriation of his work, which arguably misses its most significant contribution. Like Maslow, McGregor is criticized for creating hypotheses for which there is no proof: 'Unfortunately, there is no evidence to confirm that either set of assumptions is valid, or that accepting Theory Y assumptions and altering your actions accordingly will make employees more motivated' (Robbins et al., 2015, p.609).

However, as Jacques (2006, p.33) argues, this portrayal of McGregor as a poor 'tester of trivial hypotheses' is a misleading one. McGregor understood the value of scientific knowledge, but he was not the failed empiricist we are led to believe. Far from seeing X and Y as two hypotheses to be tested, McGregor saw them as heuristics to stimulate critical reflection. The opening pages of *The Human Side of Enterprise* are very clearly about recognising that all managerial behaviour is based upon a theory or perspective: 'The insistence on being practical really means, "Let's accept *my* theoretical assumptions without argument or test." The common practice of proceeding without explicit examination of assumptions leads, at times, to remarkable inconsistencies in managerial behaviour'. (1960, p.7, emphasis in original).

And lest we should misinterpret what McGregor was seeking to do in proposing Theory X and Y, he comes back to this message in the book's final pages: 'The purpose of this volume is not to entice management to choose sides over Theory X or Theory Y. It is, rather, to encourage the realization that theory is important, to urge management to examine its assumptions and make them explicit (p.246).'

McGregor never claimed to have empirical evidence to prove his theory. This was not his purpose, and his approach was more sophisticated than that. In popular textbook portrayals, McGregor is retrofitted into a narrative of the evolution of organizational knowledge as a 'science'. He is useful to that narrative because he was supposedly trying to think as a scientist, but proved to be not a very good one, and was therefore someone we could progress beyond as our field continued on to greater heights. This is a convenient and convincing narrative, but it is a distortion of McGregor's contribution to the field.

RECOVERING NEW FRONTIERS FOR MANAGEMENT THEORY

Lewin's CATS, Maslow's HON and McGregor's Theory X and Y have taken on a life of their own in popular management textbooks and we believe that the simplistic views promulgated by these works filter through to our field in general. For example, we have been surprised that senior management academics have resisted strongly our assertion that Lewin did not create and advocate CATS as an intervention tool. Despite there being no evidence to support the view of Lewin as a change management theorist, it is so ingrained now in management history that people have difficulty thinking it could be otherwise.

In our view, passing on an unthinking acceptance of these presentations about change management and motivation may conceal and unwittingly repress other possibilities. Inspired by the critical historical approach of Michel Foucault, the primary purpose of the counter-history presented in this chapter is to work against this kind of repression, and thereby to enable 'thinking differently' for the future. This approach encourages us to see that our history could be different; it is both questionable and malleable, so we need not be bound by it. We are freer to find alternative origins that can promote new alternative frontiers, and thus greater plurality and creativity in thinking about management. So, how might we think differently about the theorists discussed in this chapter and their ideas?

In the case of Lewin, as G.W. Allport (Allport, in Lewin, 1948, p.xiii) says in his foreword to the first volume of Lewin's works published after his death – Lewin (1951) is the second – while some elements of that collection 'outline his change experiments it is not in any sense a final report ... Others ... will [have to] carry ... forward his program [because b]efore this vital work reached the stage of completion Lewin died'. Lippitt, Schein and others carried forward the elements that became the classic foundation of change management (i.e., CATS), but freed from the idea that this is a fundamental legacy from Lewin (1947/1951), we may be encouraged to look back again, to find alternative origins, and by association new frontiers, in these works.[5]

Lewin outlines many frontiers in the 1947 paper from which CATS is developed, but the two to which he devotes the most space, and which interconnect to most of the other frontiers dear to him, are the first and the last in the article. The first is that when studying change, the unit of analysis must be the group, not the individual (as psychology might direct us), the organization (as modern management studies is want to think) or wider society (as may be the want of the sociologist). The last is a call for advances in mathematics and statistics, advances that would enable multiple variables relating to individuals and groups to be analysed as a system, so as to enable the other frontiers he has outlined to be reached. Seeing these two aims as foundations for the future could, we believe, have profound effects on research and teaching now.

To take the idea of the group as the key unit of analysis first, we might begin by considering the ideas that follow from this. Lewin's (1947a, p.6ff.) desire in this respect (which he relates to Cassirer's view that physics and other sciences generally advance as they imagine and grant existence to new units – e.g., the atom, the molecule), links to the view that while change and constancy in the life of the individual and in language may seem paradoxical, their co-existence in the life of a group is not, and that understanding the force field made up of elements promoting change and elements promoting constancy is

---

[5] Indeed, if we wanted to think differently, Allport's work would be a good cipher for Lewin, given its sympathy with his programme; its criticism of mechanistic cause-and-effect models and celebration of uniqueness (e.g., Allport, 1961, p.x-xi); its view that classifying schema are useful but lead to over-simplification, discrimination, and false judgment ('we forget these are labels and try to explain [all things] in terms of the labels' – Allport in Evans, 1970, p.9); its acceptance that there are as many ways of developing as there are individuals and its focus on the flow of becoming rather than static states. Allport (in Lewin, 1948, p.xi) notes that for Lewin, managers of change were not merely 'clever persuaders ... utilizing a few fancy tricks'.

key, as is the idea that managing change is more effective if one communicates with and involves the group rather than individuals. Indeed, all of these things were born out in the one significant empirical study of corporate change that Lewin was involved in: the Harwood Manufacturing Corporation. For example, Lewin's team (including Alex Bavelas, his graduate student from the University of Iowa, whose 'Unpublished manuscript' relating to the work at Harwood is heavily cited in Lewin's 1947 *Human Relations* article) proved here that the approach to change that met with the most success involved all stakeholders work-shopping specific processes and alternatives before agreeing the way forward (Marrow et al., 1967).

These insights are very different from those conveyed in the textbook chapters that teach managers about change.[6] And as time passes, they fade further from view. Over time, the focus has become more about the effective manager as individual change agent, responding to an increasing urgency for change in today's society (faster-paced than ever before), the resistance managers face from individual workers, and the steps and frameworks that can be used to overcome resistance and embrace the need for change. Interestingly, while the fourth and fifth editions of Robbins' textbook (1989, p.532; 1991, p.645) contain a box called 'OB Close Up', with a description of the Harwood case, by the sixth edition, the Harwood case has been replaced by a seven-step approach for 'changing attitudes with persuasive messages' (Robbins, 1999, p.671).

But what if we were to actively recover Lewin's frontier in this regard? To start with teaching, it may be that those textbook chapters on change would be called Group Dynamics, or Managing Change and Continuity, instead of Change Management with its emphasis on the individual manager overcoming resisters (Dent and Goldberg, 1999). Such chapters might begin not with society's ever-increasing need for change, or the problem of resistance, or the classic n-stage framework

---

[6] There are some exceptions beyond the mainstream, in particular Burnes (2009), who has written a very good retrospective review of Lewin and the Harwood Studies (Burnes, 2007).

that a change agent can use, but with group behaviour and how this can connect to concepts like motivation, culture and leadership, covered in earlier chapters. And, while the episteme we outlined earlier may have still steered textbooks towards reproducing frameworks that seemed relevant to managers, they need not be so crude, start with the idea of unfreezing or breaking resistance and then have the arrows all pointing in the same direction. Indeed, Lewin's works are full of diagrams, but none of them are linear n-stage forms and his key notion of the force field is depicted with arrows going in opposing directions. If these were the first things that management students learnt, their perceptions of change, and subsequently the future of the field, might form differently.

In thinking about how research might be different, we took as a sample of the latest research on change the last six volumes of the *Academy of Management Journal* (2009–14). Outside of a special issue which specifically called for 'process studies of group development' (Langley et al., 2009, p.629), all bar two of the articles published relating to change took individuals as their unit. Furthermore, even those who take a different approach pay homage to the foundational status of CATS. For example, when Lewin is cited in the Process Special Issue (Klarner and Raisch, 2012, p.163, citing Lewin 1947,no page reference given), it is as what the process authors are opposed to, those who have only 'focused on single change events and the different phases'. And while Mantere et al., (2012, p.190) present interesting new insights that relate sensemaking in group dynamics to organizational change, the framework they develop goes 'Organizational sensebreaking → Meaning void (unfreezing) → Sensegiving → Acceptance of strategy (nascent freezing)'. Lewin is not directly attributed, but he is there in the background when sensebreaking as the first phase is explained in the article (as Lewin, 1951 – no page reference given). One wonders how Mantere et al.'s framework might have been differently configured if CATS had not risen to prominence in the way we have described here, or how process views might be further advanced were Lewin seen as in their camp rather than something to be opposed – if Lewin was an early

promoter of process approaches and group dynamics, not the foundation underlying n-stage models for change agents.

A second key frontier in Lewin 1947 (39ff.) is the idea that new
mathematics will need to be developed to enable many of the other
things that Lewin, who was ahead of his time in this respect, was keen
to see advanced. The frustration that he caused the mathematicians
who worked with him at the University of Iowa is legendary. Austrian
Gustav Bergman came there to work for Lewin as a research associate,
but the association did not last long, as Bergmann became convinced
that Lewin's programme was impossible to capture (Heald, 1992).
Lewin (1947, p.10ff; 30ff.) wanted to see the effects of multiple variables relating to change: individual and group perceptions or expecta-
tions related to forthcoming change related to perceptions and
recalibrations after the event, what he called objective and subjective
or behavioural and cognitive phenomena. While such multi-variant
analysis may have been difficult in the 1940s, this is not entirely the
case now; advances in statistical techniques and computing power
offer potential to examine not only relations among many variables
at once, but also changes in these variables over time. For example,
growth modelling with latent variables, conducted with structural
equation programs like R and Mplus (Bliese and Ployhart, 2002), can
examine how latent constructs like individual beliefs are influenced
by discrete events and by other latent constructs, such as the beliefs of
other group members. Another approach that might have fascinated
Lewin is optimization, which relies on computing power to isolate the
values of variables within a predetermined equation that maximize
a desired outcome. Although optimization is often conducted with
economic (i.e., profit) and operational (i.e., production) outcomes, the
approach could be applied to maximizing (or minimizing) outcomes of
interest to Lewin, such as individual prejudice and creativity or
a group decision. Programs like MATLAB and Gurobi Python, and
even an add-on to the popular MS Excel (Mason, 2013), open up
optimization to researchers from all disciplines. While optimization
does not replace qualitative or qualitative research (as studies are

needed to identify the variables included and the distributions of those variables in the equation to be optimized), with the equation and possible values set, optimization can simulate millions of possible combinations and generate hypotheses that can be tested in subsequent observational or experimental study.

Returning to how teaching change could be made different by thinking again about Lewin's legacy with regard to this second recovered frontier, it could be that new developments and findings related to combining and analysing data from multiple sources using the latest statistical advances could be added to the set of things that Lewin has inspired at the end of those textbook chapters on change, rather than the current textbook norm of showing newer n-stage frameworks and intervention tools as simply building upon 'Lewin's classic model' and surpassing it.

Our field could also benefit from a fresh investigation of the ideas offered to us by Maslow. By understanding that workers are trying to satisfy multiple needs simultaneously, we would avoid simplistic and erroneous applications of Maslow, such as that if you pay workers enough for them to cover their basic needs, then money ceases to be important to them, or that in poorly paid and insecure employment, where workers are trying to fulfil their lower-level needs, that managers need not be concerned about providing an environment where workers are respected and feel like they belong.

Because textbooks focus exclusively on HON, it is easy to assume that this was all Maslow had to offer when, in fact, the hierarchy was only part of a more complex theory of motivation. In addition to his categorization of human needs, Maslow identified 'preconditions for basic need satisfactions' (1943, p.383), including freedom of speech, action and expression. Maslow, in arguments that resonate with our appreciation of what Adam Smith believed to be important (see Chapter Two) was adamant that these freedoms must be 'defended because without them the basic satisfactions are quite impossible, or at least, very severely endangered' (1943, p.383).

The implications of Maslow's thinking for managers and management theorists could be very different if we understood that before considering how to design work to satisfy higher-level needs, managers must ensure that these basic freedoms be respected – that a high degree of freedom is not just required for workers to self-actualize, but to satisfy even basic physiological needs.

The complexities of Maslow's theorizing were of no use to McGregor, who we can see as the equivalent to Schein in the case of Lewin – the person whose interpretations of the classic idea came to be regarded as the classic idea itself. However, McGregor acknowledges that the complexities he leaves out would only have distracted from the points he wanted to make about the danger of unreflective theorizing. Somewhat ironically perhaps, McGregor himself became subject to the processes we have analysed in this chapter – his own contributions to the field of management are distorted to represent something very different to what he might have anticipated. McGregor could have left an important legacy as one of the founders of critical reflection, rather than being portrayed a pseudo-scientific constructor of bad hypotheses that failed the test of empirical support.

Where does the evolutionary narrative of management history presented in textbooks lead us next? There are generally small excursions into the work of scholars seen to be more serious than the 'simplistic' Lewin, Maslow and McGregor. People who used behavioural or quantitative or systems approaches and actually 'used scientific research to develop theories' (Bartol et al., 2002, p.48). But the next generation of theorists following McGregor who make a major impact on the world of management are a group of pop-management consultants and academics with a new pseudo-scientific creation (but less self-reflection than McGregor), a binary that says organizations which have a strong, unified, homogeneous 'corporate culture' are good, and those that do not are bad.

8   The Invention of Corporate Culture

The development of management studies' understanding of culture reinforces a naïve, prescriptive and conservative approach to what organizations should be and aim for.

One of the latest 'truths' to emerge and be processed into the annals of management history is the notion that corporate culture has been discovered to be one of the most important enablers of, or barriers to, management success. But how did the science behind this emerge? The chapter adopts a critical perspective of the use of the term 'corporate culture' by management consultants, practicing managers and management academics since its emergence as an element of business discourse from the early 1980s. Our analysis focuses on critiques of so-called functionalist and unitarist approaches to explaining and exploiting culture in organizational contexts. We discuss how the cultural assumptions expressed by mainstream management writers and distilled into management textbooks can suppress, for example, forms of employee opposition and resistance and serve essentially to reproduce corporate ideology and propaganda, and notably so in the drive to sustain shareholder value logic and performance efficiency as the fundamental aim of management.

> Culture is a popular word in management these days ... The best organi-
> zations have strong cultures ... ones that are clear and well defined and
> widely shared among members, discourage dysfunctional work beha-
> viours and encourage positive ones ...

Campling et al. *Management* (2008, p.43)

Earlier chapters have shown how management histories have presented
a narrative whereby new theories of management have replaced (or
discontinued) the old while building on the continuity provided by
the supposed 'foundations of management'. The Hawthorne Effect
and the idea that 'a cared for worker is a busy worker' replaced
Taylorism; then we discovered that managers must show they care by
addressing workers' 'higher needs'; then we discovered it would be
better for managers who made Theory X assumptions about workers
to instead make Theory Y assumptions. So what's next? Theory Z?
In fact, that is what happens next: the first key book of the next 'wave'
of management theory is titled *Theory Z* (Ouchi, 1981).[1]

One of the most popular 'theories' in the recent history of management is the idea that organizations' shared set of underlying values
(their 'culture') is an important lever to be manipulated by management
for improved organizational performance (Bate, 1995; Davis, 1984;
Martins and Terblanche, 2003). The suggestion is that corporate culture
encompasses time-honoured values and behaviours that contributes to
the unique environment or climate of an organization, and importantly,
that a direct and causal relationship exists between a 'strong' culture
and enhanced business performance (see Deal and Kennedy, 1982, 2000;
Peters and Waterman, 1982; Schein, 1985, 1992).

The term corporate culture became widely known and extremely
popular in the business and management world from around the mid-
1980s. The assumption is that corporate culture has always existed in
the way that those early authors defined it – but we only discovered it in
the 1980s. This 'discovery' is presented in management textbooks

[1] This chapter draws from elements of Rowlinson, M. and Hassard, J. (1993).
The Invention of Corporate Culture: A History of the Histories of Cadbury. *Human
Relations*, 46(3), 299–326.

towards the end of their historical surveys, where it is often the first idea covered in subsections with titles like 'Contemporary Issues and Challenges' (Davidson et al., 2009, p.56) and 'Continuing Management Themes' (Schermerhorn et al., 2014, p.49). It is often linked to other discoveries such as Total Quality Management or 'Quality and performance excellence' (Schermerhorn et al., 2014, p.49).

The 'culture' to which these texts refer is generally defined and promoted in terms like this: 'a well-developed and business-specific culture in which management and staff are thoroughly socialized ... can underpin stronger organizational commitment, higher morale, more efficient performance ... [and] ... higher productivity' (Furnham and Gunter, 1993, p.3). So, while culture – and the theory that a strong culture is a good culture – is held up as a discovery, what it is promoted in the name of it has not changed. Culture is the latest tool to enable managers to achieve performance efficiency.

This chapter counters those characterizations. Our counter-history argues that corporate culture was invented, and is maintained, by a network of elements looking for solutions and increased legitimacy. The idea of an object called 'culture' was desirous for all of the 'knowing subjects' in this network. Rather than a scientific discovery, corporate culture, we shall argue, is another case of subject/object co-creation in management.

Moreover, we suggest that while the culture concept – with its emphasis on how habits and rituals developed over time can shape present behaviours – has promised to make organization studies more *historical*, this promise has not been fulfilled. In the years since the 'discovery' of organizational culture, the literature on management and organization studies has reflected contributions towards a 'cultural turn' for the field (Rowlinson and Hassard, 2013). Writers such as Needle (2004) examined how culture represented the collective values, beliefs and principles of organizational members and formed a distinctive intellectual product of firm history, management style, company strategy and national customs. Similarly, Ravasi and Schultz (2006) suggested that organizational culture was a set of shared anthropological assumptions that guided what happens in organiza-tions by defining appropriate behaviour for various situations. In organizational sociology, culture was said to be based on and include an organization's vision, values, norms, systems, symbols, language, assumptions, beliefs and habits (Brown, 1998), with often such argu-ments suggesting that earlier 'managerial' perspectives reflected a naïve and even utopian approach – one aimed at recommending what a culture *should be* rather than what it actually is (Parker, 2000). However, despite these contributions, the superficial view of culture that still permeates mainstream discussion makes us, we will suggest in this chapter, less historically aware, and less innovative.

Possible explanations for the failure to integrate management history and organizational studies more effectively are examined in the paragraphs that follow, and a synthesis is developed using Foucault's ideas about the ways in which histories emerge to justify present needs. We draw again on the concept of invented tradition, which we introduced in Chapter Five as part of the analysis of the institutionalization of the case method at HBS.

We find that culture is invented in response to problems encountered by management consultancies, a dissonance amongst a Western managerial class troubled by the rise of Japan as an eco-nomic power, book publishers cashing in on pop-management, uni-versity-based management academics and corporations who like the idea of creating their own corporate histories that explain the emer-gence of, and promote and justify to the world, their supposed 'strong cultures'. To illustrate this last node in the diagram of culture's creation, we show how Cadbury, a UK confectionery company well-known for its Quaker traditions, developed a corporate culture sim-ply by attributing significance to the Quaker beliefs of the Cadbury family. A counter-history is reconstructed, primarily from published sources, to demonstrate how the histories constructed by the company – including notably a centenary celebration in 1931 – were part of the process of giving meaning into the firm's labour-management institutions.

These networked elements reinforce one another to the point where the existence of corporate culture, as we have come to define it, goes unquestioned. But by highlighting how these elements emerge in combination with the notion of culture they promote, we offer a more thoroughgoing and historical critique of the creation or invention of corporate culture in the management and organization studies literature.

So, how did the science behind the *truth* about organizational culture come to pass?

MARKETING CULTURE: TO GROW A BUSINESS, YOU NEED SOMETHING TO SELL

Management histories in textbooks associate the emergence of the culture and excellence 'movements' with a series of books that became 'required reading for any manager who wanted to appear informed' (Davidson et al., 2009, p.56–7). Titles like *Theory Z* (Ouchi, 1981), *The Art of Japanese Management* (Pascale and Athos, 1981), *Corporate Cultures* (Deal and Kennedy, 1982), and *In Search of Excellence* (Peters and Waterman, 1982) are credited with creating 'pop-management'. But these books did not appear out of thin air (although some might claim that the theories they promoted did). This new wave, and the concept of culture the authors of these books (academics working with management consultants) reported on, developed as a strategic response to a particular problem. We touched on the role consultancies played in our previous chapter's discussion of the 'Will-to-sell-solutions' element of the episteme that converted the theories of prominent social scientists into management frameworks. But with respect to culture, management consultancies play an even greater role in actively inventing management knowledge.

The strategy behind the creation of culture as an important thing in management is linked to the preeminent consultancy McKinsey & Co responding to the rise of a key competitor in the 1970s. The upstart Boston Consulting Group was winning new business and growing revenues in the late 1970s by around 50 per cent year-on-year, thanks to popular new tools like the BCG matrix. McKinsey deployed a team of consultants (including Tom Peters and Robert Waterman) to Stanford and Harvard to work with professors to develop a framework of their own that they could brand.

Dovetailing with the opportunity provided by anxiety surrounding Japan seemingly turning out to be better at management than the West, they developed a model that would enable a focus on strong unitary cultures as Japanese corporations were perceived to have. This turned into the McKinsey Seven Ss framework (Systems, Staff, Structure, Strategy, Style, Skills, Shared values – which should all reinforce one another in a 'strong' culture). The Seven Ss, first published in the journal *Business Horizons* in 1980 (Waterman et al., 1980), forms the basis of Pascale (from Stanford) and Athos's (from Harvard) *Art of Japanese Management* and Peters and Waterman's *In Search of Excellence*. These publications became management's first best-sellers.

Where did the Seven Ss model in the distinctive seven-node snowflake diagram come from? Pascal, Athos, Peters and Waterman have been a little vague about this. But a few years ago, we found a small monograph called *Organizational Dynamics* written by J.P. Kotter (1978). Kotter was also a professor at Harvard at the time these meetings took place and in his 1978 monograph, there is a series of diagrams that bear a striking resemblance to the Seven Ss – although some of the names of the nodes would be altered so they all started with S (e.g., Systems remained, but Employees became 'Staff' and Organizational Arrangements became 'Structure'), providing the consultants with the catchy title for the framework.

Kotter's book was published in April 1978. Pascale and Athos (1981, p.1) claim that the Seven Ss emerged out of 'a series of meetings in June 1978' with Peters and Waterman. No mention is made of Kotter in Pascale, Athos, Peters and Waterman's writing, but they would have been aware of Kotter's work and, given the similarities, it is hard to imagine that it did not influence the Seven Ss' development. It is another example, not unlike those from our previous chapters, of the 'made up' and bric-a-brac rather than objective nature of key management theories, theories that over time we come to regard as foundations.

ACADEMIC ELEMENTS THAT SUPPORT PREVAILING VIEWS OF CORPORATE CULTURE

While it may not be surprising that management consultants and publishers seeking to maximize sales should have developed and promoted a superficial view of culture, they are not the only part of a network that sustains the creation of the 'good organizations have strong corporate cultures' theory. Academics and corporations play a role too. The following paragraphs explore how business history and organization studies scholars came to treat culture.

The promised cultural turn in management theory (outlined earlier in this chapter) suggested a change in emphasis in the study of organizations. The focus on culture was associated with a stress on the subjective realm (Alvesson, 2001), and a turn to interpretive and qualitative approaches in sociology, particularly organization sociology (Hofstede, 1986, p.254). Hence, the rise of organizational symbolism should have involved the introduction into management and organization theory of disciplines such as anthropology and literary criticism (Turner, 1990, p.83), which were unlike those that management had previously sought to connect to (especially economics and statistics). Similarly, the concept of culture was welcomed in the hope that it might induce more of 'a historical perspective' in a 'notoriously ahistorical' field (Nord, 1985, p.191).

A 'historically informed' emphasis on culture should make organizational studies 'relatively less reliant on the empirical analytical sciences and more dependent on the historical-hermeneutic sciences', it was claimed (Nord, 1985, p.191). 'History as a mode of inquiry in organizational life' was even seen as 'a liberating activity,' dereifying social structures and revealing choices to organization members (Barrett and Srivastva, 1991, p.248). Since most definitions of culture in organizations have a 'temporal dimension,' this should have opened up opportunities for historians to contribute a long-term perspective to organization studies (Dellheim, 1986, p.11). However, these promises have not been fulfilled; history, hermeneutically inclined or otherwise, and organization studies have not been drawn together significantly through the concept of culture (Rowlinson and Hassard, 2013).

The analysis further on in this chapter suggests possible reasons for the lack of integration between corporate culture and management and business history, and then attempts to rectify this by offering a case study of the history of the *invention* of a culture by Cadbury, the British chocolate confectionery manufacturer: a case that might encourage us to think differently.

Organization Studies and History

Several reasons can be suggested for the failure of organization studies to incorporate history into the concept of culture. They are similar to the problems encountered by sociologists in their efforts to erode the distinction between sociology and history. First, sociologists had become sensitized to the problems of meaning and understanding, to the view that explaining behaviour had to be embedded in the sets of meanings and orientations which actors brought to their actions. If these could best be explored by in-depth, qualitative interviewing, then dead people told no tales (Kendrick, Straw and McCrone. 1990). This methodological problem of meaning is exacerbated because corporate culture writers tend to focus on the interpersonal level and rarely accept 'the need for a macro-sociological analysis' (Thompson and McHugh, 1990, p.230). From an interpersonal perspective, 'the reality of an organization is very much influenced by values, norms, and assumptions that cannot be traced to its history' (Berg, 1985, p.288).

Schein (1985, p.7–8, 167) is a good example of a well-known corporate culture writer, inclined towards psychological analysis at the interpersonal level, who accepts that 'historical data' is vital for the study of organizational culture because culture is 'to be found only where there is a definable group with a significant history,' and so, 'one must be able to reconstruct the history of the group'. However, despite being critical of the consultant/pop-management writers on culture (in a *Sloan Management Review* article reviewing *Theory Z* and *The Art of Japanese Management*, he claimed that their arguments and methods were 'not convincing', supported by a 'meagre data base' and their 'quick fix ... prescriptions' were 'glib', 'superficial' and 'naïve' – Schein, 1981, p.59; 62; 63), Schein and other academics perpetuate many of their assumptions about the object.

Schein (1985, p.303) decides that history is methodologically more or less inaccessible because of the problem of meaning: 'Real history is fantastically complex, difficult to unravel, and itself culture bound ... cultures simplify and reinterpret the events to fit into themes that make cultural sense.' But it is worth noting that Schein relies wholly on interviews (as did Peters, Waterman and company) 'to discover key historical events and the manner in which they were handled' (1985, p.119). Like most corporate culture writers over the years, he does not seriously consider the use of documentary sources to research the history of an organization. In most organization studies, archives are not seen as part of an organization's memory, and business and management historians are dismissed as being just one among many actors in an organization's external environment trying to record its 'past performance' (Walsh and Ungson, 1991, p.66–7).

This overlooks the important role that historians play within organizations. Business historians themselves argue that history matters to managers because one important use of history is 'simply getting things, events, and facts into shared memory' (Tedlow and John, 1986, p.82). It is almost as if, because the 'culture concept has been borrowed from anthropology' (Smircich, 1983, p.339), corporate culture has been researched as if modern business organizations were illiterate tribes (cf. Smircich, 1985, p.62) which did not possess written histories. However, there is no obvious reason why the 'objective culture' that is 'written into the subjectivity of corporate members' (Fitzgerald, 1988, p.11) should not also be written into the archives and histories of a corporation. Similar problems of meaning apply both to interviews and historical documents; the subjectivity of archivists and historians is reflected in company archives and histories. In a popular novel very much concerned with time and history, Jeanette Winterson writes: 'I will have to assume that I had a childhood, but I cannot assume to have had the one I remember' (1990, p.92). Just as a child's school reports make an interesting comparison with the school-days remembered, so an organization's recorded history should provide a revealing insight into the past remembered by its members.

The second problem for sociology in relation to history is epistemological; there is a strand of thinking within sociology that is sceptical about 'the solidity of historical "events"' (Kendrick et al., 1990, p.3). Many organizational analysts (see Calás and Smircich, 1999; Hassard and Wolfram Cox, 2013 for reviews) have succumbed to the 'fatal distraction' (Thompson, 1994) of postmodernism, and postmodernism is vulnerable to the 'impositionalist claim ... that recounting the past in the form of a story inevitably imposes a false narrative structure upon it' (Norman, 1991, p.122). From this perspective, 'History cannot be rescued from deconstruction – nor should it be,' and post-modern history 'may dissolve into endlessly circulating present discourses – it can, apparently, be anything one cares to make it' (Widdowson, 1990). Such a claim for the 'legitimacy of fiction as history' is guaranteed to incur the wrath of 'professional historians' (Marwick, 1990) because: 'The emphasis on the role of the historian in the making of history tends, if pressed to its logical conclusion, to rule out any objective history at all: history is what the historian makes' (Carr, 1964, p.26).

It is this position of scepticism and subjectivism which has prevailed in the more critical approaches to culture in organizations: Events in an organization's history are raw material that members of a culture can mould into a form that both reflects and reconstitutes the culture itself. Underlying this view is the recognition that both cultures and organizational histories are socially constructed. Far from being objective descriptions, accounts of key events in an organization's history reflect differential attention, selective perception, and incomplete recall. As organizational members strive at mutually acceptable interpretations of events, distortions and omissions multiply. By the time accounts have ossified in the form of organizational stories, legends and sagas, a new reality has been socially constructed (Martin et al., 1985).

However, the reality of a past need not be abandoned simply because it has undergone a process of social construction, for to do so would result in abandoning historical research. Instead, the production of history itself, the process of social construction, can be incorporated into the historian's account. It should be accepted that there is not a clear separation between 'events' and their selection:

> Like a dike covered with ice floes at the end of the winter, the past has been covered by a thick crust of narrative interpretations; and historical debate is as much a debate about the components of this crust as about the past hidden beneath it. *(Ankersmit, 1986, p.26)*

The social construction of business archives, histories and biographies can be incorporated into historians' competing narratives. Historians have long recognized some simple guidelines, and a useful starting point is to remember that 'when we take up a work of history, our first concern should be not with the facts which it contains but with the historian who wrote it' (Carr, 1964, p.22). With company-sponsored business histories, this calls for research into the *conditions* which called for a history to be commissioned and written, as well as the *relationship* between the company and the hired historian. With Cadbury, changing conditions and different authors produced alternative histories.

Business History and the Concept of Culture

For business history, the 'boom in the study of corporate culture and the concern with the role of rituals, symbols, beliefs and myths within the corporation ... suggested new lines of inquiry' (Dellheim, 1987, p.13). Unfortunately, business history is not well-placed to take up such opportunities. Because business historians tend to avoid much theoretical and methodological reflection, they are unlikely to be able to give an adequate response to the scepticism of organization studies concerning history and culture. British business historians have been castigated by one of their own leading lights for being 'inveterate empiricists,' obsessed with simply getting the story right (Hannah, quoted in Coleman, 1987, p.141).

British business historians have complained of the absence of appropriate theoretical models for them to use (Coleman, 1987, p.151), but to some extent it is their own ideological distaste for theoretical issues, such as those raised by Marxist historians (p.149), which has effectively cut them off from wider concerns. Engagement in such debate might have led business historians to a closer understanding of the reflexive, interpretive, hermeneutic and subjective approaches expected from historians in the organizational analysis of the concept of culture. But 'objectivity' is seen as essential for the credibility of business history. Without it, 'there is the risk that the historian may become little better than an archival hired-gun fighting a rearguard action armed with index cards ... such behavior would incur the outrage of professional colleagues who would, with reason, call into question the integrity of the offender' (Dellheim, 1986, p.16).

Even when business history has been more theoretical, the preference has been for 'institutional' rather than 'psychological' history (Chandler, 1988, p.302). Strategy and structure have been considered rather than 'beliefs and symbols' (Dellheim, 1986, p.10). This tends to privilege certain kinds of data; the evidence for formal organizational structures exists, first and foremost, in the form of official organization charts (Chandler, 1962). A problem for business historians is that the usual way to gain access to the records of a company is through being commissioned to write a history of the company, and the fact remains that however scholarly, accurate, fair, objective and serious that company history, its content is necessarily shaped by the need for the author to give his client something approaching what he wants (Coleman, 1987, p.142).

In other words, the subjective, cultural requirements of companies to have written histories produced are best served by business historians professing a self-effacing 'objectivity,' which does not allow for the problems of meaning and subjectivity raised by the concept of culture to be addressed. The apparently contradictory advice given to organizations commissioning a history is that the best way to make their 'constructive accomplishments known ... encourage investor interest and, not insignificantly, spark employee pride,' is to 'strive for ... objectivity.' Apparently, the 'old-style company history, long on self-laudation but short on objectivity is no longer acceptable' because of the general scepticism about 'the objectivity and balance in "management sanctioned" corporate histories' (Campion, 1987, p.31; cf. Hannah, 1986).

Paradoxically, the strength of the Cadbury culture and the interest in the company's history, especially on the part of its former chairman Sir Adrian Cadbury, has meant that the firm has kept its archives intact and permitted relatively free access to them. This has allowed the present account to be constructed contesting the basis of the corporate culture in a company where the culture might appear all but incontestable. It might be suspected that cultures that do not allow access or criticism are not so strong. In their efforts to prove their credibility and objectivity, business historians have been keen to distance themselves from vital cultural artefacts, the old in-house histories and hagiographies. These are seen as an embarrassing legacy from the time when 'the writing of company histories was seen as a form of inferior journalistic hack-work' (Coleman, 1984, 1987, p.145; Campion, 1987, p.32).

CONSEQUENCES OF AN AHISTORICAL APPROACH TO CORPORATE CULTURE

Two consequences of the failure to integrate history and organization studies in the analysis of the concept of culture can be identified. First, instead of delving into history as such, organizational analysts of culture have tended to invoke their own culture construction, namely the 'founder.' Numerous studies offer variations on a theme, 'descriptively portraying founders as the prime movers behind historical events or prescriptively urging leaders to articulate a vision and create a culture' (Martin, Sitkin and Boehm, 1985, p.100).

In the early corporate culture literature, Schein (1985), again, draws on 'group and leadership theory' from psychology (p.50), instead of history itself, to explain the 'historical factors' concerning the origins of culture (p.148). He makes the cultural assumption that 'culture and leadership are really two sides of the same coin' (p.4), and uses 'studies of the psychodynamic make-up of leaders' (p.172) to paint an idealized picture of 'how organization founders shape culture': Firms are created by entrepreneurs who have a vision of how the concerted effort of the right group of people can create a new product or service in the marketplace (p.209).

Organizations therefore begin to create cultures through the actions of founders (p.221). All too conveniently, as the interests of 'academics' and 'practitioners' in the area of culture converged (Barley, Meyer and Gash, 1988), 'organizational studies of the culture creation process' have offered 'a seductive promise to entrepreneurs':

> namely that a founder can create a culture, cast in the founder's own image and reflecting the founder's own values, priorities, and vision of the future. Thus a founder's own perspective can be transformed into a shared legacy that will survive death or departure from the institution – a personal form of organizational immortality. *(Martin et al., 1985, p.99)*

In other words, corporate culture writers have imposed their own socially constructed narrative on history, the story of the founder. For the most part, this conforms to the rhetoric of organization studies in which social psychological theories and interview data, rather than historical evidence, are seen as persuasive. However, even when 'documentary sources' have been consulted, it is the 'founder' narrative which has been imposed upon them (Pettigrew, 1979, p.570).

A second consequence is that these elements of how culture is historicized join forces with the study of culture by less methodologically scrupulous researchers, as we described in our introduction. Two of the best-known books of the early (management consulting) corporate culture genre can be used to illustrate this. Peters and Waterman (1982) accept a neat conceptual split between history and myth. They attribute far more power to myth: 'History doesn't move us as much as does a good current anecdote (or presumably, a juicy bit of gossip)' (p.62). This is because whereas 'stories, myths and legends' can be constructed to 'convey the organization's shared values, or culture' (p.75), history is fixed and taken as given. Peters and Waterman use histories and accounts by prominent members of firms uncritically. Their material on 'IBM's philosophy,' for example, is taken almost wholly from the 1963 book *A Business and Its Beliefs: The Ideas that Helped Build IBM*, by Thomas Watson, Jr., the founder's son.

In *Corporate Cultures* (1982), Deal and Kennedy apparently placed great emphasis on *historical* sources. They wanted to find out 'what had made America's great companies not merely organizations, but successful human institutions,' and in their search, they:

> stumbled into a goldmine of evidence. Biographies, speeches, and documents from such giants of business as Thomas Watson of IBM, John Patterson (the founder of NCR), Will Durant of General Motors, William Kellogg of Kelloggs, and a host of others show a remarkable intuitive understanding of the importance of a strong culture in the affairs of their companies. *(Deal and Kennedy, 1982, p.7–8)*

As critics of the early corporate culture writings have commented however, 'what executives and managers say in words or on paper is taken as proof. There is little critical reflection on this' (Thompson and McHugh, 2009, p.165). At issue, therefore, is the status of historical evidence for culture. The view taken in this chapter is that it is not necessary to choose between either discounting company-sponsored histories out of hand, or accepting them more or less uncritically. Instead of treating the company-sponsored history as a faithful record of events – as the popular corporate writers do – it can be used as a valuable cultural artefact in its own right. The narratives constructed in such histories reveal much about the cultural concerns of companies at the time they were commissioned and written; a hagiography may reveal little about the life of a saint, but it gives a valuable insight into the hagiographer's view of saintly qualities. So in this chapter, the histories of Cadbury written to commemorate a centenary in 1931 are used as the starting point in tracing the construction of a distinctive culture in the late 1920s and early 1930s, rather than the creation of a culture in 1831.

THE CREATION OF CORPORATE HISTORIES:
A COUNTER-HISTORY OF CADBURY'S CULTURE

One objection to the corporate culture literature is that it fails to acknowledge that people are subject to more cultures than the organization, such as their social class or profession. There are many 'traditions' which might be 'a good deal older than most of our organizations,' and by implication more influential. Corporate culture writers, whether from an organization studies background or business history, have largely overlooked the wider concept of 'tradition,' which is 'not far removed, after all, from "culture"' (Thomas, 1985, p.25).

As we saw in Chapter Five when we looked at the institution of the business school, it turns out that many '"traditions" which appear or claim to be old are often quite recent in origin and sometimes invented' (Hobsbawm, 1983a, p.2). Historians have coined the term 'invented tradition.' The concept of corporate culture, as we are taught it in management, is similar to the definition of an invented tradition, which is:

> a set of practices, normally governed by overtly or tacitly accepted
> rules and of a ritual or symbolic nature, which seek to inculcate
> certain values and norms of behaviour by repetition, which
> automatically implies continuity with the past. Insofar as there is
> such reference to a historic past, the peculiarity of "invented"
> traditions is that the continuity with it is largely factitious. In short,
> they are responses to novel situations which establish their own
> past by quasi-obligatory repetition. *(Hobsbawm, 1983a, p.2)*

If the ostensibly ancient traditions of nations, such as the rituals of the British monarchy (Cannadine, 1983), turn out to have been invented in order to reinforce a cohesive national identity, then the same might well apply to many corporate cultures.

And here we find a third leg supporting the theory that good organizations have strong homogeneous corporate cultures. This is the increasingly commonplace practice of corporations employing business historians to create histories that promote the evolution of their culture. These corporate culture histories are presented as fact: and the results reinforce the rightness of their present and future actions. They are not recognized as the invented traditions which they most often are.

In the same way that historians have turned their attention to the history of the invention of traditions by nations, this last part of this chapter attempts to construct a counter-history of the invention of the Cadbury corporate culture (cf. Hobsbawm, 1983b, p.307). Cadbury is significant because as well as having a strong cultural identity, up until now, it has generally been accepted that its culture is as old as some of the company's sponsored histories have claimed it is – unlike many recent attempts to create corporate histories, Cadbury has a long history of creating corporate history so we can see the invention process over a long period of time.

The aim is not to de-mythify Cadbury, or to try to reduce its history to myth. To do so would be to claim a superior objectivity, or to deny the importance of history in the Cadbury culture, and both claims would be untenable. Instead, a competing narrative is constructed which incorporates and explains rather than refutes previous narrative histories of the company. The competing narrative is of an 'invented tradition,' instead of a story of a 'founder.' The test of the narrative will be whether the reader is persuaded that it is convincing, even in the case of a culture as strong as Cadbury's.

Cadbury Culture and the Cadbury Centenary

Cadbury, formally part of Cadbury Schweppes and since 2012 a wholly-owned subsidiary of Mondelēz International (previously Kraft Foods), is a large chocolate confectionery manufacturing company based in Britain. Until 1962, it was a private limited company, largely owned, and continuously managed by members of the Cadbury family.

The company's history is easily identified with the prominent members of the Cadbury family who founded and ran the business (Dellheim, 1986:13). It was started by John Cadbury (1801–89) in 1824, in the centre of Birmingham. It became Cadbury Brothers in 1847 when John was joined by his older brother, Benjamin Head Cadbury (1798–80), as a partner. Initially, the business was mainly concerned with the tea and coffee trade. In 1861, when John Cadbury handed over the business to his sons, Richard (1835–99) and George (1839–922), cocoa still accounted for only about a quarter of the firm's trade. Richard and George revived the firm's flagging fortunes and started to shape the business along the lines on which it has developed since, concentrating on cocoa and chocolate production. In 1879, Cadbury moved out of Birmingham city centre, Bridge Street, to a purpose-built cocoa and chocolate factory at Bournville, a greenfield site about 4 miles south of Birmingham.

The Cadbury corporate culture can be summarized as the identification of the company's distinctive labour-management policies with the Cadbury family's Quaker beliefs. This was clearly expressed in 1931 where the firm celebrated a centenary. Two publications marked the centenary: The major one was *The Firm of Cadbury* 1831–931, nearly 300 pages published by Constable. The firm paid the author, Iolo A. Williams, £350 for his work, and a Centenary Celebration Committee allocated £200–300 to advertise it; 4450 copies were given to employees with at least 10 years' service, and 450 were distributed to pensioners. The firm was pleased with the press reviews of the books, which were quoted with approval in the *Bournville Works Magazine. The Times* reviewer praised Williams for making 'a contribution of value to industrial history.' Williams was a journalist and writer, a botanist, bibliographer and an authority on early English water colours: 'Among the great interests of his life were British flora and the minor poets of the eighteenth century' (Bournville Works Magazine, February 1962). From 1905, T. B. Rogers was the full-time Editor of the *Bournville Works Magazine* (Bournville Magazine, March 1970). His more modest work, *A Century of Progress* 1831–931, was published by Cadbury, and the Advertising Department spent over £7500 to produce 180,000 copies. Cadbury's customers in Britain received a copy, and it was also used by associated companies in Australia, New Zealand and Canada.

These two histories constructed continuity between the firm's past and present policies. Both drew heavily on an unpublished book, *Personal Reminiscences of Bridge Street*, and *Bournville* 1929. This volume itself appears to have been edited, because any accounts that were less than deferential in tone were excluded from it. Some of the recollections had appeared earlier in the *Bournville Works Magazine* (September and October 1909) and others were collected in preparation for the centenary. The vocabulary used by the long-serving Cadbury workers gives a flavour of paternalism. They referred to the Cadbury brothers as 'Mr. George' and 'Mr. Richard.' One of them remembered, 'During the struggles of the 18 sixties I never knew men work harder than our masters, who were indeed more like fathers to us' (Rogers, 1931, p.27). Rogers described the reminiscences as an 'intimate history' of the firm:

> These records tell of the unflagging energy of Richard and George Cadbury to make their business succeed, and of their cheerfulness even in times when disaster faced them, but first and foremost they tell of the close human relations between master and man, who together were "like a family". *(1931, p.27)*

In their search for a unity between past and present, these histories presented precedents that are so tenuous as to almost belie the very continuity they are supposed to demonstrate. In his account of the old city centre site, Williams wrote: 'though the organization of physical training and athletics, as we understand it to-day in a factory, was a thing undreamed of then, the men were encouraged to play cricket and football' (1931, p.47).

Williams' 'postscript' concluded: throughout the century of progress and change, there has been unity – a unity brought about because during the whole period the business has been the daily personal concern of a family that has steadily tried to apply, as an employer of labour, the principles of Quaker faith (1931, p.259).

It is worth noting that it is not clear why the firm decided to celebrate a centenary in 1931. According to Williams, it was in 1931 that John Cadbury 'began the actual manufacture of cocoa and chocolate. In 1831, then, the firm of Cadbury may be said to have been born' (1931, p.6). However, in an earlier biography of Richard Cadbury, by his daughter Helen Cadbury Alexander (1906), the date for the start of cocoa manufacturing is unclear, although she believed John Cadbury started experimenting with a pestle and mortar to make cocoa and chocolate around 1835 (1906, p.36). George Cadbury's biographer (Gardiner, 1923) and other publications make no mention of 1831 as significant.

Nor is it clear when the firm decided to celebrate a centenary. There was an anniversary of the move to Bournville in 1879, and the Bournville Works Magazine explained that:

> The way in which the Jubilee should be celebrated was very carefully considered more than a year ago ... the firm had to bear in mind two facts of historical importance to them, namely, that while they would complete fifty years at Bournville in 1929, they would two years later complete their hundredth year as cocoa and chocolate manufacturers. *(1929)*

Possibly the success of the Fry bicentenary in 1928 gave the Cadburys the idea to have a centenary of their own. Fry of Bristol was another cocoa and confectionery firm. It was also owned and managed by a prominent Quaker family, the Frys. In 1919, Fry merged with, but was in effect taken over by Cadbury. Soon after the merger, Fry moved out of the centre of Bristol to a greenfield site modelled on Bournville, and its labour-management policies were directed by Cadbury.

A special issue of the *Fry Works Magazine* was produced for the bi-centenary. The opening address by Lord Riddell, 'The Chocolate Age,' outlined Fry's claims to distinction:

> For generations they have taken the keenest interest in the welfare
> of their workpeople. In furtherance of this policy they decided to
> transfer their factories from the heart of Bristol to Somerdale, a few
> miles out of the City on the banks of the Avon. *(p.13)*

A brief history of Fry told of the 'honest God-fearing Quaker founder'
who would have been alarmed by the lawlessness of the eighteenth
century (p.14), 'In the England of 1728, therefore, where excess both
in language and behaviour was the rule, the restrained and precise
lives led by the Quakers must have made them almost a race
apart' (p.19).

According to a memory of Fry in 1866:

> The personal touch was always in evidence ... This attitude was part
> and parcel – in fact the very essence – of the Fry psychology, since it
> was ingrained in the Frys not to look upon their employees as so many
> cogs in a machine for producing dividends but as human creatures
> possessed of immortal souls, for whom they were largely
> responsible. *(p.28)*

Then there was 'The Fry Spirit': 'Candour, freedom of speech
and humour are the dominant notes in our social life both at Bristol
and Somerdale ... This spirit of toleration and liberty is one of the
finest things at J.S. Fry and Sons Ltd., where one may think like an
Anarchist so long as one does one's job like a decent citizen (p.29)'.
Readers were assured that, 'the Frys of bygone years always
felt a certain responsibility for the welfare – spiritual, mental and
physical – of their employees' (p.81).

In a contribution on 'The Growth of Trade Unionism' at the
firm, the General Secretary of the Transport and General Workers'
Union, Ernest Bevin, wrote:

> It is almost impossible to believe that an institution such as Fry's
> could be 200 years old and yet be so youthful and vigorous. It has
> associated with it a great tradition, and if the record of the firm

could be produced it would make very interesting reading. (*Fry Works Magazine*, Bicentenary Number 36)

That Cadbury selected the year to mark its centenary, and Fry celebrated the labour-management policies recently imposed by the merger with Cadbury for its bicentenary, demonstrates clearly how the firms themselves decided how and when to mark certain dates with celebratory events. Organizations impose the timing and significance of historical events such as centenaries upon history; history does not impose these events upon organizations.

The Cadbury Institutions

The generally accepted view of Cadbury's labour-management policies is that they were inspired by the Cadbury family's Quaker religious beliefs (Jeremy, 1990; Corley, 1988), which created the Cadbury 'company culture' (Dellheim, 1987). Cadbury is seen as providing 'An opportunity for analysing the relationship between religious beliefs and economic action' (p.14) because:

> The Quaker beliefs of the Cadbury family shaped the ethic of the firm. The Cadbury family's social and industrial experiments were, on one level, an attempt to reconcile religious convictions and business practices ... Three main influences formed George and Richard Cadbury's beliefs in the Quaker ethic, which shaped their views of the nature and purpose of business; the experience of turning around a failing firm; and an exposure to the social problems of the industrial city ... The Quaker ethic was the cornerstone of Cadburys. *(Dellheim, 1987, p.14–5)*

Notice how the role of founder is taken by George and Richard Cadbury, even though they did not actually found the business, but took over the running of it in 1861 (Dellheim, 1986). Founder type narratives achieve this by associating those identified with the founder role with the turn-around of a company. This gets over the problem that, in the Cadbury case, associating the culture with the original founders of the business would be too tenuous. It also illustrates how founders are selected by historians retrospectively; they are not fixed by history.

An alternative account of Cadbury is that five specific labour-management institutions can be identified, and each of them was developed by the firm in response to contemporary social movements rather than Quaker inspiration. First, there is the Bournville village. In 1893, sometime after the move to Bournville, 120 acres adjacent to the factory were purchased, and the next year, house-building began. The houses were sold at cost price, with mortgages available from Cadbury. Some of the purchasers were too thrifty and sold up, making a hefty profit. George Cadbury then decided to turn the Bournville Building Estate into a Charitable Trust and on December 14 1900, the Bournville Village Trust (B.V.T.) was formed. In the view of a B.V.T. Community and Information Officer: 'It is difficult to say precisely when the concept of a Building Estate developed into that of a Garden Village, but all evidence points to the period just before the Trust was founded in December 1900' (Henselowe, 1984, p.5).

Bournville represented a departure from the earlier nineteenth century paternalist community builders (Jeremy, 1990; Jeremy, 1991). The Village Trust was nominally independent and imbued with a democratic vision (Gardiner, 1923). For this, it owed much to the nascent Garden City movement. Ebenezer Howard's book setting out a blueprint for a 'Garden City' was first published in October 1898. During 1899, the Garden City Association was started, and its first conference was held at Bournville in September 1901 (Howard, 1946). The character of the Bournville village owed more to the influence of the early town planning movement than to the inspiration of Quakerism.

The second institution to be considered is the welfare provided by the firm. The move to Bournville more or less necessitated the provision of dining rooms for workers, although these were substantially improved around the turn of the century after members of the firm visited other companies and saw their superior facilities (Marks, n.d.,; Meakin, 1905; Williams, 1931). The personnel measures undertaken in the 1900s were more substantive than anything which preceded them, and cannot be seen as ad hoc additions within a continuous policy or philosophy. There was a definite break in the history of the firm and in the development of its personnel management. This was acknowledged by George Cadbury's biographer (Gardiner, 1923). He divided the history of 'the experiments' at Bournville into two phases. The two brothers, George and Richard Cadbury, were responsible for the measures taken in the earlier phase, which were appropriate for a 'smaller enterprise'. This was 'a highly personal and in some ways a paternal effort to humanize the conditions of labour' (p.113). When Richard Cadbury died in 1899, the business was converted into a private limited company. George Cadbury was joined on the Board of Directors by his own sons, Edward (1873–948) and George Junior (1878–954), and Richard's sons, Barrow (1862–958) and William Adlington (1867–957). This marked the beginning of the second, more complicated phase, which:

> developed with the great expansion of the business, and the emergence of the new ideas in the industrial movement ... It was under this new government, later enlarged by the admission of other members of the family that the larger organized schemes of insurance, education, and so on, were developed. *(p.114)*

The 1900s were years of expansion for Cadbury. Trade increased from £977,010 in 1899 to £1,607,417 in 1909, and the Cadbury workforce rose from 2883 to 4991. It was also a period in which the Cadbury Board became increasingly aware of pressure from competitors, both at home and abroad. This was the context in which substantial welfare and personnel policies were started. These were largely derived from similar schemes which the Cadburys saw in operation at other firms. Continental firms were visited in order to study production techniques, but in 1901, George Cadbury, Jr. visited America specifically to study industrial organization. According to a short biography, he 'saw in a few enlightened firms there schemes by which employees could make known to the management their ideas and suggestions about improving products and working conditions' (Marks, n.d., p.18). He went to the National Cash Register company (N.C.R.), where the flamboyant and unorthodox president, John H. Patterson, had introduced a 'sweeping welfare program' which was already well-known among American manufacturers by 1900. The welfare plan at N.C.R.:

> had a marked impact on the development of systematic welfare work and foreshadowed the future course of welfare activity, notably the shift in emphasis from housing and community work to factory working conditions. *(Nelson 1975, p.106–7; see also Crowther, 1923; Gilman, 1899; Nelson, 1974)*

Several initiatives were undertaken at Bournville after George Cadbury, Jr. reported back to the Board on his US visit, including the introduction of a Suggestion Scheme and the publication of the *Bournville Works Magazine*. The first issue announced that, 'above all, the aim of the chapter is to promote what for lack of a better word we may describe as the Bournville "spirit"' (*Bournville Works Magazine*, Vol. 1, No. 1, November 1902). It became 'one of the great Bournville institutions,' and appeared in much the same format for 67 years (*Bournville Works Magazine*, January 1969, the last issue, p.51). N.C.R. was noted for its 'unique and highly decentralized committee system' (Gilman, 1899, p.228; Nelson, 1975, p.107–9); and in the 1900s, Cadbury also developed a committee system which was gradually extended subsequently (Cadbury, 1979; Industrial Record 1919–39, 1945; Williams, 1931).

A third institution within the Bournville factory was the rigid sexual division of labour. In common with many of the American firms which introduced extensive welfare programme before World War I, Cadbury employed large numbers of women (Nelson, 1975). In 1899, the newly formed Board made the 'marriage bar' a strict policy; it had operated loosely before. Cadbury was neither alone nor anachronistic in this (Lewenhak, 1977), and it continued to operate, as it did in the Civil Service, until the 1940s (Boston, 1980).

Those emphasizing the role of the Cadbury family's Quaker beliefs (Dellheim, 1987; Jeremy, 1990) have found it difficult to accept that the firm applied scientific management. However, it was introduced to such an extent that it can be considered as a fourth Bournville institution (Smith, Child and Rowlinson, 1990). While Edward Cadbury may have viewed Taylorism 'with caution and distrust' (Littler, 1982, p.95), his response to scientific management is best seen as an assertion that its essential elements, work measurement in particular, could be implemented without Taylor's hostility to trade unions (Cadbury, 1915, 1979). In fact, as early as 1913, Cadbury hired an American 'efficiency man' to extend and revise the piecework system, which was a long-standing feature of labour-management at Bournville (Rowlinson, 1988, p.388).

Finally, there was the Works Council scheme. Reflecting the sexual division of labour in the factory, separate councils were set up for men and women. The Bournville Works Men's Council first met on 21 November 1918. The Works Councils were introduced in response to the Whitley Reports produced by the Ministry of Labour, which advocated the setting up of Industrial Councils and Works Committees. The Cadburys wanted to pre-empt any Government intervention in industry by setting up their own scheme. Although the company secured trade union support for the Works Councils, the latter were not a forum for pay negotiations or other union matters. The Works Councils became enmeshed in the administration of welfare and educational provisions which gave them an appearance of importance. It was management which finally withdrew from the Factory Council in 1978 (Smith et al., 1990).

This outline of the institutional framework of Cadbury's labour management should be sufficient to indicate the context of each development, and to question the adequacy of invoking Quakerism as the source of inspiration. The cultural phenomenon which needs to be explained is not the influence of Quakerism on Cadbury's labour management, but how the narrative that privileged the role of Quakerism came to be constructed and accepted.

Quaker Employers

Before this question is addressed, however, the wider issue of Quakers as employers should be considered. Several accounts more or less accept the idea that Quakerism itself made Quakers better employers (Bradley, 1987; Child, 1964; Corley, 1972; 1988; Emden, 1939; Jeremy, 1990; Windsor, 1980). Child's influential study focusses on the attitudes of British Quaker employers towards industrial relations and labour management during the inter-war period. Although he situates their interest in labour management in the context of industrial and social unrest in the first quarter of this century, Child contends that the Society of Friends provided the main impetus for the formulation of 'new conceptions of industrial management' by Quaker employers (1964, p.293). The impression given is one of continuity, 'Quakerism has always stressed the need for democratic human inter-relationships' (p.304).

An earlier history of Quakers in Commerce (Emden, 1939), describes the Quakers' 'burning passion for social justice ... rooted in the Quaker tenets' (p.88). The 'middle-class respectability' of the nineteenth century Quaker merchants is praised on the grounds that:

> the English middle class was once described as the natural
> representatives of the human race, the most outstanding figure of
> which was the independent shopkeeper ... Quakerism bred men
> who did business like saints, and saints who were most efficient
> businessmen.

The Quakers therefore 'helped make England what it is: a manufacturing country,' as well as being 'the most enlightened employers that ever existed,' never losing 'sight of the human factor' (p.22).

In publicity material of the early 1980s, however, the Society of Friends was keen to dispel the view that it is a group of 'wealthy

philanthropists' (Gorman, 1981, p.3). Around the same time, a history
of *The Quaker Enterprise* by a member of the Society (Windsor, 1980),
reflects the way in which the image of the respectable middle-class
shopkeeper had lost its appeal for Quakers:

> The great Quaker entrepreneurs of the last century were true
> Victorians. They stand out as members of the new, large, self-
> satisfied, self-righteous middle-class, who regarded themselves as
> the arbiters of a civilised society and administrators to a less
> educated world ... Benevolent they may have been, charitable and
> anxious to improve the lot of mankind, but it tended to be a fatherly
> benevolence predicated on a view that they knew what was right
> and good for people. Their image was inseparable from the ideal self-
> image of their time. *(p.3)*

Against this, he stresses that although *Friends in Business* 'attained
enormous power as individuals, they chose to use that power for the
benefit of their employees, their local community, or their industry'
(Windsor, 1980, p.27). These histories show how the requirements
from history can change. For Emden (1939), the virtue of the
Quakers was that they were typical of the middle class. Very much
in response to the effect of histories such as Emden's, Windsor (1980)
tries to show that, middle class though they were, Quaker employers
were different.

To sustain the notion of continuity in the approach to labour
management by Quaker employers in general, and Cadbury in particular, an indication of a similar continuity in Quaker thinking is
needed. This view is contradicted by several histories.

The eighteenth century capitalist and Quietist Friend closely
resembled Weber's description of the 'ideal type of the capitalistic
entrepreneur' who avoids ostentation and social recognition and has
a tendency to asceticism (Weber, 1930, p.71; cf. Raistrick, 1953, p.272,
1968, p.43). Whether or not, in an earlier period, Quakerism had been,
as Marxists might see it, an important element in the dissimulatory
ideological super-structure, or else, from a Weberian viewpoint, a vital

component in the ethical basis of capitalism (cf. Birnbaum, 1965; Jeremy, 1988; Jeremy, 1990), by the end of the eighteenth century, Quakerism was losing its particular significance; Quaker industrialists 'had to conform to the new world which their own industry was creating' (Raistrick, 1968, p.344; cf. Nevaskar, 1971, p.39; Weber, 1930, p.17).

Isichei's valuable history of Victorian Quakers (1970) traces the changes within the Society of Friends. For the first half of the nineteenth century, the Society was in decline, and the number of Friends went down from an estimated 19,800 in 1800 to 13,859 in 1861. Revival came when the Society became more outward-looking and allowed Friends to marry outside the Society. Between the 1830s and the 1850s, 'Quaker attitudes to politics were transformed.' Previously, although they had been an effective pressure group, they officially deplored and had a deep distrust for elections and party politics. That distrust was almost completely abandoned, however, in what 'was one of the most rapid and complete reversals of attitude in Quaker history,' particularly over the abolition of slavery. It was a manifestation of the important change which took place within Victorian Quakerism, 'by which friends grew closer to the society in which they lived,' and this 'reflected changes in dissent in general' (p.193).

In two important respects, there was continuity in the Society. First, its solidly middle-class composition: apart from 'a glittering superstructure of great industrialists and financiers,' the average Quaker was a prosperous tradesman (Isichei, 1970, p.187). Second, moneymaking by members of the Society: 'Victorian Quakerism sanctioned and indeed encouraged the pursuit of wealth' (p.183). The Quakers' stance on various social issues reflected their class position, as did the attitudes of others towards the Quakers.

Although Quakers were later identified with the emancipation of slaves (Aykroyd, 1967; Bebbington, 1982, p.110), in the mid-eighteenth century 'Quaker nonconformity did not extend to the slave trade ... Slave dealing was one of the most lucrative investments of English as of American Quakers.' The name of a slave ship, *The Willing Quaker*, 'symbolizes the approval with which the slave trade was regarded in Quaker circles' (Williams 1964, p.43). The nineteenth century view that the anti-slavery movement represented the English middle-class at its best was the creation of British historians who 'wrote almost as if Britain had introduced Negro slavery solely for the satisfaction of abolishing it' (Williams, 1964; quoted in Aykroyd, 1967, p.62). In *The Wealth of Nations*, Adam Smith remarked that, 'the late resolution of the Quakers in Pennsylvania to set at liberty all their Negro slaves, may satisfy us that their number cannot be very great' (Galbraith, 1987, p.62). William Cobbett 'hated Quaker speculators,' (Thompson, 1980, p.833) and throughout his *Rural Rides*, 'heaped violent and vulgar abuse on Quakers and Jews alike.' For him, the Friends were a 'pestiferous sect of non-labouring, sleek and fat hypocrites' (Isichei, 1970, p.284).

In the 1900s, the Cadburys supported campaigns for old-age pensions, minimum wages, and an end to homeworking. They sponsored, carried out, and published research on *Sweating* (Cadbury and Shann, 1907; Mudie-Smith, 1906) and *Women's Work and Wages* (Cadbury, Matheson and Shann 1906), and defended, against feminist criticism, the inclusion of women in the nineteenth-century protective legislation restricting the hours of work for women and children (Cadbury et al., 1906; cf. Morris, 1986).

In contrast, earlier Quaker employers took a free trade view, and opposed the Factory Acts: 'No Quaker played a prominent part in the agitation for the limitation of factory hours. Where they appear in its history at all, it is almost always as its inveterate opponents' (Isichei, 1970, p.247). Marx had nothing but contempt for the Quaker beliefs of the manufacturers who were fined for violating the Factory Act in 1836. They had kept five boys, aged between 12 and 15 years, at work for almost 30 hours 'in the 'shoddy-hole,' the name for the hole where the woollen rags are pulled to pieces, and where a dense atmosphere of dust, shreds, etc. forces even the adult worker to cover his mouth continually with handkerchiefs for the protection of his lungs!'

(Marx, 1976, p.351–2, note 22). He also denounced the 'pro-slavery rebellion' by manufacturers against the Ten Hours Act of 1847, which restricted the hours of work for women and young children. The manufacturers told the factory inspectors that 'they would set themselves above the letter of the law, and reintroduce the old system on their own account ... Thus, among others, the philanthropist Ashworth, in a letter to Leonard Horner a factory inspector, which is repulsive in its Quaker manner' (Marx, 1976, p.400–1; cf. Cadbury et al., 1906, p.22–3).

At times, the Quakers themselves acknowledged the discontinuity in their history. In 1908, the Society of Friends held its Yearly Meeting in central Birmingham. A substantial *Handbook* was produced for those attending. Noticeable by its absence is any discussion of Bournville, or of an organized visit to the village or the factory, even though the publication was the responsibility of William A. Cadbury and another senior member of the firm, and the organizing committee of 56 included five Cadburys (*Handbook*, 1908). Two members of the Society in Birmingham wrote a 'Local history of the Society of Friends During the Last Fifty Years.' They identified three fairly clear-cut periods: 1861–75, 'Passing of the old order'; 1875–95, Period of revival and expansion; and 1895–8, 'Incoming of the modern spirit' (*Handbook*, 1908, p.66).

Given this clear discontinuity, the problem becomes one of explaining how the image of continuity has emerged in relation to both Cadbury and the Quakers as employers. Child gives a useful clue: The principle of democratic relationships in the workplace has long been held by Quakers, as Raistrick has indicated in this study of Quaker industry in the seventeenth and eighteenth centuries (1964).

Arthur Raistrick wrote three books on Quakers and industry (1953, 1968, 1977). He was a member of the Society of Friends himself, and a student of Friends' literature (Raistrick, 1968). For most of his life, he was a lecturer in civil and mining engineering at the University of Durham, but he also carried out research into a wide range of subjects, including archaeology and industrial history (Manby and Turnbull, 1986). He wrote the book cited by Child (Raistrick, 1968) while on a Fellowship at Woodbrooke College, near Bournville, which was founded by George Cadbury. Working almost near enough to the Bournville factory, founded by his co-religionists, to enjoy the sweet scent of chocolate that emanates from it, Raistrick was possibly looking for evidence to confirm the image the Cadburys had of themselves in the 1930s and 1940s. The title of his later book suggests a similar theme: *Two Centuries of Industrial Welfare: The London (Quaker) Lead Company 1692–1905* (1977).

The first of Raistrick's three books about the Quakers was on *The Darbys of Coalbrookdale* (1953), the ironmasters at the heart of the industrial revolution in Britain. It is unlikely that they could have had a similar commitment to industrial democracy in the eighteenth century as the Cadburys had in the mid-twentieth. T. S. Ashton, the eminent historian of the industrial revolution (1948), gave an account of the predominantly Quaker eighteenth-century ironmasters. Writing before Raistrick, he appears to have been oblivious to any reputation the Quakers had for industrial democracy (Ashton, 1963). Ashton's portrait leaves something to be desired for those looking for precedents for the enlightened Quaker employers of the twentieth century:

> The austerity of the ironmasters, whether cause or effect of their sectarianism, affected every side of their lives. Successful themselves, they were intolerant of what might appear weakness or inefficiency in others; and though their charities were numerous there was little of the milk of human kindness in their constitutions. At that time, more than any other, industrial leadership demanded men of an autocratic mould; and, individualists as they were both by nature and circumstance, they resented any attempt on the part of the workers to determine, in any measure, the conditions of their working life. In more than one, indeed, there was developed something approaching contempt for

the aspirations of labour ... most of the ironmasters had little time or inclination for political speculation and their main concern was that industry should be left alone: although there were among them philanthropists, and demagogues ... most of them were, apparently, content to accept social conditions as they found them. *(1963, p. 225–6)*

So the construction of a history of Quaker employers characterized by continuity and a commitment to welfare is of fairly recent origin, and in part it can be attributed to the firm of Cadbury.

The Histories of Cadbury

The first 'history' of Cadbury to come from the firm itself was *Cocoa: All About It*, a short book written by Richard Cadbury, probably for advertising purposes, and published under the pseudonym 'Historicus' (1892). He made the most of Bournville in terms of the standards of the time, stressing the separation of men and women, as well as the fact that it was a purpose-built plant. Richard Cadbury hardly mentioned welfare at the works, and neither did his daughter, Helen Cadbury Alexander, in her biography of him, although she dealt at length with his philanthropic works (1906).

A. G. Gardiner was the editor of the Liberal newspaper, the *Daily News* from 1902 to 1921. He had been appointed after George Cadbury took over the ownership of the paper (Wagner, 1987). Gardiner wrote the *Life of George Cadbury* (1923) after George's death in 1922. He discussed George Cadbury's reasons for introducing welfare at Bournville, specifically privileging a worldly, rational explanation and discounting a religious, Quaker motive:

He did not inherit a business previously well-established. He created it, and it was his deliberate conviction that the welfare policy so far from hindering the development of the firm assisted it. He based his belief, not upon the inner light or the sanctions of religion, but upon plain reasoning from cause to effect. *(1923, p.98)*

For the most part, during the period in which the Cadbury institutions were being developed, the firm identified itself with wider progressive social movements. Bournville was among the outstanding Model Factories and Villages in a survey sponsored by the firm (Meakin, 1906; Harvey, 1906). As the focus of interest shifted from the old kind of welfare, which was 'extraneous to the actual process of managing' (Child, 1969, p.36), so Cadbury projected itself as at the forefront of factory management. Edward Cadbury's *Experiments in Industrial Organization* (1979) gives a 'description of Bournville practice' before the First World War, which reads 'much like a modern personnel manual' of the 1960s (Child, 1969, p.36).

By the 1920s, the New Liberal political views adhered to by the Cadburys in the 1900s had lost their distinctiveness, 'Liberalism had become Englishness' (Smith, 1986, p.255). As the trees grew and the suburbs of the City of Birmingham expanded to surround it, Bournville probably seemed less a symbol of the 'industrial spirit' and more a reminder of a mythical rural idyll (Weiner, 1985), less ahead of than out of its time and place. This changing temporal and spatial location of the firm facilitated and called for the construction of a new identity, one which stressed its uniqueness and separation from the upheavals of the 1920s and 1930s: labour unrest and mass unemployment.

Cadbury itself was stung by the response of its workforce to the General Strike in May 1926. Nearly every union responded to the strike call and approximately 50 per cent of the male workforce, but only 12 per cent of the women, came out (Birmingham Public Libraries, 1976, p.31). The strike was short-lived at Cadbury – most of the strikers stayed out for only four of the nine days of the General Strike, and at no time did Bournville have to close. After the strike, the unions lost many of their members (Birmingham Public Libraries, 1976, p.40). Unlike other Birmingham employers, Cadbury did not victimize strikers (Branson, 1976), but the Board did insist on the removal of restrictions on non-trades unionists holding office under the Works Council Scheme. These events were later rationalized in the firm's centenary history:

> Cadbury Brothers Ltd. has never had a strike of its workpeople, directed against the firm itself; and, though many men and women were called out by their Unions in May 1926, it was generally felt that there was no personal animus against the Company. Those who were then called upon to strike felt, indeed, a very difficult opposition between two loyalties – that to their firm and that to their Trade Union. *(Williams, 1931, p.125–6)*

The *Directors' Annual Report* for 1927 summarized the previous three years, in which sales had remained practically static, as:

> the first comparatively long period in the history of the firm during which we have failed to go forward ... it is unfortunate that a failure to increase our sales has coincided with a period when other factors have been working against the fullest employment of personnel. Improvements in processes and machinery, and the shifting of the incidence of demand from products requiring a large proportion of human labour to those needing but little, have aggravated the employment position.

With some fluctuations, employment levels at Bournville continued to decrease, especially for women, from a high point in 1925 through to a low in the mid-1930s. Payments were made from the firm's Short Time and Unemployment Schemes to ameliorate the effects on the workforce.

The stability, continuity, and enduring values identified with Cadbury by the centenary publications must have been reassuring. The 'successful Centenary Year' came during a difficult period for the firm and against a background of 'national upheaval' (*Directors' Annual Report*, 1931). Both prices and wages fell in Britain during that year, but the Directors at Bournville noted that: 'No such general movement has taken place here in the standard rates of wages with the exception of Building Trades in February 1931' (p.13). If they read it, Bournville workers would have been reassured to learn from their copy of Rogers' *A Century of Progress* that even before the firm moved out to Bournville, wages were paid above the normal in Birmingham even when the business was in a precarious state, because it was recognized that standard wages were inadequate (1931, p.36).

SEEING BEYOND THE LIMITS OF CORPORATE CULTURE

The events of 1931 produced a historically specific history of Cadbury, one which has proved enduring and largely uncontested. Social psychological concepts of 'social cognition biases' may satisfactorily explain the prevalence of 'founders,' both in corporate culture and business history writings:

> Salience causes leaders to figure prominently in people's memories of events ... [and] ... attribution research suggests that people may have only minimal awareness of the situational determinants of a leader's behavior. *(Martin et al., 1985, p.101)*

However, history can complement this by explaining why the identities of founders with particular idiosyncrasies (Pettigrew, 1979) are selected at specific times in history; for example, why the Quaker beliefs of George and Richard Cadbury were given prominence in the late 1920s and 1930s, as opposed to say, George's strong Liberal political views.

The history of Cadbury based on Quakerism served the purpose of corporate cultures and 'all invented traditions' (Hobsbawm, 1983a, p.12) by providing legitimacy. In a period of 'change, crisis and dislocation' a constructed history can represent a reassuring 'preservation of anachronism' (Cannadine, 1983, p.122). In an increasingly secular society, the apparent conformity of Cadbury to a religious ideal gave the firm an identity which made it special, imbued with a morality probably perceived as lacking elsewhere. By 1931, the idea of an employer motivated by religious convictions must have appeared anachronistic, and, as it does today, more than a little quaint. The usefulness of 'invented practices' is that they tend to be:

quite unspecific and vague as to the nature of the values, rights and obligations of the group membership they inculcate ... objects or practices are liberated for full symbolic and ritual use when no longer fettered by practical use ... the wigs of lawyers could hardly acquire their modern significance until other people stopped wearing wigs. *(Hobsbawm, 1983a, p.4, 10)*

Similarly, for Cadbury, the religious affiliation of its 'founders' could be invoked with convenient significance only once secularity had ensured that few people would have had any idea about the history of the Society of Friends and what it stood for, apart from the version presented to them by the firm itself. It also ensured that there was less likelihood of sectarian hostility being aroused. Possibly this explains the apparent willingness of British businessmen to appear 'closer to the churches' than might be expected in contemporary Western socie-ties (Jeremy, 1990, p.5), why successful corporate cultures are thought to capture a 'religious tone' (Deal and Kennedy, 1982, p.195), and why, after the restructuring, downsizing and delayering of the 1980s, 1990s and 2000s (see Hassard, Morris and McCann, 2009), many companies today perhaps wish they could 'persuade workers to get religion again' (Dumaine, 1990, p.58).

If, in Selznick's readily quotable (Peters and Waterman, 1982, p.85) phrase, '"to institutionalize" is to infuse with value beyond the technical requirements of the task at hand' (1957, p.17), then the emphasis on Quakerism in the histories of the firm produced in its centenary year was a vital part of the institutionalization of Cadbury's labour-management practices. The Quaker beliefs of the Cadbury family were used to give meaning to the boundary between the firm and the troubled world outside. It should be remembered that 'the test of infusion with value is expendability' and 'when value-infusion takes place ... there is a resistance to change' (Selznick, 1957, p.18). Cadbury's labour-management practices proved to be enduring, and the firm's management found it difficult to abandon these practices when they conflicted with changes in the firm's strategy in the 1960s and 1970s (Rowlinson, 1994; Smith et al., 1990).

History is therefore part of the process of institutionalization (Hobsbawm, 1983a). Founders themselves, and the act of founding, are institutionalized by history. The founders of cultures are selected retrospectively by historians, among others, including corporate culture writers, who adhere to the widespread cultural belief in the importance of founders. It may be thought that the position of the 'cultural pragmatists,' those who 'see culture as a key to commitment, productivity, and profitability' and believe that culture can and should be managed (Martin, 1985, p.95), has already been largely undermined, but it may not be amiss to strike one more blow. The historical approach to the concept of culture in this chapter suggests that culture cannot be managed unless a relatively uncontested history can be invented.

From the Cadbury case, two points can be made. First, the company had made substantial investments in material labour-management practices well before the Cadbury culture was invented to give a firm-specific meaning to those practices. Second, in constructing a history, the firm was able to draw on appropriate and uncontested events in its past to differentiate itself from other companies. The success of the company's invented culture is indicated by the continued acceptance of its constructed history by business historians and corporate culture writers alike. This represents a considerable achievement. Those attempting to effect cultural change in the present without regard for the past want a culture on the cheap; by mere exhortation, they hope to create a firm-specific identity, without having invested in any material practices that could be given a firm-specific meaning. They may well find to their cost that, 'a company with the wrong history and myths can get itself in big trouble' (Dumaine, 1990, p.56).

In the context of this book, a number of other important observations can be drawn.

First, the network that sustains the superficial view of management theory and how it has advanced, is, as we have seen in earlier chapters, a broader coalition than we might expect. Management consultancies, publishers, managers, business schools, academics, business historians and corporations are all a part of a formation that produces certain kinds of corporate culture and management knowledge, while repressing other ways of seeing.

Second, the object of corporate culture, much like Cadbury's culture (and indeed many of the theories that management history reflects back to us as key steps along the management continuum), is an invented tradition; we (or the network we are a part of) created it. Evidence of this invention comes from observing how the over-layering of corporate culture as one of the field's latest big ideas onto the history of management in textbooks has necessitated the re-casting of earlier narratives in order to try and make sense of present needs.

Earlier, when decentralizing organizations in order to appeal to the higher needs of employees was a big idea in management, decentralization in 'freer' Western societies was seen as a progression beyond more homogenizing centralized states. As Peter Drucker (1964, p.107) put it: 'The importance of the question whether decentralization is absolutely more efficient than centralization does not lie, primarily, in its application to business management. It is actually the question whether a socialist economy can be as efficient economically as a free-enterprise economy.' (This is a background reason for the diminution of Max Weber's contribution to management – because he represented the promotion of centralization and bureaucracy, see Chapter Four). This view filtered through into textbooks that presented decentralization as an evolution in management and organization theory until the middle of the 1980s. For example:

> [The trend in America toward decentralization] hints at the
> increased diversity underlying our country. While Japan has a fairly
> homogeneous culture that allows more focused and accepted
> direction from authority, America prides itself on being a melting
> pot. A consequence in a society that supports individual rights is

that groups and individuals want to be distinct and have choices
that reflect their situations. The trend of decentralization is one
response to this diversity. *(Callahan, et al., 1986, p.592)*

By the late 1980s, with Japan and the idea that good organizations had
strong corporate cultures ascendant, and present needs changed, this
lesson in historical sociology had to change too.

Our final observation is that the current invented traditions of
management history, as they relate to the object of corporate culture
and the end of an evolutionary chain of management theories, are
harmful and confusing. They are harmful in that while their promotion of strong unitary corporate cultures, as opposed to dysfunctional
individual behaviours, may be good for incremental efficiency gains, it
cuts across the diversity and conflict that is so often the driver of
innovation and substantial creativity. Moreover, given that diversity
has come back onto the agenda as an advance in management thinking, the tail end of management histories in textbooks which outline
'Contemporary Issues and Challenges' or 'Continuing Management
Themes' often leave students with mixed messages. On the one hand,
a strong corporate culture, with everybody pointing in the same functional direction, is good. On the other hand, diversity is good because
'groups and individuals want to, and are right to, be distinct'. What
should students of management take from this?

The portrayal of the evolution of management thought, its
dumbing down and its confusion, may not be a conspiracy. These
limits on management thinking that we are linking to a network or
formation of reinforcing elements may not have been consciously
achieved. But whatever its causes may be, perhaps now, having recognized management history's invented and self-reinforcing and homogenizing nature, we should actively seek to reinvent it from the
ground up, and to do it purposefully this time, with ethical sociability,
mutual benefit, sustainability and innovation, rather than efficiency,
as our aims.

9 Remaking Management History: New Foundations for the Future

A new history of management can inspire thinking differently.

Returning to our original target (management history as it is portrayed in management textbooks), we conclude this book by asking: if we were to redesign and promote a new management history in the pages of these introductory works, what might that new history look like? What might it contain? How could it be presented? What might we define as management's fundamental purpose for a student or a manager? Furthermore, how might this new history change the way we think about management and organization studies, and – given the influence that management has on life in the twenty-first century – how might rethinking in this way help us to think differently about how we organize and measure our lives more generally?

> While participating in a Harvard Business School roundtable discussion on the value of management history, a top-level executive put it this way: "It's always hard to communicate any sort of abstract idea to someone else, let alone get any acceptance of it. But when there is some agreement on the factual or historical background of that idea, the possibilities for general agreement expand enormously."
>
> Kreitner and Cassidy, *Management* (12th ed., 2008, p.36)

Before outlining a history of management, management textbooks justify the excursion in a number of typical ways. Oftentimes, these justifications begin by acknowledging a likely reticence on the part of the reader: a reader who would probably share Robbins and others' earlier described views along the lines that 'history is of little value and thus of little interest'. Familiar acknowledgements in this respect are that:

> Some people question the value of theory and history. Their arguments are usually based on the assumptions that history has no relevance to contemporary society, and that theory is abstract and of no practical use. *(Davidson et al., 2009, p.34)*

> The problems and opportunities facing organizations today are complex and changing. All of society's institutions feel the pressure of a new and very challenging environment. But even in the rush to an exciting future, no-one should sell history short. *(Schermerhorn et al., 2014, p.36)*

Having attempted to dispel any negative predispositions, history is then justified in the following related ways:

> Understanding the historical context of management provides a sense of heritage and can help managers to avoid the mistakes of others. *(Davidson et al., 2009, p.35)*

> Knowledge gained through past experience can and should be used as a foundation for future success. *(Schermerhorn et al., 2014, p.36)*

> Understanding the origins of management thought will help you grasp the underlying contexts of the ideas and concepts presented in the chapters ahead. *(Bateman and Snell, 2009, p.41)*

> History is important because it can put current activities in perspective. *(Robbins et al., 2015, p.41)*

> Our theories about management – what it is, what it entails, what works, what doesn't – advance as we develop new ideas. *(Robbins et al., 2016, p.25)*

> An understanding of the evolution of management helps current and future managers appreciate where we are now and continue to progress toward better management. *(Samson and Daft, 2012, p.35)*

In short, management history is important because it makes initiates feel good about management's past, puts present advances in perspective, and helps us build upon these in order to continue the evolution. Kreitner and Cassidy's quotation at the head of this chapter reflects this template, but also a deeper rumination on this point. It utilizes the prestige of Harvard and the persona of a 'top-level executive' to bring home its message and explain that agreement on a historical background 'expands the possibilities for general agreement enormously'.

The counter-history we have presented in this book is written in opposition to these reasons for management history. Rather than thinking about management's past because it makes us feel good about our heritage, we argue that this may breed smugness and complacency, reduce fundamental questioning and encourage a continuation of the status quo with regard to what we assume are fundamental foundations.

Rather than just putting the past in perspective, we would rather promote a history that could blur things a little, and encourage questioning the present state of management. Is the story of management really one of evolutionary advance, for example?

Rather than using the agreed evolution as a foundation for the future, we would argue that standing on the shoulders of the shallow interpretations of giants presented in textbook histories may reduce our interest in thinking in other directions.

Rather than a history designed to help us to pin down and agree about management, we have sought to develop an alternative history that would contribute to a plurality of views, and, by association, disagreement.

Why oppose conventional views in this way? Primarily because these assumptions about the purpose of management history encourage homogeneity and agreement rather than diversity and debate; and, as we outlined in Chapter One, a contest of ideas rather than a filing cabinet of settled precedents is what drives substantive innovation. In this way, we argue that the benefits of an agreed upon history of management are outweighed by the negatives brought about by a field stagnating.

We believe that we should have the awareness and confidence as a field now to question our assumed foundations. So, for example, when Davidson et al. (2009, p.60) provide their 'Summary of Key Points' from their textbook's history and explain to readers that 'Understanding the historical context of management and precursors of management and organizations provides a sense of heritage ... Management has always been concerned with planning, leading, organizing and controlling', we think we should be able to ask the question: 'How do we know that the abstract idea "management" has always just been concerned with planning, leading, organizing and controlling?' Might it not have been concerned with other things at some point? And if so, and we are interested in diversity and the innovation that the acceptance of diversity can bring, wouldn't it be a good idea to seek these out?[1]

---

[1] Indeed, management history has a long tradition of claiming dubious empirical evidence to justify universal principles. James D. Mooney – dubbed 'the Affable Irishman' (Wren, 1972: 346ff.), set out with history professor, Alan C. Reiley, to 'expose the principles of organization, as they reveal themselves in various forms of human group movement, and to help industry protect its own growth through a greater knowledge and use of these principles'. Mooney introduced his history, titled *Onward Industry*, thus: 'Organization in the formal sense means order, and its corollary, an organized and orderly procedure. To find and correlate the formal principles that make this order is the aim of this book' (Mooney and Reiley, 1931/1947, p.ix-x). It is no surprise then that he should find formal principles of organization, and that they should be coordination, scalar hierarchy and the functional division of labour. Mooney and Reiley (1931/1947, p.4) admitted (perhaps sensing an obvious question in advance of it being asked) that Ancient people did not speak in these modern terms. But he was not fazed by this epistemological problem: 'That the great organizers of history applied these principles unconsciously proves only that their technique was inherent in their genius'. Thus, he remained confident in his claim that his principles were universal and consequently, would hold true in the future as well.

This book has aimed to promote questions like this, questions that should cause us to think again, think differently, and think otherwise about what management is, or could be.

RECAPPING A NEW HISTORY OF MANAGEMENT

We began this book by stating our view that *if we are to think differently about management, we must first rethink management history*, and signalled our intent to take aim at the conventional history of management as an unnoticed barrier to innovation: particularly in the form it is most often experienced by management initiates, management textbooks. The approach of these histories, which we have indicated again here through reviewing what such textbooks see as the purpose of management history, justifies present practices and makes it less likely that they will be challenged.

In Chapter One, we outlined our aim to develop a new history of management to counter the assumptions that this conventional view promotes; we surveyed the current narrow and homogeneous map of management history; and outlined a Foucauldian approach for a deeper and more critical historical understanding of moments that have been defined as key in management's development.

In Chapter Two, Management's Formation: The Importance of the Liberal Context, we put the case for seeing management arising not with neo-liberal or *laissez faire* economics, industrialization and increasing order and control (the causes that conventional management history recognizes), but social and moral liberalism and the decline of slavery: a factor that conventional management histories are curiously silent about. In order to do this, we looked afresh at the work of Adam Smith, so often identified as management history's first pioneer.

Smith's treatment in textbook histories is generally limited to a few sentences about his pin factory example and how Smith's 'classic economics treatise' promoted the division of labour, which then required a gradual continuity of increasing control of workers administered by a growing class of professional managers. But looking further into Smith's work reveals a different view of the role that liberalism may have played in creating the context in which management emerged and the role Smith could have in our conceptualization of management.

Smith's real intellectual innovations were not the importance of *laissez faire* economics and the efficiency that the division of labour brings, but the view that slavery and other forms of repressing a human's 'sacred freedoms', such as being able to dispense with a person's labour as he or she sees fit, were misguided: ethically, fundamentally, but also economically.

Hence, after an age where the ruling question was 'Am I leading in proper conformity to moral, natural, or divine laws?'; and then in the sixteenth and seventeenth centuries, 'Am I governing with sufficient intensity and attention to maximize our state's power against other states?', our own liberal age begins with a new problematization: 'Are we self-limiting the degree of government to enable the progress of sociability and civilization while optimizing "mutual enrichment" for all states and all people?'

In this context, the importance of management can be seen to emerge as we seek ways of governing and controlling people less, not more. In Book V of *The Wealth of Nations* (a Book seldom taken account of even by those who profess to know what Smith wrote), Smith spent some time reflecting on the nature of good management and defines it as being the opposite of force and violence: a form of persuasion that is a better means of getting things done in a modern liberal world – even though 'insolence' causes people to revert to force instead. Smith's words in this regard could form a useful basis for our understanding of management.

Following on from our reframing of the historical context that gives rise to the greater study of management, our third chapter, To What End? The Nature of Management's 'Classical' Approach, looked again at what history suggests as the aim of management theorizing. Identifying the division of labour and industrialization as origins and F. W. Taylor and the Classical Management theorists as 'fathers' identifies, by association, the aim of management theory as being to determine how greater efficiency can be achieved. But a re-investigation of the environment that led to the popularization of management in the United States in the first years of the twentieth century suggests that the foundational aim might instead be understood to be conservation, or sustainability.

The conventional historical narrative employs an efficiency-obsessed Taylor as a hero/anti-hero: a noble leader of the rise of management studies and a flawed villain whose simplistic views must be overcome. Subsequently, textbook histories tell us that management began when a highly mechanistic worldview was applied to work and organization, but since then we have developed a better, more humane understanding, culminating in recent ideas about ethics and sustainability. But by looking anew, we can see Smith's ethics of sociability as a foundation stone of management, and by looking more broadly at Taylor's Scientific Management, we can see that it captured the wider imagination through its association with a specific political issue of 1907–1912: Theodore Roosevelt and his deputy Gifford Pinchot's quest to help the American people grasp the importance of 'conservation' (or what we might call sustainability) after decades of *laissez faire* expansion in North America. How might theorizing about management happen differently if we believed (and taught) that its founding and fundamental end was not mechanistic efficiency, but rather, sustainability, or in Pinchot's words: 'the wisest use of resources for the benefit of the greatest number of people for the longest possible time'?

If the manager is the actor in the modern liberalizing context that gives rise to management studies, the organization is his or her stage. In Chapter Four, The Birth of Organization Studies: Or What We Could Learn from Sociologist Max Weber, we rethought the traditional view of Max Weber's legacy for management.

Conventional management histories deploy the character of Weber as a pioneer in organization science in two ways. First, as a serious and renowned thinker whose interest in the things that management took itself to be about added credence to the emerging field. Second, as the avid promoter of bureaucracy – his support of which has come to be seen as wrong-headed as more decentralized and 'organic' forms of organization have come to the fore. However, if we explore more of what Weber wrote, rather than just what his later interpreters chose to translate, we find a much more complex figure. Weber could see why and how bureaucracy would come to be the dominant organizational form in the early decades of the twentieth century, and the form's advantages in this context, but he was troubled by what its dominance, and its promotion of a particular part of the human psyche, would mean for humanity.

We argued that recognizing Max Weber's foundational insight as being not that bureaucracy is great, but that forms of organization emerge out of specific socio-political contexts. Influenced by this insight, and Weber's promotion of an anti-positivism when studying social action, encourages scholars of management and organization to see all cases as context specific and be wary of general theories of management.

In Chapter Five, we changed tack. While the emergence of the Business School is not covered explicitly in most histories of management, its formation promotes particular forms of management knowledge, and it is therefore key to the historical development of management studies. The Institution of the Business School developed a counter-history of this formation.

Events since the 1940s have narrowed the view of what a good business school should be and do, and the idea that Harvard is the original and best school in the business lies behind this development. But Harvard did not spring 'fully formed' into the model that we associate with it and business schools more generally today. Its form was contested and it could have turned out differently. However, this contest and these alternative pathways are overlooked in favour of a smooth evolution where the present is a continuity of the past.

One of the most interesting, potentially foundational, but now largely forgotten, relationships in the history of management is that between HBS Dean Wallace Donham and British process philosopher

A. N. Whitehead. Together, these two discussed, articulated and advanced a very different view of what a business school could be: one with a new broader type of pedagogy that would not only inspire business people, but rejuvenate Western learning and society.

Since then, this dream has been diminished and a curious discourse whereby HBS is criticized for being overly managerialist and at once aped by its competitors and opponents has emerged. Understanding how this happened and recognizing that the formation of the Business School is not an objective given, but the result of particular historical networks and contingencies, can help us think again about the form that these Schools could take.

Chapter Six formed a lynchpin in our book. The Discovery of the Human Worker is an ironic title for this chapter on Elton Mayo and the Hawthorne Studies. After the presentation of the 'classical' machine-laden influences on management, Elton Mayo's research is presented as evidence for a kinder and more scientific management theory. But what if the research on which his 'human relations' school was founded was not all that it seems? How would the good guys turning out to be not so good change our view of management's history? This chapter brings into focus the wider contextual factors influencing Mayo's research. It deconstructs and starts to critique a habitual *revelatory* narrative in textbooks: one where Western Electric – an authoritarian, bureaucratic corporation, ignorant of human factors – is enlightened by the arrival of behavioural scientists from Harvard and their 'discovery' of human relations at work.

In so doing, this counter-history describes not only how Mayo constructed a narrative for explaining the findings from Hawthorne, but also how his social networks and politics influenced the kinds of 'human relations' evidence claimed for by his Harvard Group. Mayo's political ideology was successful in that it convinced business leaders that his agenda would alleviate their concerns, with this network of influence extending to the executives of the Hawthorne Works. Contrary to the orthodox narrative of management studies, which suggests a theoretical and practical paradigm-shift in the wake of 'human relations' behavioural experimentation, the alternative impression from our analysis is that Mayo and his team did not so much turn the sociological tide at Hawthorne as swim briskly with it.

As such, we argue that Hawthorne and Mayo's legacy is a negative one for our field. Promoting the universal theory that showing human interest will make people more productive, and presenting this as an advance on the ideas of truly great thinkers like Weber and Smith, was a great leap backwards (recall that Weber warned again such general theories), and lowered the bar for subsequent management theorizing that would be slotted into the general advance of management.

Textbook Distortions, Chapter Seven, dealt with the negative consequences of having placed Mayo and Hawthorne on a pedestal. It explored how modern textbooks began to arrange seminal ideas from theorists who came after Mayo into the conventional historical narrative and simplify these ideas into easy-to-use intervention tools in the latter decades of the twentieth century. The 1970s saw the emergence of the management textbook divided into stratified chapters and sections, and illustrated in ways conducive to modern forms of lecturing large cohorts of students. Into these textbooks, management ideas from previous decades were distilled into digestible blocks, and placed in a continuum by a history of how these blocks built upon one another. However, our counter-history outlined how research by the likes of Kurt Lewin, Herbert Maslow and Douglas McGregor was twisted and compromised, and asked how our understanding of the development of management studies might be otherwise if we processed ideas like theirs differently.

The penultimate chapter of our book, The Invention of Corporate Culture, dug deeper to examine another element that can be seen as leading to the 'dumbing down' rather than the 'evolving up' of management. In addition to management textbooks presenting simple frameworks as general theories, management consultants and management academics sought to develop 'solutions' to business success for an increasingly enthusiastic market. In this way, the general theory that good organizations are those that have a strong corporate culture emerged and is presented as one of management history's latest discoveries in textbooks.

But what is the science behind this discovery? Chapter Eight developed a counter-history of the creation of 'corporate culture' since its emergence in the early 1980s and roles played by management consultants, management academics and practicing managers in this development. We discussed how the assumptions about culture produced by mainstream writers can suppress, for example, forms of employee opposition and resistance and serve essentially to reproduce corporate ideology and the status quo at the expense of critical thinking and change. In short, we argued that the development of our understanding of the importance of culture reflects a continuation of the limited Mayoist view of what a management theory should be and do.

At the time of writing this book, the latest generalizable and prescriptive management theory presented in this vein on the continuum of management history in introductory textbooks is that new thinking about sustainability should be central to the good management of an organization. But we believe there is a danger (if we do think sustainability is more than just this current decade's general theory of the 'best way') that sustainability too will be filed and superseded in keeping with the conventional form and narrative of management history as the textbooks we use roll through their umpteenth editions. The good news, however, which we have sought to stress throughout the counter-historical endeavours of this book, is that management history is not immutable. It could have been different and thus could be made different now. And promoting alternative histories of management can work as an antidote to the superficiality and complacency bred by management's conventional history.

Ultimately, the purpose of the counter-histories developed in this book was not to dismiss what we currently regard as management's history, but to provide alternatives that would stimulate more debate about management's backstory and its role in producing a certain kind of knowledge (and how this in turn may repress thinking otherwise). It was written in response to the quotations with which the book began from William Matthews and Michel Foucault, and the idea that without critical questioning, the little that we remember of our past becomes inevitable, both as the truth about the past and for our future horizons too. The effort was to encourage thinking differently about the past as a spur to thinking otherwise for the future; or to use what Gilles Deleuze (1988, p.96) called the 'culmination' of Foucault's work, 'the searing phrase [from his penultimate book]: "to get free of oneself"'. Our aim has been to help separate ourselves enough from conventional assumptions so that we may reflect back on them, unsettle and subsequently remake the foundations of our field.

PRESENTING AN ALTERNATIVE HISTORY FOR THE FUTURE OF MANAGEMENT

> And isn't the past inevitable, now that we call the little we remember of it 'the past'?

William Matthews, from the poem *Cows Grazing at Sunrise*

> The object is to learn to what extent the effort to think one's own history can free thought from what it silently thinks, and so enable it to think differently.

Michel Foucault, from *The History of Sexuality*, Vol. 2

Our specific target in this enterprise has been the form in which most management initiates or students experience management history directly: introductory textbooks. And while we have advocated throughout this book a deeper engagement with the elements that are to constitute the keys aspects of management and history (and, indeed, those that are not), we accept the fact that when teaching at this level, attention spans are short and pages in textbooks are limited. Hence, we do not expect textbook authors or lecturers to devote a massive chunk of their limited resources to management history. But we do think that encouraging thinking beyond a history that congratulates the present, to one that promotes critical questioning and alternative perspectives, one that may encourage innovative management theorizing and practice, is possible. And with this in mind, we finish this book with the presentation of an alternative management history module similar in size but not in content or formation to those found in most management textbooks.

A History for the Future of Management

Philosophical and Ethical Foundations: Adam Smith

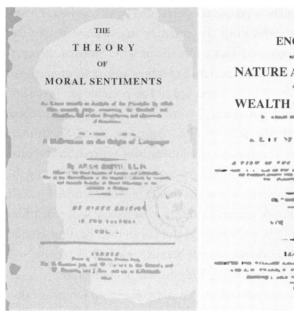
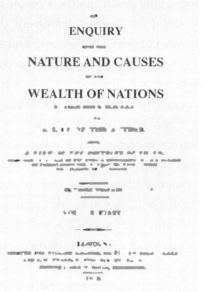

Management emerges as an alternative means of organization as liberal societies evolve and explore alternatives to traditional coercive forms of control.

Having determined management to be about the achievement of technical efficiency in the early twentieth century, histories of management claim Adam Smith as an important forebear and pick out certain aspects of his second book *The Wealth of Nations*. These are his supposed promotion of *laissez faire* economics, industrialization and the division of labour. But this focus makes far more of these aspects than Smith intended.

However, if one does want to claim Smith as a foundation, there is much of interest in his body of work with regard to management. Looking at the *Theory of Moral Sentiments*, we find useful ethical foundations for understanding why and how people cooperate and work together. *Theory of Moral Sentiments* starts from the premise that we are not selfish beings, but social beings, and seeks to explain why. Smith's theory is that we are empathetic to the experience of others and so are predisposed to be social beings, to seek to be respected and respectable (or 'loved and loveable' beings, as Smith put it) and to work together for the greater good.

Looking through the lens of *The Theory of Moral Sentiments* enables us to see that *The Wealth of Nations* was written in response to an emerging *laissez faire* economics rather than in favour of it, and the division of labour used as evidence of the theory of moral sentiments. We can divide labour and trade because we trust that people will empathize with others and want to be seen as good and fair in their dealing. Hence, we can allow a liberalization of controls because this 'fellow feeling' will hold things together while enabling the advance of civilization.

But this liberal system still needs to be managed to ensure that essential services and the gains from this economic system are delivered fairly and that those born in less fortunate circumstance still have the opportunity to rise. And this is the specific topic of Book V of *The Wealth of Nations* where Smith writes extensively about good management and defines it against more coercive approaches to getting things done in organizations.

Having Adam Smith as a founding father enables us to see that management emerges as traditional authoritarian forms of social and economic control based on birth-right and privilege decline and liberal meritocracies arise in the modern age. In these settings, we should facilitate progress through good management rather than force or coercion. And we may define management in this context as fundamentally being about *finding alternatives to coercion that help achieve progress for mutual gain.*

The Rise of the First Management Theorists

The original 'good' that management theory sought to advance was conservation, or the reduction of needless waste.

Frederick W. Taylor and his contemporaries in the early twentieth century are regarded as the first management theorists. Taylor advocated extreme forms of the division of labour designed to minimize waste.

Taylor's work gained notoriety and popularity as a solution to the biggest political problem in the United States at the turn of the twentieth century: how to stem the tide of rampant *laissez faire* industrial development. The appeal designed to combat this, developed by Gifford Pinchot and President Theodore Roosevelt, was termed 'conservation'.

As part of this campaign, lawyer Louis Brandeis gathered together a group of workplace consultants and found that Taylor's ideas repackaged under the banner of Scientific Management could make management, as a new, important subject, appear objective and politically neutral.

Conventional management histories look back with hindsight and claim efficiency of performance as management's fundamental aim. Efficiency was certainly a key part of Taylor's system, but looking more deeply at why and how management emerged, we can argue that it had the elimination of waste and a desire to achieve conservation and sustainability for the greater good as the end that efficiency aimed towards. In the words of Gifford Pinchot, we should see the aim of management as being 'to achieve the greatest good for the greatest number for the longest time'.

The Birth of Organization Science

The first social scientist of management argued that forms of organization and management were culturally specific. Therefore, we should be wary of general theories.

If Smith is the theorist who outlines the important contextual or environmental changes that lead to the rise of management; and Taylor and his network the first seen to develop a comprehensive theory of what management should do; Max Weber may be the first to theorize the organizational stages upon which management takes place.

Max Weber is identified in conventional management histories as the father of organization science because he may have been the first person to focus on the emergence of particular organizational forms. He is most famous for his extensive study of the emergence of bureaucracy within a Protestant Industrial zeitgeist, but conventional management history zeros in on him as a forebear because machine bureaucracy is seen as a match for early mechanistic and naive management theorizing. Weber is thus (mistakenly) believed to have advocated for bureaucracy as the one-best-way of organizing.

But looking at Weber more closely, a key foundational lesson that we could learn from this anti-positivist (who argued for the study of social systems through interpretive means) is that organizations emerge in particular ways in response to particular socio-cultural conditions and aims. Hence, no one type of organization may be deemed the best, general theories may be misleading, and we must adopt a contingency approach that is sensitive to local contexts.

The Global View of Management

We should appreciate a range of cultural traditions and draw insight from them for ways of organizing and managing.

Most cultures and civilizations can be seen to have developed organizations, as well as ways of achieving the greatest good for the largest number for the longest time, and ways of encouraging people to work together without coercion for mutual gain. However, conventional management history's narrow gaze focusses on management emerging in response to industrialization, performance efficiency, planning, organizing, and controlling through organizational forms like machine bureaucracies. Therefore, management's emphasis has largely been on the cultural contexts in which these ideas were formed. As a result, what people write about in management history and what management is understood to be comes mostly from an Anglo-American perspective. While this may advance agreement about what management is, it limits diversity, and, we would argue, innovation. If we believe diversity and innovation are important, we should encourage research into other sites where different forms of management may been practiced.

The Form of the Business School?

Institutions and pedagogies for teaching business have gravitated to a standard format, but this development is now being questioned.

The collegiate Business School is the institution through which most management research and instruction takes place. Following the lines of the conventional history of management, it is generally believed that business schools must have economic science at their core and pedagogy focussed on applying general management theories to solve business cases. But as Weber's research would suggest, the form of a business school will be a reflection of the beliefs and concerns of the times in which it was founded. And indeed, earlier Business Schools were configured differently.

In the late 1920s and 1930s, key thinkers considered how the form of the business school could be different from the narrow orthodoxy that was emerging. People like Wallace Donham at Harvard Business School argued for incorporating multiple perspectives beyond owners and managers of organizations, questioning assumptions about the values of business, and advocated for the reflective development of theory based on a broad view of practice as a way forward for an academy that had become too focussed on theory for its own sake. While this view did not prevail, it should give us pause for thought. How might business schools be different today if we built them according to current concerns, rather than aping traditional forms and the prestige associated with them?

A Procession of General Theories of Management Success

Management has seen a procession of general theories promoted, but while the rise and fall of these theories appears to indicate progression, from a broader historical perspective, it looks like a series of fads.

The theory that if managers show people that they care about them they will be more efficient or productive was seen as a breakthrough in the 1930s when Elton Mayo and his team of Harvard researchers promoted it.

While later researchers would find that the studies were bogus in many important respects and that it was money as much as human relations that led to the productivity gains (as earlier theorists like Taylor would have predicted), the idea that the Human Relations School was an advance stuck. The Hawthorne Studies did not alter a belief that had now seeped into the fabric of management: that its fundamental and universal aim was efficiency. It continued with and deepened this idea while providing a new universal theory for achieving this. This had the unfortunate effect of fuelling a belief in a quest for new simplistic general theories, or a 'one-best way' of management. Max Weber would have advised against this.

After Mayo's Human Relations movement proved there was a great demand for 'management science' of this sort, the conception and expansion of management as a university subject with a range of sub-disciplinary elements created a need to fill in a broader backstory of contributing theories to this new and increasingly influential 'science'.

The nuanced thinking of innovative and diligent social scientists like Kurt Lewin, Abraham Maslow and Douglas McGregor was developed and repackaged into a series of theoretical developments and advancements along the management continuum from Smith, Taylor, Weber and Mayo. However, their ideas were often transformed into general and prescriptive n-step theories for approaching management. Plugging them into an evolutionary narrative in this way does not do justice to the original material.

In the 1980s, as the bestselling management textbooks moved into the ongoing production of multiple editions, new 'advances' were added to the annals of management history.

New general theories, often developed in association with a booming management consultancy industry, follow in the footsteps of 'leaps' like the Hawthorne Studies and the distillation of the ideas of academics like Lewin and Maslow. Theories like the idea that successful organizations have a strong, unified or homogeneous culture, as 'proven' by the Excellence movement; or that successful managers follow a systems approach, are superseded in later decades and editions by assertions that good organizations and managers are now trying to be 'ethical' or interested in 'globalization' or 'diversity management'. Each of these discoveries is offered as a further advance along the continuously evolving continuum of management.

What Will Become of the Latest 'Advances'?
There is a danger that given management's now established cycle of adding the latest general theories to the pile, issues such as sustainability and ethics (which could be viewed as fundamental to management) might come to be seen as just other 'fads'.

At the time of writing this book, sustainability is the latest big idea on the chain of the management continuum.

At the end of textbook histories in 2016, readers are told that a '"New Industrial Revolution" ... not unlike the one [we] underwent in the eighteenth century ... will be led by organizations that are able to apply sustainable management practices [This] will require real change, because business-as-usual is no longer an option' (Robbins et al., 2015, p.65).

But perhaps fundamental change and innovation could come instead from less hyperbole about sustainability and ethics being new ideas that change everything, and more reflection upon how they could be regarded as the foundation stones of management that Smith and Pinchot considered them to be.

Rather than being the latest management approach on the evolutionary conveyer belt of history, taking a broader view and seeing Adam Smith's ethics and Pinchot/Brandeis/Roosevelt's aim of conservation as what management was originally built upon, could encourage more fundamental change in management theorizing and practice.

Conclusion

The purpose of our new history of management, presented above, is not to replace the conventional history; we do not propose it as a new orthodoxy that expands the possibility for general agreement about the concept of management or as something to be 'ticked off' as we rush towards a new and exciting future. This would only replicate the problem we have sought to address of how historical orthodoxy can limit horizons. Rather, we hope our alternative history might stimulate pause for thought and thinking differently and that others might be inspired to propose other histories and add new elements to our understanding of management's past.

If our new history encourages those who develop management theory or practicing managers to think a little differently about how they go about their business, then we will have achieved our aim. If it causes some of the writers of management textbooks to think twice about and alter how they present history, then we would be doubly pleased. If it achieves both of these goals from opposite aims of the spectrum of management – for those introductory students at the grassroots of the field, to seasoned professors, executives and management consultants – then it will have succeeded in being a two-fold attack upon seeing the history of management as merely an incremental series of refinements that justifies and puts the present in perspective.

We believe the timing is good with regard to a possible loosening up management history in this manner. Since we began working on *A New History of Management*, there are signs that textbook creators are amenable to rethinking their presentations. Some of the counter-historical ideas we have put forward in earlier chapters with regard to the portrayal of Max Weber's views and Elton Mayo and the

Hawthorne Studies' pre-eminence are now being incorporated. Articles such as that recently published by Prieto and Phipps (2016) are leading to a re-appraisal of the absence of ideas from people of African heritage in management history. We hope work can be incorporated that highlights alternative perspectives on management from other locations (Asia, Africa, the Middle East and South America), and promote a gender rebalance by investigating the roles played by women in developing management and organization to a far greater extent.

This 'new history' encourages our belief that instead of a circular process whereby the past is reduced and narrowed in order to achieve agreements that put the present in perspective, broadening and deepening our thinking about history can occur. This blurring of the boundaries with regard to what management could be, will, we argue, be a catalyst for substantive innovation. Think of the kind of innovation in theory and practice that could emerge from asking questions like: What if management were seen to emerge as a result of social liberalization, rather than a continuation of coercion with softer gloves?; What if the purpose of management or the end of management theory was not just increasing efficiency?; What if we as managers and management theorists actually read, and were guided by, the works of Adam Smith or Max Weber?; What if we accepted that all organizations are different and management prescriptions are not, therefore, generalizable? We believe that debating these questions can encourage thinking differently about management.

And we hope our alternative history raises many more questions too: What is the purpose of management? What is management theory seeking to advance? What if sustainability was the origin of management theory, rather than a recent trend? Why don't we look at how other societies do management differently? What else might a business school be, and how might it teach differently? What if Mayo and the Hawthorne Studies were retrograde in their promotion of lazy general theories, rather than an evolutionary landmark? What if recent management theories were inventions developed as new products rather than the discovery of objective truths about good management?

So much of how we live our lives now is shaped by metrics and strictures advanced in the name of, and what is assumed to be, 'good management': rational economic self-interest; greater efficiency; acting like we care about the work of others; thinking that we need to contribute to a positive corporate culture, conforming to what is seen to be best practice or 'one best way'. If management history can help us ask fundamental questions about how these goals were invented, the nature of our field and what it means to manage and be managed, then history can no longer be dismissed, as Adam Smith's *Wealth of Nations* once was by Walter Bagehot, as just 'a collection of curious ideas from olden times'.

More importantly, by causing us to doubt the present establishment, history becomes a living reflection of what is now at stake, an unsettling that can help us question and see alternatives to current unquestioned orthodoxies about how we live and evaluate our lives. For example, the greater accessibility to our work-lives through information technology may be a part of good management in terms of increasing efficiency and financial performance, but does it help to achieve our aims if good management is about advancing social well-being and the kind of sympathy between people that creates mutual benefits for all? Does it make us better communitarians, or more likely to be respected or respectable? Or more interested in the greatest good for the greatest number for the longest time?

In this way, a new history that promotes big questions like these can potentially lead to new thinking and liberating actions. Unless we rethink it, management history will continue to be a limit. But rethinking management history could be a great spur to achieving substantial innovation for the future.

References

Abbott, A. 2001. *Chaos of Disciplines*. Chicago: University of Chicago Press.

Academy of Management. 2013. *Announcement for Academy of Management Africa Conference, Johannesburg, South Africa, January 7–10*, 2013. http://meet ing.aomonline.org/international/southafrica/

Adair, J. G. 1984. The Hawthorne Effect: A Reconsideration of the Methodological Artifact. *Journal of Applied Psychology*, 69(2): 334–45.

Adair, J. G. 2003. Hawthorne Effect. In M. Lewis-Beck., A. E. Bryman & T. F. Liao (eds.) *The SAGE Encyclopedia of Social Science Research Methods* (Vol. II). London: Sage, 452–3.

Adams, S., & Butler, O. 1999. *Manufacturing the Future*. Cambridge: Cambridge University Press.

Albright, H. 1917. Fifty Years' Progress in Manufacturing. *Western Electric News*, November 29.

Albrow, M. 1970. *Bureaucracy*. London: Pall Mall.

Alchain, A. A., & Allen, W. R. 1964. *University Economics*. London: Wadsworth.

Aldrich, H. 1979. *Organizations and Environments*. Englewood Cliffs, NJ: Prentice-Hall.

Alexander, H. C. 1906. *Richard Cadbury of Birmingham*. London: Hodder & Stoughton.

Allen, K. 2004. *Max Weber: A Critical Introduction*. London: Pluto Press.

Allport, G. W. 1948. Foreward. In G. Lewin (ed.) *Resolving Social Conflicts: Selected Papers on Group Dynamics*. New York: Harper & Row, vii–xiv.

Allport, G. W. 1961. *Pattern and Growth in Personality*. New York: Holt, Rinehart, and Winston.

Alvesson, M. 1995. The Meaning and Meaninglessness of Postmodernism: Some Ironic Remarks. *Organization Studies*, 16(6): 1047–75.

Alvesson, M. 2001. *Understanding Organizational Culture*. London: Sage.

Alvesson, M., & Sandberg, J. 2011. Generating Research Questions through Problematization. *Academy of Management Review*, 36(2): 247–71.

Alvesson, M., & Sandberg, J. 2012. Has Management Studies Lost Its Way? Ideas for More Imaginative and Innovative Research. *Journal of Management Studies*, 50(1): 128–52.

Anderson, E. & Schiano, B. 2014. *Teaching with Cases: A Practical Guide*. Boston, MA: Harvard Business School Publishing.

Andrews, K. R. (ed.) 1953. *The Case Method of Teaching Human Relations and Administration: An Interim Statement*. Cambridge, MA: Harvard University Press.

Andrews, R. N. 2006. *Managing the Environment, Managing Ourselves: A History of American Environmental Policy*. Birmingham, NY: Yale University Press.

Ankersmit, F. R. 1986. The Dilemma of Contemporary Anglo-Saxon Philosophy of History. *History and Theory*, 25: 1–27.

Ansoff, H. I. 1991. Critique of Henry Mintzberg's 'The Design School: Reconsidering the Basic Premises of Strategic Management'. *Strategic Management Journal*, 12(6): 449–61.

Anteby, M. 2013. *Manufacturing Morals: The Values of Silence and Business School Education*. Chicago: Chicago University Press.

Anteby, M. 2014. Why Silence Is Not Enough. *Stanford Social Innovation Review*. January 22. http://ssir.org/articles/entry/why_silence_is_not_enough

Anteby, M., & Khurana, R. 2007. A New Vision: The Human Relations Movement. Baker Library Historical Collections. www.library.hbs.edu/hc/hawthorne/anewvision.html

Ashton, T. S. 1948. *Industrial Revolution, 1760–1830*. Oxford: Oxford University Press.

Ashton, T. S. 1963. *Iron and Steel in the Industrial Revolution* (3rd ed.). Manchester: Manchester University Press.

Aykroyd, W. R. 1967. *Sweet Malefactor: Sugar, Slavery and Human Society*. London: Heinemann.

Badham, R., Mead, A., & Antonacopoulou, A. 2012. Performing Change: A Dramaturgical Approach to the Practice of Managing Change. In D. M. Boje., B. Burnes., & J. Hassard (eds.) *Routledge Companion to Organizational Change*. London: Routledge, 187–205.

Bagehot, W. 1876. Adam Smith as a Person. *Fortnightly Review, 20*.

Baker Library. 2011. Western Electric Collections. Resources held at Harvard Business School.

Baldwin, N. 1996. *Edison: Inventing the Century*. New York: Hyperion.

Ballard, J. A. 2006. The Diffusion of Maslow's Motivation Theory in Management and Other Disciplines. Paper presented at the Academy of Management Annual Meeting, Atlanta, GA.

Banta, M. 1993. *Taylored Lives: Narrative Productions in the Age of Taylor, Veblen, and Ford*. Chicago: Chicago University Press.

Barley, S. R. 1992. Design and Devotion: Surges of Rational and Normative Ideologies of Control in Managerial Discourse. *Administrative Science Quarterly*, 37: 363–99.

Barley, S. R., Meyer, G., & Gash, D. C. 1988. Cultures of Commitment: Academics, Practitioners and the Pragmatics of Normative Control. *Administrative Science Quarterly*, 33: 24–60.

Barnard, C. 1938. *The Functions of the Executive.* Cambridge: Harvard University.

Barnes Z. E. 1987. Change in the Bell System. *The Academy of Management Executive* 1(1): 43–6.

Barnes, L. B., Christensen, C. R., & Hansen, A. J. 1994. *Teaching and the Case Method* (3rd ed.). Boston, MA: Harvard Business School Press.

Baron, R. A. 1983. *Behavior in Organizations: Understanding and Managing the Human Side of Work.* Boston: Allyn & Bacon.

Baron, R. A. 1986. *Behavior in Organizations: Understanding and Managing the Human Side of Work* (2nd ed.). Boston: Allyn & Bacon.

Baron, R. A., & Greenberg, J. 1990. *Behavior in Organizations: Understanding and Managing the Human Side of Work* (3rd ed.). Boston: Allyn & Bacon.

Barrett, F. J., & Srivastva, S. 1991. History as a Mode of Inquiry in Organizational Life: A Role for Human Cosmogeny. *Human Relations*, 44: 231–54.

Bartol, K., Tein, M., Matthews, G., & Martin, D. 2002. *Management: A Pacific Rim Focus* (3rd ed.). Macquarie Park: NSW: McGraw-Hill.

Barton, D. 2011. Capitalism for the Long Term. *Harvard Business Review*, 89: 84–91.

Bartunek, J. M., Rynes, S. L., & Ireland, R. D. 2006. What Makes Management Research Interesting, and Why Does It Matter? *Academy of Management Journal*, 49(1): 9–15.

Bate, P. 1995. *Strategies for Cultural Change.* Oxford: Butterworth-Heinemann.

Bateman, T. S., & Snell, S. S. 2009. *Management: Leading & Collaborating in a Competitive World* (8th ed.). Boston: McGraw-Hill.

Baumol, W. J., 1990. Entrepreneurship: Productive, Unproductive, and Destructive. *Journal of Business Venturing*, 11: 3–22.

Baumol, W. J., & Blinder, A. S. 1982. *Economics: Principles and Policy* (2nd ed.). New York: Harcourt Brace Jovanovich.

Bayón, P. S., 2013. An Approach to Regulation on Financial Derivatives in the Spanish Law. *International Journal of Business and Social Research*, 3(4): 132–38.

Bebbington, D. W. 1982. *The Nonconformist Conscience: Chapel and Politics 1870–1914.* London: Allen and Unwin.

Becher, T., & Trowler, P. 2001. *Academic Tribes and Territories* (2nd ed.). Maidenhead: The Society for Research into Higher Education and Open University Press.

Beck, R. N. 1987. Visions, Values, and Strategies: Changing Attitudes and Culture . *The Academy of Management Executive*, 1(1): 33–41.

Bedeian, A. G. 1986 *Management*. Holt, Reinhardt & Winston.

Bedeian, A. G. 2004. The Gift of Professional Maturity. *Academy of Management Learning & Education*, 3(1): 92–8.

Beer, M. 1987. Revitalizing Organizations: Change Process and Emergent Model. *The Academy of Management Executive* 1(1): 51–5.

Begg, D., Fischer, S., & Dornbusch, R. 1984. *Economics: British Edition*, McGraw-Hill.

Belich, J. 1986. *The New Zealand Wars and the Victorian Interpretation of Racial Conflict*. Auckland: Auckland University Press.

Bell, D. 1960. *The End of Ideology: On the Exhaustion of Political Ideas in the Fifties*. New York: Free Press.

Bell, D., & Kristol, I. 1981. *The Crisis in Economic Theory*. New York: Basic Books.

Bendix, R. 1956. *Work and Authority in Industry*. New York: Harper.

Bendix, R. 1966. *Max: An Intellectual Portrait*. London: Methuen.

Bennis, W. G., & O'Toole, J. 2005. How Business Schools Lost Their Way. *Harvard Business Review*, May: 96–104.

Berg, P. O. 1985. Organizational Change as a Symbolic Transformation Process. In P. J. Frost, L. F. Moore, M. R. Louis, C. C. Lundberg, & J. Marin (eds.) *Organizational Culture*. London: Sage, 281–300.

Bettis, R. A., & Prahalad, C. K. 1995. The Dominant Logic: Retrospective and Extension. *Strategic Management Journal*, 16(1): 5–14.

Bidanda, B., Warner, R. C., Warner, P. J. & Billo, R. E. 1999. Project Management and Implementation. In S. A. Irani (ed.) *Handbook of Cellular Manufacturing Systems*. New York: John Wiley & Sons, 413–52.

Bilton, C. & Cummings, S. 2010. *Creative Strategy: Reconnecting Business and Innovation*. Oxford: Wiley.

Birmingham Public Libraries. 1976. *The Nine Days in Birmingham: The General Strike 4–12 May, 1926*. Birmingham.

Birnbaum, N. 1965. The Rise of Capitalism: Marx and Weber. In N. J. Smelser (ed.) *Readings on Economic Sociology*. London: Prentice Hall, 2–16.

Bliese, P. D., & Ployhart, R. E. 2002. Growth Modelling Using Random Coefficient Models: Model Building, Testing, and Illustrations. *Organizational Research Methods*, 5: 362–87.

Bodenstar, W. H. 1918. *The Journal of the American Medical Association*, p. 12.

Bonansinga, J. 2004. *The Sinking of the Eastland: America's Forgotten Tragedy*. New York: Citadel Press.

Boston, S. 1980. *Women Workers and the Trade Union Movement*. Davis-Poynter.

Bottom W. 2006. Before the Ford Foundation: Development of the Research-based Model of Business Education. Paper presented at the Academy of Management Annual Meeting, Atlanta, GA.

Bourke, H. 1982. Industrial Unrest as Social Psychology: The Australian Writings of Elton Mayo. *Historical Studies*, 20: 217–33.

Boyd, W. 1961. *Education in Ayrshire through Seven Centuries*. London: University of London Press.

Bradley, I. C. 1987. *Enlightened Entrepreneurs*. London: Weidenfield & Nicholson.

Bramel, D. & Friend, R. 1981. Hawthorne: The Myth of the Docile Worker and Class Bias in Psychology. *American Psychologist*, 36: 867–78.

Brandeis, L. D. 1910. Letter to F. W. Taylor, December 7, 1910. Stevens Institute of Technology, New Jersey, F. W. Taylor. Archive, File no. 098J022.

Brandeis, L. D. 1911. *Scientific Management and the Railroads*. Engineering Magazine: New York.

Brandeis, L. D. 1914. *Business: A Profession*. New York: Small, Maynard & Co.

Brandes, S. 1976. *American Welfare Capitalism, 1880–1940*. Chicago: University of Chicago Press.

Branson, J. 1976. The General Strike at Cadburys 1926. Unpublished B.A. dissertation, Birmingham University School of History.

Braverman, H. 1974. *Labor and Monopoly Capital: The Degradation of Work in the Twentieth Century*. New York: NYU Press.

Bridgman, T. 2010. Beyond the Manager's Moral Dilemma: Rethinking the 'Ideal Type' Business Ethics Case. *Journal of Business Ethics*, 94: 311–22.

Bridgman, T., Cummings, S., & McLaughlin, C. 2015. The Case Method as Invented Tradition. Revisiting Harvard's History to Reorient Management Education. In J. Humphreys' (ed.) *Proceedings of the 75th Annual Meeting of the Academy of Management*, Vancouver, August 7–11, 2015.

Bridgman, T., & McLaughlin, C. 2012. *The Battle for 'Middle-Earth': A Quest for National Identity in an Industrial Dispute*. Paper presented at the Academy of Management Annual Meeting, Boston: MA.

Brookes, J. 1976. *Telephone: The First Hundred Years*. New York: Harper and Row.

Brotman, R. 1958. *Book Review: The Dynamics of Planned Change* by R. Lippitt; J. Watson; B. Westley *American Sociological Review* 23(3): 341–2.

Brown, A. 1988. *Organization Culture* (2nd ed.). London: Pearson.

Bruce, K. 2006. Henry S. Dennison, Elton Mayo, and Human Relations Historiography. *Management & Organizational History*, 1(2): 177–99.

Bruce, K. & Nyland, C. 2011. Elton Mayo and the Deification of Human Relations. *Organization Studies*, 32: 383–405.

Bruton, G. D., Fried, V. H., & Manigart, S. 2005. Institutional Influences on the Worldwide Expansion of Venture Capital. *Entrepreneurship Theory & Practice*, 29(6): 737–60.

Buchan, J. 2006. *Adam Smith and the Pursuit of Perfect Liberty*. London: Profile Books.

Buenker, J., Burnham, J., & Crunden, R. 1986. *Progressivism*. Cambridge, MA: Schenkman.

Burke, W. W. 1982 *Organization Development: Principles and Practices*. Boston: Little Brown.

Burke, W. W. 1987. From the Editor. *The Academy of Management Executive*, 1(1): 5.

Burnes, B. 2004. Kurt Lewin and the Planned Approach to Change: A Re-appraisal. *Journal of Management Studies*, 41(6): 977–1002.

Burnes, B. 2007. Kurt Lewin and the Harwood Studies: The Foundations of OD. *The Journal of Applied Behavioral Science*, 43(2): 213–31.

Burnes, B. 2009. *Managing Change*. London: Prentice Hall.

Burnes, B., & Cooke, B. 2012. Review Article: The Past, Present and Future of Organization Development: Taking the Long View. *Human Relations* 65(11): 1395–429.

Burns, T., & Stalker, G. 1961. *The Management of Innovation*. London: Tavistock

Burrell, G. 1988. Modernism, Postmodernism and Organizational Analysis 2: The Contribution of Michel Foucault. *Organization Studies*, 9(2): 221–35.

Burrell, G., & Morgan, G. 1979. *Sociological Paradigms and Organizational Analysis*. London: Heinemann.

Cadbury, E. 1914. The Case against Scientific Management. In *Scientific Management in Industry*. 1915; a discussion reprinted from the *Sociological Review*.

Cadbury, E. 1979. *Experiments in Industrial Organization*. New York: Arno Press (first published in 1912).

Cadbury, E., Matheson, M. C., & Shann, G. 1906. *Women's Work and Wages*. London: T. Fisher Unwin.

Cadbury, E. & Shann, G. 1907. *Sweating*. London: Headley Brothers.

Calas, M., & Smircich, L. 1999. Past Postmodernism? Reflections and Tentative Directions. *Academy of Management Review*, 24: 649–71.

Callahan, R. E., Fleenor, C. P., & Knudson, H. R. 1986. *Understanding Organizational Behavior: A Managerial Viewpoint*. Columbus, OH: Merrill Publishing Company.

Campion, F. D. 1987. How to Handle the Corporate History. *Public Relations Journal*, 43: 31–2.

Campling, J., Poole, D., Wiesner, R., & Schermerhorn, J. R. 2008. *Management* (3rd Asia-Pacific ed.). Australia: John Wiley & Sons.

Cannadine, D. 1983. The Context, Performance and Meaning of Ritual: The British Monarchy and the 'Invention of Tradition'. In E. Hobsbawn & T. Ranger (eds.) *The Invention of Tradition*. Cambridge: Cambridge University Press.

Carey, R. 1863. *Narrative of the Late War in New Zealand*. London: Bentley.

Carey, A. 1967. The Hawthorne Studies: A Radical Criticism. *American Sociological Review* 32: 403–16.

Carr, E. H. 1964. *What Is History?* Harmondsworth: Penguin Books Ltd.

Chandler, A. D. 1959. The Beginnings of 'Big Business' in American Industry. *Business History Review*, 33(1): 1–31.

Chandler, A. D. 1962. *Strategy and Structure: Chapters in the History of the American Industrial Enterprise*. Cambridge, MA: MIT Press.

Chandler, A. D. 1973. Review of The Evolution of Management Thought by Daniel A. Wren. *Business History Review*, 47(3): 393–5.

Chandler, A. D. 1977. *The Visible Hand: The Managerial Revolution in American Business*. Cambridge, MA: Harvard University Press.

Chandler, A. D., 1988. Business History as Institutional History. In T. K. McCraw (ed.) *The Essential Alfred Chandler: Essays towards a Historical Theory of Big Business*. Cambridge, MA: Harvard Business School Press.

Chandler, A. D. 1990. *Scale and Scope: The Dynamic of Industrial Capitalism*. Cambridge, MA: Belknap Press of Harvard University Press.

Chetkovich, C., & Kirp, D. L. 2001. Cases and Controversies: How Novitiates Are Trained to Be Masters of the Public Policy Universe. *Journal of Policy Analysis and Management*, 20: 282–314.

Chia, R. 2005. The Aim of Management Education: Reflections on Mintzberg's Managers Not MBAs. *Organization*, 26: 1090–2.

Child, J. 1964. Quaker Employers and Industrial Relations. *Sociological Review*, 12: 293–315.

Child, J. 1969. *British Management Thought: A Critical Analysis*. London: Allen & Unwin.

Child, J. 1972. Organizational Structure, Environment and Performance: The Role of Strategic Choice. *Sociology*, 6: 1–22.

Child, J. 2005. *Organization: Contemporary Principles and Practice*. Oxford: Blackwell.

Childs, M. 2002. Master-Slave Rituals of Power at a Gold Mine in Nineteenth-century Brazil. *History Workshop Journal*, 53: 43–72.

Clark, P., & Rowlinson, M. 2004. The Treatment of History in Organisation Studies: Towards an 'Historic Turn'? *Business History*, 46(3): 331–52.

Clark, T., & Wright, M. 2009. So, Farewell Then … Reflections on Editing the Journal of Management Studies. *Journal of Management Studies*, 46: 1–9.

Clegg, S. R. 1990. *Modern Organizations: Organization Studies in a Postmodern World*. London: Sage.

Clegg, S. R. 1992. Postmodernism and Postmodernity in Organizational Analysis. *Journal of Organizational Change Management*, 5: 8–25.

Clegg, S. R. 2005. Puritans, Visionaries and Survivors. *Organization Studies*, 26(4): 527–45.

Clegg, S. R., Kornberger, M., & Pitsis, T. 2008. *Managing & Organizations: An Introduction to Theory and Practice*. London: Sage.

Clutterbuck, D., & Crainer, S. 1990. *Makers of Management*. London: Macmillan.

Coleman, D. C. 1984. Historians and Businessmen. In D. C. Coleman and P. Mathias (eds.) *Enterprise and History: Essays in Honour of Charles Wilson*. Cambridge: Cambridge University Press.

Coleman, D. C. 1987. The Uses and Abuses of Business History. *Business History*, XXIX, 141–56.

Collins, D. 1998. *Organizational Change: Sociological Perspectives*. Routledge: London.

Collinson, D., & Tourish, D. 2015. Teaching Leadership Critically: New Directions for Leadership Pedagogy. *Academy of Management Learning & Education*, 14(4): 576–94.

Contardo, I., & Wensley, R. 2004. The Harvard Business School Story: Avoiding Knowledge by Being Relevant. *Organization*, 11: 211–31.

Cooke, B. 2003. The Denial of Slavery in Management Studies. *Journal of Management Studies*, 40(8): 1895–918.

Cooke, B., & Alcadipani, R. 2015. Towards a Global History of Management Education: The Case of the Ford Foundation and the São Paulo School of Business Administration, *Academy of Management Learning & Education*, 14(4): 482–99.

Cooke, B., & Mills, A. J. 2008. The Right to Be Human and Human Rights: Maslow, McCarthyism and the Death of Humanist Theories of Management. *Management & Organizational History*, 3(1): 27–47.

Cooke, B., Mills, A. J., & Kelley, E. S. 2005. Situating Maslow in Cold War America: A Recontextualization of Management Theory. *Group & Organization Management*, 30(2): 129–52.

Copeland, M. T. 1958. *And Mark an Era: The Story of the Harvard Business School*. Boston, MA: Little Brown and Company.

Copley, F. B. 1923. *Frederick W. Taylor: Father of Scientific Management* (Vol. II). New York: Harper & Brothers.

Corley, T. A. B. 1972. *Quaker Enterprise in Biscuits: Huntley and Palmers of Reading 1822–1972*. London: Hutchinson Co.

Corley, T. A. B. 1988. How Quakers Coped with Business Success: Quaker Industrialists, 1860–1914. In D. J. Jeremy (ed.) *Business and Religion in Britain*. Aldershot: Gower.

Cornelissen, J., & Floyd, S. W. 2009. The Future Ahead: Imagination, Rigour and the Advancement of Management Studies. *Journal of Management Studies*, 46: 11–15.

Cotter, A. 1913. The Conservation of the Worker. *Engineering Magazine*, 45: 489–505.

Covey, S. R. 2004. *The Eighth Habit*. New York: Free.

Cozine, A. 2005. Czechs and Bohemians. *Encyclopedia of Chicago*, www.encyclopedia.chicagohistory.org/pages/153.html

Crane, A. 2013. Modern Slavery as a Management Practice: Exploring the Conditions and Capabilities for Human Exploitation. *Academy of Management Review*, 38(1): 49–69.

Crowther, S. 1923. *John H. Patterson: Pioneer in Industrial Welfare*. Garden City, New York: Doubleday, Page & Co.

Cruikshank, J. L. 1987. *A Delicate Experiment: The Harvard Business School 1908–1945*. Boston, MA: Harvard Business School Press.

Cummings, S. 1995. Centralization and Decentralization: The Never-Ending Story of Separation and Betrayal. *Scandinavian Journal of Management*, 11: 103–17.

Cummings, S. 2002. *Recreating Strategy*. London: Sage.

Cummings, S., & Bridgman, T. 2011. The Relevant Past: Why the History of Management Should Be Critical for Our Future. *Academy of Management Learning & Education*, 10(1): 77–93.

Cummings, S., & Bridgman, T. 2016. The Limits and Possibilities of History: How a Wider, Deeper and More Engaged Understanding of Business History Can Foster Innovative Thinking. *Academy of Management Learning & Education*, 15(2): 1–18.

Cummings, S., Bridgman, T., & Brown, K. 2016. Unfreezing Change as Three Steps: Rethinking Kurt Lewin's Legacy for Change Management. *Human Relations*, 69(1): 33–60.

Cunliffe, A. L. 2004. On Becoming a Critically Reflexive Practitioner. *Journal of Management Education*, 28(4): 407–26.

Cunliffe, A. L. 2009. The Philosopher Leader: On Relationalism, Ethics and Reflexivity: A Critical Perspective to Teaching Leadership. *Management Learning*, 40(1): 87–101.

Currie, G., Knights, D., & Starkey, K. 2010. Introduction: A Post-crisis Critical Reflection on Business Schools. *British Journal of Management*, 21: S1–S5.

Currie, G., & Tempest, S. 2008. Moving towards Reflexive Use of Teaching Cases. *International Journal of Management Education*, 7: 41–50.

Daft, R. L. 2015. *Management* (13th ed.). Cengage Learning.

Dale, E. 1967. *Organization*. New York: American Management Association.

Danielian, N. 1939. *AT&T*. New York: Vanguard Press.

Datar, S. M., Garvin, D. A., & Cullen, P. G. 2010. *Rethinking the MBA: Business Education at a Crossroads*. Boston, MA: Harvard Business Press.

Davidson, P., Simon, A., Woods, P., & Griffin, W. W. 2009. *Management* (4th Australasian ed.). Milton, QLD: Wiley.

Davis, K. 1957. *Human Relations at Work*. New York: McGraw-Hill.

Davis, S. M. 1984. *Managing Corporate Culture*. Cambridge, MA: Ballinger.

Deal, T. E., & Kennedy, A. A. 1982. *Corporate Cultures: The Rites and Rituals of Corporate Life*. Reading, MA: Addison-Wesley (reissued by Perseus Books, 2000).

Decker, S. 2013. The Silence of the Archives: Business History, Post-colonialism, and Archival Ethnology. *Management and Organizational History*, 8(2): 155–73.

Dellheim, C. 1986. Business in Time: The Historian and Corporate Culture. *The Public Historian*, 8: 9–22.

Dellheim, C. 1987. The Creation of a Company Culture: Cadburys, 1861–1931. *The American Historical Review*, 92: 13–44.

Delves Broughton, P. 2008. *Ahead of the Curve: Two Years at Harvard Business School*. New York: Penguin Press.

Deleuze, G. 1988. *Foucault*. Minneapolis: University of Minnesota Press.

Dent, E. N., & Goldberg, S. G. 1999. Challenging 'Resistance to Change'. *The Journal of Applied Behavioral Science*, 35(1): 25–41.

Desrenaudes, M. B. 1802. Review of Garnier's The Wealth of Nations. *La decade philosophique, litteraire and politique*, no. 36.

Dewing, A. S. 1931. An Introduction to the Use of Cases. In M. P. McNair (ed.) *The Case Method at the Harvard Business School*. New York: McGraw-Hill, 1–5.

Dilliard, I. 1941. *Mr. Justice Brandeis*. St. Louis: Modern View.

Dingley, J. 1997. Durkheim, Mayo, Morality and Management. *Journal of Business Ethics*, 16: 1117–29.

Donald, A. D. 2007. *Lion in the Whitehouse: A Life of Theodore Roosevelt*. New York: Basic Books.

Donham, W. B. 1921a, 10 February. Letter to F. C. Hood. Box 13, Folder 13–11. *Office of the Dean (Donham) Records, (AA1.1)*. Harvard Business School Archives, Baker Library, Harvard Business School.

Donham, W. B. 1921b, 27 April. Letter to H. Elliott. Box 13, Folder 13–11. *Office of the Dean (Donham) Records, (AA1.1)*. Harvard Business School Archives, Baker Library, Harvard Business School.

Donham, W. B. 1922. Business Teaching by the Case System. *The American Economic Review*, 12: 53–65.

Donham, W. B. 1924, 4 January. Letter to F. C. Hood. Box 13, Folder 13–11. *Office of the Dean (Donham) Records, (AA1.1)*. Harvard Business School Archives, Baker Library, Harvard Business School.

Donham, W. B. 1927. The Social Significance of Business. *Harvard Business Review*, 5: 406–19.

Donham, W. B. 1931. *Business Adrift*. New York: McGraw-Hill.

Donham, W. B. 1933. The Failure of Business Leadership and the Responsibilities of the Universities. *Harvard Business Review*, 11: 418–35.

Dreyfus, H. L., & Rabinow, P. 1983. *Michel Foucault: Beyond Structuralism and Hermeneutics*. Chicago, IL: University of Chicago Press.

Drucker, P. F. 1964. *The Concept of the Corporation*. New York: Mentor.

Drucker, P. F., & Maciariello, J. A. 1973/2008. *Management* (revised ed.). New York: Collins.

Drury, H. B. 1915. *Scientific Management: A History and Criticism*. New York: Columbia University Press.

DuBrin, A. J. 1984. *Foundations of Organizational Behaviour: An Applied Perspective*. Englewood Cliffs, NJ: Prentice-Hall.

Du Gay, P. 2000. *In Praise of Bureaucracy*. London: Sage.

Dumaine, B. 1990. Creating a New Company Culture. *Fortune*, January 15: 55–58.

Duncan, W. J. 1989. *Great Ideas in Management: Lessons from the Founders and Foundations of Managerial Practice*. San Francisco, CA: Jossey-Bass.

Durepos, G., & Mills, A. J. 2012a. Actor-Network Theory, ANTi-History and Critical Organizational Historiography. *Organization*, 19(6): 703–21.

Durepos, G., & Mills, A. J. 2012b. *Anti-history: Theorizing the Past, History, and Historiography in Management and Organization Studies*. Charlotte, NC: Information Age Publishing.

Dyck, B., & Neubert, M. 2008. *Management: Current Practices and New Directions*. Boston, MA: Cengage Learning.

Ebbinghaus, B., & Manow, P. 2001. *Comparing Welfare Capitalism: Social Policy and Political Economy in Europe, Japan and the USA*. London: Routledge.

Edward, P., & Montessori, N. M. 2011. A Critical Return to Lewin: Exposing Discourse and Identification in a Participative Action Research Project. Paper presented at Critical Management Studies 7, Naples, Italy.

Ellet, W. 2007. *The Case Study Handbook: How to Read, Discuss and Write Persuasively about Cases*. Boston, MA: Harvard Business School Press.

Elliott, H. 1921, April 21. Letter to W.B Donham. Box 10, Folder 10–31. *Office of the Dean (Donham) Records, (AA1.1)*. Harvard Business School Archives, Baker Library, Harvard Business School.

Elliott, H. 1921, April 30. Letter to W.B. Donham. Box 10, Folder 10–31. *Office of the Dean (Donham) Records, (AA1.1)*. Harvard Business School Archives, Baker Library, Harvard Business School.

Ellis, P. D., & Zhan, G. 2011. How International Are International Business Journals? *International Business Review*, 20: 100–12.

Ellis, R. J. 2012. *The Development of the American Presidency*. London: Routledge.

Elshtain, J. 2002. *Jane Addams and the Dream of American Democracy*. New York: Basic Books.

Emden, P. H. 1939. *Quakers in Commerce: A Record of Business Achievement*. London: Sampson Low.

Eribon, D. 1991. *Michel Foucault*. Cambridge, MA: Harvard University Press.

Erikson, K. 1976. *Everything in Its Path*. New York: Simon and Shuster.

Esch, E., & Roediger, D. 2009. One Symptom of Originality: Race and the Management of Labour in the History of the United States. *Historical Materialism*, 17(4): 3–43.

Etzioni, A. 1964. *Modern Organizations*. New York: Prentice Hall.

Evans, G. W. 1970. *Gordon Allport: The Man and His Ideas*. New York: Dutton.

Evans, J. A. 2008. Electronic Publication and the Narrowing of Science and Scholarship. *Science*, 321(5887): 395–9.

Evans, R. 1997. *In Defence of History*. London: Granta.

Fagen, M. (ed.) 1975. *A History of Engineering and Science in the Bell System: Volume 1 The Early Years (1875–1925)*. New York: The Bell Telephone Laboratories.

Fagen, M. (ed.) 1978. *A History of Engineering and Science in the Bell System: Volume 2 National Service in War and Peace (1925–1975)*. New York: The Bell Telephone Laboratories.

Festinger, L. (ed.) 1980. *Retrospections on Social Psychology*. New York: Oxford University Press.

Fink, L. 2001. *Major Problems in the Gilded Age and Progressive Era*. Boston: Houghton Mifflin.

Fitzgerald, T. H. 1988. Can Change in Organizational Culture Really Be Managed? *Organizational Dynamics*, 17(2): 5–15.

Flexner, A. 1930. *Universities: American, English, German*. New York: Oxford University Press.

Florence, M. 1984. Foucault, Michel, 1926—. In G. Gutting (ed.) *The Cambridge Companion to Foucault*. Cambridge: Cambridge University Press, 314–19.

Force, P. 2003. *Self-interest before Adam Smith: A Genealogy of Economic Science* (Vol. LXVIII). Cambridge: Cambridge University Press.

Force, P. 2004. From Amour-propre to Égoïsme: The French Translations of The Wealth of Nations, *Gimon Conference on French Political Economy (1650–1848)*, Stanford University, April 2004.

Foucault, M. 1970. *The Order of Things: An Archaeology of the Human Sciences*. London: Tavistock.

Foucault, M. 1976a. *The Archaeology of Knowledge*. New York: Harper Colophon.

Foucault, M. 1977a. *Discipline and Punish: The Birth of the Prison*. London: Allen Lane.

Foucault, M. 1977b. *Language, Counter-memory, Practice*. Ithaca, NY: Cornell University Press.

Foucault, M. 1980a. *Power/Knowledge. Selected Interviews and Other Writings 1972–77*. Brighton: Harvester Press.

Foucault, M. 1980b. *The History of Sexuality: Volume One*. New York: Pantheon.

Foucault, M. 1985. *The History of Sexuality: Volume Two: The Use of Pleasure*. New York: Pantheon.

Foucault, M. 1988. An Interview with Michel Foucault Conducted by Michael Bess, San Francisco (3 November 1980). *History of the Present*, 4 (Spring 1988): 1–13.

Foucault, M. 2008. *The Birth of Biopolitics*. London: Palgrave Macmillan.

Fox, M. 2008. Herd Mentality Rules in Financial Crisis. *San Diego Union Tribune*, September 30.

Franke, R., & Kaul, J. 1978. The Hawthorne Experiments: First Statistical Interpretations. *American Sociological Review*, 43: 623–43.

Freeman, D. S. 1935. *R. E. Lee: A Biography*. New York: C. Scribner's Sons.

French, J. R. P. 1950. Field Experiments: Changing Group Productivity. In J. G. Miller (ed.) *Experiments in Social Process: A Symposium on Social Psychology*. New York, NY: McGraw-Hill.

French, W. L., & Bell, C. H. 1973. *Organization Development* (1st ed.). Englewood Cliffs, NJ: Prentice-Hall.

French, W. L., & Bell, C. H. 1990. *Organization Development* (4th ed.). Englewood Cliffs, NJ: Prentice-Hall.

French, W. L., & Bell, C. H. 1995. *Organization Development* (5th ed.). Englewood Cliffs, NJ: Prentice-Hall.

French, W. L., Bell, C. H., & Zawacki, R. A. 2005. *Organization Development and Transformation*. New York: McGraw-Hill.

Fulop, L., & Linstead, S. 1999. *Management: A Critical Text*. Macmillan Education.

Furnham, A., & Gunter, B. 1993. *Corporate Assessment: Auditing a Company's Personality*. Routledge, London.

Galbraith, J. K. 1987. *A History of Economics: The Past as the Present*. London: Hamish Hamilton.

Galbraith, J. K. 2014. *The End of Normal: The Great Crisis and the Future of Growth*. New York: Simon & Schuster.

Garatty, J. 1986. *The Great Depression*. San Diego: Harcourt Brace.

Gardener, B. B. 1945. *Human Relations in Industry*. Chicago: Irwin.

Gardiner, A. G. 1923. *Life of George Cadbury*. London: Cassell & Co.

Garel, G. 2013. A History of Project Management Models: From Pre-models to the Standard Models. *International Journal of Project Management*, 31(5): 663–9.

Garnier, G. M., Stewart, D., & Wakefield, E. G. 1805. *An Inquiry into the Nature and Causes of the Wealth of Nations*. At the University Press, Printed by and for J. & J. Scrymgeour, and for Mundell & Son, and A. Constable & Company, Edinburgh.

Garvin, D. A. 2003. Making the Case: Professional Education for the World of Practice. *Harvard Magazine*, 106: 56–65.

George, C. S. 1968/1972. *The History of Management Thought*. Englewood Cliffs, NJ: Prentice-Hall.

Gerth, H. H., & Mills, C. W. 1948. *Max Weber: Essays in Sociology*. London: Routledge & Kegan Paul.

Gerth, H. H., & Mills, C. W. 1954. *Character and Social Structure, the Psychology of Social Institutions*. London: Routledge & Kegan Paul.

Ghoshal, S. 2005. Bad Management Theories are Destroying Good Management Practices. *Academy of Management Learning & Education*, 4(1): 75–91.

Gilbreth, F. B. 1912. *Primer of Scientific Management*. New York: D. Van Nostrand Company.

Gillespie, R. 1991. *Manufacturing Knowledge: A History of the Hawthorne Experiments*. Cambridge: Cambridge University Press.

Gilman, N. P. 1899. *A Dividend to Labor: A Study of Employers' Welfare Institutions*. New York: Houghton Mifflin & Co.

Gilson, M. 1940. Book Review: 'Management and the Worker'. *American Journal of Sociology*, 46: 98–101.

Glad, P. 1966. Progressives and the Business Culture of the 1920s. *Journal of America History*, 53: 75–89.

Glassie, H. H. 1999. *Material Culture*. Bloomington, IA: Indiana University Press.

Gordon, R., & Howell, J. 1959. *Higher Education for Business*. New York: Columbia University Press.

Gorman, G. H. 1908. Introducing Quakers. London: Quaker Home Service, 1981. *Handbook of the Yearly Meetings of the Society of Friends*. Birmingham.

Gotfried, A. 1962. *Boss Cermak of Chicago: A Study in Political Leadership*. Seattle: University of Chicago Press.

Gragg, C. 1940. Because Wisdom Can't Be Told, *HBS Case No. 9–451–005*. Harvard Business School.

Grandon Gill, T. 2011. *Informing with the Case Method: A Guide to Case Method*. Santa Rosa, CA: Informing Science Press.

Grant, J. 1876. *History of the Burgh Schools of Scotland*. London: William Collins & Sons.

Grant, J. D., & Mills, A. J. 2013. The Quiet Americans: Formative Context, the Academy of Management Leadership, and the Management Textbook, 1936–1960. *Management & Organizational History*, 1: 201–24.

Green, A., & Troup, K. 1999. *The Houses of History: A Critical Reader in Twentieth-century History and Theory*. Manchester: Manchester University Press.

Greenberg, J., & Baron, R. A. 1993. *Behavior in Organizations: Understanding and Managing the Human Side of Work* (4th ed.). Boston: Allyn & Bacon.

Greenberg, J., & Baron, R. A. 1995. *Behavior in Organizations: Understanding and Managing the Human Side of Work* (5th ed.). Englewood Cliffs, NJ: Prentice-Hall.

Greenberg, J., & Baron, R. A. 1997. *Behavior in Organizations: Understanding and Managing the Human Side of Work* (6th ed.). Upper Saddle River, NJ: Prentice-Hall.

Greenberg, J., & Baron, R. A. 2000. *Behavior in Organizations: Understanding and Managing the Human Side of Work* (7th ed.). Upper Saddle River, NJ: Prentice-Hall.

Greenberg, J., & Baron, R. A. 2003. *Behavior in Organizations: Understanding and Managing the Human Side of Work* (8th ed.). Upper Saddle River, NJ: Prentice-Hall.

Greenberg, J., & Baron, R. A. 2008. *Behavior in Organizations: Understanding and Managing the Human Side of Work* (9th ed.). Upper Saddle River, NJ: Pearson Prentice-Hall.

Greenwood, R., Bolton. A., & Greenwood, R. 1983. Hawthorne a Half Century Later: Relay Assembly Participants Remember, *Journal of Management*, 9: 217–31.

Greif, A. 1993. Contract Enforceability and Economic Institutions in Early Trade: The Maghribi Traders' Coalition. *The American Economic Review*, 83(3): 525–48.

Greiner, L. E. 1972. Evolution and Revolution as Organizations Grow. *Harvard Business Review*, 50(4): 37–46.

Grey, C. 2004. Reinventing Business Schools: The Contribution of Critical Management Education. *Academy of Management Learning & Education*, 3(2): 178–86.

Grey, C. 2010. Organizing Studies: Publications, Politics and Polemic. *Organization Studies*, 31: 667–94.

Gross, B. M. 1964. *The Managing of Organizations: The Administrative Struggle.* New York: Macmillan.

Haber, S. 1964. *Efficiency and Uplift: Scientific Management in the Progressive Era 1890–1920.* Chicago: University of Chicago Press.

Haire, M. 1969. The Social Sciences and Management Practices. In M. S. Wortman & F. Luthans (eds.). *Emerging Concepts in Management*. London: Macmillan: 162–72.

Hamel, G. 2007. *The Future of Management*. Harvard Business Press.

Hammond, J. S. 1976. Learning by the Case Method. *HBS Case No. 9–376–241.* Harvard Business School.

Hammond, J. S. 2009. *Learning by the Case Method.* Boston: MA: Harvard Business Publishing.

Hannah, L. 1986. Corporate Histories: Limited Liability Offers a 1980s Boom. *Financial Times*, November 19.

Harbaugh, W. H. 1967. *The Life and Times of Theodore Roosevelt.* New York: Galaxy Books.

Harvey, A. 1906. *The Model Village and Its Cottages: Bournville.* London: B. T. Batsford.

Harvey, C., & Press, J. 1991. *William Morris: Design and Enterprise in Victorian Britain*. Manchester: Manchester University Press.

Harvey, C., & Press, J. 1996. *Databases in Historical Research*. London: Macmillan Education.

Hassard, J. S. 2012. Rethinking the Hawthorne Studies: The Western Electric Research in Its Social, Political and Historical Context. *Human Relations*, 65(11): 1431–61.

Hassard, J., Morris, J., & McCann, L. 2009. *Managing in the Modern Corporation: The Intensification of Managerial Work in the USA, UK and Japan.* Cambridge: Cambridge University Press.

Hassard J. S., & Rowlinson, M. 2010. Historical Methods in Management and Organisation Studies. Paper presented at the Management History Research Group conference, St Andrews, Scotland, July.

Hassard, J., & Wolfram Cox, J. 2013. Can Sociological Paradigms Still Inform Organizational Analysis? A Paradigm Model for Post-paradigm Times. *Organization Studies*, 34(11): 1701–28.

Hawthorne Works Museum. 2010. Exhibits and material sources (various). Morton College, Cicero, Illinois.

Hayek, F. 1960. *The Constitution of Liberty*. London: Routledge and Kegan Paul.

Hayek, M., Novicevic, M. M., Humphreys, J. H., & Jones, N. 2010. Ending the Denial of Slavery in Management History: Paternalistic Leadership of Joseph Emory Davis. *Journal of Management History*, 16: 367–79.

Hays, S. P. 1959. *Conservation and the Gospel of Efficiency: The Progressive Conservation Movement, 1890–1920*. Boston: Harvard University Press.

Heald, W. 1992. From Positivism to Realism: The Philosophy of Gustav Bergmann. *Books at Iowa*, 56 (April): 25–46.

Hemmerly, W. D. 1915. Letter to Kempton Taylor, August 28, 1915, Stevens Archive, File no. 014N001.

Hendley, B. 2002. In Search of the Elusive Whitehead: A Cautionary Tale. *Process Studies*, 31(2): 51–63.

Henisz, W. J. 2011. Leveraging the Financial Crisis to Fulfill the Promise of Progressive Management. *Academy of Management Learning & Education*, 10(2): 298–321.

Henselowe, P. 1984. *Ninety Years On: An Account of the Bournville Village Trust*. Birmingham: The Bournville Village Trust.

Hicks, A. 1999. *Social Democracy and Welfare Capitalism*. Ithaca, NY: Cornell University Press.

Hill, S. 1981. *Competition and Control at Work*. Cambridge, MA: MIT Press.

Hilton, G. 1995. *Eastland: Legacy of the Titanic*. Stanford, CA: Stanford University Press.

Historicus (Cadbury, R.). 1892. *Cocoa: All about It*. London: Sampson, Low, Marston & Co.

Hitt, M. A., Black, J. S., Porter, L. W., & Hanson, D. 2007. *Management*. Frenchs Forest, NSW: Pearson Education Australia.

Hobsbawm, E. 1983a. Introduction: Inventing Traditions. In E. Hobsbawm, and T. Ranger (eds.) *The Invention of Tradition*. Cambridge: Cambridge University Press, 1–14.

Hobsbawm, E. 1983b. Mass-producing Traditions: Europe, 1870–1914. In E. Hobsbawm, & T. Ranger (eds.) *The Invention of Tradition*. Cambridge: Cambridge University Press, 215–230.

Hobson, J. A. 1965. *Imperialism: A Study*. Ann Arbor: University of Michigan Press.

Hoffman, E. 1999. *The Right to Be Human: A Biography of Abraham Maslow* (revised ed.). New York: McGraw-Hill.

Hofstede, G. 1986. Editorial: The Usefulness of the 'Organizational Culture' Concept. *Journal of Management Studies*, 23(3): 253–7.

Hogan, D. 1978. Education and the Making of the Chicago Working Class, 1880–1930, *History of Education Quarterly*, 18: 227–70.

Hood, F. C. 1921, 28 January. Letter to W. B Donham. Box 13, Folder 13–11. *Office of the Dean (Donham) Records, (AA1.1)*. Harvard Business School Archives, Baker Library, Harvard Business School.

Hood, F. C. 1923, 21 December. Letter to W. B Donham. Box 13, Folder 13–11. *Office of the Dean (Donham) Records, (AA1.1)*. Harvard Business School Archives, Baker Library, Harvard Business School.

Hood, F. C. 1924, 11 January. Letter to W. B Donham. Box 13, Folder 13–11. *Office of the Dean (Donham) Records, (AA1.1)*. Harvard Business School Archives, Baker Library, Harvard Business School.

Howard, E. 1946. *Garden Cities of To-Morrow*. London: Faber & Faber (first published in 1898, reissued with slight revisions in 1902).

Hughes, T. P. 2004. *American Genesis: A Century of Invention and Technological Enthusiasm, 1870–1970*. Chicago: University of Chicago Press.

Hunger, J. D., & Wheelen, T. L. 1980. A Performance Appraisal of Undergraduate Business Education. *Human Resource Management*, 19(1): 24–31.

Huse, E. 1975. *Organizational Development*. New York: West Publishing.

Industrial Record 1919–1939. Bournville: Cadbury Brothers, 1945.

Isichei, E. 1970. *Victorian Quakers*. Oxford: Oxford University Press.

Israel, P. 1992. *From Machine Shop to Industrial Laboratory: Telegraphy and the Changing Context of American Invention, 1830–1920*. Baltimore: Johns Hopkins University Press.

Jackson, J., & Morgan, C. 1982. *Organization Theory* (2nd ed.). Englewood Cliffs, NJ: Prentice-Hall.

Jackson, N., & Carter, P. 2000. *Rethinking Organizational Behaviour*, London: Prentice Hall.

Jackson, S. E., Joshi, A., & Erhardt, N. L. 2003. Recent Research on Team and Organizational Diversity: SWOT Analysis and Implications. *Journal of Management*, 29: 801–30.

Jacoby, S. 1985. *Employing Bureaucracy: Managers, Unions and the Transformation of American Industry, 1900–1945*. New York: Columbia University Press.

Jacoby, S. 1986. Employee Attitude Testing at Sears, Roebuck and Company, 1938–1960. *Business History Review*, 60: 602–32.

Jacoby, S. 1997. *Modern Manors: Welfare Capitalism since the New Deal*. Princeton, NJ: Princeton University Press.

Jacques, E. 1951. *The Changing Culture of a Factory: A Study of Authority and Participation in an Industrial Setting*. London: Tavistock.

Jacques, R. 1996. *Manufacturing the Employee: Management Knowledge from the 19th to 21st Centuries*. London: Sage.

Jacques, R. S. 2006. History, Historiography and Organization Studies: The Challenge and the Potential. *Management & Organizational History*, 1(1): 31–49.

Jenkins, K. 2003. *Refiguring History: New Thoughts on an Old Discipline*. London: Routledge.

Jeremy, D. J. (ed.) 1988. *Business and Religion in Britain*. Aldershot: Gower.

Jeremy, D. J. 1990. *Capitalists and Christians: Business Leaders and the Churches in Britain, 1990–1960*. Oxford: Clarendon Press.

Jeremy, D. J. 1991. The Enlightened Paternalist in Action: William Hesketh Lever at Port Sunlight. *Business History*, 33: 58–81.

Jevons, W. S. 1888. *The Theory of Political Economy*. London: Macmillan.

Johansson, F. 2006. *Medici Effect: What You Can Learn from Elephants and Epidemics*. Cambridge, MA: Harvard Business Press.

Jones, S. R. 1990. Worker Interdependence and Output: The Hawthorne Studies Reevaluated. *American Sociological Review*, April: 176–90.

Jones, S. R. 1992. Was There a Hawthorne Effect? *American Sociological Review*, November: 451–68.

Jones, G., & Khanna, T. 2006. Bringing History (Back) into International Business. *Journal of International Business Studies*, 37: 453–68.

Kanigel, R. 1997. *The One Best Way: Frederick Winslow Taylor and the Enigma of Efficiency*. New York: Viking.

Katz, D., & Kahn, R. 1966. *The Social Psychology of Organizations*. New York: Wiley.

Kaul, N. 2007. *Imagining Economics Otherwise: Encounters with Identity/ Difference*. London: Routledge.

Kavanagh, D. 2013. Problematizing Practice: MacIntyre and Management. *Organization*, 20(1): 103–15.

Kay, B. 2000. *Cicero: The First Suburb West*. Chicago: Arcadia Books.

Kearney, E., & Gebert, D. 2009. Managing Diversity and Enhancing Team Outcomes: The Promise of Transformational Leadership. *Journal of Applied Psychology*, 94: 77–89.

Kelman, H. C. 1958. Compliance, Identification, and Internalization: Three Processes of Attitude Change. *The Journal of Conflict Resolution* 2(1): 51–60.

Kendrick, S., Straw, P., & McCrone, D. 1990. *Interpreting the Past, Understanding the Present*. London: Macmillan.

Kenrick, D. T., Griskevicius, V., Neuberg, S. L. & Schaller, M. 2010. Renovating the Pyramid of Needs: Contemporary Extensions Built upon Ancient Foundations. *Perspectives on Psychological Science*, 5(3): 292–314.

Kent, R. T. 1932. The Taylor Society Twenty Years Ago. *Bulletin of the Taylor. Society*, 17: 39–41.

Khurana, R. 2007. *From Higher Aims to Hired Hands: The Social Transformation of American Business Schools and the Unfulfilled Promise of Management as a Profession*. Princeton, NJ: Princeton University Press.

Kinicki, A., & Williams B. K. 2009. *Management: A Practical Introduction* (4th ed.). Boston: McGraw-Hill.

Kirkman, B., & Law, K. 2005. International Management Research in AMJ: Our Past, Present, and Future. *Academy of Management Journal*, 48(3): 377–86.

Klarner, P., & Raisch, S. 2012. Move to the Beat – Rhythms of Change and Firm Performance. *Academy of Management Journal*, 56(1): 160–84.

Klein, N. 2015. *This Changes Everything: Capitalism vs the Climate*. New York: Simon & Schuster.

Knights, D., & Willmott, H. 2007. *Introducing Organizational Behaviour and Management*. London: Thomson Learning.

Knights, D., & Willmott, H. 2012. *Introducing Organizational Behaviour and Management* (2nd ed.). Cengage Learning, Hampshire, UK.

Koestler, A. 1970. *The Act of Creation*. London: Hutchinson.

Kolb, D. A., & Frohman, A. L. 1970a. Organizational Development through Planned Change: A Development Model. *MIT Working Paper Series*: 453–70.

Kolb, D. A., & Frohman, A. L. 1970b. An Organization Development Approach to Consulting. *Sloan Management Review*, 12(1): 51–65.

Koontz, H. 1961. The Management Theory Jungle. *Academy of Management Journal*, 4(3): 174–88.

Koontz, H. 1980. The Management Theory Jungle Revisited. *Academy of Management Review*, 5(2): 175–88.

Koontz, H., & O'Donnell, C. 1974. *Essentials of Management*. New York: McGraw-Hill.

Kotter, J. P. 1978. *Organizational Dynamics: Diagnosis & Intervention*. Reading, MA: Addison-Wesley.

Kotter, J. P. 1995. Leading Change: Why Transformation Efforts Fail. *Harvard Business Review* 73(2): 59–67.

Kotter, J. P., & Cohen, D. S. 2002. *The Heart of Change: Real-life Stories of How People Change Their Organizations*. Boston, MA: Harvard Business Press.

Kotter, J. P., & Rathgeber, H. 2006. *Our Iceberg Is Melting: Changing and Succeeding under Any Conditions*. London: Macmillan.

Kraft, P., Drozd, F., & Olsen, E. 2008. Digital Therapy: Addressing Willpower as Part of the Cognitive-affective Processing System in the Service of Habit Change. *Persuasive Technology*, 5033: 177–88.

Kraft, P., Drozd, F., & Olsen, E. 2009. ePsychology: Designing Theory-based Health Promotion Interventions. *Communications of the Association for Information Systems*, 24(1): 24.

Kreitner, R., & Cassidy. C. 2008. *Management* (11th ed.). Cengage Learning.

Kuhn, M. H. 1951. Lewin, Kurt. Field Theory of Social Science: Selected theoretical papers. In: D. Cartwright (ed.) *The ANNALS of the American Academy of Political and Social Science*, 276(1): 146–7.

Kuhn, T. 1970. *The Structure of Scientific Revolutions*. Chicago: Chicago University Press.

Kurtzman, J. 2013. How Adam Smith Revived America's Oil Patch. *Wall Street Journal*, June 19.

Kweder, M. A. 2014. *Whose Welfare? A Critical Discourse Analysis of Harvard Business Publishing Cases*. Paper presented at the annual meeting of the Academy of Management, Philadelphia.

Landsberger, H. 1958. *Hawthorne Revisited*. Ithaca, NY: Cornell University.

Langley A., Smallman. C., Tsoukas, H., & Van de Ven, A. H. 2009. Process Studies of Change in Organization and Management. *Academy of Management Journal* 52(3): 629–30.

Lasswell, H. D. 1952. Book Review: Field Theory in Social Science. *Human Relations* 5(1): 99–100.

Latour B. 2005. *Reassembling the Social: An Introduction to Actor-Network Theory*. Oxford: Oxford University Press.

Lawrence, P., & Lorsch, J. 1967. *Organization and Environment*. Cambridge, MA: Harvard.

Layton, A. P., Robinson, T. J., & Tucker, I. B. 2011. *Economics for Today*. Mason, OH: Cengage.

Leavitt, H., & Kaufman, R. 2003. Why Hierarchies Thrive. *Harvard Business Review*, 81(3): 96–102.

Lee, R. E. [Jr.]. 1905. *Recollections and Letters of General Robert E. Lee*. New York.

Leontiades, M. 1989. *Myth Management: An Examination of Corporate Diversification as Fact and Theory*. Oxford: Blackwell.

Lerner, M. 1939. *Ideas are Weapons: The History and Uses of Ideas*. New Brunswick, NJ: Transaction Books.

Lewenhak, S. 1977. *Women and Trade Unions*. London: Ernest Benn.

Lewin, K. 1920. Die sozialisierung des Taylorsystems: Eine grundsätzliche untersuchung zur arbeits-und betriebspsychologie. *Gestalt Theory*, 3: 129–51.

Lewin, K. 1931. The Conflict between Aristotelian and Galileian Modes of Thought in Contemporary Psychology. *The Journal of General Psychology*, 5(2): 141–77.

Lewin, K. 1947a. Frontiers in Group Dynamics: Concept, Method and Reality in Social Science; Equilibrium and Social Change. *Human Relations*, 1(1): 5–41.

Lewin, K. 1947b. Group Decision and Social Change. In T. M. Newcomb & E. L. Harley (eds.) *Readings in Social Psychology*. New York: Henry Holt, 330–44.

Lewin, K. 1948 in G. Lewin (ed.) *Resolving Social Conflicts: Selected Papers on Group Dynamics*. New York: Harper & Row.

Lewin, K. 1949. Cassirer's Philosophy of Science and the Social Sciences. In P. A. Schilpp (ed.) *The Philosophy of Ernst Cassirer*. Evanston, IL: Library of Living Philosophers, 269–288.

Lewin, K. 1951 in D. Cartwright (ed.) *Field Theory in Social Science: Selected Theoretical Papers*. New York: Harper & Row.

Li, P. P. 2012. Toward an Integrative Framework of Indigenous Research: The Geocentric Implications of Yin-Yang Balance. *Asia Pacific Journal of Management*, 29(4): 849–72.

Liang, N., & Wang, J. 2004. Implicit Mental Models in Teaching Cases: An Empirical Study of Popular MBA Cases in the United States and China. *Academy of Management Learning & Education*, 3: 397–413.

Likert, R. 1947. Kurt Lewin: A Pioneer in Human Relations Research. *Human Relations*, 1: 131–40.

Lindberg, R. 1997. *Ethnic Chicago*. Lincolnwood, IL: Contemporary Books.

Lindzey, G. 1952. Review of 'Field Theory in Social Science'. *Journal of Abnormal and Social Psychology*, 47(1): 132–3.

Linstead, S., Fulop, L., & Lilley, S. 2004. *Management and Organization: A Critical Text*. Basingstoke: Palgrave.

Lipartito, K., & Sicilia, D. B. 2004. *Constructing Corporate America: History, Politics, Culture*. Oxford: Oxford University Press.

Lippitt, G. 1973. *Visualizing Change: Model Building and the Change Process*. La Jolla, CA: University Associates.

Lippitt, R. 1947. Kurt Lewin, 1890–1947. Adventures in the Exploration of Interdependence. *Sociometry*, 10(1): 87–97.

Lippitt, R., Watson J., Westley, B., & Spalding, W. B. 1958. *The Dynamics of Planned Change: A Comparative Study of Principles and Techniques*. New York: Harcourt Brace.

Lipset, S. M. 1969. The End of Ideology. In C. Waxman (ed.) *The End of Ideology Debate*. New York: Simon and Schuster.

Littler, C. R. 1982. *The Development of the Labour Process in Capitalist Societies*. London: Heinemann.

Locke, E. 1982. Critique of Bramel and Friend (Comment). *American Psychologist*, 37: 858–9.

Locke, R. 1989. *Management and Education since 1940: The Influence of America and Japan on West Germany, Great Britain, and France*. Cambridge: Cambridge University Press.

Luthans, F. 2010. *Organizational Behavior* (12th ed.). New York: McGraw-Hill /Irwin.

Lux, K. 1991. *Adam Smith's Mistake: How a Moral Philosopher Invented Economics and Ended Morality*. Boston: Shambhala Publications.

Lynn, L. E. 1999. *Teaching and Learning with Cases: A Guidebook*. New York: Seven Bridges Press.

Lyotard, J. F. 1984. *The Postmodern Condition: A Report on Knowledge*. Manchester: Manchester University Press.

MacIntyre, A. C. 1984. *After Virtue*. Notre Dame, IN: University of Notre Dame Press.

MacRae, D. G. 1974. *Weber*. London: Fontana.

Maltby, J., & Rutterford, J. 2006. 'She Possessed Her Own Fortune': Women Investors from the Late Nineteenth Century to the Early Twentieth Century. *Business History*, 48(2): 220–53.

Manby, T. G., & Turnbull, P. (eds.) 1986. *Archaeology in the Pennines: Essays in Honour of Arthur Raistrick*. British Archaeological Reports, British series 158.

Mangaliso, M., & Lewis, A. 2013. Strategic Management Research in Developing Nations: How Relevant? In *Academy of Management Proceedings*. http://meet ing.aomonline.org/international/southafrica/

Mantere, S., Schildt, H. A., & Sillince, J. A. A. 2012. Reversal of Strategic Change. *Academy of Management Journal*, 55(1): 172–96.

March, J., & Sutton, R. I. 1997. Organizational Performance as a Dependent Variable. *Organization Science*, 8(6): 698–706.

Marens, R. 2010. Destroying the Village to Save It: Corporate Social Responsibility, Labour Relations, and the Rise and Fall of American Hegemony. *Organization*, 17(6): 743–66.

Marglin, S. A. 1976 [1974]. What Do Bosses Do? The Origins and Functions of Hierarchy in Capitalist Production. In A. Gorz (ed.) *The Division of Labour and Class Struggle in Modern Capitalism*. Harvester: Sussex.

Marks, W. (in collaboration with Cadbury, C.). *George Cadbury Junior 1878–1954*. Private publication, n.d.

Marrow, A. J. 1947. In Memoriam: Kurt Lewin, 1890–1947. *Sociometry*, 10(2): 211–12.

Marrow, A. J. 1969. *The Practical Theorist: The Life and Work of Kurt Lewin*. New York: Basic Books.

Marrow, A. J., Bowers, D. G. & Seashore, S. E. 1967. *Management by Participation*. New York: Harper & Row.

Marshak, R. J., & Heracleous, L. 2004. Organizational Development. In S. Clegg & J. Bailey (eds.) *International Encyclopaedia of Organization Studies*. Los Angeles: Sage, 1047–52.

Martin, J. 1985. Can Organizational Culture Be Managed? In P. J. Frost, L. F. Moore, M. R. Louis, C. C. Lundberg, & J. Martin (eds.) *Organizational Culture*. London: Sage, 95–8.

Martin, J., Sitkin, S. B., & Boehm, M. 1985. Founders and the Elusiveness of a Cultural Legacy. In P. J. Frost L. F. Moore, M. R. Louis, C. C. Lundberg, & J. Martin (eds.) *Organizational Culture*. London: Sage, 99–124.

Martin, R. 2009. *The Design of Business*. Boston, MA: Harvard Business Press.

Martins, E. C., & Terblanche, F. 2003. Building Organizational Culture that Stimulates Creativity and Innovation. *European Journal of Innovation Management*, 6(1): 64–74.

Marwick, A. 1990. Letter to the editor. *The Times Higher Education*. December (Suppl. 7).

Marx, K. 1976. *Capital* (Vol. I). Harmondsworth: Penguin.

Maslow, A. H. 1943. A Theory of Human Motivation. *Psychological Review*, 50(4): 370–96.

Maslow, A. H. 1954. *Motivation and Personality*. New York: Harper & Row.

Maslow, A. H. 1970. *Motivation and Personality* (2nd ed., W. G. Holtzman & G. Murphy eds.). New York: Harper & Row.

Maslow, A. H. 1987. *Motivation and Personality* (3rd ed., R. Frager & J. Fadiman eds.). New York: Harper & Row.

Mason, A. J. 2013. SolverStudio: A New Tool for Optimisation and Simulation Modelling in Excel. *INFORMS Transactions on Education*, 14: 45–52.

Mason, A. T. 1946. *Brandeis: A Free Man's Life*. New York: Viking Press.

Matthews, W. 1982. *Flood: Poems*. Little Brown & Company.

Mayer, J. P. 1943. *Max Weber and German Politics*. London: Faber & Faber.

Mayhew, L. H. (ed.) 1982. *Talcott Parsons: On Institutions and Social Evolution*. Chicago: University of Chicago Press.

Mayhew, A. 2009. *Narrating the Rise of Big Business in the USA: How Economists Explain Standard Oil and Wal-Mart*. New York: Routledge.

Mayo, E. 1933. *The Human Problems of an Industrial Civilization*. New York: Macmillan.

Mayo, E. 1935. The Blind Spot in Scientific Management. Sixth International Management Congress: Reports and Proceedings. London: P S King.

Mayo, E. 1945. *The Social Problems of an Industrial Civilization*. London: Routledge & Kegan Paul.

McEachern, W. A. 2011. *Macroeconomics: A Contemporary Introduction* (9th ed.). Cengage Learning.

McGee, W. J. 1909. *Proceedings of a Conference with Governors*. Washington, DC: Government Printing Office.

McGrath, P. 2005. Thinking Differently about Knowledge Intensive Firms: Lessons from Medieval Irish Monasticism. *Organization*, 12(4): 549–66.

McGrath, P. 2007. Knowledge Management in Monastic Communities of the Medieval Irish Celtic Church. *Journal of Management History*, 13(2): 211–33.

McGregor, D. M. 1957. 'The Human Side of Enterprise' in A. M. Shafritz & J. S. Ott (eds.) *Classics of Organizational Theory*. Fort Worth, TX: Harcourt Brace & Co, 176–82.

McGregor, D. M. 1960. *The Human Side of Enterprise*. New York: McGraw-Hill.

McKenna, J. F. 1989. Management Education in the United States. In W. Bryt (ed.) *Management Education: An International Survey*: London: Routledge, 18–54.

McKinlay, A. 2002. 'Dead Selves': The Birth of the Modern Career. *Organization*, 9: 595–614.

McLaughlin, C. 2013. Corporate Social Responsibility and Human Resource Management. In R. Carberry & C. Cross (eds.) *Human Resource Management: A Concise Introduction*: Palgrave Macmillan: Basingstoke, 224–39.

McLaughlin, C., & Prothero, A. 2014. Embedding a Societal View of Business among First Year Undergraduates. In A. Murray (ed.) *Inspirational Guide for the Implementation of PRME: UK & Ireland Edition*. Sheffield: Greenleaf Publishing.

McNair, M. P. 1954. *The Case Method at the Harvard Business School*. New York: McGraw-Hill.

McQuarrie, F. A. E. 2005. How the Past Is Present(ed): A Comparison of Information on the Hawthorne Studies in Canadian Management and Organizational Behaviour Textbooks. *Canadian Journal of Administrative Sciences*, 22(3): 230–42.

Meakin, B. 1905. *Model Factories and Villages: Ideal Conditions of Labour and Housing*. London: T. Fisher Unwin.

Mee, J. F. 1963. *Management Thought in a Dynamic Economy*. New York: New York University Press.

Merseth, K. K. 1991. The Early History of Case-based Instruction: Insights for Teacher Education Today. *Journal of Teacher Education*, 42: 243–9.

Mesny, A. 2013. Taking Stock of the Century-long Utilization of the Case Method in Management Education. *Canadian Journal of Administrative Sciences*, 30: 56–66.

Metcalf, H. C., & Urwick, L. 1940. *Dynamic Administration: The Collected Papers of Mary Parker Follett*. New York: Harper & Brothers.

Metz, I., & Harzing, A. 2009. Gender Diversity in Editorial Boards of Management Journals. *Academy of Management Learning & Education*, 8(4): 540–57.

Meyer, K. E. 2006. Asian Management Research Needs More Self-confidence. *Asia Pacific Journal of Management*, 23: 119–37.

Miller, J. 1993. *The Passion of Michel Foucault*. New York: Simon & Schuster.

Mills, A., & Durepos, G. 2010. ANTi-history'. Entry in Mills A. Durepos, G., & Wiebe, E. (eds.) *Sage Encyclopaedia of Case Study Research*. London: Sage.

Mills, A. J., Weatherbee, T. G., & Durepos, G. 2014. Reassembling Weber to Reveal the-Past-as-History in Management and Organization Studies. *Organization*, 21(2): 225–43.

Mills, A. J., Weatherbee, T. G., Foster, J., & Helms Mills, J. 2015. The New Deal for Management and Organization Studies: Lessons, Insights and Reflections. In P. G. McLaren, A. J. Mills & T. G. Weatherbee (eds.) *The Routledge Companion to Management and Organizational History*. Oxford, UK: Routledge, 265–84.

Mintzberg, H. 1991. Learning 1, Planning 0 Reply to Igor Ansoff. *Strategic Management Journal*, 12(6): 463–6.

Mintzberg, H. 2004. *Managers Not MBAs: A Hard Look at the Soft Practice of Managing and Management Development*. San Francisco: Barrett-Koehler.

Monin, N. 2012. *Management Theory: A Critical and Reflexive Reading*. Oxford, UK: Routledge.

Montes, L. 2003. Das Adam Smith Problem: Its Origins, the Stages of the Current Debate, and One Implication for Our Understanding of Sympathy. *Journal of the History of Economic Thought*, 25(01): 63–90.

Moody's Magazine. 1911. *The International Investors' Monthly* (Vol. XI). New York: Ferrin (republished in one volume by NABU Public Domain Records).

Mooney, J. D. & Reiley, A. C. 1931/1947. *Onward Industry! The Principles of Organization*. New York: Harper & Row.

Morgan, G. 2006. *Images of Organization*. Thousand Oaks, CA: Sage.

Morris, J. 1986. *Women Workers and the Sweated Trades: The Origins of Minimum Wage Legislation*. Aldershot: Gower.

Mosson, T. 1967. Introduction. In *Teaching the Process of Management: The Proceedings of an International Seminar*. London: Harrap.

Mudie-Smith, R. 1906. *Sweated Industries: Being a Handbook of The 'Daily News' Exhibition*. London: Bradbury, Agnew.

Murrow, E. R. 1961. *Broadcasted Comments after President John F. Kennedy's Inaugural Address* (20 January 1961).

Nadler, D. A., & Tushman, M. L. 1989. Organizational Frame Bending: Principles for Managing Reorientation. *Academy of Management Executive*, 3(3): 194–204.

Nadworny, M. J. 1955. *Scientific Management and the Unions, 1900–1932: A Historical Analysis*. Cambridge, MA: Harvard University Press.

Nattermann, P. M. 2000. Best Practice Does Not Equal Best Strategy. *McKinsey Quarterly*, 2, May: 22–31.

Needle, D. 2004. *Business in Context: An Introduction to Business and Its Environment*. London: Thomson.

Nelson, D. 1974. The New Factory System and the Unions: The National Cash Register Company Dispute of 1901. *Labour History*, 15: 163–78.

Nelson, D. 1975. *Managers and Workers: Origins of the New Factory System in the United States 1880–1920*. Madison, WI: University of Wisconsin Press.

Nelson, D. 1980. *Frederick Winslow Taylor and the Rise of Scientific Management*. Madison, WI: University of Wisconsin Press.

Nevaskar, B. 1971. *Capitalists without Capitalism: The Jains of India and the Quakers of the West*. Connecticut: Greenwood Publishing.

Newcomb, T. M., & Hartley, E. L. (eds.) 1947. *Readings in Social Psychology*. New York: Holt.

Noujain, E. G. 1987. History as Genealogy: An Exploration of Foucault's Approach to History. In A. P. Griffiths (ed.) *Contemporary French Philosophy*. Cambridge: Cambridge University Press, 157–174.

Nord, W. R. 1985. Can Organizational Culture be Managed? In P. J. Frost., L. F. Moore., M. R. Louis., C. C. Lundberg., & J. Martin (eds.) *Organizational Culture*. London: Sage: 187–96.

Norman, A. P. 1991. Telling It like It Was: Historical Narratives on Their Own Terms. *History and Theory*, 30(2): 119–35.

Nyland, C. 1996. Taylorism, John R. Commons and the Hoxie Report. *Journal of Economic Issues*, 30: 985–1016.

Nyland, C., & Bruce, K. 2012. Democracy or Seduction? The Demonization of Scientific Management and the Deification of Human Relations. In N. Lichtenstein., & E. Shermer (eds.) *The Right and Labor in America: Politics, Ideology and Imagination*. Philadelphia: University of Pennsylvania Press, 42–76.

Nyland, C., & Heenan, T. 2005. Mary van Kleeck, Taylorism and the Control of Knowledge, *Management Decision*, 43: 1358–74.

Nyland, C., & McLeod, A. 2007. The Scientific Management of the Consumer Interest. *Business History*, 49: 717–35.

O'Connor, E. 1999. The Politics of Management Thought: A Case Study of the Harvard Business School and the Human Relations School. *Academy of Management Review*, 24: 117–31.

O'Connor, E. S. 2001. Back on the Way to empowerment: The Example of Ordway Tead and Industrial Democracy. *Journal of Applied Behavioral Science*, 37: 15–32.

O'Connor, E. 2011. *Creating New Knowledge in Management: Appropriating the Field's Lost Foundations.* Stanford: Stanford University Press.

Oliver, W. H. 1981. *The Oxford History of New Zealand.* Oxford: Oxford University Press.

Olsen, R., Verley, J., Santos, O. L., & Salas, C. 2004. What We Teach Students about the Hawthorne Studies: A Review of Content with a Sample of I-O Psychology and Organizational Behavior Textbooks. *Industrial-Organizational Psychologist*, 41(3): 23–9.

Orcutt. W. D. 1911. The Conservation of the Worker. *The Harpers Monthly*, February: 432–6.

O'Rourke, P. J. 2007. *On the Wealth of Nations: Books that Changed the World.* New York, NY: Grove.

Oswick, C., Fleming, P., & Hanlon, G. 2011. From Borrowing to Blending: Rethinking the Processes of Organizational Theory Building. *Academy of Management Review*, 36(2): 318–37.

Ouchi, W. 1981. *Theory Z.* Reading, MA: Addison Wesley.

Oxford Compact English Dictionary (1996). Oxford: Oxford University Press.

Page, A. 1941. *The Bell Telephone System.* New York: Harper.

Palmer, I., Benveniste, J., & Dunford, R. 2007. New Organizational Forms: Towards a Generative Dialogue. *Organization Studies*, 28(12): 1829–47.

Palmer, I., & Dunford, R. 2008. Organizational Change and the Importance of Embedded Assumptions. *British Journal of Management*, 19(1): 20–32.

Palmer, I., Dunford, R., & Akin, G. 2009. *Managing Organizational Change: A Multiple Perspectives Approach.* New York: McGraw-Hill Irwin.

Papanek, M. L. 1973. Kurt Lewin and His Contributions to Modern Management Theory. *Academy of Management Proceedings*, August: 317–22.

Parker, M. 1992. Getting Down from the Fence: A Reply to Haridimos Tsoukas. *Organization Studies*, 13(4): 651–3.

Parker, M. 2000. *Organizational Culture and Identity.* London: Sage.

Parolo, P. D. P., Pan, R. K., Ghosh, R., Huberman, B. A., Kaski, K., & Fortunato, S. 2015. *Attention Decay in Science. Journal of Informetrics*, 9: 734–45.

Parsons, T. 1929. 'Capitalism' in Recent German Literature: Sombart and Max Weber II. *Journal of Political Economy*, 37(1): 31–51.

Parsons, T. 1933. *Lecture Outline*. 3 May 1933. 7 pages (typed notes). Course material: lecture notes, outlines, reading lists, etc. 1930s-1960s (HUG (FP) – 15.65 Box 1).

Pascale, R., & Athos, A. 1981. *The Art of Japanese Management*. New York: Warner.

Payne, S. C., Youngcourt, S. S., & Watrous, K. M. 2006. Portrayals of F. W. Taylor across Textbooks. *Journal of Management History*, 12(4): 385–407.

Pearce, J. A., & Robinson, R. B. 1989. *Strategic Management*. New York: Random House.

Pearce, K. A. & Hoover, K. D. 1995. After the Revolution: Paul Samuelson and the Textbook Keynesian Model. *History of Political Economy*, 27: 183–216.

Pellegrin, R. F. & Coates, C. H. 1957. Executives and Supervisors: Contrasting Definitions of Career Success. *Administrative Science Quarterly*, 1(4): 506–17.

Perry, B. 1921. *Life and letters of Henry Lee Higginson*. Boston: Atlantic Monthly Press.

Person, H. S. 1929. The Origin and Nature of Scientific Management. In H. Person (ed.) *Management in American Industry*. New York: Harper & Brothers, 25–45.

Peters, T. J., & Waterman, R. H. 1982. *In Search of Excellence: Lessons from America's Best-run Companies*. New York: Harper & Row.

Petriglieri, G., & Petriglieri, J. 2009. Business Schools Need a Broader Mandate. *Businessweek*, Viewpoint, June 1.

Petriglieri, G., & Petriglieri, J. 2010. Identity Workspaces: The Case of Business Schools. *Academy of Management Learning & Education*, 9(1): 44–60.

Pettigrew, A. M. 1979. On Studying Organizational Cultures. *Administrative Science Quarterly*, 14: 570–81.

Pfeffer, J. 1987. The Theory-Practice Gap: Myth or Reality? *The Academy of Management Executive*, 1(1): 31–2.

Pfeffer, J., & Fong, C. 2002. The End of Business Schools? Less Success than Meets the Eye. *Academy of Management Learning & Education*, 1: 78–95.

Phillipson, N. 2011. *Adam Smith: An Enlightened Life*. London: Penguin.

Pierson, F. 1959. *The Education of American Businessmen: A Study of University-Collegiate Programs in Business Education*. New York: McGraw-Hill.

Pinchot, G. 1910. *The Fight for Conservation*. New York: Doubleday.

Pinchot, G. 1937. How Conservation Began in the United States. *Agricultural History*, 11(4): 255–65.

Pinchot, G. 1947. *Breaking New Ground*. Washington, DC: Island Press.

Pitcher, B. 1981. The Hawthorne Experiments: Statistical Evidence for a Learning Hypothesis. *Social Forces*, 59: 133–9.

Polanyi, M. 1981. 'The Creative Imagination'. In D. Dutton & M. Krausz (eds.) *The Concept of Creativity in Science and Art*. Netherlands: Springer, 91–108.

Pollack, E. H. 1956. *The Brandeis Reader*. New York: Oceana Publications.

Pollard, S. 1965. *The Genesis of Modern Management: A Study of the Industrial Revolution in Great Britain*. Cambridge, MA: Harvard University Press.

Poole, E. 1911. Brandeis: A Remarkable Record of Unselfish Work Done in the Public Interest. *American Magazine*, February: 481–93.

Porter, L. W., & McKibbin, L. E. 1988. *Management Education and Development: Drift or Thrust into the 21st Century?* Highstown, HJ: McGraw-Hill.

Prahalad, C. K., & Bettis, R. A. 1986. The Dominant Logic: A New Linkage between Diversity and Performance. *Strategic Management Journal*, 7(6): 485–501.

Prahalad, C. K., & Ramaswamy, V. 2004. Co-creation Experiences: The Next Practice in Value Creation. *Journal of Interactive Marketing*, 18(3): 5–14.

Price Waterhouse Change Integration Team. 1995. *Better Change: Best Practices for Transforming Your Organization*. New York: Irwin Professional Publishing.

Prieto, L. C., & Phipps, S. T. A. 2016. Re-discovering Charles Clinton Spaulding's 'The Administration of Big Business": Insight into Early 20th Century African-American Management Thought. *Journal of Management History*, 22(1): 73–90.

Raffnsøe, S., Gudmand-Høyer, M., & Thaning, M. S. 2016. Foucault's Dispositive: The Perspicacity of Dispositive Analytics in Organizational Research. *Organization*, 23(2): 272–98.

Raistrick, A. 1953. *Dynasty of Iron Founders: The Darbys of Coalbrookdale*. London: Longmans Green & Co.

Raistrick, A. 1968. *Quakers in Science and Industry: Quaker Contributions to Science and Industry during the Seventeenth and Eighteenth Centuries*. Newton Abbott: David & Charles Holdings (first published 1950).

Raistrick, A. 1977. *Two Centuries of Industrial Welfare: The London (Quaker) Lead Company 1692–1905*. Trowbridge & Esher.

Raphael, D. D. (ed.) 1991. *The Wealth of Nations*. London: Random Century Group.

Ravasi, D. & Schultz, M. 2006. Responding to Organizational Identity Threats: Exploring the Role of Organizational Culture. *Academy of Management Journal*, 49(3): 433–58.

Reich, L. 1985. *The Making of American Industrial Research: Science and Business at GE and Bell, 1876–1926*. Cambridge: Cambridge University Press.

Rice, B. 1982. The Hawthorne Defect: Persistence of a Flawed Theory. *Psychology Today*, February: 70–4.

Riley, F. P. 1922. *General Robert E. Lee. after Appomattox*. New York: Macmillan.

Ritzer, G. 1996. *The McDonaldization of Society: An Investigation into the Changing Character of Contemporary Social Life.* Thousand Oaks, CA: Pine Forge Press.

Robbins, S. P. 1979. *Organizational Behaviour: Concepts and Controversies* (1st ed.). Englewood Cliffs, NJ: Prentice-Hall.

Robbins, S. P. 1983. *Organizational Behaviour: Concepts, Controversies, and Applications,* (2nd ed.). Englewood Cliffs, NJ: Prentice-Hall.

Robbins, S. P. 1986. *Organizational Behaviour: Concepts, Controversies, and Applications* (3rd ed.). Englewood Cliffs, NJ: Prentice-Hall.

Robbins, S. P. 1989. *Organizational Behaviour: Concepts, Controversies, and Applications* (4th ed.). Englewood Cliffs, NJ: Prentice-Hall.

Robbins, S. P. 1991. *Organizational Behaviour: Concepts, Controversies, and Applications* (5th ed.). Englewood Cliffs, NJ: Prentice-Hall.

Robbins, S. P. 1993. *Organizational Behaviour: Concepts, Controversies, and Applications* (6th ed.). Englewood Cliffs, NJ: Prentice-Hall.

Robbins, S. P. 1994. *Management* (4th ed.). Englewood Cliffs, NJ: Prentice Hall.

Robbins, S. P. 1997. *Managing Today.* Upper Saddle River, NJ: Prentice Hall.

Robbins, S. P. 2001. *Organizational Behaviour: Concepts, Controversies, and Applications* (9th ed.). Upper Saddle River, NJ: Prentice-Hall.

Robbins, S. P., Bergman, P., Stagg, I., & Coulter, M. 2006. *Management* (4th ed.). Sydney, NSW: Pearson Australia.

Robbins, S. P., Bergman, P., Stagg, I., & Coulter, M. 2012. *Management* (6th ed.). Sydney, NSW: Pearson Australia.

Robbins, S. P, Bergman, P., Stagg, I., & Coulter, M. 2015. *Management* (7th ed.). Sydney, NSW: Pearson Australia.

Robbins, S. P., & Coulter, M. K. 2002. *Management* (7th ed.). Upper Saddle River, NJ: Prentice-Hall.

Robbins, S. P., & Coulter, M. K. 2005. *Management* (8th ed.). Upper Saddle River, NJ: Prentice-Hall.

Robbins, S. P., DeCenzo, D. A., Coulter, M., & Woods, M. 2016. *Management: The Essentials* (3rd ed.). Melbourne, Vic: Pearson Australia.

Robbins S. P., & Judge, T. A. 2009. *Organizational Behaviour: Concepts, Controversies, and Applications* (13th ed.). Upper Saddle River, NJ: Prentice-Hall.

Robbins, S. P., Judge, T. A., Odendaal, A., & Roodt, G. 2009. *Organizational Behaviour: Global and Southern African Perspectives* (2nd ed.). Capetown: Pearson.

Robbins, S. P., & Mukerji, D. 1990. *Managing Organizations: New Challenges and Perspectives.* New York: Prentice-Hall.

Rodrigues, L. L., Gomes, D., & Craig, R. 2004. The Portuguese School of Commerce, 1759–1844: A Reflection of the 'Enlightenment'. *Accounting History*, 9: 53–71.

Roethlisberger, F. 1941. *Management and Morale*. Cambridge, MA: Harvard. University Press.

Roethlisberger, F. J. 1954. *Training for Human Relations*. Boston: Harvard Business School.

Roethlisberger, F., & Dickson, W. 1939. *Management and the Worker*. Cambridge, MA: Harvard University Press.

Rogers, T. B. 1931. *A Century of Progress 1831–1931*. Bournville: Cadbury Brothers Ltd.

Rollinson, D. 2008. *Organisational Behaviour and Analysis: An Integrated Approach* (4th ed.). London: Pearson.

Ronken, H. O. 1953. What One Student Learned. In K. Andrews (ed.), *The Case Method of Teaching Human Relations and Administration: An Interim Statement*. Cambridge, MA: Harvard University Press, 46–65.

Roosevelt, T. D. 1914. *Theodore Roosevelt – An Autobiography*. New York: Macmillan.

Rose, M. 1970. *Industrial Behaviour: Theoretical Developments since Taylor*. Harmondsworth: Penguin.

Rowlinson, M. 1988. The Early Application of Scientific Management by Cadbury. *Business History*, 30(4): 377–95.

Rowlinson, M. 1994. Strategy, Structure and Culture: Cadbury, Divisionalization and Merger in the 1960s. British Academy of Management Sixth Annual Conference, Bradford University.

Rowlinson, M., & Carter, C. 2002. Foucault and History in Organization Studies. *Organization*, 9(4): 527–47.

Rowlinson, M., & Delahaye, A. 2010. The Cultural Turn in Business History. *Entreprises et histoire*, 2: 90–110.

Rowlinson, M., & Hassard, J. 1993. The Invention of Corporate Culture: A History of the Histories of Cadbury. *Human Relations*, 46(3): 299–326.

Rowlinson, M., & Hassard, J. 2013. History and the Cultural Turn in Organization Studies. In M. Bucheli & D. Wadhwani (eds.), *Organizations in Time: History, Theory, Methods*. Oxford: Oxford University Press, 147–67.

Rowlinson, M., Hassard, J., & Decker, S. 2014. Research Strategies for Organizational History. A Dialogue between Organizational Theory and Historical Theory. *Academy of Management Review*, 39(3): 250–74.

Rowlinson, M., & Proctor, S. 1997. Efficiency and Power: Organizational Economics Meets Organization Theory. *British Journal of Management*, 8: S31–S42.

Rubin, R. S., & Dierdorff, E. C. 2009. How Relevant Is the MBA? Assessing the Alignment of Required Curricula and Required Managerial Competencies. *Academy of Management Learning & Education*, 8: 208–24.

Rue, L. W., & Byars L. L. 2009. *Management: Skills and Applications* (13th ed.). Boston: McGraw-Hill.

Ruef, M. 2008. Book Review: From Higher Aims to Hired Hands: The Social Transformation of American Business Schools and the Unfulfilled Promise of Management as a Profession by Rakesh Khurana. *Administrative Science Quarterly*, 53(4): 745–52.

Rutterford, J., & Maltby, J. 2006. 'The Widow, the Clergyman and the Reckless': Women Investors in England, 1830–1914. *Feminist Economics*, 12(1–2): 111–38.

Salvemini, G. 1939. *Historian and Scientist: An Essay on the Nature of History and the Social*. Boston, MA: Harvard University Press.

Samson, D., & Daft, R. L. 2012. *Management (4th Asia Pacific ed.)*. Australia: Cengage Learning.

Samuelson, P. A. 1980. *Economics* (11th ed.). McGraw-Hill.

Sandberg, J., & Tsoukas, H. 2011. Grasping the Logic of Practice: Theorizing through Practical Rationality. *Academy of Management Review*, 36(2): 338–60.

Sass, S. A. 1982. *The Pragmatic Imagination: A History of the Wharton School, 1881–1981*. Philadelphia, PA: Wharton.

Schein, E. H. 1961. Management Development as a Process of Influence. *Industrial Management Review*, 2(2): 59–77.

Schein, E. H. 1969. *Process Consultation: Its Role in Organization Development*. Reading, MA: Addison-Wesley.

Schein, E. H. 1981. Does Japanese Management Style Have a Message for American Managers? *Sloan Management Review*, 23(1): 55–68.

Schein, E. H. 1985. *Organizational Culture and Leadership*. San Francisco: Jossey-Bass.

Schein, E. H. 1992. *Organizational Culture and Leadership* (2nd ed.). San Francisco: Jossey-Bass.

Schein, E. H. 1996. Kurt Lewin's Change Theory in the Field and in the Classroom: Notes toward a Model of Managed Learning. *Systems Practice*, 9(1): 27–47.

Schein, E. H. 2010. *Organizational Culture and Leadership* (4th ed.). San Francisco: Wiley.

Schein, E. H., & Bennis, W. G. 1965. *Personal and Organizational Change through Group Methods: The Laboratory Approach*. New York: Wiley.

Schermerhorn, J. R., Davidson, P., Poole, D., Woods, P., Simon, A., & McBarron, E. 2014. *Management: Foundations and Applications* (2nd Asia-Pacific ed.). Milton, QLD: Wiley.

Schilpp, A. (ed.) 1949. The Philosophy of Ernst Cassirer. Evanston, IL: Library of Living Philosophers. *Sciences*, 1(2): 145–77.

Schmalenbach, E. 1919. Selbstkostenrechnung, *ZfhF*: 13, 257–99.

Schwartz, D. 1980. *Introduction to Management: Principles, Practices, and Processes*. New York: Harcourt Brace.

Schwarzkopf, S. 2012. What Is an Archive – And Where Is It? Why Business Historians Need Constructive Theory of the Archive. *Business Archives*, 105: 1–9.

Scott, R. 2003. *Organizations: Rational, Natural, and Open Systems* (5th ed.). New York: Prentice Hall.

Seldes, J. 1917. *American Efficiency* in England. *Bellman*, 22: 122–3.

Selznick, P. 1957. *Leadership in Administration. A Sociological Interpretation*. Evanston, IL: Row, Peterson & Co.

Senft, P. 1960. Review of 'The Dynamics of Planned Change'. *International Journal of Psychiatry*, 5: 315–16.

Sennett, R. 2006. *The Culture of the New Capitalism*. New Haven, CT: Yale University Press.

Shea, J. P. 1951. Logico-Mathematics: Field Theory in Social Science by Kurt Lewin Review. *The Scientific Monthly*, 71(1): 65–6.

Shenhav, Y. 2002. *Manufacturing Rationality: The Engineering Foundations of the Managerial Revolution*. New York: Oxford University Press.

Shepherd, D. A., & Sutcliffe, K. M. 2011. Inductive Top-Down Theorizing: A Source of New Theories of Organization. *Academy of Management Review*, 36(2): 361–80.

Shils, E. 1987. Max Weber and the World since 1920, in W. Mommsen and J. Oesterhammel (eds.) *Max Weber and His Contemporaries*. London: Allen and Unwin.

Shin, S. J., & Zhou, J. 2007. When Is Educational Specialization Heterogeneity Related to Creativity in Research and Development Teams? Transformational Leadership as a Moderator. *Journal of Applied Psychology*, 92: 1709–21.

Shrimpton, A. W., & Mulgan, A. E. 1930. *Maori & Pakeha: A History of New Zealand*. Auckland: Whitcombe & Tombs.

Simon, H. A. 1967. The Business School a Problem in Organizational Design. *Journal of Management Studies*, 4(1): 1–16.

Simons, R. 2013. The Business of Business Schools: Restoring a Focus on Competing to Win. *Capitalism and Society*, 8(1), Article 2.

Skinner, A. (ed.) 1970. *The Wealth of Nations*. Harmondsworth: Penguin.

Sklar, K. 1995. *Florence Kelley and the Nation's Work: The Rise of Women's Political Culture, 1830–1900*. New Haven and London: Yale University Press.

Skousen, M. 1997. The Perseverance of Paul Samuelson's Economics. *Journal of Economic Perspectives*, 11(2): 137–52.

Smircich, L. 1983. Concepts of Culture and Organizational Analysis. *Administrative Science Quarterly*, 28: 339–58.

Smircich, L. 1985. Is the Concept of Culture a Paradigm for Understanding Organizations and Ourselves? In P. J. Frost, L. F. Moore, M. R. Louis, C. C. Lundberg, & J. Martin (eds.) *Organizational Culture*. London: Sage, 55–72.

Smith, A. 2010. *The Theory of Moral Sentiments* (Sen, A., Introduction). Harmondsworth: Penguin Classics.

Smith, A. 2014. *The Wealth of Nations* (K. Sutherland ed.). Oxford University Press.

Smith, C., Child, J., & Rowlinson, M. 1990. *Reshaping Work: The Cadbury Experience*. Cambridge: Cambridge University Press.

Smith, D. 1986. Englishness and the Liberal Inheritance after 1886. In R. Colls & P. Dodd (eds.) *Englishness. Politics and culture 1880–1920*. London: Croom Helm, 254–282.

Smith, G. E. 2007. Management History and Historical Context: Potential Benefits of Its Inclusion in the Management Curriculum. *Academy of Management Learning & Education*, 6(4): 522–33.

Smith, J. A., & Ross, W. D. 1908. *The Works of Aristotle*. Oxford: Clarendon.

Smith J. H. 1998. The Enduring Legacy of Elton Mayo. *Human Relations* 51: 221–49.

Smith, M. 2007. *Fundamentals of Management*. New York: McGraw-Hill.

Smith, M. B. 1951. Review of 'Field Theory in Social Science: Selected Theoretical Papers'. *Psychological Bulletin*, 48(6): 520–1.

Smith, W. K., & Lewis, M. 2011. Toward a Theory of Paradox: A Dynamic Equilibrium Model of Organizing. *Academy of Management Review*, 36(2): 381–403.

Söderlund, J., & Lenfle, S. 2013. Making Project History: Revisiting the Past, Creating the Future. *International Journal of Project Management*, 31(5): 653–62.

Sonnenfeld, J. A. Shedding Light on the Hawthorne Studies, *Journal of Occupational Behavior*, April: 111–30.

Sorenson, O., & Audia, P. G. 2000. The Social Structure of Entrepreneurial Activity: Geographic Concentration of Footwear Production in the United States, 1940–1989. American *Journal of Sociology*, 106(2): 424–62.

Sowell, T. 2006. *On Classical Economics*. New Haven, CT: Yale University Press.

Stacey, R. D. 2007. *Strategic Management and Organisational Dynamics: The Challenge of Complexity* (5th ed.). Harlow, UK: Prentice Hall.

Stambaugh, J. E. & Trank, C. Q. 2010. Not So Simple: Integrating New Research into Textbooks. *Academy of Management Learning & Education*, 9(4): 663–81.

Starkey, K., & Tempest, S. 2009. The Winter of Our Discontent: The Design Challenge for Business Schools. *Academy of Management Learning & Education*, 8(4): 576–86.

Starkey, K., & Tiratsoo, N. 2007. *The Business School and the Bottom Line*. Cambridge: Cambridge University Press.

Steiger, M. B., & Roy, R. K. 2010. *Neo-liberalism: A Very Short Introduction*. Oxford: Oxford University Press.

Steiner, P. 2003. 'Physiocracy and French Pre-Classical Political Economy' in W. J. Samuels., J. E. Biddle and J. Davis (eds.) *A Companion to the History of Economic Thought*. Oxford: Blackwell, 61–77.

Stephen, L. 1902. *History of English Thought in the Eighteenth Century* (Vol. II). London: Putnam.

Stigler, G. J. 1971. Smith's Travels on the Ship of State. *History of Political Economy* 3(2): 265–77.

Stoner, J. A. F., Freeman, R. E., & Gilbert, D. R. 1995. *Management* (6th ed.). London: Prentice-Hall.

Strum, P. 1989. *Louis D. Brandeis: A Justice for the People*. New York: Schocken Books.

Suddaby, R., Foster, W. M. & Trank, C. Q. 2010. Rhetorical History as a Source of Competitive Advantage. In J. Baum (ed.) *The Globalization of Strategy Research, Advances in Strategic Management* (Vol. XXVII). Emerald Group Publishing Limited, 147–73.

Suddaby, R., Hardy, C., & Huy, Q. N. 2011. Where Are the New Theories of Organization? *Academy of Management Review*, 36(2): 236–46.

Sundararajan, L. 2015. Indigenous Psychology: Grounding Science in Culture, Why and How? *Journal for the Theory of Social Behaviour*, 45(1): 64–81.

Taylor, F. W. 1903. *Shop Management*. New York: Harper & Row.

Taylor, F. W. 1910. Letter to James M. Dodge, Nov. 8, 1910, Stevens Institute of Technology, New Jersey, F. W. Taylor. Archive, File no. 098J008.

Taylor, F. W. 1911a. *The Principles of Scientific Management*. New York: Harper & Row.

Taylor, F. W. 1911a. Letter to H. Crozier April 11, Stevens Archive, 1911 TP185B.

Tead, O. 1921. The Problem of Graduate Training in Personnel Administration. *Journal of Political Economy*, 29: 353–67.

Tead, O. 1933. *Human Nature and Management* (2nd ed.). New York: McGraw-Hill.

Tead, O. 1953. Book Review: The Case Method of Teaching Human Relations and Administration. *Personnel Journal*, July/August: 105–6.

Tead, O. 1960. The Evaluative Point of View. *Improving College and University Teaching*, 8(1): 4–10.

Tead, O. 1964. Character and the College Teacher. *The Journal of Higher Education,* 35: 269–72.

Tedlow, R. S., & John, R. R. 1986. *Managing Big Business: Essays from the Business History Review.* Boston, MA: Harvard Business School Press.

Terjesen, S., Hessels, J., & Li, D. 2016. Comparative International Entrepreneurship: A Review and Research agenda. *Journal of Management,* 41(1): 299–344.

The Harvard Crimson. 1932. Dean Donham's Speech, September 21.

Thomas, M. 1985. In Search of Culture: Holy Grail or Gravy Train? *Personnel Management,* September, 17: 24–7.

Thompson, C. B. 1917. *The Theory and Practice of Scientific Management.* Boston: Houghton Mifflin.

Thompson, E. P. 1980. *The Making of the English Working Class.* Harmondsworth: Penguin.

Thompson, P. 1994. Fatal Distraction: Post-Modernism and Organisational Analysis. In J. Hassard & M. Parker (eds.) *Towards a New Theory of Organisations.* London: Routledge, 183–203.

Thompson, P. 2003. Disconnected Capitalism: Or Why Employers Can't Keep Their Side of the Bargain. *Work, Employment and Society,* 17: 359–78.

Thompson, P. 2013. Financialization and the Workplace: Extending and Applying the Disconnected Capitalism Thesis. *Work, Employment and Society,* 27: 472–88.

Thompson, P., & McHugh, D. 1990. *Work Organizations: A Critical Introduction.* London: Macmillan.

Thompson, P. & McHugh, D. 2001. *Work Organisations: A Critical Introduction* (3rd ed.). London: Palgrave.

Thompson, P & McHugh, D. 2009. *Work Organization: A Critical Introduction* (4th ed.). London: Palgrave.

Thomson, A. 2001. The Case for Management History. *Accounting, Business & Financial History,* 11(2): 99–115.

Tichy, N. M. & Devanna, M. A. 1986. *The Transformational Leader: The Key to Global Competitiveness,* New York: John Wiley & Sons.

Time. 1931. *Review of Business Adrift,* 17(14): 45–6.

Tone, A. 1997. *The Business of Benevolence: Industrial Paternalism in Progressive America.* Ithaca, NY: Cornell University Press.

Trahair, R. 1984. *The Humanist Temper: The Life and Work of Elton Mayo.* London: Transaction.

Tredennick, H. 1935. *Aristotle's Metaphysics.* Cambridge, MA: Harvard University.

Tribe, K. 1988. Translator's Introduction, in W. Hennis, *Max Weber, Essays in Reconstruction.* London: Allen & Unwin.

Tribe, K. 1999. Adam Smith: Critical Theorist? *Journal of Economic Literature*: 609–32.

Trist, E., Emery, F., & Murray, H. (eds.) 1997. *The Social Engagement of Social Science: A Tavistock Anthology*, The Socio-ecological Perspective (Vol. III). Philadelphia, PA: University of Pennsylvania Press.

Trist, E., & Murray, H. (eds.) 1990. *The Social Engagement of Social Science: A Tavistock Anthology*, The Socio-ecological Perspective (Vol. I). Philadelphia, PA: University of Pennsylvania Press.

Trist, E., & Murray, H. (eds.) 1993. *The Social Engagement of Social Science: A Tavistock Anthology*, The Socio-ecological Perspective (Vol. II). Philadelphia, PA: University of Pennsylvania Press.

Tsoukas, H., & Chia, R. 2002. On Organizational Becoming: Rethinking Organizational Change. *Organization Science* 13(5): 567–82.

Tsoukas, H., & Cummings, S. 1997. Marginalization and Recovery: The Emergence of Aristotelian Themes in Organization Studies. *Organization Studies*, 18(4): 655–83.

Tsui, A. S. 2007. From Homogenization to Pluralism: International Management Research in the Academy and Beyond. *Academy of Management Journal*, 50(6): 1353–64.

Turner, B. 1990. The Rise of Organizational Symbolism. In J. Hassard % D. Pym (eds.) *The Theory and Philosophy of Organizations: Critical Issues and New Perspectives*. London: Routledge.

Tushman, M. 1974. *Organizational Change: An Exploratory Study and Case History*. Ithaca, NY: ILR Press, Cornell University.

Urofsky, M. I., & Levy, D. W. 1972. *Letters of Louis D. Brandeis* (Vol. II), Albany, NY: State University of New York Press.

Urwick, L. 1947. *Elements of Administration*. London: Pitman.

Urwick, L. 1956. *The 'Golden Book' of Management*. London: Millbrook Press.

Urwick, L. & Brech, E. F. L. 1951. *The Making of Scientific Management– Volume I: Thirteen Pioneers*. London: Pitman.

Urwick, L. & Brech, E. F. L. 1953. *The Making of Scientific Management – Volume II: Management in British Industry*. London: Pitman.

Usdiken, B., & Kipping, M. 2014. History and Organization Studies: A Long-Term View. In Bucheli, M. & Wadhwani, R. D. (eds.) *Organizations in Time: History, Theory, Methods*. Oxford: Oxford University Press, 33–55.

Vaara, E. & Whittington, R. 2012. Strategy as Practice: Taking Social Practices Seriously. *Academy of Management Annals*, 6(1): 285–336.

Vanderbroeck, P. 2012. Crises: Ancient and Modern Understanding an Ancient Roman Crisis Can Help Us Move beyond our Own. *Management & Organizational History*, 7(2): 113–31.

Van Fleet, D. D. 1982. The Need-Hierarchy and Theories of Authority. *Human Relations*, 9 (Spring): 111–18.

Van Fleet, D. D., & Wren, D. A. 2005. Teaching History in Business Schools: 1982–2003. *Academy of Management Learning & Education*, 4(1): 44–56.

van Merte, T. W. 1954. *A History of the Graduate School of Business, Columbia University*. New York: Columbia University Press.

Veblen, T. 1918. *The Higher Learning in America: A Memorandum on the Conduct of Universities by Businessmen*. New York: B. W. Huebsch.

Visker, R. 1995. *Michel Foucault: Genealogy as Critique*. London: Verso.

Vogel Carey, T. 2009. Don't Blame Adam Smith. *Philosophy Now*, 73: 19–22.

Wachholz, T. 2005. *The Eastland Disaster*. Chicago: Chicago Historical Society.

Waddell, D. M., Creed, A., Cummings, T. G., & Worley, C. G. 2014. *Organizational Change: Development and Transformation* (5th ed.). Melbourne: Cengage.

Wadhwani, R. D., & Bucheli, M. 2014. The Future of the Past in Management and Organization Studies. In Bucheli, M. & Wadhwani, R. D. (eds.) *Organizations in Time: History, Theory, Methods*. Oxford: Oxford University Press, 3–30.

Wagner, G. 1987. *The Chocolate Conscience*. London: Chatto & Windus.

Wagner-Tsukamoto, S. 2007. An Institutional Economic Reconstruction of Scientific Management: On the Lost Theoretical Logic of Taylorism. *Academy of Management Review*, 32(1): 105–17.

Wahba, M. A., & Bridwell, L. G. 1976. Maslow Reconsidered: A Review of Research on the Need Hierarchy Theory. *Organizational Behavior and Human Performance*, 15: 212–40.

Walsh, J. P., & Ungson, G. R. 1991. Organizational Memory. *Academy of Management Review*, 16: 57–91.

Walter Camp Papers. (Various). Held at Yale University, New Haven, CT. Reel 15.

Warner, W. L., & Lunt, P. S. 1941 *The Social Life of a Modern Community*. New Haven, CT: Yale University Press.

Waterman, R. H., Peters, T. J., & Phillips, J. R. 1980. Structure Is Not Organization. *Business Horizons*, 23(3): 14–26.

Watson, T. J. 1963. *A Business and Its Beliefs: The Ideas that Helped Build IBM*. New York: McGraw-Hill.

Wearne, B. C. 1989. *The Theory and Scholarship of Talcott Parsons to 1951: A Critical Commentary*. Cambridge: Cambridge University Press.

Weber, M. 1930. *The Protestant Ethic and the Spirit of Capitalism*. London: Allen-Unwin.

Weber, M. 1947. *The Theory of Social and Economic Organizations*. Translated by A. M. Henderson & T. Parsons. New York: Free Press.

Weber, M. 1948. *From Max Weber: Essays in Sociology*. Translated by H. Gerth & C. W. Mills. London: Routledge.

Weber, M. 1975. *Max Weber: A Biography*. New York: John Wiley.

Weick, K. E., & Quinn, R. E. 1999 Organizational Change and Development. *Annual Review of Psychology*, 50(1): 361–86.

Weiner, M. J. 1985. *English Culture and the Decline of the Industrial Spirit*. Harmondsworth: Penguin.

Weiss, B. 1981. *American Education and the European Immigrant*. Urbana: University of Illinois Press.

Weiss, R. M. 1983. Weber on Bureaucracy: Management Consultant or Political Theorist? *Academy of Management Review*, 8(2): 242–8.

Welch, C., Piekkari, R., Plakoyiannaki, E., & Paavilainen-Mäntymäki, E. 2011. Theorising from Case Studies: Towards a Pluralist Future for International Business Research. *Journal of International Business Studies*, 42(5): 740–62.

Wensley, R. 2011. Getting Too Close to the Fire: The Challenge of Engaging Stories and Saving Lives. *British Journal of Management*, 22: 370–81.

Western Electric News. 1915a. 'Foreword', H. B. Thayer, President, Western Electric Company, *Western Electric News*, 4(6): 1–2.

Western Electric News. 1915b. 'The Story of July Twenty-fourth', *Western Electric News*, 4(6): 3–8.

Western Electric News. 1915c. 'What the Survivors Tell', *Western Electric News*, 4(6): 22–5.

Western Electric News. 1915d. 'The Experiences of a Hawthorne Nurse', *Western Electric News*, 4(6): 19–20.

Western Electric News. 1915e. Comment, *Western Electric News*, 4(6): 16.

Western Electric News. 1915f. 'How the Hawthorne Hospital Staff Worked', *Western Electric News*, 4(6): 18.

Wheelen, T. L., & Hunger, J. D. 1983. *Strategic Management and Business Policy*. Reading, MA: Addison-Wesley.

Whetten, D. A., Felin, T., & King, B. 2009. The Practice of Theory Borrowing in Organizational Studies: Current Issues and Future Directions. *Journal of Management*, 35: 537–63.

White, M., & Gribbin, J. 2005. *Einstein: A Life in Science*. New York: Free Press.

Whitehead, A. N. 1925. *Science and the Modern World*. New York: Macmillan.

Whitehead, A. N. 1927, 7 May. Letter to W. B. Donham. Box 38, Folder 38–3. *Office of the Dean (Donham) Records, (AA1.1)*. Harvard Business School Archives, Baker Library, Harvard Business School.

Whitehead, A. N. 1928. Universities and Their Function. *Bulletin of the American Association of University Professors*, 14: 448–50.

Whitehead, A. N. 1931. 'On Foresight' in *Business Adrift* (W.B. Donham). New York: McGraw-Hill, xi–xxix.

Whitehead, A. N. 1933. *Adventures of Ideas*. New York: Macmillan.

Whitehead, A. N. 1942. The Professionalization of Business. *Harvard Business School Alumni Bulletin*, Summer: 235–6.

Whitehead, T. North. 1938. *The Industrial Worker*. Cambridge MA: Harvard University Press.

Whitley, R. 1984. *The Intellectual and Social Organization of the Sciences*. Oxford: Clarendon Press.

Whyte, W. F. 1959. *Man and Organization: Three Problems in Human Relations in Industry*. New York, NY: Irwin.

Whyte, L. 1977. Hawthorne: 75 – WE's Oldest Plant Celebrates Its Diamond Anniversary. *Western Electric Magazine*, January–February: 22.

Widdowson, P. 1990. Perspective: The Creation of a Past. *The Times Higher Education Supplement*, November 30.

Williams, I. A. 1931. *The Firm of Cadbury 1831–1931*. London: Constable & Co. Ltd.

Williams, E. 1964. *Capitalism and Slavery*. London: Andre Deutsche.

Williams, K. Y., & O'Reilly, C. A. 1998. Demography and Diversity in Organizations: A Review of 40 Years of Research. In B. M. Staw & R. Sutton (eds.) *Research in Organizational Behaviour, 20*. Greenwich, CT: JAI, 77–140.

Windsor, P. B. 1980. *The Quaker Enterprise: Friends in Business*. London: Frederick Muller Ltd.

Winterson, J. 1990. *Sexing the Cherry*. London: Vintage.

Wolf, W. B. 1973. The Impact of Kurt Lewin on Management Thought. *Academy of Management Proceedings*, August: 322–5.

Worrell, D. L. 2009. Assessing Business Scholarship: The Difficulties in Moving beyond the Rigor-Relevance Trap. *Academy of Management Learning & Education*, 8: 127–30.

Worren, N. A., Ruddle, K., & Moore, K. 1999. From Organizational Development to Change Management: The Emergence of a New Profession. *The Journal of Applied Behavioral Science*, 35(3): 273–86.

Wrege, C. 1976. Solving Mayo's Mystery: The First Complete Account of the Origin of the Hawthorne Studies. Paper presented at the Management History Division, Academy of Management meeting, Kansas: MO.

Wrege, C. 2008. Hawthorne's Films: Clues to Hawthorne's Secrets. Working paper (available from author).

Wrege, C. D. 1986. *Facts and Fallacies of Hawthorne: A Historical Study of the Origins, Procedures, and Results of the Hawthorne Illumination Tests and Their Influence upon the Hawthorne Studies*. New York: Garland.

Wrege C. D., & Greenwood, R. 1982. Mary B. Gilson—A Historical Study of the Neglected Accomplishments of a Woman Who Pioneered in Personnel Management, *Business and Economic History*, 11: 35–42.

Wrege C. D., & Greenwood, R. 1991. *Frederick W. Taylor, the Father of Scientific Management: Myth and Reality*. Homewood, IL: Business One Irwin.

Wrege, C. D., & Hodgetts, R. 2000. Frederick W. Taylor's 1899 Pig Iron Observations: Examining Fact, Fiction, and Lessons for the New Millennium. *Academy of Management Journal*, 43(6): 1283–91.

Wrege, C., & Perroni, A. 1974. Taylor's Pig Tale: A Historical Analysis of Frederick W. Taylor's Pig-Iron Experiments. *Academy of Management Journal*, 17: 6–27.

Wrege, C. D. & Stotka, A. M. 1978. Cooke Creates a Classic: The Story behind F. W. Taylor's Principles of Scientific Management. *Academy of Management Review*, 3(4): 736–49.

Wren, D. 1972. *The Evolution of Management Thought*. New York: The Ronald Press Company.

Wren, D. 1979. *The Evolution of Management Thought* (2nd ed.). New York: John Wiley & Sons.

Wren, D. 1985. Industrial Sociology: A Revised View of Its Antecedents. *Journal of the History of the Behavioral Sciences*, 21: 310–20.

Wren, D. A. 1987a. Management History: Issues and Ideas for Teaching and Research. *Journal of Management*, 13(2): 339–50.

Wren, D. 1987b. *The Evolution of Management Thought* (3rd ed.). New York: John Wiley & Sons.

Wren, D. 1994. *The Evolution of Management Thought* (4th ed.). New York: John Wiley & Sons.

Wren, D. 2000. Medieval or Modern? A Scholastic's View of Business Ethics, circa 1430. *Journal of Business Ethics*, 28(2): 109–19.

Wren, D. 2005. *The History of Management Thought* (5th ed.). New York: John Wiley & Sons.

Wren, D., & Bedeian, A. 2009. *The Evolution of Management Thought* (6th ed.). New York: John Wiley & Sons.

Wren, D., & Greenwood, R. 1998. *Management Innovators: The People and Ideas that Have Shaped Modern Business*. New York: Oxford University Press.

Wren, D. A., & Hay, R. D. 1977. Management Historians and Business Historians: Differing Perceptions of Pioneer Contributors. *Academy of Management Journal*, 20(3): 470–6.

www.archiver.rootsweb.ancestry.com/th/read/CHICAGO-BOHEMIANS/2004-11/1100481270

www.inficad.com/~ksup/welectric.html

Yerkes, R. 1922. What Is Personnel Research? *Journal of Personnel Research*, June, 56–63.

Yogev, E. 2001. Corporate Hand in Academic Glove: The New Management's Struggle for Academic Recognition – The Case of the Harvard Group in the 1920s. *American Studies International*, 39: 52–71.

Yorks, L., & Whitsett, D. 1985. Hawthorne, Topeka, and the Issue of Science versus Advocacy in Organizational Behavior. *Academy of Management Review*, 10: 21–30.

Yunker, G. W. 1993. An Explanation of Positive and Negative Hawthorne Effects: Evidence from the Relay Assembly Test Room and Bank Wiring Observation Room Studies. Paper presented at Academy of Management Annual Meeting, August 1993, Atlanta, GA.

Zey-Ferrell, M. 1979. *Dimensions of Organizations*. Glenview, IL.: Scott, Foresman.

Index

Kotter, John P., 236, 249, 252, 274
Kotter's eight-step change framework, 249

labour process theory, 34, 35
labour-management, 272, 286, 288, 290, 291, 294, 305, 306
laissez faire economics, 46, 50, 52, 82, 313
leadership, 85, 116, 123, 129, 146, 151, 156, 231, 252, 265, 281, 300
Lee, General Robert E., 149, 151
legitimacy, 158, 165, 168, 177, 180, 193, 271, 278, 304
Lewin, Kurt, 44, 226–30, 232, 234–53, 255, 256, 260–8, 318
Lewinian change theory, 245
  freezing, 238, 240, 245, 246, 265
  Lewin's three-step model of change (CATS), 249
  Unfreezing, 228, 238, 240, 245, 246, 248, 265
liberalism, 43, 46, 48, 49, 53, 54, 73, 80, 127, 313
  cultural liberalism, 127
  economic liberalism, 73, 127
  humanist liberalism, 127
  liberal governance, 73, 74
  moral liberalism, 43, 49, 73, 313
  political liberalism, 73
  social liberalism, 43, 49, 73, 313
Likert, Dennis, 239, 355
Lippitt, Gordon, 246
Lippitt, Ronald, 239, 243, 248

Macintyre, Alasdair, 88
managerial autonomy, 170
Marrow, Alfred, 239, 240, 242, 264
Marxism, 34, 35, 280
Maslow, Abraham, 44, 226, 227, 229, 230, 235, 236, 253, 255, 256, 258, 259, 260, 261, 262, 267, 268, 318
Maslow's pyramid/hierarchy of needs, 253
Mayo, Elton, 44, 84, 126, 181–94, 204, 210–16, 221, 222, 224, 225, 226, 253, 317, 318, 331, 332
Mayoist, 319
McGregor, Douglas, 44, 226, 227, 229, 230, 236, 255, 256, 258, 259, 260, 261, 262, 268, 318
McKinsey & Co, 236, 273
  seven-S model, 236
mechanization, 43, 82

industrial mechanization, 43
mechanistic physics, 66
'Medici effect', 5
modern management, 8, 32, 34, 63, 69, 71, 84, 88, 102, 186, 226, 227, 228, 234, 260, 263
modernity, 38, 39
morality, 48, 66, 73, 79, 80, 217, 304, 343, 356
Morgan, Gareth, 91, 113, 120, 185, 189
motivation, 197, 211, 227, 229, 234, 253, 259, 262, 265, 267

neo-liberalism, 48, 53, 54
  neo-liberal economics, 43, 49, 54
New Nationalism (of T D Roosevelt), 107
Newtonian approach, 66

objectivity, 184, 280, 281, 285
optimization, 266, 267
organizational behaviour, 121, 191, 210, 218–21, 232, 247
organizational development, 233, 234, 235, 246, 249
organizational symbolism, 275

panopticon metaphor, 38
paternalism, 190, 213, 215, 216, 217, 225, 287
Peters, Tom, 274
philosophy, 13, 54, 60, 74, 104, 167, 170, 177, 188, 196, 200, 215, 224, 237, 242, 283, 292
Pierson, Frank, 12, 26, 64, 65, 66, 68, 149, 150, 151, 168, 233
Pinchot, Gifford, 32, 81, 91, 92, 93, 94, 95, 96, 97, 103, 105, 106, 107, 109, 110, 111–16, 315
Pinchot–Ballinger controversy, 95, 97, 103, 116
Pollard, Sidney, 9, 47, 69, 363
pop-management, 231, 232, 236, 252, 268, 272, 273, 276
Porter, Michael, 149, 150
post-modernism, 278
problem solving, 4
productivity, 59, 79, 86, 174, 220, 271, 306
progress (notions of), 8, 35, 36, 38, 47, 54, 60, 70, 71, 73, 74, 76, 79, 80, 88, 90, 99, 105, 106, 111, 123, 124, 144, 146, 167, 186, 192, 226, 228, 262, 287, 311, 314
progressive taxation, 51